MW00463000

THE ITALIAN CANTATA
IN VIENNA

Publications of the Early Music Institute

PAUL ELLIOTT, EDITOR

THE ITALIAN CANTATA
IN VIENNA

Entertainment in the Age of Absolutism

Lawrence Bennett

INDIANA UNIVERSITY PRESS

Bloomington & Indianapolis

This book is a publication of

Indiana University Press
Office of Scholarly Publishing
Herman B Wells Library 350
1320 East 10th Street
Bloomington, Indiana 47405 USA

iupress.indiana.edu

Telephone orders   800-842-6796
Fax orders   812-855-7931

Manufactured in the United States of America

Cataloging information is available from the Library of Congress.

ISBN 978-0-253-01018-6 (cloth)
ISBN 978-0-253-01034-6 (ebook)

1 2 3 4 5   18 17 16 15 14 13

For Nancy,
whose patience provided the support that made this book a reality

CONTENTS

PREFACE

This book is the culmination of many years of work by a lover of vocal chamber music. That love began in 1969, when I cofounded The Western Wind vocal ensemble, a sextet dedicated to a cappella music of all periods. About the time that The Western Wind gave its first concert, I began my search for a Ph.D. dissertation topic in music history at New York University. Strongly attracted to the great madrigals of Claudio Monteverdi, Giaches de Wert, and Luca Marenzio, I at first considered a topic focused on an aspect of the Italian madrigal. Noticing, however, that many outstanding scholars were already working in this field, I wondered if perhaps there was a seventeenth- or eighteenth-century topic in accompanied vocal chamber music that merited exploration. Scholars such as Owen Jander, Gloria Rose, and Eleanor Caluori were producing groundbreaking studies and thematic catalogs for important secular cantata composers such as Alessandro Stradella, Giacomo Carissimi, and Luigi Rossi, but the sheer vastness of the extant cantata repertoire made it evident that much work still needed to be done. My search for a topic eventually led me to the music of the Bononcini brothers, Giovanni and Antonio Maria, and more specifically to their secular cantatas.

In the spring of 1969 I learned that I had received a Fulbright Fellowship to study the Bononcini cantatas housed in the great libraries of Vienna. That summer I traveled to Massachusetts, where I received valuable advice from Jander, a professor at Wellesley College, and met Lowell Lindgren while working in the Loeb Music Library at Harvard University. To my surprise, Lindgren informed me that he too was starting out on a dissertation about the music of the Bononcinis. After the initial shock, we decided to split the topic: Lindgren would concentrate on the operas, and I would work on the cantatas. Lindgren has gone on to write a dissertation and to publish many meticulously prepared articles.

For my study of the Bononcini cantatas, I had chosen Vienna because of its central location, naively hoping that I would be able to travel to libraries and archives all over Europe. Because of travel restrictions and limited funds, I concluded within a few weeks after arriving in Vienna that it would be impossible to realize my dream of collecting all the Bononcini cantatas in a single year. Regular visits to the music collections of the Österreichische Nationalbibliothek and the Gesellschaft der Musikfreunde made me aware that there was more than enough to do in Vienna. I learned that the Bononcini brothers were only two of many Italian composers who spent all or large portions of their careers in the service of the imperial family. I therefore refocused my topic to concentrate on the cantatas written for Vienna by composers employed by the Habsburgs during the baroque era. I rewrote my dissertation proposal and was fortunate to receive a one-year renewal of my Fulbright Fellowship.

I soon learned that the music-loving Habsburg emperors took great pains to preserve the works composed in their honor and for their entertainment. Thus the music libraries of the emperors Leopold I, Joseph I, and Charles VI contain beautiful copies of operas, oratorios, cantatas, and other works prepared for them by professional scribes on high-quality paper. The sturdy bindings of parchment or leather often display elaborate imprints decorated with gold that identify the specific emperors who had ordered the archival copies. The majority of the cantatas are housed in the music collection of the Österreichische Nationalbibliothek, but I discovered that the library of the Gesellschaft der Musikfreunde also preserves many cantatas, including autograph copies by Habsburg composers such as Marc Antonio Ziani and Antonio Caldara. Over time I also located manuscript copies of cantatas composed for Vienna in libraries such as the Deutsche Staatsbibliothek in Berlin and the Max-Reger-Institut in Meiningen.

Manuscripts, yes, but what of printed Italian cantata collections? After all, many volumes of cantatas were published in Italy during the baroque era. Of the dozens of composers employed by the Habsburgs between 1658 and 1740, only one—Carlo Agostino Badia—appears to have received permission to publish a volume of secular cantatas. The Habsburg emperors asserted strict ownership of works composed in their honor and in general did not permit much of the music to circulate beyond the imperial court.

The Viennese libraries contain manuscripts with countless cantatas by composers who never received Habsburg appointments. No doubt some of these cantatas were performed in Vienna. My task eventually became one of isolating the cantatas specifically written for Vienna by composers employed there. The work was somewhat mitigated by the fact that composers such as Antonio Draghi, Filippo Vismarri, Carlo Cappellini, and Badia spent most of their careers in the service of the imperial family. The Habsburgs' pride in preserving archival copies of cantatas by composers with imperial appointments also enabled me to identify many works pertinent to my topic. Giovanni Bononcini posed a special problem. Giovanni composed large numbers of cantatas before and after his service in Vienna. Would it be possible to separate the cantatas written for Vienna from the rest? Many Bononcini cantatas exist in multiple copies spread throughout Europe and the United States. For some time I attempted to create a thematic catalog with concordances of the Bononcini cantatas. This work was eventually expanded and completed by Lindgren; the text incipits with sigla for libraries containing Bononcini cantatas are given by Lindgren in the articles for Giovanni and Antonio Bononcini published in the 2001 edition of *The New Grove Dictionary of Music and Musicians*. Five cantatas by Giovanni are found in unique archival copies from the period of his first imperial service (1698–1712), and I therefore concluded that they were composed for Vienna.

I returned to New York in the summer of 1971. My dissertation advisors at New York University, David Burrows and Jan LaRue, gave helpful suggestions as the project moved forward. At first I intended to include the cantatas composed for Vienna for the entire baroque era. Observing that such a project could take a lifetime to complete, LaRue wisely recommended that I limit the dissertation to the cantatas composed from roughly 1700 to 1711, the final years of the emperorship of Leopold I and the brief reign of Joseph I. Confining the dissertation to this period made perfect sense because it coincided with the influx of new composers who brought the late baroque style to Vienna.

Following an American Musicological Society conference in the 1990s, Robert Kendrick strongly encouraged me to consider a book about the cantatas composed for Vienna. *The Italian Cantata in Vienna: Entertainment in the Age of Absolutism* is the result of my current research.

A book of this scope would not be possible without the support of many colleagues. I am especially grateful to Steven Saunders and Andrew Weaver for their generous advice in helping me to shape the introductory chapter; to Lowell Lindgren for sharing innumerable valuable suggestions and details; and to the Austrian scholars Martin Eybl, Herbert Seifert, and Theophil Antonicek for their insights. I also wish to acknowledge the music library staff at the Österreichische Nationalbibliothek, especially Günter Brosche and Thomas Leibnitz, the former and current directors; Otto Biba and the library staff at the Gesellschaft der Musikfreunde; Herta Müller and Maren Goltz, the former and current music librarians at the Max-Reger-Institut in Meiningen; and the staff of the William and Gayle Cook Music Library at Indiana University, especially David Lasocki and Carla Williams, the former and current reference librarians. I am also grateful for the support of the library staff at Wabash College, especially Diane Norton, John Lamborn, and Deborah Polley, and for the suggestions of my colleague in the Music Department, Peter Hulen. Lucia Marchi painstakingly proofread the entire manuscript, and Steven Winkler helped to prepare the seventy-five music examples with the Finale program. Finally, I would like to thank Raina Polivka and the staff at Indiana University Press for the care with which they helped me to complete this book.

The abbreviations for voices and instruments and for bibliographical citations used throughout this book are those found in *The New Grove Dictionary of Music and Musicians* (2001). The sigla for libraries are those provided by Répertoire International des Sources Musicales (RISM). The bibliographical abbreviations and the sigla are given below.

At present I envision a second book, *The Italian Cantata in Vienna: Entertainment in the Age of Emperor Charles VI,* which will sum up my research of cantatas by important composers such as Antonio Caldara, Francesco and Ignazio Conti, Giuseppe Porsile, Georg Reutter Jr., Leopold Timmer, and Luca Predieri. I hope that my work will lead to future studies that will shed more light on the rich history of the Italian cantata.

BIBLIOGRAPHICAL ABBREVIATIONS

AcM	*Acta Musicologica*
AMf	*Archiv für Musikwissenschaft*
AnMc	*Analecta musicologica*
CHM	*Collectanea historiae musicae*
DBI	*Dizionario biografico degli italiani*
DTOe	*Denkmäler der Tonkunst in Österreich*
EDM	*Das Erbe deutscher Musik*
EitnerQ	R. Eitner, *Biographisch-bibliographisches Quellen-Lexikon*
EMc	*Early Music*
ES	*Enciclopedia dello spettacolo*
FAM	*Fontes artis musicae*
FétisB	F. J. Fétis, *Biographie universelle des musiciens*
JAMS	*Journal of the American Musicological Society*
JM	*Journal of Musicology*
KJb	*Kirchenmusikalisches Jahrbuch*
La MusicaD	Guido Maggiorino Gatti and Alberto Basso, eds., *La musica: Dizionario*
MD	*Musica disciplina*
Mf	*Die Musikforschung*
MGG	*Die Musik in Geschichte und Gegenwart*
ML	*Music & Letters*
MQ	*Musical Quarterly*
MR	*Music Review*
MT	*Musical Times*
NA	*Note d'archivio per la storia musicale*
NG	*The New Grove Dictionary of Music and Musicians*
NGDO	*The New Grove Dictionary of Opera*
NRMI	*Nuova rivista musicale italiana 4*
ÖMz	*Österreichische Musikzeitschrift*
RIM	*Rivista italiana di musicologia*
RISM	Répertoire International des Sources Musicales
RMI	*Rivista musicale italiana*

SchmidlD   C. Schmidl, *Dizionario universale dei musicisti*
SchmidlS   C. Schmidl, *Dizionario universale dei musicisti* suppl.
SIMG   *Sammelbände der internationalen Musikgesellschaft*
SMw   *Studien zur Musikwissenschaft*
VMw   *Vierteljahrsschrift für Musikwissenschaft*
WE   Wellesley Edition
WECIS   Wellesley Edition Cantata Index Series
ZMw   *Zeitschrift für Musikwissenschaft*

RISM SIGLA

A-GÖ	Göttweig, Benediktinerstift, Musikarchiv
A-Imf	Innsbruck, Tiroler Landesmuseum Ferdinandeum
A-Wgm	Vienna, Gesellschaft der Musikfreunde
A-Wm	Vienna, Minoritenkonvent
A-Wn	Vienna, Österreichische Nationalbibliothek, Musiksammlung
A-Ws	Vienna, Schottenabtei, Musikarchiv
B-Bc	Brussels, Conservatoire Royal, Bibliothèque, Koninklijk Conservatorium, Bibliotheek
B-MAR	Denée, Abbaye de Maredsous
CZ-KR	Kroměříž, Knihovna Arcibiskupského Zámku
D-Bsb	Berlin, Staatsbibliothek zu Berlin Preussischer Kulturbesitz
D-Dl	Dresden, Sächsische Landesbibliothek- Staats- und Universitäts-Bibliothek, Musikabteilung
D-DS	Darmstadt, Hessische Landes- und Hochschulbibliothek, Musikabteilung
D-Kl	Kassel, Gesamthochschul-Bibliothek, Landesbibliothek und Murhardsche Bibliothek, Musiksammlung
D-Mbs	Munich, Bayerische Staatsbibliothek
D-MEIr	Meiningen, Meininger Museen, Abteilung Musikgeschichte/Max-Reger-Archiv
D-MÜd	Münster, Bischöfliches Diözesanarchiv (now in D-MÜp)
D-Rp	Regensburg, Bischöfliche Zentralbibliothek, Proske-Musikbibliothek
D-SHm	Sondershausen, Schlossmuseum
D-SHs	Sondershausen, Schlossmuseum, Bibliothek [in SHm]
D-W	Wolfenbüttel, Herzog August Bibliothek, Handschriftensammlung
F-Pn	Paris, Bibliothèque Nationale de France
GB-CDp	Cardiff, Public Libraries, Central Library
GB-Cfm	Cambridge, Fitzwilliam Museum, Department of Manuscripts and Printed Books
GB-Lam	London, Royal Academy of Music, Library
GB-Lbl	London, British Library
GB-Lgc	London, Guildhall Library

GB-Lk	London, King's Music Library [in Lbl]
GB-Ob	Oxford, Bodleian Library
I-Baf	Bologna, Accademia Filarmonica, Archivio
I-Bc	Bologna, Civico Museo Bibliografico Musicale
I-BGc	Bergamo, Biblioteca Civica Angelo Mai
I-Bsp	Bologna, Basilica di S Petronio, Archivio Musicale
I-Fas	Florence, Archivio di Stato, Biblioteca
I-Fc	Florence, Conservatorio Statale di Musica Luigi Cherubini
I-Mc	Milan, Conservatorio di Musica Giuseppe Verdi, Biblioteca
I-MOe	Modena, Biblioteca Estense e Universitaria
I-Nc	Naples, Conservatorio di Musica S Pietro a Majella, Biblioteca
I-Nf	Naples, Biblioteca Oratoriana dei Gerolamini (Filippini)
I-Rsc	Rome, Conservatorio di Musica S Cecilia
I-Rvat	Rome, Biblioteca Apostolica Vaticana
I-Vmc	Venice, Museo Civico Correr, Biblioteca d'Arte e Storia Veneziana
I-Vnm	Venice, Biblioteca Nazionale Marciana
SI-Lf	Ljubljana, Frančiškanski Samostan, Knjižnica
S-L	Lund, Universitet, Universitetsbiblioteket, Handskriftsavdelningen
S-Skma	Stockholm, Statens Musikbibliothek
S-Uu	Uppsala, Universitetsbibliotekek
US-CA	Cambridge, Mass., Harvard University, Harvard College Library

THE ITALIAN CANTATA
IN VIENNA

1

Introduction

Cantiam, cantiamo un poco
e in armonie canore
passiam gioconde l'ore
di questo lieto dì.[1]

—Antonio Draghi, *Lo specchio*, 1676

The Role of Music in the Daily Lives of the Habsburgs

Thus begins Antonio Draghi's cantata entitled *Lo specchio*, composed for the birthday (18 November) of the Habsburg empress dowager Eleonora (1628–86) in 1676. Widow of the emperor Ferdinand III (1608–75), Eleonora herself sang these opening lines, and she was joined in the performance by four aristocratic ladies of the court. The sheer delight in singing celebrated in these verses encapsulates the Habsburg family's deep affection for the art of music. From the time of Maximilian I (r. 1493–1519), music had held a special place in the daily lives of the imperial family. Once the Habsburgs established the home of their empire along the Danube River in Vienna early in the seventeenth century, their fondness for music grew in a grand crescendo. In Habsburg lands throughout the late seventeenth and early eighteenth centuries, music could be heard everywhere: in cathedral and palace, monastery and church, summer garden and private imperial chamber.

For Ferdinand and his successors—Leopold I (1640–1705), Joseph I (1678–1711), and Charles VI (1685–1740)—music was not just a pastime, it was a passion. As patrons they dueled with other European monarchs for the most gifted composers, singers, instrumentalists, librettists, and theater designers of their age. Countless poets and composers glorified their names in music. As collectors, they amassed vast libraries of music manuscripts and prints that can be viewed today in the Musiksammlung of the Österreichische Nationalbibliothek in Vienna. Professional scribes were hired to prepare beautiful archival copies of music performed for the entertainment of the imperial family and their guests; these manuscripts form the nucleus of the music libraries named for the emperors.

But the Habsburg interest in music was not limited to patronage. As youthful heirs to the imperial throne, Ferdinand, Leopold, Joseph, and Charles received thorough training in music. All four tried their hand at composition.[2] Ferdinand and Leopold proved to be the most talented and prolific. Only a few works by Joseph have survived, and none of the compositions by Charles is extant.[3] The emperors also participated often in performances of works at court. Ferdinand danced in court festivities and took part in equestrian ballet. Leopold was proficient on both harpsichord and flute; a fuller appreciation of his historical place as a composer and patron of music is given in chapter 2 of this book. Joseph, too, played the flute and performed with other family members for special celebrations. Charles excelled on the harpsichord and is known to have directed performances from the keyboard.

Other members of the Habsburg family played prominent roles as patrons and performers. Notable among these are Archduke Leopold Wilhelm (1614–62), brother of Ferdinand III, who took the lead in drawing Italian musicians to the Habsburg court and assembled his own vast collection of manuscripts, as well as the empress dowager, who not only sang but also joined Leopold Wilhelm in his efforts to foster a Viennese literary academy where music was often heard. The daughters of Emperor Leopold, Archduchesses Maria Elizabeth and Maria Anna, and of Charles, Archduchesses Maria Theresia and Maria Anna, delighted the court with their singing. The future empress of Austria, Maria Theresia, was especially esteemed for her fine soprano voice.

The Habsburgs' growing appetite for music required a constant supply of large and small vocal works with instrumental accompaniment. For grand occasions such as a coronation, birthday, or wedding, court composers provided elaborate operas with brilliant scenic effects, epitomized most spectacularly by Antonio Cesti's *Il pomo d'oro*, performed for the seventeenth birthday of Empress Margaret Theresa (1651–73) in 1668, or by Johann Joseph Fux's *Costanza e fortezza*, composed for the coronation of Charles VI as king of Bohemia and for the birthday of Empress Elizabeth Christina (1691–1750) in 1723. Ample opportunities for dramatic music were provided during Carnival season, followed by Lent, when dramatic oratorios replaced secular performances. A special type of Viennese oratorio, the *sepolcro*, was reserved for Maundy Thursday and Good Friday of Holy Week. A plethora of more modest sacred and secular vocal works, including Italian cantatas, could be heard throughout the year.

During the period 1658–1711 the cantata and related works served as a source of elite entertainment for the imperial rulers and their guests. Many cantatas provided amusement during banquets and academic meetings. Others paid homage to members of the Habsburg family for birthdays, name days, and special occasions such as a military victory and even a coronation. Using the age-old topic of love—especially the unrequited type—poets provided an endless supply of alluring texts set to music by composers favored at court and performed by singers who learned well the technique of charming an aristocratic audience. With regard to the cantatas with love poetry, the degree of seriousness varied considerably: some texts were frivolous, others merely playful, still others earnest. No doubt the emphasis on jealousy and infidelity reflected the promiscuous practices of an age that boasted a Louis XIV of France, a Charles II of England, and a Joseph I of Austria. At academic meetings topics of love were often intertwined with questions of social etiquette. Filippo Vismarri (1635–1706?) composed a handful of cantatas based on moral topics, following a tradition dating back more than a century. Several longer texts of occasional cantatas also portrayed heroes of mythology and ancient history but in grand terms clearly aimed at flattering the honorees.

THE SCOPE OF THE BOOK

This study focuses on the evolution of the Italian cantata in Vienna during the reigns of emperors Leopold I and Joseph I. It highlights those cantatas that were specifically written for performance at the imperial court by composers who held appointments there. Rather than concentrating on the cantatas of a single composer, I have chosen to examine the cantatas of many composers active in a single city over a period of more than fifty years. The vast majority of these cantatas are concentrated in just two libraries: the Musiksammlung of the Österreichische Nationalbibliothek and the Gesellschaft der Musikfreunde, both in Vienna.[4] Vienna is a particularly apt choice for such a study because the wealthy Habsburgs were able to attract exceptionally talented musicians who served them over long stretches of time. Many composers and performers came to Vienna as young men and remained in the service of the emperors throughout their entire careers. In short, the music-loving Habsburgs provided the kind of professional encouragement and financial support that created a stable environment. To be sure, wars and the plague often interrupted the usual schedule of performances and delayed payments to musicians, but after each period of financial stress the Habsburgs resumed their vast outlays for music, a trend that declined dramatically after the death of Charles VI in 1740.

THE SECONDARY LITERATURE

In 1920 Jakob Torbé completed a pioneering study of the cantata in Vienna, "Die weltliche Solokantate in Wien um die Wende des 17./18. Jahrhunderts." Torbé's dissertation offers many stylistic insights. However, it almost completely lacks documentation, musical background, and historical perspective. In some respects Torbé's list of composers and sources is too complete: while men such as Legrenzi, Lotti, Gasparini, and Mancini dedicated works to Habsburg emperors, present research indicates that they never resided in Vienna. Moreover, Torbé does not include important sources preserved not only in Austria but also elsewhere in Europe. In deciding to consider only solo cantatas with continuo accompaniment, Torbé omitted a significant number of ensemble cantatas and works with obbligato instruments. Because the period 1700–1711 witnessed a major increase in the use of obbligato accompaniments, such cantatas take on added significance. In short, the pieces included by Torbé represent only a small percentage of the total output of cantatas composed in Vienna during the years 1658–1711.

Sixty years after Torbé's dissertation, I completed a study of early eighteenth-century cantatas written for Vienna, "The Italian Cantata in Vienna, c.1700–c.1711." In this dissertation I considered one hundred chamber cantatas, some with obbligato instruments, others with basso continuo accompaniment only. At that time I decided not to include four grand cantatas, but these works are discussed in this book. Since I began work on my dissertation in the 1970s, a remarkable number of scholars have contributed books, articles, and editions that have greatly enriched our knowledge of the Viennese cantata repertoire. Here I name only a few: Lowell Lindgren, Hermine Williams, Brian Pritchard, Herbert Seifert, and Theophil Antonicek. Their work and my own continuing research have made it possible to create a much fuller understanding of the cantata's importance to the musical life of the Habsburg court during the age of absolutism.

Cantata Terminology

No study of the Italian cantata can long avoid complex questions of terminology. Like the words *sonata* and *concerto,* the term *cantata* was used by several generations of baroque composers writing in a wide variety of styles and working in many European courts. Composers did not apply the term with great consistency, sometimes used hybrid terms, and often omitted genre designations altogether. David Burrows has indicated, for example, that none of the Cesti pieces that present-day scholars refer to as cantatas was actually given the designation *cantata* in a manuscript prepared during the composer's lifetime.[5] In the most basic terms, the cantata in Vienna during the years 1658–1711 can be described as a secular vocal composition with an Italian text intended for one or a few solo singers accompanied by continuo instruments only or by continuo and a few concertato instruments. The cantata consists of several contrasting sections; contrast is achieved not only through structural variety but sometimes also by changes in voicing and instrumentation. Viennese cantatas are essentially chamber music; this is reflected by the limited overall dimensions and by the usually modest forces required to perform them. Most cantatas were performed in intimate surroundings such as private rooms in the imperial residences, which were ideally suited to chamber music. These cantatas were not conceived of as elaborate theatrical compositions and did not include scenery, costumes, or detailed dramatic representation.

Giovanni Valentini (1582/83–1649) probably became the first composer in Vienna to use the indication *di camera* for a printed collection of vocal pieces when it appeared in the title for his *Musiche di camera* in 1621. A tradition of accompanied vocal music intended specifically for performance in private chambers thus existed in Vienna from the early reign of Ferdinand II. Later Viennese composers such as Bertali, Sances, and Vismarri continued to use descriptive markings such as *di camera* and *per camera*. After the death of Joseph I (1711) Viennese composers wrote an increasing number of unusually long ensemble cantatas that require groups of soloists and richly varied instrumental accompaniment. Thus, for example, Francesco Conti's *cantata allegorica* titled *Fermate i vostri passi* (1720) and Antonio Caldara's *cantata a quattro soprani* titled *Il giuoco del quadriglio* (1734) stretch the limits of pure chamber music and approach the realm of the one-act opera. For such pieces Caroline and Efrim Fruchtman have suggested the helpful term *grand cantata*, a suggestion that has been adopted in this study.[6] Large numbers of grand cantatas were not composed until the reign of Charles VI; I have located only four such pieces from 1700 to 1712: Carlo Badia's *La Pace e Marte supplicanti avanti al trono della Gloria* (1701); Marc'Antonio Ziani's *L'Ercole vincitor dell'invidia* (1706); A. M. Bononcini's *La Fortuna, il Valore e la Giustizia* (1706); and Badia's *Il sacrificio di Berenice* (1712). These pieces are from four to nine times as long as an average cantata from the early eighteenth century; they require from three to five singers accompanied by a small orchestra; and they have rudimentary dramatic plots. Thus, in addition to its normal role as pure chamber music, the cantata in Vienna gradually also assumed a more grandiose function, often associated with specific celebrations such as name days. Since the expanding role of the cantata is central to an understanding of the evolution of the genre in Vienna, both types—the chamber cantata and the grand cantata—are discussed here.

Also considered are ten *accademie* by Giovanni Battista Pederzuoli, two by Antonio Draghi, and two by Marc'Antonio Ziani. The designation *accademia*, like so many seventeenth-century terms, seems to have been used in Vienna in different ways over an extended period of time. Thus, the Florentine ambassador to Vienna reported having heard what he called a sung *accademia* about Adam, Eve, Cain, and Abel in March 1659.[7] The text of this early work seems to place it closer in spirit to the oratorio than the cantata. Later *accademie* are exclusively settings of secular poetry. Closely resembling contemporary Viennese cantatas, these *accademie* follow an Italian practice of presenting in music philosophical debates about love and general questions of life. Exactly when composers began to set such discourses to music is unclear, but a tradition of holding verbal debates on themes about love at academic sessions had existed in Italy at least since the early seventeenth century. Such debates were held, for example, at the meetings of the Accademia degli Unisoni, founded by Giulio Strozzi at Venice in 1637.[8] During the second half of the seventeenth century, the term *accademia* came to refer not only to a formally constituted body such as the renowned Accademia Filarmonica of Bologna (or to a less formal gathering such as the ones that took place in Rome and Modena, where poetic and musical entertainments were provided for visiting dignitaries) but also to a composition performed for an academic meeting. William Klenz indicates that vocal compositions such as cantatas were called *accademie* by the 1680s, if not earlier. Some works designated as *accademie* were occasional pieces. Many others seem to have been musical extensions of the earlier tradition of verbal discourses or literary debates. Klenz cites several examples by G. B. Vitali that survive in the Estense collection at Modena: "The subjects reflect the absolutist philosophy and atmosphere, being carefully chosen to avoid political implications or inferences."[9]

In Vienna the earliest music to survive in which the term *accademia* appears is Pederzuoli's six *Accademie-cantate per l'anno 1685, ovvero problemi diversi*. From this title and from the undated *Cantate per l'accademia per sua M.tà Ces.a Dell'Imp:ce Eleonora*, also by Pederzuoli, it is obvious that the concepts of cantata and *accademia* were intimately bound together in the composer's mind. The Viennese *accademie* tended to be ensemble works accompanied by slightly larger groups of instruments than those used in most cantatas written for nonacademic occasions. The *accademie*, however, are basically chamber compositions, not theatrical works, and their texts are philosophical, not dramatic.

In general, I have excluded compositions with designations such as *serenata, servizio di camera, scherzo musicale,* and *musica di camera*. It is worth noting that some of the earliest examples of the serenata were performed in Vienna. Michael Talbot indicates that serenata performances in a variety of European cities took place in the open air at night, that singers wore costumes set against a scenic background, that the librettos were usually divided into two roughly equal parts, and that, in general, the serenata "sits uncomfortably between stage and concert hall."[10] After thoroughly examining the secular vocal works by Antonio Draghi with their extant librettos, Herbert Seifert concluded that, with exceptions, Draghi's serenatas were not staged.[11] In any event, the terms *serenata* and *cantata* were rarely used interchangeably in Vienna. Giovanni Bononcini's *L'Euleo festeggiante nel ritorno d'Allessandro Magno dall' Indie* is typical of the Viennese serenata at the turn of the century; it was presented on the evening of 9 August 1699, "fin a mezza notte, sopra il Vivaio sopra un vago Teatro di bellissima architettura e maestro lavoro, eretto nella Paschiera del Cesareo Giardino della Favorita" (until midnight, next to the greenhouse in a lovely theater of beautiful architecture and skillful work, built near the fish pond of the imperial garden of the Favorita).

The precise nature of the *servizio di camera* has not yet been thoroughly investigated. While the term itself implies a chamber-music type of performance, examination of a half-dozen Viennese examples of the *servizio di camera* reveals that it was usually a work of greater length than most cantatas, requiring orchestral accompaniment and a story that invited at least rudimentary staging. With the *servizio di camera,* then, we encounter a genre that lies midway between theater music and pure chamber music. The fine distinction between cantata and *servizio di camera* is reflected by the occasional use of hybrid designations that combine both terms, for example, M. A. Ziani's *cantata per servizio di camera* titled *L'Ercole vincitor dell'invidia* (1706). During the reign of Charles VI, composers such as Antonio Caldara also occasionally used the hybrid term *cantata a servizio di camera*.

What were the social contexts of the *servizio di camera,* and why were compositions such as Ziani's *cantata per servizio di camera* commissioned for important occasions instead of more overtly theatrical works? Answers to questions such as these may eventually help us to understand some of the fine distinctions in terminology. On the basis of an incomplete survey, it is possible to make one hypothesis: the *servizio di camera* often replaced larger theatrical entertainments during periods when the court was in mourning or at times when it became difficult for the court to mount elaborately staged productions. Thus, for example, Cappellini's *A servizio di camera nel giorno del nome dell'Imperatore Leopoldo* and the same composer's *La fama illustrata* (for the empress dowager Eleonora's birthday) were composed while the court was absent from Vienna because of the plague. The emperor and a substantial part of the court left Vienna on 14 August 1679 and traveled to Prague, where they arrived on 23 November. Cappellini's work paid tribute to Leopold for his name day, 15 November, but the manuscript (A-Wn, 16282) clearly indicates that the performance took place "in Praga"; therefore, the celebration was probably delayed until the court actually arrived in Prague. In any event, the temporary and inconvenient circumstances of the court probably account for the fact that Cappellini was commissioned to write only brief theatrical works for occasions usually honored with major dramatic compositions. Similarly, Ziani's *L'Ercole* was composed for Joseph I's name day on 19 March 1706; at that time the court was still officially in mourning for Leopold, and all large theatrical presentations were forbidden.

A term closely related to *servizio di camera* is *musica di camera,* used in Vienna after 1658 for small chamber operas. Examples are Pederzuoli's undated *L'Ozio ingannato* and Badia's *Il commun giubilo del mondo* (1699), more extended and theatrically ambitious works than the cantatas by either composer. *Scherzo musicale* also appears as a genre designation in several middle and late baroque sources. Earlier the term had been used for light Italianate pieces such as Monteverdi's *Scherzi musicali* (1607), but in the later periods in Vienna it came to mean a small one-act, secular dramatic composition. Particularly intriguing is Pederzuoli's *Scherzo musicale in modo di scenica rappresentazione* (Carnival 1685), a description that leaves open the question of just how much staging actually took place. A hybrid composition without a genre designation but closely related to the chamber cantata is *L'Oracolo d'Apollo* (1707) by Giovanni Bononcini. This work consists of three arias, each of which is followed by a substantial ballet.

FORERUNNERS OF THE CANTATA IN VIENNA

The term *cantata* or *cantata per camera* began to appear in Viennese manuscripts after Leopold assumed the throne in 1658, but the origins of accompanied secular Italian vocal music in Habsburg lands can be traced back much earlier.[12] Many of the earliest developments north of the Alps took place in centers such as Graz, Innsbruck, Salzburg, and Prague.

In general, the forerunners of the cantata in Vienna derived from three basic genres in Italy: monody, continuo madrigal/dance-song, and elaborate concertato compositions, all of which found acceptance in Habsburg lands only a few years after they had been introduced in Italy. Monody found early favor in Graz at the thoroughly Italianized court of Archduke Ferdinand (the future Ferdinand II, 1578–1637). In 1615 Ferdinand became the dedicatee of the *Parnassus Musicus Ferdinandaeus*, a famous collection of fifty-seven sacred concerti for one or a few voices with continuo accompaniment; of the thirty-two composers represented, nine were in the service of Ferdinand, and among their compositions are a substantial number written in monodic style.[13] Francesco Rasi (1574–1621), an acclaimed tenor, poet, and composer, probably first introduced the style of monody to an imperial audience in 1612, when he visited Prague to perform in honor of the new emperor, Matthias (r. 1612–19). A pupil of Caccini who sang in Peri's *Euridice* (1600), Gagliano's *Dafne* (1608), and probably Monteverdi's *Orfeo* (1607), Rasi published three extant collections of monodies and dialogues between 1608 and 1620.[14] On his journey back to Italy at the end of 1612, Rasi sang for the prince-archbishop of Salzburg, Count Marcus Sitticus (1574–1619), to whom he dedicated a manuscript collection of monodies, *Musica di camera et chiesa*.[15] Not long after Rasi's journey to Prague and Salzburg, at least two other Italian monodists entertained Austrian nobility. In 1616 the Veronese composer Camillo Orlandi (fl. early seventeenth century) appeared in Salzburg, and he later dedicated a book of arias (*Arie*, Venice, 1616) for one to three voices to Marcus Sitticus.[16] The virtuoso tenor Francesco Campagnolo (1584–1630) first sang in Salzburg in the same year; six years later he delighted members of the imperial family with his singing during the Diet of Oedenburg (Sopron). He also served as theater Kapellmeister at the archducal court in Innsbruck during the war of the Mantuan succession.[17] On the whole, however, monody in northern Austria remained the specialty of visiting Italian singers and gained no strong footing there.[18]

In sharp contrast, continuo madrigals and secular pieces in more elaborate *stile concertato* became popular in Vienna during the first half of the seventeenth century. Once Ferdinand II had transferred his progressive court from Graz to Vienna in 1619, Italian composers residing in Vienna contributed richly to this varied repertoire. The love of vocal and instrumental contrasts is already evident in the sacred music of the imperial Kapellmeister Christoph Strauss (ca. 1575/80–1631). After Ferdinand II succeeded Matthias as emperor, he released the members of Matthias's chapel and replaced Strauss with the Venetian Giovanni Priuli (ca. 1575–1626), who had served him as Kapellmeister in Graz since 1612. In the hands of composers like the Kapellmeister Priuli and Valentini, the assistant Kapellmeister Pietro Verdina (ca. 1600–1641), and the court organist Giovanni Giacomo Arrigoni (1597–1675), concertato contrasts in Viennese sacred music reached a new level of brilliance and complexity.[19] It seems an inevitable development that composers such as Priuli and Valentini would transfer these techniques to secular vocal genres.

Recent scholars have documented the musical connections and exchanges between Vienna and northern Italian centers such as Mantua and Venice. Certainly the Mantuan connection to Vienna was very strong. The second wife of Ferdinand II and the third wife of Ferdinand III, both named Eleonora, were Mantuan princesses of the house of Gonzaga. When the conflict over the Gonzaga succession erupted in the late 1620s, several Mantuan musicians fled to Vienna. Herbert Seifert has detailed the journeys of the seminal composer Claudio Monteverdi (1567–1643) to Habsburg lands and has identified works by the Italian master that were performed for imperial occasions and/or dedicated to members of the royal family.[20] The most famous collection dedicated to a reigning Habsburg is Monteverdi's *Madrigali guerrieri, et amorosi*, Book VIII (1638). Originally intended for Ferdinand II, who died in February 1637, the printed copy of the eighth book of madrigals bears a dedication to his successor, Ferdinand III. Although Monteverdi refers to the music as "new," at least some of the works in Book VIII, including the renowned *Ballo delle ingrate*, date from his Mantuan years.

Margaret Mabbett has argued persuasively that stylistic trends and influences flowed both ways across the Alps.[21] For example, many of the compositions in Book VIII seem specifically intended for performance in Vienna or for one of the other imperial cities. Mabbett deduces this from style characteristics found in Book VIII that are prevalent in Vienna and concludes that, "compared with contemporary madrigalists in Italy, the composers active in Vienna employ larger forces, make greater use of melodic instruments within their works and seek out the means to create more extended formal structures."[22] She points out the facts that the Italian madrigalists active in Vienna required a variety of bowed string instruments to reinforce the bass line rather than the chitarrone, the preferred instrument in Italy; that composers in Austria more often integrated the instrumental lines into the vocal texture; that the greater variety of textures in Austria enabled the madrigalists to create broader, often experimental structures based on longer texts; and that the Austrian madrigalists were among the first to use repetitive bass patterns and dance rhythms. Mabbett emphasizes that both Monteverdi and the Italians in Vienna often blurred the genre distinction between the madrigal and the *canzonetta alla napolitana*. She even indicates that Arrigoni may have preceded Monteverdi in the use of *stile concitato*, albeit with voices rather than instruments.[23] Peter Holman also discusses the Viennese connection to Book VIII. Noting the odd scorings and frequent consecutive octaves, he suggests that Monteverdi may have had an "assistant" at the Habsburg court who prepared the string parts.[24]

Many of the features found in Book VIII can also be seen in the music of Priuli and Valentini. An organist who published instrumental as well as sacred and secular vocal music, Priuli embraced a wide range of styles, from polychoral sacred pieces to conservative compositions in *stile antico,* from few-voiced motets and monodies to elaborate concertato madrigals. Priuli's tendency to simulate the styles of Monteverdi and Giovanni Gabrieli (ca. 1554–1612) is apparent already in his *Il terzo libro de madrigali a 5 voci, di due maniere, l'una per voci sole, l'altra per voci & istromenti* (Venice, 1612), which was published while he was still active in Venice. Priuli requires, however, that all the madrigals be performed "con Partitura," that is, with supporting continuo accompaniment. Although less radical than Monteverdi, Priuli used many of the more celebrated composer's experimental and affective techniques, including *parlando* passages, virtuoso ornaments, and choral recitative (*falsobordone*), as in Monteverdi's madrigal "Sfogava con le stelle" (Book IV, 1603). After he began his service in Vienna, Priuli published two other collections of accompanied vocal chamber music: *Musiche concertate . . . libro quarto* (Venice, 1622) for twenty-nine voices and instruments and *Delicie musicali* (Venice, 1625) for two to ten voices and instruments.[25] In both volumes continuo accompaniment is obligatory, and in the *Delicie musicali* the element of vocal and instrumental contrasts becomes especially important.

Beginning in 1614 Valentini served at the Graz court of Archduke Ferdinand. When the archduke became Emperor Ferdinand II in 1619, Valentini received an appointment as the highest paid court organist. He succeeded Priuli as Kapellmeister on 15 June 1626 and was ennobled in the following year. After the accession of Ferdinand III in 1637 he was reelected Kapellmeister, and he continued to lead the imperial musicians until his death in 1649. Between 1616 and 1625 Valentini published at least six anthologies of vocal chamber music.[26] These collections include many selections with continuo accompaniment only, as well as numerous examples with concerted instrumental accompaniment. In both his sacred and his secular music, Valentini became a leading exponent of the *stile concertato* in Austria. He experimented with chromatic keyboard harmony while still at Graz, participated in the earliest operas performed in Vienna, penned the libretti for the first *sepolcri,* and composed early examples of the dramatic dialogue. In their evaluation of Valentini's style, Hellmut Federhofer and Steven Saunders emphasize that "much of his music employs a modern concertato idiom that reveals a highly adventurous, even avant-garde composer."[27] Joachim Steinheuer echoes this evaluation of Valentini's music, arguing that Valentini was one of the most original and advanced composers of the 1610s and 1620s. Steinheuer points to the rich variety of voicings, formal types (including ostinato and dance models), daring pictorial effects, and concertizing instruments.[28] Yet Valentini's sacred music sometimes reveals a more learned and conservative approach, and in his fifth book of madrigals (1625; "per cantarsi senza istromento") the composer actually returned to the a cappella style of the previous generation.

With the exceptions of notable periods of innovation and change such as the 1620s, the 1660s, and the 1700s, Vienna did indeed remain a stronghold of conservative style throughout the baroque era, partly no doubt because of the tastes of the emperors themselves. The pattern of innovation and stability is one of the most fascinating aspects of Viennese baroque music history. A period of change corresponded with the accession or rise of a new monarch, who inherited his predecessor's chapel but frequently encouraged a fresh circle of artists. Those composers who emerged as an emperor's favorites were rewarded with prestigious posts, high salaries, and long tenures. Isolated from the most current developments in Italy and secure in their abilities to please their patron, the favored composers did not always continue to experiment and thus grew increasingly insular and conservative. Valentini's thirty-year residence in Vienna set a precedent that was paralleled or surpassed by imperial composers such as Antonio Bertali, Felice Sances, Antonio Draghi, Carlo Agostino Badia, Francesco Conti, Johann Joseph Fux, and Antonio Caldara.

In the mid-seventeenth century, the two leading composers of vocal chamber music in Vienna were Antonio Bertali (1605–69) and Giovanni Felice Sances (ca. 1600–1679). Each served the Habsburgs for more than forty years; together Bertali and Sances contributed a vast amount of sacred and secular vocal music. Born in Verona, Bertali appears to have arrived in Vienna in 1624, probably with a recommendation from his early mentor, Stefano Bernardi, who had entered the service of Ferdinand II's brother, Archduke Carl Joseph, bishop of Breslau and Bressanone, in 1622. Rather early in his Viennese service, Bertali seems to have earned a coveted position as a composer, for he was chosen to compose the cantata *Donna real* for the marriage of the future emperor Ferdinand III to the Spanish infanta Anna Maria in 1631, and he continued to provide music for significant occasions in the lives of the Habsburgs. On 1 October 1649 Bertali succeeded Valentini as Kapellmeister, and he retained the appointment until his death in April 1669. During his tenure Bertali encouraged the growth of Italian opera at the Viennese court and solidified his reputation as one of the leading violinists of his generation. Two collections of instrumental music were published posthumously.[29]

An early catalog of Leopold I's library (*Distinta specificatione dell'archivio musicale per il servizio della cappella e camera cesarea*) now at A-Wn lists some six hundred compositions by Bertali.[30] The inexplicable loss of nearly all of this music remains a permanent mystery. Venetian influence is evident in the extant liturgical music, operas, and oratorios. Of the approximately 600 compositions referred to in the early catalog no fewer than 188 are designated as works belonging to the realm of secular Italian vocal chamber music. This total is divided under three main entries: (1) *40 compositioni morali e spirituali per la camera* for one to six voices with a variety of instruments; (2) *14 compositioni proprie;* and (3) *134 compositioni amorose* for one to eight voices, some with instruments.

From the information provided by the catalog entries we can draw several conclusions. The *40 compositioni morali e spirituali per la camera* were probably similar to chamber cantatas composed on moral topics by the court singer Filippo

Vismarri and dedicated to Leopold I, perhaps in the 1660s or 1670s. Unlike many stylistically related motets of the same period, these pieces were written in Italian, not Latin, and were intended for performance in the imperial chambers, not in church. Bertali's *14 compositioni proprie* were secular pieces undoubtedly written for specific court occasions. Whether or not these works were given scenic and/or dramatic representation cannot be determined, but the fact that they are inventoried as a group rather than individually suggests that they may have been compositions of fairly modest, cantata-like dimensions. The *134 compositioni amorose* for one to eight voices clearly belong to the realm of vocal chamber music. This group probably included many continuo madrigals and other ensemble chamber works representing the transition from madrigal to cantata that was taking place during the first half of the seventeenth century. The variety of voicing in these pieces and in the *compositioni morali e spirituali* reinforces the overall impression that Bertali was strongly influenced by the Venetian school.

Bertali's secular Italian compositions would greatly increase our knowledge of the early cantata north of Italy; therefore, it is particularly unfortunate that only a few have come down to us. At least three are preserved in the Düben-Sammlung managed by the Department of Musicology at the University of Uppsala.[31] Of the four members of the Düben family who served as *Hofkapellmeister* at the Royal Swedish Court from 1640 to ca. 1726, Gustav Düben the elder (1628–90) appears to have assembled most of this vast vocal and instrumental music collection. According to information given in the University of Uppsala catalog, the three Bertali pieces date from the last years of his life.

A native of Rome, Sances began his career at a rather early age as a boy soprano at the Collegio Germanico. He is known to have served Nicolò Sagredo in Venice and the Marquis Pio Enea degli Obizzi in Padua before he received an appointment as a tenor in the chapel of Ferdinand II not later than December 1636. From 1 October 1669 Sances held the post as Kapellmeister, an appointment he retained until his death in 1679.[32]

Sances was an astonishingly prolific composer of both sacred and secular music. A large percentage of his motets and cantatas were published, and present-day scholars have therefore been able to obtain a more complete picture of his work than that offered by the relatively few extant sources of Bertali's music. Table 1 includes the known titles of Sances's cantata prints. Facsimiles of the *Cantade,* Book 2, Part I, of cantatas and arias from Book 4, and of the *Capricci poetici* have recently been made available online.[33] The *Distinta specificatione* lists manuscript copies of 37 *compositioni morali et spirituali* for one to eleven voices, 22 *compositioni proprie,* and 273 *compositioni amorose* for one to six voices, the vast majority of which are lost. Peter Weberhofer also refers to numerous lost cantata manuscripts.[34]

From the numbering in the titles of Sances's prints of secular vocal music, it is evident that he published at least six volumes with more than one hundred pieces.

TABLE 1.1. TITLES OF PRINTED CANTATA COLLECTIONS BY GIOVANNI FELICE SANCES

Cantade . . . a voce sola, commode da cantarsi sopra tiorba, clavicembalo, arpa, o altro simile instrumento, libro secondo, parte prima (Venice: Bartolomeo Magni, 1633). Dedicated to Pio Enea degli Obizzi.[1]

Cantade . . . a doi voci, commode da cantarsi sopra tiorba, clavicembalo, arpa, o altro simile instrumento con un dialogo a tre, libro secondo, parte seconda (Venice: Bartolomeo Magni, 1633). Also dedicated to Obizzi.

Il quarto libro delle cantate, et arie a voce sola . . . commode da cantarsi sovra spinetta, tiorba, arpa, o altro instrumento, con due canzonette a due, e una aria a tre voci nel fine (Venice: Alessandro Vincenti, 1636).[2]

Capricci poetici . . . a una, doi e tre voci (Venice: Gardano, 1649). Dedicated to Nicolò Sagredo.

Trattenimenti musicali per camera a 2.3.4.5. . . . libro primo, opera sesta (Venice: F. Magni, 1657). Dedicated to Emperor Ferdinand III.

Notes
1. Modern facsimile edition in *Italian Secular Song 1606–1636, Venice II,* ed. Gary Tomlinson (New York, 1986). Concerning this collection, see especially Paolo Cecchi, "Le 'Cantade a voce sola' (1633) di Giovanni Felice Sances," *Rassegna Veneta di studi musicali* 5–6 (1989–90): 137–80.
2. Selections in *La Flora,* ed. Knud Jeppesen, vols. 2–3 (Copenhagen, 1949).

The first volume appears to be entirely lost, and I have not located any references to a title. The *libro secondo* (Venice, 1633) was issued in two parts containing a total of thirty-six pieces.[35] Among the extant cantata prints, there are no exemplars of a *libro terzo,* and it may be that this collection is also lost; on the other hand, Sances may have decided to leap ahead in the numbering to *libro quarto* (Venice, 1636) because each of the two parts of the *libro secondo* represented a substantial volume in its own right. *Libro quarto* consists of twenty-two pieces. Volumes 1–4 were all printed before Sances began his service in Vienna in 1637; even after receiving an appointment at the imperial court, he evidently maintained close associations with Venetian music publishers. A total of at least nine books of motets and cantatas were printed by B. Magni, F. Magni, Gardano, and Vincenti between 1638 and 1657. The two cantata volumes from this time are the *Capricci poetici* (Venice, 1649), which includes twenty-three pieces, and the *Trattenimenti musicali per camera* (Venice, 1657), with sixteen compositions.

Sances's vocal music shows the influence of both the contemporary experimentalists and the traditional Roman school. During his youthful career as a singer in Rome he may have associated with the progressive circle that included Mazzochi, Sabbatini, and Michi. On the whole, the monodic influence is more apparent in his soloistic sacred music and operas than in his cantatas, many of which reveal his solid grounding in the contrapuntal tradition. Sances was one of the earliest composers to use the term *cantata;* a degree of independence may also be reflected by the terms that he preferred in his last two collections: *capriccio* and *trattenimento*. In general, Sances's cantatas are representative of the middle baroque trend away from the many-voiced compositions in *stile concertato* toward the solo or few-voiced cantatas with continuo accompaniment. This more intimate version of the cantata became the standard one throughout the middle and late baroque era in Austria, as in Italy. However, with regard to structure, many of the pieces in these early *Cantade* collections are strophic bass songs and do not closely resemble the multisectional cantatas written for Vienna in the second half of the seventeenth century. Ironically, some of the pieces in the *Capricci poetici* are more like the later cantata than selections with the designation *cantada,* a symptom of the fluidity of genre terminology.

It is this fluidity that makes it difficult to pinpoint which works should be identified as cantatas, and it therefore seems unwise to adopt a strictly semantic approach to terminology. Joachim Steinheuer has demonstrated that a secular work such as Sances's *Dialogo a 3 voci* from the *Capricci poetici,* in which the composer assigns direct speech to a narrator, is quite similar to the cantata.[36] Similarly, John Whenham's discussion of *Tirsi morir volea* from Sances's *Cantade . . . Libro Secondo, Parte Seconda* stresses both the role of a narrator and the contrasts between recitative and arioso typical of the cantata, though he argues that the *dialogo* should be considered an independent genre.[37] Often even larger works composed for Vienna, such as the early operas, *sepolcri,* and *balli*—works that often include alternation of recitative and aria texts—seem to have more in common with the cantata than Seicento song.

In the hands of Bertali and Sances, vocal chamber music became one of the most important ingredients in the musical life of the imperial court. Both set poetry published in collections by Archduke Leopold Wilhelm and Emperor Leopold I as vocal chamber music. Just how popular the cantata and related genres had become in Austria in the middle of the seventeenth century can be seen from an inventory of the Innsbruck court's music holdings in 1665, the year in which control of that court reverted back to the imperial crown.[38] The inventory shows that the Innsbruck court had acquired published copies of vocal chamber music by Valentini, Rigatti, Strigoni, Piochi, Banchieri, Crivelli, Grandi, Agazzari, Steffano Bernardi, d'India, and Filippi. It is hardly surprising that composers like Antonio Cesti (1623–69) and Pietro Andrea Ziani (ca. 1616–84) were welcomed in Innsbruck in the early 1660s.

Some of the cantatas by Bertali and Sances undoubtedly date from the reign of Leopold I, though these composers seem to have concentrated increasingly upon the composition of larger dramatic works in their later years of Viennese service. After the conclusion of the financially draining Thirty Years' War, the elderly Ferdinand and the young Leopold I could devote more attention to costly and ostentatious entertainments that glorified them. Significantly, Sances published his last volume of vocal chamber music in 1657, shortly before the accession of Leopold. His four operas written for Vienna (1662–70) all date from the reign of Leopold, as do all six known oratorios (1666–76). It also seems likely that after the success of Bertali's first operas in the 1650s the aging composer turned increasingly to larger sacred and secular dramatic music. Nevertheless, at least a few of his vocal chamber works listed in the *Distinta specificazione* were composed during the reign of Leopold, as evidenced by the three Bertali compositions preserved in the Düben-Sammlung.

PART ONE

THE CANTATA IN VIENNA,

1658–1700

2

The Political and Cultural Milieu

Historical Background

During the successive reigns of Leopold I (r. 1658–1705) and his sons, Joseph I (r. 1705–11) and Charles VI (r. 1711–40), the principles of dynastic power and absolute monarchy within the Habsburg Empire were essentially unchallenged.[1] The old Habsburg dream of unifying the German Empire under one crown had been shattered by the Thirty Years' War. The Treaty of Utrecht (1648) enabled each provincial German ruler to establish the religion of his convictions within his own boundaries and to emulate the absolutism already practiced successfully by the French monarchy.

Prepared for the priesthood and educated by the Jesuit Neidhart (Nitardi), Leopold was unexpectedly placed in the role of successor to his father, Ferdinand III, when his older brother, Ferdinand, died in 1654. Physically unattractive, deeply religious, disinclined to war, often halting and indecisive, Leopold formed a distinct contrast to his cousin, Louis XIV. Yet under his forty-seven-year rule—one of the longest in European history—the Habsburg Empire enjoyed one of its most brilliant epochs.

Freed from the pressures of the Thirty Years' War, Leopold concentrated upon strengthening the position of Catholicism within his own diverse lands. During the second half of the seventeenth century, he also gradually improved the political position of the Danubian monarchy, particularly in eastern Europe. From 1658 to 1682 he maintained an uneasy peace with the Ottoman Empire. In 1664 he negotiated a treaty that enabled him to continue the status quo by paying the Turks an annual sum of money. As soon as the treaty expired, however, the Turks began to prepare for the devastating Siege of Vienna, which took place in 1683. With the help of the Polish king Jon Sobieski, the imperial forces were able to defeat the Turks decisively by September 1683. By the end of the seventeenth century, armies led by Prince Eugene of Savoy had also driven Turkish forces from Hungary. In the Treaty of Carlowitz (1699), the Habsburgs regained control of Hungary as well as Transylvania. Benefiting from a remarkable series of military successes and a gradual economic recovery, Leopold's image as the docile inheritor of the Habsburg dynasty changed in the years following the siege to one of a more assertive leader evermore glorified by the visual arts, the written word, and theatrical and musical spectacles.[2]

As in other German states, the cultures of France and Italy exerted a considerable amount of influence upon Austria during the baroque era. However, unlike Prussia and most other North German states, where French taste appears to have prevailed, Austria adopted the Italian style to a greater degree than the French. To be sure, no part of Germany escaped the influence of France. Louis XIV, the leading protagonist of absolutism and the dominant figure of his era, provided a model that was envied and imitated by every German prince, however modest his means.[3] In Austria, fashions and imported goods from France remained popular throughout the baroque era. Dancers trained in France began to receive appointments early in the reign of Leopold, and their numbers increased during the next hundred years.[4] A French as well as an Italian influence is evident in dance music written by the Austrians Johann Heinrich Schmelzer (ca. 1620–80), Anton Andreas Schmeltzer (1653–1701), and Joseph Hoffer (1666–1729) for operas, ballets, and equestrian ballets performed at the imperial court. However, courtly dance music in Austria never attained the extraordinary popularity that it enjoyed in France.[5]

An Italian influence was felt not only in Austria. The late seventeenth century witnessed a remarkable dissemination of Italian genius throughout Europe. This process had begun already in the Renaissance but was slowed somewhat by the exigencies of the Thirty Years' War. After the middle of the seventeenth century, however, Italian artists readily found employment at courts in most parts of Europe. "By the first half of the eighteenth century colonies of Italian artists, architects, and musicians, scattered from Moscow to Boston, from Stockholm to Budapest, were disseminating the culture of Italy."[6] At no court did the Italians achieve fuller supremacy than at the Habsburg court in Vienna.

One of the factors that led to the preeminence of Italian culture in Vienna was the frequent intermarriage of Habsburgs with members of prominent Italian families. The second wife of Ferdinand II and the third wife of Ferdinand III, Mantuan princesses of the house of Gonzaga, encouraged the influence of Italian culture in Austria; in particular, they helped Italian opera and oratorio become an established part of the imperial court life. Leopold's stepmother, the empress dowager Eleonora (1629–86), continued to play a leading role at the Austrian court long after her husband's death in 1657.[7] She frequently participated in political maneuvering, ably maintained her own court, and lavishly supported the arts. Still another Habsburg empress of Italian descent was the second of Leopold's three wives, Anna Claudia Felicitas of Tyrol (1613–76), granddaughter of Cosimo de' Medici.

A second reason for the Austrian assimilation of Italian culture was the prolongation of the Counter-Reformation, which continued throughout the seventeenth century. By 1650 many Protestant noblemen had lost their titles and had taken refuge in other parts of Germany. In their places, numerous merchants and landowners—frequently Italians seeking their fortunes in Habsburg lands—were rewarded with new titles of nobility for their fidelity to the emperor and to the Catholic Church. Often derided by the older members of the aristocracy, these newcomers, who included the princes Montecuccoli, Bucelini, and Piccolomini, among others, soon found favor with Leopold as political advisors and influential members of the military.[8] Similarly, a large number of Italian artists, architects, poets, and musicians emigrated from Italy to Vienna during the seventeenth century. Many found permanent employment in the service of the emperor as members of the official court.

During the reign of Leopold, Italian became the preferred language of the Habsburg court and was spoken by members of the imperial family, the aristocracy, and the intelligentsia. Leopold himself, fluent in at least four languages, was recognized for his skill in writing Italian verse.[9] "One of Leopold's pastimes, when he was not busy with his royal duties, was to play a game with these two elders [his stepmother, Eleonora, and his uncle, Archduke Leopold Wilhelm] of improvising Italian sonnets, each one of the trio speaking a couplet, to be continued by the next one."[10] Moreover, the first Italian journal to be published in Vienna, *Il corriere ordinario,* began to appear in 1677; it thus preceded the earliest German-language newspaper, the *Wienerisches Diarium,* by nearly thirty years.

Another indication of increased Italian influence following the Thirty Years' War was the creation of a literary academy modeled after the ones that flourished in Italy in the seventeenth century. The prime mover in this effort was Leopold Wilhelm, who ranks among the most important and enthusiastic patrons of the arts in the entire history of the Habsburg dynasty.[11] He played a central role in attracting Italian musicians to the imperial court. Two agents who served the archduke for this purpose were Friedrich, landgrave of Hessen-Darmstadt, and the Jesuit Theodorico Bechei, both of whom maintained especially strong ties to Rome. Leopold Wilhelm supported young Italian musicians in his service who studied at the German college in Rome. One of the most prominent musicians who trained at the college was Francesco Foggia (1604–88), who became *maestro di cappella* at the Austrian court of the youthful Leopold Wilhelm in the 1620s.[12] The archduke served as a military commander and general during the Thirty Years' War. On 11 April 1647 he took up residence in Brussels, where he assumed the post as governor of the Low Countries. During his ten-year service in Brussels, he became a great patron of the arts, employing the renowned Flemish painter David Teniers the Younger, who assisted him in collecting a vast number of paintings that were later taken to Vienna and are now housed at the Kunsthistorisches Museum. In 1647 Leopold Wilhelm attempted repeatedly to attract the great Roman oratorio and cantata composer Giacomo Carissimi (1605–74). Letters to Carissimi from Friedrich and Bechei on behalf of the archduke reveal the generous terms offered to the composer, but after some deliberation, Carissimi declined, preferring to remain in Rome.[13] An idea of Leopold Wilhelm's lively interest in Italian music can be gleaned from an inventory of his vast collection now in the Viennese Hofkammerarchiv. In addition to a list of musical instruments and books of sacred music, the inventory lists more than 250 titles of works *per servicio di tavola,* including madrigals, dialogues, serenatas, and cantatas.[14]

Herbert Seifert has written in detail about the origin and evolution of academic meetings in Vienna during the reign of Leopold.[15] By the beginning of 1656, Leopold Wilhelm and the field marshal Count Raimondo Montecuccoli had founded the Accademia dei Raffinati at Brussels. In that year the archduke assembled and published a collection of Italian poetry, *Diporti del Crescente,*[16] which he dedicated to his elder brother, Emperor Ferdinand III, who likewise wrote and published poetry.[17] Returning to Vienna, Leopold Wilhelm hoped to continue what had already been established in Brussels. His idea of founding a literary academy was supported by the emperor and empress, and the first session was held on 7 January 1657. The assistant Kapellmeister, Sances, composed vocal music for early meetings of the newly founded academy.

From the outset, the Viennese academy was dominated by noble Italian diplomats and military figures who adopted playful names such as il Distillato (Montecuccoli), lo Sprezzato, il Sitibondo, and l'Errante. Ferdinand III assumed the name l'Occupato, and Eleonora became known as l'Immutabile. Held in imperial chambers of the Hofburg palace, the chief residence of the imperial family, the early meetings took place during Fasching (Carnival) and continued into Lent. Activities included speeches by the members, poetry, and music. Seifert reveals that Sances composed a work that specifically played upon the academic names of the emperor, the empress, and Montecuccoli. However, the death of Ferdinand III on 3 April 1657 brought all court celebrations, including academic sessions, to a halt.

The year 1668 witnessed the founding of the Accademia degl'Illustrati by the empress dowager Elonora Gonzaga. Instead of diplomats and military leaders, the members of the Accademia degl'Illustrati were Italian men of letters. Thus, the membership included the historian Count Galeazzo Gualdo Priorato, as well as the librettists Francesco Sbarra and Girolamo Branchi, whose cantata texts were set to music by Carlo Cappellini. Held in a grand hall of the Hofburg on Sundays during Fasching, the meetings of 1668 were open to all *persone civili,* but the empress established strict rules of seating and protocol for the participating members. Three sessions were held in 1669, but a fire at the Hofburg prevented further meetings there. However, additional sessions took place that year at the Favorita, Eleonora's summer residence. Records indicate that Eleonora sponsored additional academic meetings during Fasching in 1677, 1684, and 1685. The four sessions of 1677 honored Leopold I on the occasion of his third marriage. Vocal music by Antonio Draghi entertained the participants during the 10 February session. Giovanni Battista Pederzuoli's six *accademie: cantate per l'anno 1685* are the earliest extant Viennese secular compositions for which the term *accademia* appears in the title. From this title and from his four undated *cantate per l'accademia,* it is obvious that the concepts of cantata and *accademia* were intimately bound together in Pederzuoli's mind.[18]

In time Leopold I founded his own academy, which held its initial meeting on 7 January 1674. The members included Count Priorato, Nicolò Minato, and Filippo Sbarra, son of the court librettist, as well as Count Montecuccoli, who changed his academic name to l'Incerto. Leopold himself assumed the name that his father, Ferdinand III, had chosen: l'Occupato. Draghi was chosen to provide music for meetings on 3 February 1693, 15 November 1697, and 11 February 1698. The meeting on 15 November 1697 appears to be the only academic session that celebrated a specific family festival, namely, the emperor's name day. An element of competition seems to have played an important role in Leopold's academy. While the topics were frequently banal, the participants were expected to debate with eloquence and erudition. For the emperor's name day in 1697, five noble Italian ladies debated whether luck or merit is more useful in life. A decision in favor of merit was handed down by Archduchess Maria Elisabeth. By the 1690s the competitive aspect seems to have extended to musical performances. In December 1691 noble ladies and gentlemen competed with one another in singing and in playing musical instruments. And in May 1699 a host of virtuosos, including the cellist Giovanni Bononcini and the castrato Vincenzo Ulivicciani, performed during an academy held in the emperor's quarters at Schloss Laxenburg.[19]

Seifert emphasizes the fact that the academies did not carry the same meaning for the artistic and scientific life of Vienna that they did for Italy. Primarily they served as entertainment for the imperial family and their noble guests. A secondary purpose of the academies was the encouragement of Italian poetry, written both by resident poets and by members of the aristocracy. The number of meetings in a given year was quite small, and their occurrence from year to year can be traced only sporadically.

Topics chosen for debate were apolitical and often concerned playful aspects of love. That so many academic texts were lighthearted can be attributed in part to the fact that they were performed mostly during Carnival season or in the summer. Typical subjects included whether the beauty of the body is preferable to the beauty of the soul, whether jealousy is a pleasant or a cruel companion of love, whether a man is more attracted to a beautiful woman by her singing or by her weeping, and whether a lover in the presence of his lady should pale or blush—topics that undoubtedly reflected the reality of courtly life. At Carnival a comic theme was introduced: if Amor should visit the court, what office should be assigned to him? Minato concluded that every office in the court was suitable for the god of love. Occasionally a session focused on a more serious topic such as whether death should be loved or hated.

Erika Kanduth delves deeper into the style of poetry by Leopold Wilhelm and Emperor Ferdinand III.[20] She offers quotes from selected poems, her interpretations, and a discussion of the various genres of poetry found in Leopold Wilhelm's collection. On the whole, she finds the archduke's poetry superior to the emperor's verse, emphasizing that all the poetry in their collections was conceived for immediate entertainment and consumption within the context of court decorum. Kanduth concludes that Vienna was not a major literary center in the seventeenth century and describes the noble poets as *Versenschreiber* rather than *Dichter*.[21]

LEOPOLD I AS PATRON AND COMPOSER

Much of the cultural growth that took place in Austria during the late seventeenth century was encouraged by Leopold himself. A student of science, philosophy, history, and the arts, Leopold increased the manuscript and print holdings of the imperial library by approximately ten thousand volumes. For the purpose of expanding the library, he engaged the scholar Peter Lambeck (Lambecius) as court librarian from 1663 to 1680. The extant portion of Leopold's music library, the Collezione Leopoldina, is preserved in the Musiksammlung at A-Wn.[22] In a fascinating article, Josef Gmeiner has traced the history of Leopold's impressive private collection of music manuscripts, the Schlafkammerbibliothek.[23] This collection was strictly for Leopold's personal use so that he could follow along the scores when he himself was not at the harpsichord. The library was kept in Leopold's private bedroom on the first floor of the Schweizerhof, not in the Leopoldinischertrakt (Leopold Wing) of the Hofburg, as formerly assumed.[24] Gmeiner indicates that the extant collection consists of 524 volumes, which can be identified by their original call numbers. He discusses in detail the bindings, imprints, and copyists before tracing the history of the collection, which lay in obscurity after the death of Charles VI until it was rescued and cataloged by Moritz Graf Dietrichstein in 1825. Gmeiner then follows the history of the collection up to 1920, when it was transferred to the Musiksammlung in the Albertina.[25]

Leopold's interests in the arts were unusually diverse, but he especially favored music, to which he gave his attention throughout his long reign.[26] As a patron, he paid the personnel of his large chapel as much as ten thousand florins annually, a vast expenditure in the seventeenth century. Franz Hadamowsky verifies that imperial musicians were well paid, though not as extravagantly as sometimes assumed; thus, for example, the Kapellmeister earned sixty times as much as a vineyard worker, while an imperial music student received six times as much.[27] Leopold showed personal concern for the well-being of individual musicians, notably Antonio Draghi, and he himself laid down rules for their organization and conduct.[28] Through unusual outlays of money, he provided for the construction of theaters and opera houses. The abundance of court entertainments astonished foreign visitors.[29] The vast array of musical works dedicated to Leopold includes compositions by prominent seventeenth-century musicians such as Ercole Bernabei, Carissimi, Legrenzi, Pasquini, Stradella, and Giovanni Bononcini. The volumes are preserved in the Collezione Leopoldina.

Leopold not only supported musicians generously, but he himself was an accomplished performer on the harpsichord and recorder. His keyboard instructors were Marcus and Wolfgang Ebner. He appears to have studied composition with Bertali and was active as a composer throughout his adult life. Of the four emperor-composers, he was by far the most prolific and probably the most naturally gifted. He created at least nine sacred dramatic works, eleven secular dramatic compositions (written in Italian or German), a variety of liturgical pieces, more than one hundred dances for violin and continuo, and a handful of vocal chamber pieces. In addition, he composed a large number of individual arias that were inserted in specific dramatic works by a variety of composers.[30]

Seifert documents an undated two-part *cantata dell'accademia* by Leopold, but unfortunately the music is no longer extant.[31] Otherwise, Leopold's compositions closest in spirit and style to the cantata are his madrigal and four canzonettas. The canzonettas date from 1655 to 1657 and clearly belong to his list of student compositions. They survive in A-Wn, 18831, a manuscript devoted to the music of the young Leopold and assembled by Wolfgang Ebner, one of his keyboard instructors.[32] The source, *Spartitura compositionum,* is divided into three basic parts: sacred music, vocal pieces "per la camera" (i.e., the canzonettas), and sonatas. The canzonettas appear in the manuscript in the order given in Table 2.1. The dates are written in Leopold's own hand.[33] *Guerra, alla Guerra, o alma,* written in the year before Leopold ascended the throne, is representative of these youthful compositions. Scored for two tenors and continuo, this canzonetta consists of an initial binary ritornello *con cembalo solo* followed by three ariettas and a final duet. For the meter of the ritornello Leopold selected $\frac{3}{2}$, the most common choice of the Bertali-Sances generation, and each section typically ends with hemiola. Repeated notes in the bass of the ritornello provide a conventional illustration of *guerra*. In the binary arietta that follows, the first tenor urges his soul to war, while the second tenor counters with an exhortation to peace. In separate ariettas the tenors reiterate their arguments for war and peace. The second-tenor aria continues as a duet in which the singers assert that the greatest triumph is to rest in God. The tenors join in long sustained tones that nicely portray the final line of text, "goder gioir e riposar in Dio." The religious conclusion of this canzonetta places it in the tradition of vocal chamber music with moral and spiritual topics found in numerous works by Bertali and Sances and in the *cantate morali* of Filippo Vismarri.

Leopold's only madrigal, "Sideree luci, ond'io sospiro," is the final piece in A-Wn, 16589, the source that also preserves two serenatas and a *dialogo musicale.* No date is provided for any of the works in this collection, but the rather ambitious

TABLE 2.1. CANZONETTAS BY LEOPOLD I IN A-WN, 18831

FOLIOS	VOICES/INSTRUMENTS	DATE	TEXT INCIPIT
52–58	T, vl, bc	November 1655	*Oimè, son perso*
58–64	S 1–2, bc	July 1656	*Patienza, mio core*
64–69	S 1–2, B, vl 1–2, bc	September 1656	*Rio destin, crudo laccio*
69–73	T 1–2, bc	February 1657	*Guerra, alla Guerra, o alma*

dimensions of the dramatic pieces suggest that they were composed during Leopold's mature years, after he had assumed his responsibilities as emperor in 1658. The madrigal is a continuo composition *a 3*. Its poetry, like the texts of the canzonettas, may well have been written by Leopold himself. The style of the canzonettas and madrigal belongs to the tradition of the continuo madrigal and *scherzo musicale* initiated by early baroque composers such as Monteverdi and Grandi and continued in Vienna by mid-seventeenth-century composers such as Bertali and Sances.

The manuscript A-Wn, 16023 contains Leopold's *Musica per la festa delle / Serenissime Arciduchesse e Signore Dame / Composta da sua Maestà Cesarea / . . . 1695,* a late piece of vocal chamber music that demonstrates the emperor's growth as a composer. Written for Carnival, this charming work introduces Turkish characters and exploits a mixture of Italian, Spanish, German, and Latin for humorous effects. Ritornellos alternate with recitatives, ariosos, strophic arias, and a duet, unfolding in a style similar to multisectional occasional pieces from the same period by Antonio Draghi. Leopold's strongest suit is his intelligent formal planning, which reveals a sophisticated level of variety and originality. The structure of the fifth aria is especially interesting. It consists of two strophes separated by a ritornello; each strophe is ternary (ABA), but the music for the second strophe is a variation of the first. Less varied are Leopold's rhythmic patterns and melodies, obviously composed for dilettante singers whose brief coloratura passages illustrate words such as *bella, lieta, variabile,* and *mutabile.* Recitatives are quite simple, dynamics are entirely lacking, and tempo indications are limited to allegro and adagio. Leopold supplies figuration for first-inversion chords and for suspensions. The bass line itself functions almost exclusively as harmonic support, and harmonies throughout are basic and clear, each aria beginning and ending in the same key with limited tonal movement internally.

HABSBURG MUSIC CHAPELS, 1658–1700

Although the term *chapel* has become standard in describing court musical institutions in the early modern period, the imperial Kapelle had lost its purely sacred character already by the early seventeenth century. Thus, during the combined reigns of Ferdinand II and Ferdinand III (1618–57), Habsburg composers provided approximately twenty-five secular dramatic works for performances at court. The Mantuan wives of these two emperors were largely responsible for instigating the performances, which usually took place on the birthday or name day of the emperor. However, the financial restraints imposed because of the Thirty Years' War prevented the Habsburgs from actually reproducing the costly splendor of the operas to which the Mantuan princesses were accustomed. Shortly after Leopold assumed power, opera became established on a secure footing in Vienna. Court performances of secular vocal and instrumental chamber music also increased gradually during the second half of the seventeenth century.

In this study, the term *chapel* is used to designate not only the court institutions but also the total music personnel engaged by the Habsburgs: administrators, composers, male and female singers, *Singerknaben,* instrumentalists, instrument makers, even servants. During the first half of Leopold's reign (1658–82), the number of musicians employed at the Habsburg court did not increase significantly over the total engaged by Ferdinand III.[34] For the Regensburg Diet of 1653, Ferdinand had taken with him some sixty musicians, the highest number known to have been employed during his reign. After 1658 Leopold appears to have increased expenditures not for the purpose of augmenting his chapel but rather for producing lavish performances of dramatic music. As pressure from the Turkish wars receded after 1683, the number of *kayserliche Hof-Musici* increased slowly but steadily. By 1705, the last year of Leopold's reign, the total number of court musicians had grown to 102.[35] With regard to nationality, the chapel consisted mainly of Italians and native Austrians. The percentage of Italians increased steadily throughout the late seventeenth century. Moreover, Italians continued to hold most of the important posts.

During the years 1658–86 the imperial court actually supported two music chapels, one maintained by the emperor himself and a second patronized by the empress dowager Eleonora.[36] While the membership of each chapel appears to have been distinct, interchange of musicians for performances was common. Eleonora engaged a smaller number of musicians than the emperor, but these included some of the most influential composers. Her chapel consisted almost entirely of Italians, many of whom she recruited from her native Mantua. After her death in 1686, Eleonora's chapel was absorbed by the emperor.

Italian composers active at the Habsburg courts from 1658 to 1700 include important figures such as Giuseppe Tricarico (1623–97), Antonio Cesti (1623–69), Pietro Andrea Ziani (ca. 1616–84), Antonio Draghi (1634–1700), Filippo Vismarri (before 1635–1706?), Antonio Maria Viviani (before 1630?–1683), Giovanni Bonaventura Viviani (1638–ca. 1692), Carlo Cappellini (before 1635–84), and Giovanni Battista Pederzuoli (before 1650–after 1691). At least five of these composers wrote cantatas for Habsburg entertainment. On the whole, a composer's nationality defined his duties. Italian composers provided dramatic music (opera, oratorio, and cantata), while Austrians concentrated upon instrumental ensemble pieces (including ballet music for dramatic works), keyboard music, liturgical compositions, and music for the Jesuit dramas. This separation of duties was not entirely strict. Thus, for example, court keyboard composers included not only Austrians such as Johann Caspar Kerll (1627–93) and Ferdinand Tobias Richter (1649–1711) but also Italians such as Alessandro Poglietti (d. 1683), and Kerll is known to have composed at least two Italian cantatas. Nevertheless, a close relationship between a composer's nationality and the kind of music he was expected to provide persisted until the end of the seventeenth century.

OCCASIONS, PLACES OF PERFORMANCE, AND PERFORMERS

Some information about the occasions and places of cantata performance has come to light. Leopold's private chamber in the Schweitzerhof not only housed his personal library but was also the scene of many musical performances attended by a select group of invited guests. In short, the Schlafkammer became the ideal space for *musica da camera,* including cantatas.

Academic sessions often provided occasions for musical performances. According to Seifert, Antonio Draghi may have composed music for a meeting of the Accademia degl'Illustrati on 10 February 1677, one of the sessions that honored Leopold on the occasion of his third marriage.[37] Music by Giovanni Battista Pederzuoli with poetry by Nicolò Minato was definitely performed before and after the discussions at sessions held in Eleonora's private living quarters in January and February 1685. The modest level of difficulty evident in Pederzuoli's four undated *accademie* found in MS 18872 implies that they were written for two ladies and gentlemen of the court. Eleonora herself probably sang the soprano part. The earliest surviving music for one of the meetings of Leopold's academy appears to be Draghi's *Seconda accademia* of 1693. From the title of Draghi's *Intramezzo di musica in una accademia di Dame* (1697) it is clear that aristocratic ladies performed this work; on the title page Draghi further indicates that the vocal parts were sung by "Quattro Dame Sotto Nome / di Confidenza. Speranza. Avvertenza. Prud:[enz] a." Draghi collaborated with his son, Carlo Domenico, in the composition of the *Terza accademia* in 1698, the year in which Archduke Charles (the future Emperor Charles VI) is first named as a participant in academic activities. Seifert indicates that the *Terza accademia* probably took place during Fasching because of a notice in the *Corriere ordinario* reporting the attendance of the emperor and empress at an academy that year.[38]

An explanation for Draghi's preoccupation with ensemble rather than solo cantatas lies in the fact that at least some of them were intended for performance by members of the imperial family and the Viennese aristocracy, who loved to participate in dramatic entertainments of the late seventeenth century. In the case of *Lo specchio,* composed for Eleonora's birthday (18 November) in 1676, participation by the empress dowager and four countesses is actually documented on the title page, where the list of performers appears:

Sua Altezza Seren:[ma] [Eleonora]
Cont.[sa] Lamboin
Cont.[sa] Rapach
Cont.[sa] Prainerin
Cont.[sa] Sera:[?]

Participation by members of the nobility in one or more of the other Draghi canatas seems likely, although it was customary to list imperial and aristocratic participants in the manuscripts. The roles named on the title page of the undated *Forza d'un bel volto* are "Due occhi. La bocca. Il crine. Il volto," and those for the *Terza accademia* are "Due Innamorati P:[o] e 2:[do] et Amore."

With regard to professional performers of specific cantatas, our knowledge is somewhat limited. Ludwig Ritter von Köchel provides a list of singers engaged at the imperial court during the periods 1657–79 and 1680–1711, with details about the durations of their appointments.[39] Vismarri, a highly esteemed soprano castrato, may have performed his own cantatas and ariettas, all scored for soprano and continuo. That the alto castrato Paolo Castelli authored the poetry of one of Vismarri's ariettas suggests that he too may have performed cantatas.

A recent study by Janet Page has greatly enriched our understanding of the importance of female singers at the Habsburg court during the seventeenth century.[40] Page has demonstrated that female professional musicians were engaged at the Habsburg court in Vienna as early as 1617. In her table 1 she identifies no fewer than sixteen singers employed between 1617 and 1686. Other women, named only as "musicians," may also have sung in chamber music performances. Many of them were wives of court musicians, relatives of musicians or other court employees, or simply young girls with singing talent. The usual salary of a female singer, including Maria Betali, the wife of the Kapellmeister Antonio Bertali, was 360 florins.

Foremost among the female singers during the reign of Leopold I was Giulia Masotti (ca. 1650–1701), the focus of Page's essay. She established a career as a star soprano in Venice during the 1660s and early 1670s. Giulia was appointed to the court of Empress Claudia Felicitas as a chamber musician in 1673. The empress herself was admired for her skill as a singer and a performer on the harpsichord and lute. Initially Giulia sang at Innsbruck on 5 September in a serenade that marked the imperial engagement of Leopold and Claudia Felicitas. She traveled with Antonio Maria Viviani, the empress's Kapellmeister, from Innsbruck, arriving in Vienna by December. Her close association with Viviani suggests that she may have sung several of his cantatas. Giulia's extraordinary salary of 1,500 florins plus perks—higher than that of the leading castrati engaged at the imperial court—is indicative of her star status. According to Page, Giulia "performed frequently for [Leopold and Claudia Felicitas's] personal entertainment in 'Haus Concerten' (chamber music) often with the soprano castrato Vincenzino, sometimes with the empress herself, sometimes with other singers."[41] Did some of the *Haus Concerten* in fact include Italian cantatas? (It is worth noting that Giulia's performances in Vienna were not limited to chamber music. The singing of Giulia and another female singer in Antonio Draghi and Nicolò Minato's opera *Il ratto delle Sabine* on 9 and 10 June 1674 breached the imperial tradition of prohibiting women from appearing on the stage.)

The music-loving empress dowager Eleonora Gonzaga also engaged at least two female singers.[42] Did these women or perhaps even Giulia sing in the *accademie* by Pederzuoli? No specific details identifying the names of musicians who played in Italian cantatas have come to light, but Köchel lists a host of instrumentalists who may have participated.[43] The keyboard player Carlo Cappellini perhaps participated in private performances of his cantatas either for Leopold or for his patroness, the empress dowager.

LIBRETTISTS

A handful of librettists for cantatas by Vismarri, Cappellini, Pederzuoli, and Draghi have been identified, but none for Viviani or Kerll. The mid-seventeenth-century Roman Giovanni Lotti, the poet of no. 4 in Vismarri's collection of *cantate e ariette per camera,* is known also as the librettist for cantatas by Luigi Rossi, Savioni, Cesti, and possibly Carissimi. In addition to Lotti, four other librettists, ostensibly gentlemen of the court, are named: Marc'Antonio Signorini (nos. 1, 5, 11, and 22), Domenico Manzini (no. 21), Carlo Marcheselli (no. 23), and Paolo Castelli (no. 24). For no. 22 (*Gioverà cangiar pensiero*) Signorini provided a title: *Contro l'ambizione di donna invecchiata.* He also penned librettos for at least five oratorios performed in Vienna between 1694 and 1703.[44] Marcheselli gave the enigmatic title *In lontananza di B.D.* to no. 23 (*Luci belle, miei soli*). Castelli, the poet of no. 24 in Vismarri's anthology, sang at the imperial court from 1 October 1662 until his death in December 1685.[45] As dilettante poets rather than court-appointed librettists, Signorini, Manzini, Marcheselli, and Castelli did not receive commissions for large secular dramatic works.[46]

The two poets identified in the manuscript of Cappellini's *cantate per camera,* Giberto Ferri (nos. 1, 3, 4, 6, and 7) and Girolamo Branchi (nos. 5 and 8), were, like the composer, associated with the court of Eleonora. The fourth cantata is the only one given a title: *Che la Ruggiada è Pianto dell'Aurora.* Between 1670 and 1674 Ferri supplied librettos for two *sepolcri* and one oratorio, all with music by Draghi and performed in Eleonora's private chapel.[47] Branchi wrote the text for a *festa musicale* set to music by Pederzuoli and offered for Eleonora's birthday on 18 November 1677; he was also named by Eleonora as a member of the Accademia degl'Illustrati in 1670 and 1675.[48]

Certainly one of the most important librettists of the late seventeenth century was Nicolò Minato (ca. 1630–98), court poet in Vienna from 1669 until his death. Following a successful career as a librettist and impresario in Venice, Minato became the leading poet at the Habsburg court, writing more than 210 texts for sacred and secular dramatic works by Draghi, Pederzuoli, Marc'Antonio Ziani, Giovanni Bononcini, and Leopold I, among others.[49] As a cantata poet, Minato wrote the texts for Draghi's *Lo specchio* (1676) and for Pederzuoli's six *accademie* composed for sessions of the Accademia degl'Illustrati in 1685.

In a recent article, Beatrice Barazzoni discusses in detail the texts of three cantatas by Draghi, one in the manuscript A-Wn, 16299 (*Lo specchio*) and two in A-Wn, 16315 (*Forza d'un bel volto* and *Di tre Amanti*). Barazzoni makes the reasonable conjecture that Minato, Draghi's most frequent collaborator, authored not only the cantata attributed to him in 16299 but also the two cantatas in 16315.[50] She describes the differences and similarities between *Lo specchio* and the other two cantatas. While *Lo specchio* belongs to the elevated allegorical tradition of seventeenth-century cantatas, *Forza d'un bel volto* and *Di tre Amanti* evince the more relaxed lyrical poetry dealing with aspects of love. All three cantata texts reflect the popular style of the Neapolitan poet Giambattista Marino (1569–1625), whose extravagant conceits, use of antithesis, and lavish descriptions influenced several generations of Italian poets.[51] Barazzoni stresses the great variety of metrical and prose forms that translate naturally into musical variety, allowing Draghi to treat the texts flexibly, sometimes actually subverting the poetic structures.

In view of the fact that Leopold spoke Italian fluently and occasionally wrote Italian verse, the possibility that the emperor himself created several cantata texts should not be overlooked. He may well be the author of the poetry for his own youthful canzonettas and madrigal.

3

The Composers

The early years of Leopold's reign must be counted among the most fruitful for music in the entire history of the Habsburg court. After a generation of relative stability marked by the long tenures of Bertali and Sances, the 1660s in particular witnessed an unusual amount of artistic innovation and musical activity. An influx of strong new musical personalities added to the cultural life of the court. These included the composers Giuseppe Tricarico (1623–97), Antonio Cesti (1623–69), Pietro Andrea Ziani (ca. 1616–84), and Antonio Draghi (1634–1700), men who brought to Vienna a mixture of contemporary Italian styles. Among these four significant musical personalities, only Draghi was to remain in the service of the Habsburgs after 1669. Cesti died in that year, Tricarico had departed for Gallipoli by 1664, and Ziani had probably already returned to Venice in 1668.

Composers Who May Have Written Cantatas for Vienna during the Early Reign of Leopold I

The first of the new wave of Italians who arrived in Vienna shortly after the accession of Leopold was Giuseppe Tricarico, who had established a solid reputation as a composer in Rome and Ferrara during the 1640s and 1650s.[1] In 1656 he followed his brother, a violinist, to Vienna and soon received an appointment as Kapellmeister at the court of the empress dowager, a position he retained until 1662, when he was succeeded by Ziani. Tricarico's significance rests mainly upon his role as an early harbinger of the mid-seventeenth-century Roman style north of Italy. For Vienna he composed three operas, three oratorios, and a variety of sacred works.[2] However, there is no clear evidence that Tricarico composed vocal chamber music during his Viennese residence. All of the cantatas known to me are preserved in the Conservatorio di Musica at Naples.[3] If not an active cantata composer in Vienna, Tricarico nevertheless advanced the Roman style and may have influenced late seventeenth-century cantata composers employed by Leopold.

Born in the Tuscan city of Arezzo, the tenor Antonio Cesti enjoyed his first successes as an opera composer in Venice. He became one of the most renowned and successful opera composers of his generation, and his presence in Austria from as early as December 1652 undoubtedly stimulated fresh interest in Italian dramatic music among all of the Habsburg princes.[4] In that year he received an appointment as *maestro di cappella di camera* at the Innsbruck court of Archduke Ferdinand Charles, a second cousin of Leopold. In 1658 Cesti was in Rome; by June 1659 he was again in Innsbruck, but he returned to Rome by 1 November of that year.[5] At Florence in 1661 he sang in opera performances honoring the marriage of Cosimo III de' Medici, the nephew of Ferdinand Charles's wife. He returned with the archduke to Innsbruck early in February 1662. After the deaths of Ferdinand Charles (30 December 1662) and his successor, Sigmund Franz (24 June 1665), control of Tyrol reverted to the imperial crown, and the Innsbruck music establishment was largely absorbed by the Habsburg chapel in Vienna.[6]

It is evident that Cesti's music had begun to circulate in Vienna some years before his arrival in 1666. Ties between Innsbruck and Vienna had been strong throughout the early seventeenth century. Leopold himself had joined Archduke Ferdinand Charles in interceding with Pope Alexander VII (Chigi) on Cesti's behalf in 1661. Cesti was appointed *cappellano d'honore* and *intendente delle musiche teatrali*, a post subsequently held by Draghi, on 1 January 1666, although he did not arrive in Vienna before 22 April. Later in the same year Cesti became assistant Kapellmeister, an appointment he held simultaneously with Sances.[7] His list of secular works for Vienna comprises at least five compositions, one of which was originally written for Innsbruck. The most famous Viennese opera is *Il pomo d'oro* (12 and 14 July 1668), a colossal allegorical work that climaxed the resplendent festivities in connection with the marriage of Leopold and the infanta Margaret Theresa of Spain.[8] Following the performances, Leopold granted Cesti's request to return to Tuscany for reasons of family and health, not anticipating that the composer would never return.[9]

In addition to more than a dozen large secular dramatic works, some seventy-five chamber cantatas and a few sacred pieces by Cesti come down to us.[10] His possible activity as a cantata composer in Vienna remains difficult to document. Several vocal works by Cesti were performed as table music on 11 August 1667 on the occasion of Empress Margaret Theresa's first visit to the imperial picture gallery in the Stallburg. Herbert Seifert believes that these compositions were almost certainly chamber cantatas, although no specific titles are identified.[11] While a few cantatas from his total output can be dated with some precision, a clear chronology has not yet been established.[12] Not a single cantata can be assigned to the Viennese period with certainty. Only two extant cantata manuscripts (D-Mbs, Mus. ms. 1527 and A-GÖ, Ms. 4091) appear to be of Viennese origin. The manuscript in D-Mbs was presumably intended for the personal use of the elector Max Emanuel (1662–1726), who had married archduchess Maria Antonia (1669–92), the daughter of Leopold I and Margaret Theresa, in 1685. It contains sixteen cantatas and one arietta. Of the three cantatas by Cesti, two are also found in I-MOe.[13] Ms. 4091 at A-GÖ preserves thirty-one Italian cantatas. One of the two by Cesti is found also in I-Rvat; the other is in D-MÜs.[14]

If Cesti neglected the cantata during his three-year engagement at Vienna, the reason for this neglect was probably his constant preoccupation with the composition of larger secular dramatic works not only for Vienna but also for Venice. Nevertheless, because of his probable activity as a cantata composer during his residence in Innsbruck, Cesti may already have stimulated interest in the cantata among other composers in Austria. In any event, the emergence of the middle baroque, bel canto style, with its smooth melodic contours and diatonic harmonies, can be traced in Viennese vocal music from the time of Cesti's employment in Austria.

A third musician who contributed significantly to the artistic growth of Vienna during the 1660s was Pietro Andrea Ziani, a native of Venice and one of the foremost opera composers of his generation.[15] The year 1660 marked the beginning of a decade of close ties between Ziani and the Habsburg family. In that year F. Magni engraved his *Sacrae Laudes complectentes Tertiam*, op. 6, which Ziani dedicated to Archduke Ferdinand Charles of Tyrol.[16] About this time his vocal chamber works were also known in Tyrol; the Innsbruck inventory of 1665 includes an entry for Ziani's first published work, the *Fiori musicali* of 1640.[17] With the performance of the opera *La Galatea* at Vienna in 1660, Ziani also began his association with the imperial court. He was definitely in Innsbruck in 1662, and in autumn of that year he was called to Vienna by the emperor. By the end of 1662 he had received an appointment as *maestro di capella* at the court of the empress dowager, who generously provided special recommendations and financial assistance.[18] Perhaps the most valuable recommendation given to Ziani by Eleonora was a flattering letter of reference that he carried with him when he left Vienna toward the end of 1668; the letter undoubtedly helped him to obtain the post as first organist at Saint Mark's in Venice, succeeding Francesco Cavalli on 20 January 1669.

Most of Ziani's efforts during his stay in Austria were devoted to large-scale secular and sacred dramatic works. Although copies of his vocal chamber music circulated in Habsburg lands, Ziani does not seem to have given much attention to cantata composition during the 1660s. None of the extant manuscripts of vocal chamber music is preserved in a Viennese library.[19] Ziani, like Cesti, may have stimulated interest among composers who remained in Austria after 1670 not only in the progressive opera style but also in the composition of smaller secular vocal works.

Antonio and Carlo Draghi

Among the four important composers to arrive in Vienna early in the reign of Leopold, only Antonio Draghi appears to have written cantatas specifically for Vienna.[20] Unlike Tricarico, Cesti, and Ziani, the youthful Draghi did not begin his

Viennese residence already in possession of an impressive record as a successful composer. Instead, he had established his reputation in northern Italy as a singer, first as a boy soprano, then as a bass. His earliest creative efforts as a composer took place in Vienna, where he was employed continuously for forty-two years. Nearly everything that Draghi composed was written for the Viennese court or for festivities connected with the lives of the Habsburgs during their visits to other cities.

Draghi began his Viennese career in 1658, first as a singer at the court of the empress dowager and then as a librettist. In 1661 he provided the texts for a *sepolcro* by Bertali and for *L'Almonte,* a *componimento drammatico* by Tricarico. During the 1660s Draghi supplied additional librettos for dramatic works by Bertali, Tricarico, and Ziani, as well as for his own compositions. The earliest music that can definitely be attributed to him is the *compositione drammatica* entitled *La mascherata* (4 March 1666). After 1669 he no longer penned libretti but turned his attention entirely to musical composition. By 1670 he had composed at least twelve additional secular dramatic works, two oratorios, two *sepolcri,* and a serenata.[21] The earliest source that gives information about an official title held by Draghi is the score of *La mascherata,* where he is named "musico dell'Imperatrice [Eleonora]." In 1668 he became assistant Kapellmeister at Eleonora's court, and between April and June 1669, following Ziani's final departure for Venice, Draghi received the appointment as Kapellmeister.[22] In this year he composed no fewer than five dramatic works for Vienna, and his remarkable productivity continued unabated until the final years of the seventeenth century. Already during Sances's service as Kapellmeister in the 1670s, the number of Draghi's dramatic works produced in Vienna exceeded the total by all other composers combined. In 1673 Leopold rewarded Draghi by giving him the additional title "intendente delle musiche teatrali di S.M.C.," an appointment Cesti had received in 1666.[23]

After the death of Sances (24 November 1679), Leopold selected J. H. Schmelzer as his Kapellmeister. Schmelzer was the only non-Italian Kapellmeister during the period 1619–1715. However, Schmelzer's death early in 1680 again left the position vacant. The emperor did not make a new appointment for nearly two years; because of the plague, he and the entire court were absent from Vienna throughout 1680 and most of 1681. Draghi eventually succeeded Schmelzer on 1 January 1682; he remained in the post for eighteen years. Since Leopold did not fill the post of assistant Kapellmeister until 1697, he left virtual control of both administrative and artistic matters in Draghi's hands. Because of Draghi's illness in 1697, Leopold finally engaged Antonio Pancotti to assist him. Two days after his death on 16 January 1700, Draghi was buried in Saint Michael's Church in Vienna.

During a remarkably long period—from the late 1660s to 1700—Draghi completely overshadowed all other composers employed by the Habsburgs. By 1682 he had acquired a relationship with the emperor that closely paralleled the relationship between Jean-Baptiste Lully and Louis XIV; he enjoyed a virtual monopoly in the composition of dramatic music for court entertainment.[24] Centralization of dramatic music in the hands of one composer can be viewed historically in terms of the influence of absolute monarchy. This concentration of the arts and other court activities was a logical outgrowth of a system in which all power belonged to a single individual. Draghi obviously adapted perfectly to the conditions of his age; he was able to win and to retain the complete confidence and esteem of his patron. Seifert and Max Neuhaus give abundant information to illustrate the emperor's high regard for his Kapellmeister.[25] Leopold himself contributed individual arias to many of Draghi's dramatic works.

The immediate influences upon Draghi in Vienna during the formative years of his career would have been Bertali, Sances, and the mature Venetian composers Cesti and Ziani.[26] Draghi composed his first works at a time when the innovations of the mid-seventeenth-century Italian opera composers were being introduced to Vienna. However, the style of composers such as Cesti and Ziani was itself a retrenchment, a search for greater stability following the radical experiments of Monteverdi and his generation. Once Draghi had assimilated the characteristics of the younger generation's music, he mainly adhered to them for the remainder of his career. Indeed, Rudolf Schnitzler concludes that, at least with regard to the sacred dramatic works, Draghi's music underwent very little stylistic development.[27] On the other hand, by comparing Draghi's two versions of the opera *Leonida in Tegea* (1670 and 1694), Seifert demonstrates that Draghi did indeed absorb some of the more progressive style characteristics of his younger contemporaries, notably the use of violin and flute as obbligato instruments for arias and the adoption of the standard da capo aria form.[28] If on the whole Draghi's style remained essentially conservative, it no doubt corresponded with the tastes of the emperor. In short, after a brief period of sudden growth and rich artistic innovation in the 1660s, Vienna settled into a long generation of insularity. While the music of Draghi's younger contemporary Giovanni Battista Pederzuoli anticipated the style of the eighteenth century, the introduction and absorption of the newer style in Vienna had to await the arrival of a generation led by Carlo Agostino Badia, Giovanni Bononcini, and Marc'Antonio Ziani.

Draghi composed a vast number of secular and sacred dramatic compositions, masses, and hymns and a Stabat Mater. His operas, oratorios, and liturgical music have been the subjects of modern studies.[29] Cantata composition consumed only a small fraction of the prolific Draghi's energy. The term *cantata* appears as the genre designation in the manuscripts of his works only twice. Many other vocal chamber compositions lie somewhere between the cantata and full-fledged opera. Written for important occasions in the lives of the Habsburgs such as weddings, birthdays, and name days, these multisectional works often include sinfonias or sonatas, double choruses and elaborate ensembles for up to eight vocal parts with instruments, and an array of recitatives, ariosos, and arias. Genre designations for works of this type include *applauso per musica* (a congratulatory composition), *concerto musicale*, *epitalamio musicale* (a wedding piece), *musica di camera*, *introduzione*, *servizio di camera*, *capriccio*, *composizione per musica*, *trattenimento musico*, *serenata*, *intramezzo di musica*, *accademia*, and *dialogo*. Of these, the works stylistically closest to the standard cantata of the late seventeenth century are three *academie* and a *dialogo*. Only these four pieces and the two cantatas will be considered in the discussion of text and music in chapter 5.

Three arias from Draghi's *Terza accademia* (1698) are specifically attributed to his son, Carlo Domenico, who had begun study with the court organist Ferdinand Tobias Richter in 1688. In 1692 Carlo received a travel allowance of sixty florins per month; the stipend enabled him to "perfect" his art in Italy.[30] Returning to Vienna by 1697, he was appointed court organist on 1 October 1698. He married twice and continued in his post until his death in May 1711.[31] As a composer, Carlo is known only by the arias he contributed to three dramatic works by his father: the revised version of *Sulpizia* (1697); *La forza dell'amor filiale* (1698); and the *Terza accademia*. He may have composed the arias to help his ailing father, who became ill in 1697, the year in which Pancotti was named assistant Kapellmeister. Antonio may also have used the opportunities to advance his son's career at the imperial court.[32]

Filippo Vismarri

Besides the examples by Antonio Draghi, cantatas were contributed by four little-known Italian composers employed in Vienna in the late seventeenth century: Abate Antonio Maria Viviani (before 1630?–83), the soprano castrato Filippo Vismarri (before 1635–1706?), and the organists Carlo Cappellini (before 1635–84) and Giovanni Battista Pederzuoli (before 1650–after 1692?). Cantatas far more typical of the late seventeenth-century repertoire than those by Draghi survive in a volume devoted to the music of Vismarri, a singer and composer active at the Viennese court for thirty years.[33] Vismarri began receiving a monthly stipend of sixty guilders as a soprano castrato at the Habsburg court on 1 April 1650. In addition to his salary, Vismarri received numerous sums from the emperors Ferdinand III and Leopold I and from the empress dowager Eleonora. In 1655, for example, he was given 150 guilders to send for his sister from Italy so that she could marry the court singer Baldassare Poggioli.[34] Three years later the Kapellmeister Bertali supported Vismarri's request for financial aid by citing his industry and general excellence in the theater.[35] His monthly salary increased by fifteen guilders in 1659 and again in 1671. The increase of 1659 was followed by professional success: in 1660 he sang in Leopold's *Il sagrificio d'Abramo* and was honored by a court production of his own opera, *L'Orontea*, a setting of the famous libretto by G. A. Cicognini that was first set to music by Cesti (Venice, 1649) and served as the basis of several other operas.[36] Vismarri's setting adheres closely to the version of the libretto set by Cesti in the 1650s and published by Michael Wagner, the court printer at Innsbruck, in 1656.[37] Along with Antonio Bertali's *La magia delusa*, Vismarri's *L'Orontea* is one of the two oldest opera scores for the imperial court that are actually dated.

In 1679 Vismarri fled from the plague with the entire court; somewhat earlier he must have taken holy orders, for from this date on he is referred to as "Don" Filippo Vismarri. In February 1683 Draghi, by then Kapellmeister, upheld Vismarri's request for a pension by referring to the singer's thirty-four-year period of service.[38] He became an honorary member of the chapel when he retired that year, and the pension that he began to receive then continued to be paid until 1706. His disappearance from court records after this date suggests that he died in that year.

In addition to *L'Orontea,* the extant works of Vismarri include the undated oratorio *Giuda disperato* (text by Sentinello), ten sacred works, and twenty-four *Cantate e ariette per camera.*[39] The cantatas and ariettas come down in a single volume at A-Wn (MS 17753). On the front cover of the binding Vismarri is identified as *Musico di camera di sua Maestà Cesarea.* The contents of this source suggest a Roman influence. At least one of the anonymous texts was possibly also set by Carissimi, and another was definitely also set by Luigi Rossi.[40] Moreover, two other texts survive in anonymous settings preserved in the Vatican library.[41] Further evidence of Roman influence can be inferred from the ascription of one of the texts to the Roman librettist Giovanni Lotti. Cantata texts by Lotti were set to music by important Roman composers such as Luigi Rossi, Savioni, and possibly Carissimi, as well as by Cesti. No detailed information about the precise time and the extent of a Roman influence upon Vismarri's cantatas has yet come to light. His cantata style and choice of texts may simply reflect the influence of Cesti and Tricarico, both of whom had been active at Rome.

Carlo Cappellini

Another musician who showed interest in vocal chamber music at Vienna in the late seventeenth century was the composer and organist Carlo Cappellini, who was born in Brescia.[42] A certain Michelangelo Cappellini served in Mantua, but no evidence has yet turned up to document a family relationship with Carlo Cappellini.[43] A relationship between Carlo and Pietro Paolo Cappellini, a mid-seventeenth-century Roman composer, also has not been documented.[44]

Cappellini was organist at the Accademia della Morte in Ferrara from 1653 to January 1654. Seifert indicates that he was subsequently employed as organist at the electoral court in Dresden from 1656 until roughly 1658 before beginning his Viennese service, perhaps as early as 1659, the year in which he composed *balli* for Giuseppe Tricarico's *La Virtù guerriera.*[45] Cappellini is the first in a long list of Viennese composers to be named in a printed libretto as the composer of the ballet music but not the opera itself. From 1659 he served as organist in the chapel of the empress dowager Eleonora before receiving the appointment as a court organist on 27 April 1665 with a monthly salary of seventy-five guilders. In the following year he received an increase of thirty guilders per month and was granted a *Hofscholar.* In 1669 Eleonora rewarded him with the substantial sum of 225 guilders. Leopold also appears to have favored him, for his fellow organist, Alessandro Poglietti, applied without success at least three times between 1667 and 1673 for a raise that would have made his income equal to Cappellini's.[46] The year 1679 seems to have been the most important in Cappellini's career as a composer; he produced his oratorio, *Il serafino della terra,* for Eleonora's chapel (only the libretto survives), and in Prague, to which he fled from the plague with the entire court, he received commissions for chamber operas honoring Leopold's name day (15 November) and Eleonora's birthday (18 November). Ironically, after returning to Vienna, Cappellini died of the plague in June 1683.

Only the libretto of the oratorio *Il serafino della terra,* now in the Biblioteca Nazionale Marciana, is extant.[47] The scores of both chamber operas (*A servizio di camera nel giorno dell' . . . nome . . . dell'Imperatore Leopoldo* and *La fama illustrata*) are found at A-Wn. The eight *cantate per camera* survive in an undated source in the same library (MS 17768).[48]

Giovanni Battista Pederzuoli

Still another composer who contributed vocal chamber music to the Viennese repertoire in the second half of the seventeenth century was the organist Giovanni Battista Pederzuoli.[49] He was *maestro di cappella* at Santa Maria Maggiore in Bergamo from 12 February 1664 until 26 January 1665.[50] In 1677 he began his service in Vienna as organist at the court of the empress dowager. Five years later he succeeded Draghi as Eleonora's Kapellmeister, a position he retained until her death in 1686. Pederzuoli may have continued his stay in Vienna as a member of the emperor's chapel, but only one work attributed to him (the 1692 oratorio *L'anima in transito*) bears a date later than 1686. No other records of his activity after 1686 have come to light.

During Pederzuoli's service in Vienna, music at the Habsburg court was almost entirely dominated by the prolific Draghi. Nevertheless, except for Draghi, Pederzuoli composed more sacred dramatic works than any other musician engaged by the Habsburgs in the late seventeenth century. For Eleonora's chapel, he provided a new *sepolcro* each year from 1683 through 1686. Three additional oratorios survive. Between 1677 and 1686 Pederzuoli also composed at least fourteen secular dramatic works for Vienna. His list of other extant compositions includes ten *accademie,* an undated *trialogo nel natale del signore,* and a *sonetto per le felicissime nozze* (of Maria Antonia, archduchess of Austria, and Maximilian II Emanuel, elector of Bavaria, in 1685); the scores of all these works are preserved at A-Wn. Elsewhere, a madrigal *a 5* is attributed to Pederzuoli.[51]

Compositions such as the *Scherzo musicale* (Carnival, 1685), the *servizio di camera* entitled *Ragguaglio della fama* (18 November 1680), and the *Sonetto* (1685) as well as undated works such as the *Trialogo*, the madrigal, and the *musica di camera* named *L'ozio ingannato* give evidence of Pederzuoli's lively interest in vocal chamber music. Yet the only pieces that closely resemble the typical late seventeenth-century cantata are the ten *accademie*, which represent the earliest surviving examples of this hybrid genre written for Vienna. Even these works are unusual, because some of them begin with four-part sinfonias in dance forms. They were performed at sessions of the Accademia degl'Illustrati founded by Eleonora Gonzaga in 1668, to which Pederzuoli's chief librettist (Minato) also belonged. Pederzuoli arrived in Vienna in 1677, or approximately at the time when the term *accademia* was becoming current in northern Italy, where he had been employed. The ten *accademie* written for Vienna come down in the manuscripts A-Wn, 16909 and 18872.

Antonio Maria and Giovanni Buonaventura Viviani

Antonio Maria Viviani led a varied career as organist, singer, composer, court official, and priest. He was the older cousin of the better-known and more prolific composer Giovanni Buonaventura Viviani (1638–after 1692).[52] Antonio Maria was already at the Innsbruck court of Archduke Ferdinand Charles before 1648, where he wrote the music for an *introduzione drammatica* performed in 1652 during a tournament.[53] At Innsbruck he received appointments as first organist, chaplain, and secretary to the archduke, who ennobled him in 1654. He served Ferdinand Charles as an agent by engaging Italian artists, traveling often to Venice for that purpose. His association with Cesti is well documented.[54] In 1660 he became superintendent of the Italian chamber musicians at court. From time to time from as early as 1667, the emperor summoned Antonio Maria to Vienna, and the composer may have written part of the Spanish opera *Aun vencido vence Amor, o El Prometeo*, performed at the imperial court in 1669. If so, this work as well as two Spanish arias with refrain definitely attributed to him were undoubtedly composed to please Leopold's first wife, Margaret Theresa of Spain, who often wished to hear Spanish music.[55] Following the death of Margaret Theresa in 1673, Antonio Maria went with the retinue of the widowed archduchess Anna of Innsbruck to Vienna, where he became *maestro di musica* to her daughter, Empress Claudia Felicitas, Leopold's second wife. After the young empress's death only three years later, Leopold continued to employ Antonio Maria as a singer and poet. The two Spanish arias with refrain, three cantatas, and two duets attributed to "Abbate Viviani" survive in a manuscript belonging to the Biblioteca Leopoldina.

Giovanni Buonaventura Viviani served as Kapellmeister at the Innsbruck court of Eleonora Maria (1653–97), widow of King Michael Wisniowiecki of Poland (d. 1673), wife of Charles of Lorraine (d. 1690), and stepsister of Emperor Leopold. There is no evidence that any of his vocal chamber music was composed for Viennese performances. Of his eight published works, only the last three contain secular vocal chamber music, but they were engraved long after his stay in Innsbruck, which probably ended in 1666.[56] The strophic aria "Ch'io ami et arda amante" found on folios in the manuscript A-GÖ, 4089, and attributed "del Viviani" could be a composition of either A. M. or G. B. Viviani.[57]

German-Speaking Composers

Beyond the few vocal chamber works by Bertali and the cantatas by Draghi, A. M. Viviani, Vismarri, Cappellini, and Pederzuoli, the number of extant cantatas composed specifically for Vienna during the period 1658–1700 appears to be quite small. Of course, as we have seen, the emperor Leopold himself showed some interest in composing vocal chamber music. Apart from Leopold's few secular vocal chamber works, the cantata and related genres written for Vienna remained almost exclusively the province of Italian composers. Yet there is evidence that two prominent German-speaking composers, the violinist Johann Heinrich Schmelzer and the organist Johann Caspar Kerll (1627–93), occasionally experimented with brief compositions in the Italian language. As a young man, Schmelzer may have learned the devices of contemporary Italian style from his probable mentor, Antonio Bertali. He spent his entire career in the service of the Habsburgs, was appointed assistant Kapellmeister in 1671, and succeeded Sances as Kapellmeister eight years later. Three Italian cantatas (all lost) are attributed to him in the catalog of Leopold's private collection, the *Distinta specificatione*.[58]

Kerll holds an important place in the music history of both Munich and Vienna.[59] A student of Giovanni Valentini in Vienna, he served from 1647 to 1656 as an organist at the Brussels court of Archduke Leopold Wilhelm, who encouraged Kerll by sending him to study in Rome. Kerll's long service at the court of Elector Ferdinand Maria in Munich (1656–73) was followed by a decade in Vienna. Even before he took up residence in Vienna Kerll had established close contact with the imperial court by composing the mass for the coronation of Leopold I, who ennobled him in 1664. In Vienna he received a pension in 1675 and an appointment as one of the court organists two years later. Friedrich Wilhelm Riedel and Leonhard Riedel have identified two Italian secular cantatas attributed to Kerll in A-GÖ, Ms. 4089.[60] In addition, Richard Schaal lists three small pieces among Kerll's secular vocal music: a duet for two sopranos and continuo ("Il mio cor è un passaggiero"); an aria for bass accompanied by two violins, two oboes, three trumpets, timpani, and continuo ("In tanta solennitate"); and a "Cantata a voce sola, Soprano o Tenore" (*So rühret die Trumme*).[61] The use of the term *cantata* is particularly enticing; it indicates the composer's specific interest in vocal chamber music. The secular text may be a German imitation of the Marinists, or it could even be a translation. In any event, whether any of these pieces cited by Schaal was composed for Vienna has not been established.

4

Repertoire and Sources

THE REPERTOIRE

It is difficult to assess the amount of cantata activity in Vienna during the first half of Leopold's reign, roughly 1658–80. Vast numbers of lost vocal chamber works by Bertali and Sances may have been composed between 1658 and their deaths in 1669 and 1679, respectively.[1] The performances of several Cesti cantatas in 1667 tantalizingly suggest that this pivotal composer may have written additional cantatas for Vienna. The cantatas by A. M. Viviani undoubtedly date from this period, as well as perhaps some of those by Draghi, Vismarri, and Cappellini. If so, then these years spawned a rich array of vocal chamber music. A different picture emerges for the second half of Leopold's reign. Extant sources and available information about occasions, librettists, and performers indicate that, in general, composers employed by the Habsburgs during these years devoted only sporadic attention to the cantata at a time when countless cantatas were being composed in Italy. Several reasons can be advanced to explain why so few were written for Vienna.

First of all, Leopold was preeminently interested in sustaining opera on a permanent basis.[2] This tendency can already be detected from the repertoire performed during the last years of the reign of Ferdinand III. Costly and splendid, baroque opera was an art form perfectly suited to the needs of an indulgent monarch. The conclusion of the war freed the Habsburgs—at least until the Siege of Vienna in 1683—from enormous external pressures and expenses and enabled Leopold to turn his attention increasingly to more ostentatious entertainments. Thus, the degree of political and economic pressure had a direct influence upon the types of works commissioned.

A second reason why cantata activity may have declined after 1680 is the virtual monopoly on important commissions that Draghi enjoyed during the period 1670–1700. He composed at least six cantatas, but they represent only a tiny portion of his enormous output. Is it possible that the cantata simply held little interest for Draghi? Perhaps, but it seems more likely that he was too preoccupied with the steady stream of commissions for larger sacred and secular dramatic works and with his duties as the sole administrator of the emperor's chapel to be able to devote time to smaller works not specifically related to prestigious court occasions. In a letter to Antonio Perti dated 9 June 1688, Draghi apologized for failing to answer an inquiry from Perti and, as a reason for his tardiness, cited the "gravissime occupazioni" of his service.[3] Thus, the composition of cantatas may have been left to less prestigious figures such as Vismarri, Cappellini, and Pederzuoli.

A third reason for the lack of interest in the cantata is the stylistic preference of the emperor himself. Beyond his love of opulent entertainment, which baroque opera ideally satisfied, Leopold seems to have had rather conservative musical tastes. In view of his early preparation for an ecclesiastical career, it is not surprising that as a composer he devoted a considerable amount of his attention to sacred music. Many of his compositions reveal the plaintive and serious aspects of his nature.[4] Leopold's secondary musical interests were the ballet and the equestrian ballet, in which he participated. The cantata lacked the overtly ceremonial or religious significance of other genres and perhaps held little appeal for the emperor. To a certain extent, it thrived under the umbrella of the Viennese academies, of which Leopold was of course a member. At least thirteen cantatas of this period were written for academic occasions. As for Eleonora, she too seems to have preferred compositions of a strictly ceremonial or religious nature.

Finally, a margin of error must be recognized. The Habsburgs may have been less careful about preserving music not specifically related to important court occasions. However, Leopold's own attitude toward expanding the imperial library and preserving sources does not bear out this conclusion. In any event, the extant cantatas considered in this chapter provide a glimpse of a varied and charming aspect of entertainment during the late seventeenth century in Vienna.

A total of fifty-eight extant cantatas composed for performance at the Habsburg court during the period 1658–1700 have been identified.[5] The three surviving Bertali cantatas identified in chapter 1 are preserved at S-Uu. Fifty-three cantatas created by five Italian composers working in Vienna survive at A-Wn in ten core sources—manuscripts that are (1) clearly of Viennese origins and (2) dated or assignable to the approximate period 1658–1700 on the basis of internal evidence. In addition, a manuscript at A-GÖ preserves two cantatas by Johann Caspar Kerll. To be sure, a large number of manuscripts dating from this period with cantatas by composers who did not work or reside in Vienna are also preserved at A-Wn. Perhaps some of these cantatas entertained members of the imperial family, but because specific performances in Vienna have not been documented, they have been excluded for the present study. Also excluded are individual cantatas and cantata anthologies (both manuscripts and prints) dedicated to the Habsburgs by composers who did not receive appointments at the imperial court or were not employed in Vienna at the time that they dedicated the cantatas.[6]

TABLE 4.1. TOTAL EXTANT CANTATAS IN CORE VIENNESE SOURCES

COMPOSER	NO. OF CANTATAS IN CORE SOURCES
J. C. Kerll	2
A. M. Viviani	5
Draghi	6
Vismarri	24
Cappellini	8
Pederzuoli	10
Total	55

TABLE 4.2. CHRONOLOGY OF CANTATAS BY ANTONIO DRAGHI

TITLE	GENRE	MS	DATE OF COMPOSITION
Lo specchio	cantata	16299	22 November 1676
Forza d'un bel volto	dialogo	16315	before 1682
Di tre Amanti (Era l'aurora)	cantata	16315	before 1682
Seconda accademia	accademia	17926	3 February 1693
Intramezzo di musica in una accademia di dame	accademia	16316	15 November 1697
Terza accademia	accademia	16027	11 February 1698

Table 4.1 summarizes the number of core cantatas by Kerll, A. M. Viviani, Draghi, Vismarri, Cappellini, and Pederzuoli. The six works by Antonio Draghi pertinent to this study are preserved as unica in five manuscripts at A-Wn.[7] Table 4.2 gives the chronology of Draghi's cantatas based on the historical and source evidence. Of the five sources with Draghi cantatas, only MS 16315 is undated. It seems plausible that Draghi composed the two cantatas in this manuscript before he assumed his duties as the emperor's Kapellmeister in 1682; the works are similar in scope and style to the cantata in MS 16299, dated 1676. The compositions in 16315 may have been written either during Draghi's service at the court of the empress dowager or during the journeys of the court at the time of the plague (1679–81).[8] Draghi composed the *seconda accademia* in 1693, the *intramezzo di musica* in 1697, and the *terza accademia* in the following year. No *prima accademia* has been identified.[9]

Table 4.3 lists the five manuscripts at A-Wn that contain cantatas by A. M. Viviani, Vismarri, Cappellini, and Pederzuoli. *Un tiranno di foco*, the final duet attributed to Viviani in MS 18762, is ascribed to Luigi Rossi in the library of the Conservatorio Luigi Cherubini in Florence.[10] With two exceptions, all the other cantatas in these manuscripts appear to be unica.[11] Notational details such as the use of baritone clef in the *dialogo* and black notation for numerous hemiola cadences in the cantatas by Viviani suggest that they date from a slightly earlier period than most of the cantatas by Vismarri and Cappellini. They may have been composed during

TABLE 4.3. MANUSCRIPTS AT A-WN CONTAINING CANTATAS BY A. M. VIVIANI, VISMARRI, CAPPELLINI, AND PEDERZUOLI

COMPOSER	MANUSCRIPT	NO. OF CANTATAS	DATE
A. M. Viviani	18762	5	between 1667 and 1676?
Vismarri	17753	24	before 1683
Cappellini	17768	8	before 1683
Pederzuoli	16909	6	1685
Pederzuoli	18872	4	between 1677 and 1686

his early visits to Vienna, beginning about 1667, or during his three-year tenure as *maestro di cappella* to the empress Claudia Felicitas. The twenty-four *cantate e ariette per camera* by Vismarri in MS 17753 represent the single largest collection of cantatas by a Habsburg composer employed between 1658 and 1700.[12] Presumably Vismarri composed these works before he retired in 1683, but it has not been possible to establish the dates of individual cantatas. The collection may well be a compilation of works composed and performed by the castrato himself over a period of years. It seems even more likely that Cappellini assembled the eight *cantate per camera* in MS 17768 over a number of years before his death in 1683.[13] This is especially evident from the widely ranging styles, from the anachronistic final duet, recalling the experiments of the Monteverdi generation, to works typical of cantata style in the third quarter of the seventeenth century. Pederzuoli's six *Accademie: Cantate per l'anno 1685, ovvero problemi diversi* with texts by Minato are preserved in MS 16909, and the four *Cantate, per l'Accademia per Sua M.ta Ces:a dell'Imp:ce Eleonora* with anonymous texts survive in MS 18872, an undated source that obviously predates the death of the empress dowager in 1686.

THE SOURCES

The Core Sources

Appendix B is a catalogue raisonné that begins with detailed descriptions of the ten core sources from 1658 to 1700.[14] All these manuscripts are cropped archival copies. The sources with cantatas by Draghi, Pederzuoli, and Viviani belong to the group of 524 manuscripts from Leopold's Schlafkammerbibliothek discussed by Gmeiner. Lacking the usual elaborate imprints, the cantata collections by Vismarri and Cappellini probably do not belong to this select group. There are no autograph scores of cantatas by composers working in Vienna during this time. The five sources containing Draghi cantatas and the two with Pederzuoli *accademie* are in standard upright format. The manuscripts with cantatas by Vismarri, Cappellini, and Viviani are in the oblong format more characteristic of the next generation. Eight of the manuscripts are bound in white parchment, the preferred binding material at the Habsburg court in the late seventeenth century. All these bindings are in good condition, with the exception of Cappellini's collection, MS 17768, with its soiled parchment, nails protruding from three edges of the front cover, and indications of missing straps that must have held the manuscript together at one time. The binding of Vismarri's collection, MS 17753, consists of brown leather over cardboard. Here too there are signs that straps once bound the manuscript. Also unusual is MS 16027, which lacks the usual imprints and consists of modern heavy cardboard held together with red tape over early red paper with gold decorations; the date (1698) is written in the original scribe's hand.

Various faded gilt imprints appear on the front and/or back bindings. Not surprisingly, the most elaborate imprints are found on the bindings of works by the most prestigious composer, Antonio Draghi. In general, the most common imprint for front covers is the image of Leopold (16299, 16316, 16909, 18762, and 18872), sometimes surrounded with laurel. The best-known symbol of the Habsburg Empire, the Aquila, is a two-headed eagle with crown, representing the dual aspects of church and state. The Aquila appears on the front and back covers of 16315 and on the back covers only of 16316 and 16909. Elsewhere another common symbol of the period, the Eye of God (the sun shining through clouds onto a crowned earth, with hands holding sword and scepter on opposite sides), appears on the back covers of 16299, 18762, and 18872. Additional gilt decorations include floral patterns, scrolls, or simple lines around the edges of the bindings. The thickest manuscript, 16909, also displays simple decorations on the spine.

The medium-light to medium-heavy papers of the core manuscripts are in good to fair condition. The copyists of the manuscripts in upright format have prepared the cantatas by Draghi and Pederzuoli on sheets of ten or twelve staves. The cantatas in oblong format by Vismarri and Cappellini are written on paper lined with four staves. MS 18762 is a compilation of works by several composers, including Viviani, bound together and copied on several papers with six or eight staves. Original foliation is found only in the manuscripts with cantatas by Vismarri and Cappellini. A modern hand has supplied folio numbers for all the other manuscripts except 16299, which lacks foliation altogether. In 16027 numbers appear only for folios 10, 20, 30, 40, and 42.

Throughout the baroque era, Viennese scribes developed a handwriting style that was passed along from one generation to the next. As professional copyists, these scribes were also members of the *kaiserliche Hofmusikkappelle*. With the exceptions of MSS 16027, 16316, and 18762, a single scribe penned each of the pertinent manuscripts. The copyist of Vismarri's, Cappellini's, and Viviani's cantatas, as well as the early examples by Draghi in MSS 16299 and 16315, may have been Alessandro Riotti, employed at the imperial court from at least 1658 to 1672, or Gottfried Alois Gebauer, identified in the *Obersthofmeisteramtakten* of 1670–79 as a copyist and trombonist.[15] MS 18762 is a pastiche of scribes and papers assembled with a white

TABLE 4.4. ITALIAN SECULAR WORKS BY ANTONIO BERTALI IN THE DÜBEN-SAMMLUNG

TITLE	MANUSCRIPT NO.
Deh volgetemi un guardo	S-Uifm, vmhs 047:020
Mortali vedete	S-Uifm, vmhs 047:021
Già dai monti	S-Uifm, vmhs 047:022

parchment binding typical of the Biblioteca Leopoldina. In this pastiche at least seven different scribes copied the music on three distinct papers. Some of the handwriting of the first five items, which are not by Viviani, appears very hasty and may in fact be autograph. In his catalog of the manuscripts at A-Wn, Joseph Mantuani lists only eleven items, but Mantuani's no. 6 actually consists of two separate Spanish arias, so that the manuscript contains a total of twelve pieces. The compositions by A. M. Viviani, nos. 6–12, are all written on one paper by a single scribe, probably Riotti or Gebauer. Viviani is not identified by his name for nos. 11–12, the scribe preferring simply to indicate "del Med:[esi]mo" ("the same"). The other composers in this pastiche are anonymous (no. 1), Alessandro Melani (1639–1703, no. 2), and G. M. Pagliardi (1638–92, nos. 3–5). Possible scribes of the Draghi manuscripts of the 1690s are the violinists J. A. Salchi and Andreas Abendt.[16] That MSS 16316 and 16027 are the work of more than one scribe is evident from the variety of distinct handwriting.

The Düben-Sammlung Manuscripts

Table 4.4 lists the titles and manuscripts for the three Italian compositions by Antonio Bertali pertinent to this study. Like the sources with cantatas by Draghi and Pederzuoli, the manuscripts in the Düben-Sammlung are preserved in standard upright format. Unlike the core sources, however, the Bertali cantatas have been copied in part-books rather than in score. Bindings and imprints are completely lacking, but original paper wrappers enclose the parts for *Già dai monti* and for *Mortali vedete*, the *Lamento della Regina d'Inghilterra*. The individual parts for all three compositions are preserved on one or two pages or, more frequently, in one to three gatherings consisting of two to four pages each. The widths of the pages vary from 195 to 223 mm, and the lengths range from 264 to 293 mm. The facsimiles of selected pages provided online for *Mortali vedete* and for the *Lamento della Regina d'Inghilterra* reveal that the papers are yellowish brown, worn, and spotted. No facsimiles are given for *Già dai monti*. In the database catalog of the Düben-Sammlung, the anonymous scribes have been identified by the code numbers H-207 and H-208. The copying appears to be that of Viennese scribes. It is similar to that found in manuscripts with cantatas by Carlo Cappellini and G. B. Pederzuoli, although there is no perfect match.[17] The ornamental capital letters at the beginnings of cantata texts resemble not only those found in the manuscripts of cantatas by Cappellini and Pederzuoli but also those in sources with cantatas by Vismarri and Draghi. Elsewhere the scratchy copying of cantata texts appears to have been hastily prepared. The prevailing watermark in these manuscripts is, according to the online catalog, the pinecone or a variant such as the pinecone in shield with fleur-de-lis. These part-books may have been prepared for actual performances.

5

Text and Music

In order to gain a fuller appreciation of the richness and variety of the cantatas composed for Vienna in the last half of the seventeenth century, it is essential to examine in detail the style of a number of specific works by Bertali, Kerll, A. M. Viviani, Vismarri, Cappellini, Pederzuoli, and Draghi. While the works of these seven composers share some basic style features, a closer look reveals their individual approaches to aspects such as melody, harmony, rhythm, broad formal plans, aria designs, the relationship of the vocal and bass lines, the use of obbligato instruments, and the importance of counterpoint. With regard to harmony, their music falls within the fascinating transitional period that lies between mode and key.[1] While the term *key* is generally avoided here, a clear sense of tonality and tonal relationships is, with few exceptions, evident in the cantatas analyzed in this chapter.

Antonio Bertali and Johann Caspar Kerll

Bertail had arrived in Vienna already in 1624, decades before any of the other composers discussed in this chapter. Because on the whole the style of his music belongs to an earlier generation, his vocal chamber music will be discussed only in passing here. Three pieces in the Düben-Sammlung that date from the end of Bertali's life offer a tiny glimpse of what appears to have been a large oeuvre of cantata-like compositions. *Deh volgetemi un guardo* for two sopranos and basso continuo and the serenata *Già dai monti* for five voices, two violins, and continuo probably belong to the category *compositioni amorose*.[2] *Mortali vedete*, the *Lamento della Regina d'Inghilterra* with a text by Archduke Leopold Wilhelm, probably written originally upon the death of Charles I of England, was composed by Bertali in 1669 on the death of Queen Henrietta Maria, wife of Charles I, and therefore belongs to the group of *compositioni proprie*.[3] The text found in Bertali's setting varies somewhat from the original. The model for this lament was undoubtedly Monteverdi's *Lamento d'Arianna*. Bertali's striking setting features soprano soloist (accompanied by continuo, with bass viol) and bass soloist (accompanied by four viols). Andrew Weaver provides a detailed analysis of text and music online in the Web Library of Seventeenth-Century Music (WLSCM). I have not examined the two cantatas by Kerll, but in a recent study Friedrich Wilhelm Riedel and Leonhard Riedel offer a brief analysis of Kerll's *D'un occhio brillante* and *Mio cor ti perdersi*.[4]

ANTONIO MARIA VIVIANI

In comparison with the vocal chamber works of Vismarri, Cappellini, Draghi, and Pederzuoli, the cantatas and duets of Antonio Maria Viviani are rather modest examples of the genre both in scope and in content. The first cantata attributed to Viviani in MS 18762 (no. 8) is a *dialogo a due* for soprano and baritone; it is followed by four more Viviani works: two cantatas for soprano, one for bass, and a duet for soprano and alto, all accompanied by basso continuo. The vocal ranges for soprano, alto, baritone, and bass do not make unusual demands on the singers. Apart from a single ritornello in the soprano-baritone *dialogo Lilla e Lidio* and a few brief tags at the ends of aria segments, there are no independent instrumental sections. The composer provides the usual figuration for suspensions, raised thirds, and first inversions. On the whole, the bass lines function as pure harmonic support without entering into thematic or motivic material. However, in the soprano cantata *Adorate mie bellezze* (no. 10 in the manuscript), Viviani uses the head-motive at the beginning of the first brief aria both as a source of imitation between bass and soprano and as a device to unify the entire cantata.

Only two tempo markings, adagio and allegra [*sic*], appear in the scores, and dynamics are limited to a few instances of *piano*. The unusual use of four-against-three rhythm occurs twice in *Lilla e Lidio*. The composer avoids awkward melodic leaps and elaborate coloratura passages, though he writes a few vocal flourishes for key words such as *affetto* and *piove* and vigorous runs for the singers and bass line near the end of *Lilla e Lidio*. Viviani establishes clear tonal centers (G, E, C, D, and E) for the five chamber pieces, explores closely related tonalities within arias and larger sections, and reaffirms the central tonalities in the final cadences. Aria components and larger sections are often separated by clear articulations. Viviani's harmonies are seldom daring. Typical Phrygian cadences, found also in the cantatas of Vismarri and Cappellini, conclude recitative passages, and an occasional Neapolitan sixth highlights a particular word such as *amore* in *Adorate mie bellezze*.

Viviani also shares with Vismarri and Cappellini the tendency to devise a different formal scheme for each cantata or duet. The simplest plan can be seen in the duet *Un tiranno di foco* (no. 12). Here the composer divides the music into two equal parts based upon the two long poetic stanzas; part 2 repeats the music of part 1 verbatim. He subdivides each part into three sections, all anchored in e minor. A strict metrical pulse in $\frac{3}{2}$ unifies sections 1 (thirty-three measures) and 3 (thirty-nine measures); both are developed by sequence and are repeated, but in other respects their music is different. The much shorter contrasting middle section in $\frac{4}{4}$ (nine measures) alternates soprano and alto phrases in recitative before concluding with an arioso duet. In the bass cantata *Perché mio cor, perché* (no. 11), a rondo pattern emerges, with the threefold statement of a miniature ABA aria serving as the rondo refrain. A single musical-poetic phrase, "Uccidetemi tormenti, uccidetemi sì sì," supplies the unifying refrain in the soprano cantata *Su la riva d'un ruscello* (no. 9). It first appears as the A portion of an AABA aria; when B returns, it has new text, but the repetition of A retains the original verse. On a broad scale, however, this cantata has an open form because the refrain does not recur at the end. The most through-composed cantata is *Adorate mie bellezze,* which consists of a series of recitatives and metrical passages without a unifying refrain. The cantata closes with an ABA[1] aria in which A[1] encapsulates several phrases from A but extends them with new music.

In all five vocal chamber pieces, Viviani prefers ternary designs to strophic structures. This is most evident in the duet *Lidio t'intendo affè,* entitled *Lilla e Lidio,* the longest and most complex work in the set of five cantatas. No fewer than four distinct sections display ternary patterns. The cantata opens with a short aria in strict ABA form, sung by Lilla. She continues with another three-part section; united only by their $\frac{3}{2}$ meter, the first and third parts of this section are separated by a short syllabic passage in $\frac{4}{4}$. Lidio's introductory aria mirrors the ABA design of Lilla's entrance aria. For the relatively long concluding duet, Viviani uses modified da capo form. The initial A (measures 1–26) begins in g minor and modulates to B♭ major; B (measures 27–48) continues in B♭ but returns to the tonic. A[1] (measures 49–61) is an abbreviated version of A that reestablishes the original tonality. The complete ABA[1] is then repeated. In this duet, soprano and baritone alternate long and short phrases before joining in parallel tenths. Other sections unfold more freely, mixing repetitious and sequential passages, meters, and vocal styles.

FILIPPO VISMARRI

Vismarri's lovely, well-crafted cantatas and ariettas deserve to be far better known. What distinguishes a cantata from an arietta in Vismarri's collection appears to be the absence of recitative between arias or ariosos in the ariettas. Using this as a criterion, then, nos. 3, 7–9, 11, and 19–21 fit the genre designation arietta. Vismarri labels five of the cantatas in his collection (nos. 1, 4–5, 11, and 15) as *cantate morali.* The tradition of Italian vocal chamber music based on moral topics that began in the Renaissance continued to flourish at the religious court of Leopold, as evidenced not only by Vismarri's examples but also by forty lost *compositioni morali e spirituali per la camera* attributed to Bertali in the *Distinta specificatione.* In view of Vismarri's career as a castrato who eventually sought the priesthood, it is not surprising that he chose to include several cantatas with moral topics.

In all other respects the twenty-four soprano cantatas and ariettas form a unified set of vocal chamber music. The soprano range is normally not greater than d^1–g^2 but dips down to b in *Sì sì voglio morir* (no. 17) and rises to a climactic b^2 in *Sopra le proprie pene* (no. 12).[5] That the composer intended the free use of obbligato instruments is clear from indications in the score for ritornellos *a piacere*. A phrase in treble clef for an unidentified instrument and marked *si suona* appears between vocal phrases near the end of *Care selve, frondosi ricetti* (no. 10), and an entire section for treble and bass instruments marked *si suona* occurs in *Occhi se sete infidi* (no. 16). Passages marked *tasto solo* in *Sopra le proprie pene* and *Là muta voi fate il sordo faro* (no. 24) provide additional timbral variety. The sparse dynamic indications are limited to *piano* and *forte*.

Bass figuration is fairly detailed, especially for raised thirds of dominant chords, first inversions, and all suspensions. The bass line often interacts with the voice as an equal partner by sharing motivic material, participating in imitation, or exchanging short phrases. From the perspective of tonality, Vismarri's cantatas are in step with the progressive style found in works by his better-known contemporaries working in Italy. The harmonic patterns and tonal relationships are usually clear; arias and sections of arias begin and end in the same "key." At times the tonal rhythm is very fast, as harmonies move rapidly through a series of tonal centers in a typical middle baroque style. Circle-of-fifth progressions are common.

The barring of Vismarri's cantatas is often inconsistent, but the composer's intention is easy enough to discern. A scribal error occurs in the second aria of *Gioverà cangiar pensiero* (no. 22) where the vocal line is written in $\frac{3}{8}$—the intended meter—simultaneously with a bass line in $\frac{3}{2}$. Vismarri's sensitivity to text setting is abundantly clear throughout the collection. For example, frequent hemiolas reinforce poetic rhythms. Arias in $\frac{3}{2}$ typically cadence with hemiola, often written out as a single measure of $\frac{3}{1}$, with black notation for the final whole note. Tempo markings, limited to adagio, allegro, più allegro, presto, and più presto, are used not only for arias and ariosos but even for recitatives.

Repetition and sequence are of course stock-in-trade, but Vismarri's melodic sequences are not always predictable or simple. In *Maledetto sia quel dì* (no. 2), for example, the composer subtly varies the sequential pattern in each repetition (example 5.1). He cleverly combines long- and short-range sequence in *Luci belle, miei soli* (no. 23) and thereby creates a broader structure. Rather than functioning as an end in itself, coloratura is often integrated into the complete melodic arch (example 5.2). Vismarri sometimes heightens the intensity of a final phrase by combining a rising melodic line with increased rhythmic activity. Ariosos typically evolve out of recitatives. Metrical arioso flourishes are not always placed at the ends of recitatives but rather reflect Vismarri's immediate responses to textual details.

The composer draws upon many expressive melodic and harmonic effects. Affective intervals such as diminished thirds, fourths, and sevenths are fairly com-

EX. 5.1. Vismarri, *Maledetto sia quell dì*, mm. 27–30.

mon. The unusual ascending and descending tritones of the strophic aria in *Male-detto sia quel dì* aptly underscore the bitter sentiment of the poetry, offering the singer a special vocal and dramatic challenge (example 5.3). Many of the clichés of the north Italian cantata repertoire of the mid-seventeenth century are found also in Vismarri's works. Thus, for example, he renders *morirai* with repetitive languid sighs, portrays *piangendo* with a drooping melodic line in steady half notes, evokes *naufragi* with harmonic restlessness, and depicts stock words such as *rai, s'asconde, l'ali,* and *vittoria* with elaborate ornaments and coloratura. Amusingly, the word *os-tinato* prompted the composer to use motivic repetition in *Occhi ohimè* (no. 18), and the words *torna indietro* at the beginning of the initial aria of *Scioglieasi baldanzoso* (no. 1) predictably lead to a recall of the aria near the end of the cantata. The final cantata in the set features some expressive chromatic harmony. Neapolitan-sixth chords are common, though extreme chromaticism and unprepared dissonance are not characteristic of Vismarri's style.

Perhaps the most fascinating aspect of Vismarri's cantatas is their remarkable formal variety. While most consist of a free intermingling of recitatives, ariosos, and brief arias, no two unfold in the same way. Even the lengths of cantatas vary considerably. Consisting of only two sections (AA[1]), the brief arietta *Io son preg-gio di natura* (no. 20) contrasts sharply with sprawling pieces such as *Care selve, frondosi ricetti,* which comprises twelve separate sections. Working in a somewhat amorphous, mid-seventeenth-century style, Vismarri is nevertheless skillful at creating formal unity. Nos. 2, 16, and 24, for example, use the refrain principle, a technique found even more commonly in cantatas by Cappellini. In several Vismarri cantatas, an entire aria heard at the beginning returns in the middle or

EX. 5.2. Vismarri, *Gioverà cangiar pensiero,* mm. 1–8.

near the end. Others take on a specific rounded pattern such as A–R–BBA (no. 17), ABCDA (no. 22), AB–R–AB (no. 8), or AABC–R–AABC (no. 3). Sometimes a small melodic motive unifies an entire cantata. In *Là muta voi fate* (no. 24) Vismarri's opening refrain motive, a descending fourth followed by an ascending second, recurs in the final aria and—slightly altered—in the central aria. Variation techniques are found in *Fu che fuor di te* (no. 15) and *Sì sì voglio morir* (no. 17). A rhapsodic, multisectional cantata such as *Luci belle, miei soli* contains no literal repetitions but recycles fragments of earlier material quite freely. And *Se troppo perfidi* (no. 5) is through-composed, its continuously flowing music derived entirely from the text.

EX. 5.3. Vismarri, *Maledetto sia quell dì*, mm. 31–39.

A closer examination of two cantatas demonstrates Vismarri's thoughtful approach to form based upon text. *Lasci d'amar chi non ha sorte* (no. 7) consists of ten clearly delineated sections. These are divided into two groups of five separated by an instrumental ritornello. The first and fifth sections are identical in both text and music. Section 6 repeats the music of sections 1 and 5 but with new text. Sections 7, 8, and 9 repeat the music of sections 2, 3, and 4, respectively, this time with new poetry. Finally, section 10 repeats the music heard in sections 1, 5, and 6 using the text of section 6; section 10 is then repeated. A less obvious method occurs in *In amor ci vuol patienza* (no. 14), a cantata grounded in a minor. The opening aria contains five lines of poetry, the fifth verse identical to the first.

> In amor ci vuol patienza;
> chi non l'ha non sarà nulla.
> La bellezza è una fanciulla
> che non piace violenza;
> in amor ci vuol patienza.[6]

The music of line 1 cadences in the tonic in measure 5; when it returns at the end of the aria, it is considerably altered (examples 5.4a–b). The conventional recitative that follows becomes metrical when the music of line 1 of the aria reappears, but this time as an extended, subtle combination of the two earlier versions (example 5.4c). After a second recitative, the combined version is heard again. The first stanza of the ensuing strophic aria is followed by a complete reprise of the initial aria, but the second stanza ends with only a simplified five-measure variant of line 1 (example 5.4d). An extended recitative gradually becomes more metrical before leading to a final statement of the combined version of line 1 (example 5.4c).

The aria types found in Vismarri's cantatas are nearly as varied as the broad formal plans. Strophic arias with two stanzas are quite common. The music of the second strophe is often, but not always, a literal repetition. The expressive central aria of *Là muta voi fate* is a rare example of strophic variations. Several arias are miniature da capos, either ABA or ABA[1], a pattern that is also used for individual strophes. In *Innamoratevi del sommo bene,* the return of A is not written out but indicated by the words *da capo,* which would become customary by the end of the century. Repetition and sequence often determine the internal structures. "Troppo afflitto amante," the central aria of *Sa il mio core* (no. 9), is a modified da capo, but the middle section actually consists of a long, balanced, two-part sequence. The length of this aria is also unusual, extending to more than one hundred measures.

EX. 5.4a–d. Vismarri, *In amor ci vuol patienza,* mm. 1–5, 13–16, 29–36, and 160–64.

EX. 5.4a

EX. 5.4b

Arias derived from text without regard to specific patterns of repetition can be seen in the cantatas *Occhi, se sete infidi* and *Gioverà cangiar pensiero*.

On the whole, Vismarri's style is both more in step with contemporary Italian style and more progressive than Draghi's. This can be seen not only from his preference for solo soprano plus continuo but also from features such as the clear separation of recitative and aria, the occasional da capo aria, and the frequent imitation between bass and vocal lines. This last feature—a thematic relationship between the two parts—became a standard one in the arias of contemporary north Italian composers.

CARLO CAPPELLINI

The first five cantatas of Carlo Cappellini's collection feature the soprano voice accompanied by basso continuo. The composer reserves the end of the volume for three duets, two for a pair of sopranos and a final duet for soprano and alto that harks back to the more experimental style of the early seventeenth century. Numerous indications for ritornellos throughout the collection suggest that melodic instruments were to be added freely. As in Vismarri's cantatas, Cappellini's soprano vocal range remains comfortably within the span of d^1–g^2, occasionally rising to a^2 and infrequently dipping down to c^1; the alto range of the final duet spans a tenth, from g to b^1. Dynamics are restricted to *piano* indications for echo effects.

The bass line chiefly supplies harmonic support, either with long-held notes or steady, beat-marking motion. The static basses at the beginnings of recitatives

EX. 5.4C

or ariosos act as pedal points beneath declamatory, sometimes dissonant soprano phrases, possibly reflecting the composer's experience as an organist (example 5.5).[7] In the opening ten-bar refrain of *Pensieri, amerò!* (no. 5), the bass moves slowly under animated dotted figures in the voice until the final measures, where the roles of the two parts are reversed, the bass suddenly becoming active beneath a sustained vocal a[1] on the last syllable of *amerò*. In the cantata *Ancor sazia non sei* (no. 1), a rare instance of imitation between soprano and bass occurs at the beginning of the aria "Chi segue Cupido," an obvious play on words. Elsewhere the bass participates only occasionally in motivic material or as a partner with the soprano in a dramatic flourish, as in *Occhi miei, non vi struggete* (no. 2). Cappellini is consistently careful

EX. 5.4d

to indicate 4–3 suspensions; otherwise figuration is limited to raised and lowered thirds, a few 7–6 suspensions, first inversions, and a rare dominant seventh.

Each cantata is anchored in a clear tonality. The composer's choices for the eight cantatas (c, a, G, B♭, A, g, d, and g) are wider ranging than those in the Vismarri volume, but within the typically short sections the tonal rhythm is often steadier. The first aria of *Pensieri, amerò* begins as if in f♯ minor but cadences in the central tonality of A major at the end.

Cappellini draws almost entirely upon a few typical tempo markings such as presto, allegro, and adagio. In *Ancor sazia non sei* he creates a dramatic effect by prescribing an extreme shift from adagiatissimo to presto. Barring in his cantatas is clear and consistent. While his choice of meter is also usually straightforward, in two instances he specifies unusual time signatures: $\frac{4}{3}$ for an aria in the first cantata and $\frac{8}{3}$ for a similar aria in the third cantata. In both pieces, he clearly intends $\frac{6}{8}$; both show the influence of dance, so that the upper number of the time signature may indicate the grouping of measures, while the lower number denotes the subdivision of each half measure. The influence of dance is evident in other arias written in compound meters. This becomes explicit from the indication *come corrte* at the head of the aria "Chi segue Cupido." Here the composer establishes the lilting rhythm of dotted eighth–sixteenth–eighth, then adapts it to the rhythm of the verse with appropriate syncopations and hemiolas. The soprano's playful syncopations in the aria "Non più assalti" from *Pensieri, amerò!* make this the most rhythmically complex passage in the entire Cappellini collection. Like Vismarri, Cappellini is able to coordinate the increasing rhythmic intensity with a rising melodic line, reaching the peak of a^2 three times in the final four measures (example 5.6).

EX. 5.5. Cappellini, *Ancor sazia non sei,* mm. 1–9.

Cappellini also shares with Vismarri a fondness for expressive leaps such as diminished thirds, fourths, and sevenths. In *Cinto d'oscure bende,* he responds to the emotionally charged words "in forma di ruggiada i miei tormenti" by writing a long, tortured vocal line that includes the increasingly difficult descending intervals of the minor sixth, tritone, minor seventh, and minor tenth (example 5.7). As the fourth cantata, *Cinto d'oscure bende* forms a virtuoso showpiece in the middle of the set. The exceptionally long-breathed coloratura passages for the words *scioglie* and *volo* demand a singer of considerable skill, suggesting that Cappellini may have composed this cantata with a particular singer in mind. Throughout the collection, brief flourishes on words such as *fulminarla, volate, augelli,* and *vivendo* are relatively common. Some of the word painting is overtly entertaining. For example, the rising and falling melodic line at the beginning of *Prendi l'arco, o Cupido* (no. 3) represents the arching of Cupid's bow, and the ensuing repetitions of "Su, su, perfido, all'armi, ch'a battaglia mortal" belong to the time-honored clichés of battle music. In *Pensieri, amerò!,* the "knotted" sixteenth-note turns on the word *catene* aptly depict the lover's chains.

Cappellini's cantatas are multisectional works, like Vismarri's, but the number of sections is generally fewer. Moreover, unlike the castrato, Cappellini does not

EX. 5.6. Cappellini, *Pensieri amerò!*, mm. 83–89.

indicate in the score which segments are recitatives, arias, or ariosos. Many sections hover between recitative and arioso. The clearest overall plans are those that depend upon a musical-poetic refrain. In the third cantata, for example, the initial line ("Prendi l'arco Cupido che vuo' teco provarmi") occurs musically at the beginning, at the end of the second section, and again at the end of the complete cantata. The second and third statements of the refrain are not written out but are indicated by *da capo,* a term that in the next generation will refer specifically to the third section of a da capo (ABA) aria, whether written out or not. *Pensieri, amerò!* has a particularly clear design. Four statements of a refrain alternate with three brief arias; these are followed by an extended passage of recitative and arioso, an instrumental ritornello, and a final aria with refrain.

Similar, though less predictable patterns of repetition and variety can be found in other cantatas and in the first and second duets (nos. 6 and 7). In these two duets, Cappellini primarily avoids a specific aria type such as strophic, da capo, or binary; instead, a line of text spun out in sequence is followed by another line treated in a similar manner. The use of a refrain is quite straightforward in *Sensi miei, sospirate* (no. 7), but in *Così, bella, mi lasci* (no. 6) the composer varies the device by giving new text to a musical phrase heard earlier or by starting the recurrence literally, then breaking free with new music. Quasi-ostinato bass lines and overlapping imitation between the two sopranos in this duet help to shape and unify individual sections. Jarring minor seconds between the two equal voices and strident sevenths and ninths with the bass line are obvious responses to the expressive possibilities suggested by the poetry. Such dissonant passages characteristically conclude with sweet-sounding phrases in parallel thirds.

EX. 5.7. Cappellini, *Cinto d'oscure bende,* mm. 68–75.

Cappellini prefers free arioso patterns to closed forms, but there are a few strophic songs and da capo arias. *Cinto d'oscure bende* contains not one but two strophic arias, each with two stanzas. For the pair of strophes sung in succession by the two sopranos near the end of *Sensi miei, sospirate* the composer provides different music for each singer. "Volate, sparite," the fifth section of *Ancor sazia non sei,* comes as close to being a true ternary aria as any piece in the whole cantata collection.

The duet for soprano and alto, *Cieli, non posso più* (no. 8), merits special consideration. Placed at the end of the collection, this duet seems stylistically anachronistic and thus quite different from the other cantatas. There are no refrains, and the simple overall plan of the piece focuses attention on the expressive content of the music. Duets at the beginning and end of the cantata frame two extensive solos, the first for soprano and the second for alto. The soprano solo begins with a delightful, rhythmically free passage in *stile rappresentativo* for the voice over a sustained G in the bass. The vocal F♯s that clash with the bass are reminiscent of similar effects in the operas of Monteverdi and Cavalli (example 5.8). The ensuing alto solo opens with a rising chromatic line on the word *langue* over another

EX. 5.8. Cappellini, *Cieli, non posso più,* mm. 29–33.

sustained G, then proceeds with a presto passage filled with repetitious sixteenth-note patterns on the word *raddoppia.* Both solos mix recitative and arioso freely.

GIOVANNI BATTISTA PEDERZUOLI

Pederzuoli composed the ten cantatas in MSS 16909 and 18872 exclusively for academic occasions.[8] The four undated cantatas with anonymous poetry in MS 18872 show both the progressive and conservative traits of his style. These charming pieces form a kind of textually unified "cantata cycle," in which the first cantata is scored for alto, the second and fourth for soprano, and the third for tenor—a rare instance in the entire Viennese repertoire of the late seventeenth and early eighteenth centuries. In the first cantata the shepherd Fileno poses the question to be resolved: Should he believe that he is loved by Filli, yes or no? The singers in the second and third cantatas adopt opposing views. In the second cantata the soprano argues that the greatest contentment comes when a lover simply accepts that he is loved. But in the third cantata the tenor argues that it is better to be dubious than to be made a fool. The final cantata restates the conflict and concludes with a decision: "It is best to navigate according to the wind" (Voglio sol navigar' secondo il vento).

This cantata cycle seems ideally suited to the abilities of dilettante court singers. The alto cantata at the beginning of the set seems particularly easy, with its range of little more than one octave (a–b♭¹) and its predominantly syllabic setting. The ranges for soprano (c¹–g²) and tenor (c–g¹) are wider but not extreme, and though their parts include occasional smooth sequential runs, they never reach a level of professional virtuosity. The composer specifies the tempo markings presto, allegro, and adagio for the second, third, and fourth cantatas, respectively, but he gives no other tempo indications and no dynamics at all.

In each cantata of 18872 the accompaniment consists of basso continuo without any obbligato instruments. The composer provides scarcely any figuration and only a few bass-line ritornellos derived from the arias that precede them in the third and fourth cantatas. Pederzuoli varies the bass-line function from aria to aria. In the first aria of the third cantata, for example, the active bass melody has its own motivic material; it begins in quasi-ostinato fashion but turns to imitation of the tenor in the last section. In the first aria of the fourth cantata, the composer supports the soprano with a sequential, nonmotivic bass in steady eighths that continues unabated until the final cadence.

The forward-looking features of this cantata cycle include the use of a da capo aria, the presentation of a *Devise* at the beginning of an aria, the assignment of thematic material to the bass line (including imitation with the voice), the complete absence of black notation for hemiola, and the predilection for "modern" meters (notably $\frac{3}{4}$ in place of $\frac{3}{2}$, still common in the works of Vismarri, Cappellini, and A. M. Viviani).[9] The tendency toward alternation of recitative and aria is also apparent though not yet firmly established. The less progressive side of Pederzuoli's style can be seen in his sometimes confused treatment of harmony; several arias begin with no clear tonal focus and only after three or four measures settle into a basic tonality.

As in his larger dramatic works, Pederzuoli includes virtually no arioso patterns in the recitatives of the cantatas in MS 18872. Hence, the *semplice* recitatives are strictly functional, with minimal melodic and harmonic interest. The arias contain many clichés characteristic of mid-seventeenth-century style: frequent hemiola patterns, recurrent Phrygian cadences (especially for questions), and melismatic flourishes on words such as *baleno, burlato,* and *tanto.* Consistent with the prevailingly simple style, the aria melodies move mostly in conjunct lines interspersed with easy leaps such as fourths and fifths, though the tenor cantata includes descending tritones and a rather dramatic ascending octave leap for emphasis of the words *no, no.* Pederzuoli is perhaps most successful with lilting, stepwise, bel canto arias written in $\frac{6}{8}$, such as the lovely "Nel pensiero il più vero contento si trova," which concludes the second cantata. Rhythm is one of the most interesting aspects of his style. In the second cantata, for example, the composer creates flexible motion, almost reminiscent of Renaissance rhythm, by favoring agogic rather than metrical accents, coupling these with a delightful interplay between vocal and bass lines (example 5.9). Using a different technique in one of the tenor arias, the composer sets a lively syncopated vocal figure against a chromatic but rhythmically steady bass line (example 5.10).

Besides the da capo aria (used only once), rondo and strophic forms occur in MS 18872. In strophic arias Pederzuoli usually separates the individual stanzas with

EX. 5.9. Pederzuoli, *Son felice e so perché*, mm. 43–52.

EX. 5.10. Pederzuoli, *Non ti credo, non ti fido*, mm. 11–18.

written-out ritornello bass lines, but his remark at the end of stanza 1 of the second aria of cantata no. 3 is especially revealing with regard to contemporary Viennese performance practice: "Si suona un poco e poi da capo." The instruction confirms the basic role of improvisation in the performance of seventeenth-century music at Vienna.

The six cantatas in MS 16909 with texts by Minato were composed for sessions of the Accademia degl'Illustrati held in 1685, the year before Eleonora Gonzaga's death. An apolitical problem is posed at the beginning of each *accademia* in this manuscript. The first cantata investigates whether inspiration or education is more important for fulfillment in life. The second asks what is most easily lost: love, time, loneliness, or ingratitude. The third searches for the truest sign of friendship. The fourth probes whether a gentleman can be sensitive if in order to obey his lady he offends another. The fifth queries if it is more glorious to conquer an indifferent heart or one inclined to the love of another. The sixth cantata seeks to determine which of two lovers deserves more compassion: one who enjoys the pleasure of frequently seeing his lady, by whom, however, he is despised, or one who is alone without hope of ever seeing his lady but by whom he has the certainty of being tenderly loved. In short, the sessions were organized for amusement and entertainment rather than serious intellectual discourse. That they also dealt with contemporary aspects of class and social conduct seems apparent.

Pederzuoli divides each *accademia* into an *introduzione* and a *seconda parte*. All but the third and fourth cantatas of this set begin with an instrumental *sinfonia avanti*. From the ranges of the individual lines, the probable combination of instruments is strings *a 4* (violins 1–2, viola, and cello), but a fifth line, identical to the cello part except for the addition of figuration, is obviously intended for the supporting keyboard continuo instrument. The sinfonias for the first, second, and sixth cantatas begin with short, stately sections in common time; the first sinfonia continues with a corrente in $\frac{3}{2}$, the second with an allemanda in $\frac{4}{4}$, and the sixth with a binary presto, also in common time. The fifth cantata opens with a corrente in $\frac{3}{2}$ and closes with a gigue in $\frac{6}{8}$. All the dances are binary with repeats; characteristic rhythmic figures and balanced phrases suggest that these pieces may indeed have been danced. Pederzuoli often infuses the texture with imitation. In the Presto of the sixth sinfonia he also demonstrates his fine skill at part writing. The second half of the Presto begins with sequential motion, leading from the tonal center of G through F to D; the pattern is repeated, with the tonal center moving to B♭ before returning to G, but the parts are completely redistributed. Pederzuoli manages to keep each part active and independent throughout.

During the sections with text, the composer achieves a considerable amount of instrumental variety. For many ritornellos, which generally appear between stanzas of the numerous strophic arias, he retains four-part writing with a separate continuo bass line. Unlike the ritornellos found in many works by his Viennese contemporaries, Pederzuoli's instrumental parts are often entirely written out. This is true also for the accompaniments of most duets, trios, and quartets and also for at least one aria in the fifth cantata. Occasionally the instrumental accompaniments marked *a 4* for vocal trios and quartets are not written out, except for the continuo line, and are probably meant to double the vocal parts. In the third *accademia* the composer limits the accompaniment to basso continuo, even for the ensembles. The ritornello between stanzas of one of the arias in the *seconda parte* is specifically marked *col cembalo*.

The first three cantatas include vocal parts for soprano, alto, tenor, and bass, but the last three omit the vocal bass. A part for bass in the first cantata occurs only in the final quartet. The second cantata features each vocal soloist, including the bass, but the four never join in a single ensemble. Frequent duets and trios add to the variety of all the cantatas. Each cantata concludes with an ensemble. Given the richness of vocal and instrumental sonorities, it is a little surprising that MS 16909 lacks detailed dynamics and tempo markings.

The degree of difficulty for the singers in these six academic cantatas is fairly modest. Soprano and tenor ranges do not rise above $g\sharp^2$ and g^1, respectively, and the alto range does not exceed c^2. Occasionally lengthy florid passages requiring good breath control place greater demands upon an individual singer. Interestingly, the vocal parts often become most challenging and florid in the ensemble numbers.

Pederzuoli is fond of imitation and counterpoint, especially in the large ensembles but also sometimes in the ritornellos. He draws upon a variety of contrapuntal techniques, including paired imitation, inversion, and stretto. The fugal tutti at the end of the fifth cantata demonstrates his skillful technique of working out a variety of motives. His interest in counterpoint is also evident in ensembles such as the quartet at the beginning of the *seconda parte* of the third cantata and the trios that conclude both sections of the sixth cantata, which will be discussed below in more detail.

Pederzuoli's grasp of tonality is firmer in these *accademie* than in the cantata cycle of MS 18872, and he uses clear tonal relationships in shaping long-range formal designs. The narrative poetry of each *accademia* determines the sequence of recitatives, ariosos, arias, ensembles, and ritornellos. The first *accademia* admirably illustrates how the composer weaves together all these components in constantly varying patterns. The second proceeds somewhat differently. After the sinfonia each singer presents an argument, mostly in recitative, in favor of one of the four things most easily lost (love, time, loneliness, or ingratitude). A succession of three strophic arias with ritornellos leads to a trio that completes the *introduzione*. The *seconda parte* continues the debate with short metrical passages and recitative, followed by a triumphant strophic aria for the winner and a trio finale.

Although strict da capo arias rarely occur, Pederzuoli creates numerous ternary patterns in which the middle section consists of recitative, a plan that is also found occasionally in arias of the early eighteenth century. For example, the *introduzione* of the third *accademia* begins with a trio followed by recitative and a da capo of the complete trio. A similar format appears at the beginning of the *seconda parte*, but with a quartet instead of a trio. In the same *parte*, an aria and its da capo are separated by a duet. An A section in the *seconda parte* of the fifth *accademia* leads to a recitative and an abbreviated da capo (A^1). The composer sometimes extends these repetitious patterns beyond simple ternary designs. In the *seconda parte* of the fourth *accademia*, a series of alternating recitatives and ariosos generate patterns such as abcb¹. In the same *accademia* Pederzuoli uses a subtler means to unify a pair of arias: the second aria inverts the melodic ideas of the first.

The final cantata in MS 16909 is also the most elaborate. The soprano and tenor assume the roles of the despised lover and the exiled lover, while the alto acts as an objective commentator. The lovers express their complaints in their first duet, an ABA¹ in which they sing individually in the outer sections, then together in the contrasting middle section. Each lover is given one strophic aria in the *introduzione* and one in the *seconda parte*. The alto's only aria, "Quel arciero, che nudo va," illustrates Pederzuoli's typical way of extending form. He begins with a three-bar phrase repeated sequentially down a fourth and proceeds with a new three-bar phrase treated sequentially up a major third. Each strophe begins firmly in e minor and cadences in the parallel major. The imitation between vocal and bass lines is taken up by all four instrumental parts in the ritornello. The tendency to use the bass in imitation with the voice can be seen also in the soprano's first aria, "Io son Tantalo, ch'a l'onda," where the interval of imitation is sometimes as much as two full measures of common time. The soprano's final aria, "Spezza cor le tue catene," consists of two strophes, each a precise ABA with equal distribution of the lines of poetry. In the ritornello of this aria imitative entrances are sometimes separated by one-half measure, at other times by only one beat. Tied notes for the words *le tue catene* provide a charming bit of wordplay.

The trio at the end of the *introduzione* of the sixth *accademia* stands out as one of Pederzuoli's most impressive achievements. The piece opens with the three voices and five-part instrumental ensemble performing in homophony. At measure 3 the composer launches an extensive fugue based upon the setting of the text "gode udir favellar delle tempeste" (example 5.11). Beginning with voices and basso continuo only, the initial alternation of subject and answer proceeds as follows:

> T: g minor, two measures, moving from quarters to eighths to sixteenths
>> A: d minor, real answer plus two free measures
>>> S: g minor, with less literal sixteenth-note motion

An extension based upon the second half of the subject (*delle tempeste*) ends with a cadence in d minor. The entrance of the four string instruments dovetails with this cadence; all four enter at once, but violin 2 has the first half of the subject, while violin 1 plays the second half. After two bars, the voices reenter, and the instruments are temporarily silent:

> S: B♭, two measures, but the answer comes after one measure
>> A: subject at the same pitch level (B♭)
>>> T: again in B♭
>>>> S: now in g minor
>>>>> violin 2: E♭ major

EX. 5.11. Pederzuoli, *Sesta accademia, prima parte,* mm. 3–6. Fugal subject.

A one-measure extension overlaps with the beginning of a new, increasingly florid vocal series:

S: c minor

   A: g minor

      T: g minor

After a one-measure extension the instruments reenter at the cadence, combining the two halves of the subject. The voices return with stretto entrances of the second half only. The instruments join in as the whole ensemble reaches a final cadence in g minor. This ensemble must surely have pleased the imperial family, who consistently admired and appreciated the intricacies of counterpoint.

The vocal and instrumental ensemble at the conclusion of the *seconda parte* receives a similar fugal treatment. If this finale is not quite as impressive as the closing movement of the *introduzione,* it still draws upon a wide range of contrapuntal devices, including contrary motion, and confirms Pederzuoli's outstanding command of part writing. The composer's strong grasp of the *prima prattica* probably reflects his own background as an organist as well as the tastes of the imperial court.

ANTONIO AND CARLO DRAGHI

The six works by Draghi pertinent to this study are preserved in five manuscripts at A-Wn.[10] All six Draghi cantatas, like Pederzuoli's, are rather unorthodox when compared with those composed in Italy during the late seventeenth century or with those written by his Viennese colleagues Vismarri, Cappellini, and Viviani. The rather sizable dimensions and performing forces betray the composer's greater interest in larger dramatic works. All six are "ensemble cantatas": two trios, three quartets, and one quintet. It is true that chamber duets were quite common throughout this period in Italy, but cantatas employing three or more voices were exceptions. In some respects, therefore, Draghi's works do not belong to the mainstream of seventeenth-century cantata literature. Table 5.1 shows that the Kapellmeister exploited a variety of vocal and instrumental colors in these chamber works. The two quintets and the *Intramezzo di musica* are provided with continuo accompaniment only, without obbligato instruments. The most elaborate instrumentation is found in the score of the *Terza accademia*, which calls for two violins, alto viola, and basso di viola, in addition to continuo. The *Seconda accademia* has obbligato parts for two violins, and the trio *Di tre amanti* includes parts for two treble instruments, perhaps also violins. In the latter piece, written-out parts occur only in the final trio, but one or both treble instruments may have played in the ritornellos of the arias. In fact, in many scores Draghi provides spaces for ritornellos but does not give details. He occasionally specifies that ritornellos should be played and leaves several bars of blank staves for treble and continuo lines to be filled in by the performers.[11]

Lo specchio is an elaborate compliment to the empress dowager on her birthday. Eleonora and four ladies of the court sing the praises of the mirror, which "does not pretend and does not lie." The mirror thus becomes a symbol of justice, prudence, and constancy, ostensibly the same virtues evident in Eleonora herself. In the story of *Forza d'un bel volto,* the face, the mouth, and the eyes compete in an effort to break down the resistance of the stubborn heart. Each of these three protagonists sings of its own fine qualities that will lead the heart to surrender in the end. The moral of the story is given in the final lines: "It's better to love for love's sake than to be forced to love" (Meglio è amar per amor ch'amar per forza). In *Di tre amanti* each of three lovers recalls the time of day when he first found himself in love: in the morning at daybreak, at midday when the sun's rays are strongest, or in the evening when the stars fade into the sea. Finally, all three confess: "It's no use hoping to find shelter from Love's sorties, whether in the morning, midday, or evening" (Sì, sì, ch'esser sicuro dal insidie d'Amor invan si spera su'l mattin', su'l meriggio, su la sera).[12]

Among the Draghi cantatas, *Forza d'un bel volto* offers a good example of his earlier cantata style. The piece consists of a free alternation of recitatives, ariosos, brief arias, and ensembles. Only the opening aria, written for *occhio primo,* unfolds in the da capo design that would overtake all other aria forms later in the century. However, Draghi does not set up the kind of key tension found in later da capo arias; all sections begin and end in G major. Virtually all the other arias and ensembles are cast in the strophic form still popular in the 1670s. For the duet assigned to *primo e secondo occhio,* Draghi cleverly combines the strophic and da capo principles. This duet consists of two strophes separated by a recitative that concludes with the instruction *Da Capo con la 2.a Stanza dell'Aria.*

Draghi's melodies are predominantly conjunct, and the recitatives are quite simple. In contrast to the more extreme cantatas by Cappellini, Draghi's *Forza d'un bel volto* does not include unusual or dramatic leaps other than the octave. Both soprano parts include long-breathed coloratura passages extending to as much as five measures in common time but carefully calculated for singing because of their stepwise motion and short sequential patterns. The bass aria also makes consider-

TABLE 5.1. VOCAL AND INSTRUMENTAL FORCES IN CANTATAS BY ANTONIO DRAGHI

TITLE	VOICES	INSTRUMENTATION
Lo specchio (1676)	SSSSS	bc
Forza d'un bel volto (before 1682)	SSATB	bc
Di tre amanti (before 1682)	SAT	2 treble instruments (vl 1–2), bc
Seconda accademia (1693)	SSAT	vl 1–2, bc
Intramezzo di musica in una accademia di dame (1697)	SSSS	bc
Terza accademia (1698)	SSA	vl 1–2, alto viola da gamba, bass viola da gamba, bc

able demands on the singer, but the alto and tenor parts are much less virtuosic. Similarly, the fairly large range of a twelfth found in both soprano and bass parts is greater than the limited ranges for alto and tenor. Draghi uses *fioriture* for obvious play on words such as *strali, sparge, guance,* and *trionfar,* and he paints "delle trage-die tue misera scena" in the central trio with an expressive descending line and a succession of tied rhythms.

In *Forza d'un bel volto,* the composer's preference for meters such as $\frac{4}{4}$, $\frac{3}{4}$, and $\frac{6}{8}$ instead of those with the half note as the beat reveals a more modern aspect of his style. Draghi exploits the use of hemiola for cadences, so common in the cantatas of Vismarri and Cappellini, only in the final two-voiced *choro,* where the play be-tween $\frac{6}{4}$ and $\frac{3}{2}$ brings the cantata to a dance-like conclusion. Throughout the cantata there is a modest amount of continuo figuration, primarily for raised and lowered thirds, first-inversion chords, and suspensions. No ritornellos between numbers are indicated, either written out or implied by blank measures. Even initial ritornellos for arias and ensembles are lacking, though brief bass-line passages are used to articulate formal sections derived from text. The role of the bass line varies. In the opening aria the bass of the A section is a rhythmic quasi ostinato, but in many arias and ensembles the bass mainly provides harmonic support. In the aria for *Il volto* the instrumental bass is a kind of *basso seguente,* sometimes duplicating the vocal bass line, at others playing a simplified version, and at still others ornament-ing the singer's melody. Motivic interplay between vocal and bass lines is limited but occurs effectively in the tenor aria for *Il crine,* with its delightful exchange of syncopated rhythmic fragments.

Many style features seen in *Forza d'un bel volto* can be found also in *Di tre amanti* and in *Lo specchio.* In *Di tre amanti* a rounded ABA[1] musical structure oc-curs for every stanza of the strophic arias. The designation *da capo* is given at the end of each stanza of the g-minor aria for the *terzo amante,* but, rather unusually, the reprise in this aria is not written out. Always derived from the preceding vocal music, two-voiced ritornellos occur between strophes and after the da capo aria. Typically, the copyist provides only the beginning of the treble part and several measures more of the bass line of these ritornellos. The degree of vocal virtuosity is much more modest than in *Forza d'un bel volto;* even the final trio is short and simple. The instrumental bass performs its usual function as pure harmonic support, occasionally participating in imitation, as in the final trio, where the composer humorously portrays *mattin, meriggio,* and *sera* with rising and falling figures. The F-major aria for the *secondo amante* is a true duet for alto and bass line, the two sharing equally in lively $\frac{6}{8}$ rhythms.

Of the three cantatas composed before 1682, *Lo specchio* may in fact be the earliest. In its greater use of arioso and dependence on strophic aria form (with the exception of one binary aria), *Lo specchio* most closely resembles the cantatas of Vismarri and Cappellini. Ensembles grow out of preceding solo sections, often without formal articulations. Four of the arias have strophes with the rounded form found in *Forza d'un bel volto* and *Di tre amanti,* in which—much like Vismarri's *In amor ci vuol patienza*—the A¹ section recalls only the first line of text and cadences in the appropriate tonality.

Eleonora's G-major aria is a fine example of a piece with strophes in ABA¹ form. The aria features two distinct motives, one in quarters and the other in eighths, heard in a sprightly exchange between voice and bass line during long stretches of music. In the middle section the quarter-note motive moves in the opposite direction. Although the aria is rather static tonally, it pleases because of its clear construction, charming wordplay, and agreeable exploitation of hemiola—a device used much more frequently in *Lo specchio* than in the cantatas of MS 16315.

A favorite device in *Lo specchio* is the inverted pedal point, a sustained tone for the singer over an active bass line. Continuo figuration is unusually sparse, and there are no ritornellos except for a rare extension at the end of an arioso or short phrases used to punctuate aria forms. In general, the vocal lines of *Lo specchio* are fairly florid, especially in the music for the empress dowager, and patterns are more regularly sequential than in the cantatas of the 1690s. In such passages, the bass line supports the active vocal line with steady rhythm; similarly, it provides a steady pulse in the more complex quartet and quintet. Several arias include imitation between voice and bass, but Draghi's counterpoint never approaches the complexity found in Pederzuoli's *Sesta accademia.*

In her discussion of *Lo specchio, Forza d'un bel volto,* and *Di tre amanti,* Beatrice Barazzoni takes a middle stance with regard to the question of whether the musical style of Draghi's early cantatas is conservative or forward-looking.[13] She rightly considers his aria structures—strophic and tripartite with only a brief da capo—as forms that were already becoming obsolete by the late 1670s. On the other hand, she identifies Draghi's melodic style as one sign of the future by contrasting the gentle contours of his graceful melodies with the more angular and declamatory lines found in cantatas by Vismarri, Cappellini, and Pederzuoli. Barazzoni cites the use of a *Devise* and dance rhythms in *Lo specchio* as other progressive style

TABLE 5.2. PROBLEMS STATED IN DRAGHI'S *ACCADEMIE* OF THE 1690S

ACCADEMIA	PROBLEM
Seconda accademia	Whether a person with an eccentric disposition prefers to find a lover who is similar or one who is calm[1]
Intramezzo di musica	Whether fortune or merit is more helpful[2]
Terza accademia	Whether it is more sorrowful to lose the favor of a lover because of one's own guilt or because of another's slander[3]

Notes
1. "Se un Humore Stravagante ami più trovare / un simile overo un placido nell'Amore."
2. "Se sia più giovenale la Fortuna / ò il Merito."
3. "Se sia più doloroso il perdere la gratia della / sua Innamorata per propria colpa ò per altrui calunnia."

features. Rather than viewing the quasi-ostinato bass of a slow aria in $\frac{3}{2}$ in *Di tre amanti* as a relic of the past, she sees it as a revival of the early seventeenth-century Venetian lament but reintroduced in a late seventeenth-century Viennese context. She points out that even though Draghi often exploits virtuosic vocal passages for conventional effects, he also uses style elements to create more general affects in the manner of late baroque music. As examples she cites a chromatic motive in the aria "Sei avinto, sei legato" from *Forza d'un bel volto* to depict Cupid's capture of a recalcitrant lover and the light coloratura brushstrokes in the aria "Della tigre cessa l'ira" from *Lo specchio* to portray a tiger that amusingly loses his characteristic rage when he sees himself in the mirror.

A hiatus of nearly twenty years separates the cantatas of the 1670s from the *accademie* of the 1690s. As usual, a problem is stated at the beginning of each academic cantata (see table 5.2). The *Intramezzo di musica* of 1697 was obviously composed for dilettante singers. Occasional coloratura phrases require a modest level of skill, but even these passages are not very demanding. Vocal ranges too are modest, lying almost exclusively within an octave. Draghi clearly knew the strengths and limitations of his aristocratic singers. The entire spirit of this composition is one of pleasure and amusement, evident from the playful treatment of text. The words *viene e va* in Prudenza's first aria, for example, are separated by rests and repeated twice. In the same aria Draghi chooses repeated dotted quarter notes and a single d^2 for the second syllable of *costante* and then contrasts this setting with an agitated rhythmic figure and flighty coloratura for *incostante*.

The *Intramezzo* is divided into *prima e seconda parte*, each of which is subdivided into two sections. The style is not significantly different from the early cantatas. Yet Draghi seems less dependent upon arioso, and he sometimes uses a ritornello to introduce an aria as well as to delineate phrases. Avvertenza's aria in the second section of the *prima parte* exemplifies Draghi's adherence to the mid-seventeenth-century ABA[1] format in which only the first line of text is reprised, but

Speranza's aria in the *seconda parte* is a bona fide da capo, though still lacking the tonal tension characteristic of da capo arias by contemporary composers working in Italy. Elsewhere Draghi varies the aria forms somewhat, drawing upon binary and text-based structures for variety. He effectively coordinates the "Corelli clash" and hemiola at several cadences.

The *Terza accademia* is divided into an *introduzione* and a *conclusione*. Herbert Seifert cites Draghi's use of obbligato instruments and the da capo aria in the second version of *Leonida in Tegea* (1697) as progressive features, and it may be that the expanded instrumental forces of the *Terza accademia* support this conclusion. Numbers such as the final trio of this end-of-the-century composition are marked *a 6,* the complete vocal ensemble probably understood as the sixth part. Other aspects of style provide hints that Draghi had become aware of more current trends toward the end of his life. The percentage of recitatives and ariosos, for example, is much smaller than in cantatas like *Lo specchio,* with the result that much greater emphasis is placed on the aria. The increased number of ritornellos and the greater use of the *Devise* are also signs of late seventeenth-century practice.

Draghi's late cantatas show little of the tonal ambiguity found in music of the previous generation. In this respect the composer is in step with developments of composers like Corelli. Harmonies are clear and stable, and especially in the arias and ensembles, modulations and overall key schemes are remarkably logical, showing a clear grasp of the usual tonal relationships. For his chord choices, Draghi continues to draw upon triads in root position and in first inversion, as well as dominant seventh chords, but he occasionally uses coloristic chords such as the Neapolitan sixth. Draghi usually supplies some figuration for his bass lines, especially for the numerous expressive suspensions. In general, he conceives of the bass line as harmonic support, but he occasionally uses it as an independent voice that enters into imitation with the vocal line.

Two arias from the *Terza accademia* are especially noteworthy. The *Primo innamorato*'s C-major aria in the *introduzione* unfolds in a rondeau-like scheme: rit.–A–rit.–A^1–rit.–B–rit.–A^2–rit. The written-out ritornellos for first and second violins and alto viola occur not only between sections but also at the beginning and at the end. Draghi selects modulations to closely related keys such as the dominant, relative minor, and mediant. Amore's c-minor aria in the *conclusione* is a modified written-out da capo. Starting without a ritornello, the voice enters alone, followed in imitation by the bass. The anticipated ritornello comes at the end of the A section, which concludes in E♭ major. The B section also begins in E♭ and consists of two vocal sections with ritornellos related to one another but not to the ritornello of A. Draghi explores the dominant minor before returning to c minor. The da capo duplicates the A section, except that the final ritornello is modified to end in the tonic key.

The degree of vocal virtuosity varies somewhat in this *accademia;* the most difficult writing is always assigned to Amore, who also sings the highest part in the trios and may have been a professional singer. In a manner similar to the contrapuntal ensembles in Pederzuoli's *Sesta accademia,* Draghi concludes the *introduzione* and *conclusione* with fugal trios. The D-major theme of the first trio is heard in imitation four times: (1) voices cadencing in a minor; (2) instruments with similar imitation ending in b minor; (3) voices again in invertible counterpoint and with cadences in f♯ minor and a minor; (4) voices in a minor joined after two measures by instruments leading to an Adagio and a concluding cadence in D major. The second trio follows a similar series of imitative sections for voices and instruments. Draghi's trios demonstrate his mastery of counterpoint, but they do not attain the degree of complexity found in Pederzuoli's fugal ensembles.

Each of the three arias by Carlo Draghi in the *Terza accademia* unfolds in the three-part form used so often by his father. Each begins with a *Devise* and contains points of imitation between the voice and the bass line. The vocal writing is simple and mostly stepwise.

While Antonio Draghi's late works do reveal evidence of a more progressive style, when contrasted with the cantatas of composers like Carlo Badia and Giovanni Bononcini, both of whom had arrived in Vienna by 1698, they still seem rather old-fashioned. The regular alternation of recitative and aria, found almost universally in Italian vocal music of the 1690s, was not adopted by the aging Kapellmeister. The full da capo aria, the dominant type by the end of the seventeenth century, turns up rarely even in his late cantatas. In the final analysis, it is important to appreciate Draghi's music for its own qualities rather than placing too much emphasis on the question of progressive versus conservative style.

PART TWO

THE CANTATA IN VIENNA,

1700–1711

6

The Political and Cultural Milieu

Historical Background

Emperor Leopold I's successor, Joseph I (1678–1711), proved to be one of the most energetic, forceful, and intelligent leaders in the entire history of the Habsburg dynasty.[1] His early death at the age of thirty-two, after only six years on the throne, can be counted as a major blow to the Austrian Empire. Charles VI, his brother and successor, lacked Joseph's decisiveness, financial aptitude, and personal charm. Even before he assumed his role as emperor, Joseph had selected his own, more secular advisors. Reconstituting the Aulic Council, he delegated many of the affairs of state to his most trusted councilors.

Joseph was the eldest son of Leopold and his third wife, Eleonore Magdalena Theresia of the Palatinate-Neuburg. Since neither of Leopold's first two marriages had produced a surviving male heir, Joseph's birth was received with special rejoicing. In several ways his childhood and early training contrasted sharply with his father's. Thus, he was not prepared for an ecclesiastical career, as Leopold had been. And in spite of his mother's austerely religious inclinations, Joseph's education was not entrusted to the influential and conservative Jesuits. Instead, he received a rather practical and liberal education directed by Karl Dietrich Otto, prince of Salm, with special training in history, politics, and military strategy. His instructors included Prince Eugene of Savoy, the imperial military hero. Especially gifted as a linguist, Joseph spoke French fluently; he was also proficient in Latin, Italian, Spanish, Czech, and Hungarian.

Only a few years after Joseph's birth, Leopold began to set the stage for his son's eventual assumption of the full imperial powers. At Bratislava on 9 December 1687, Joseph became inheritor of the kingdom of Hungary, and at Augsburg on 26 January 1690, at the age of eleven, he was crowned king of the Romans. His marriage to Amalia Wilhelmina of Braunschweig-Lüneburg, whose sister Carlotta had married Duke Rinaldo I of Modena, took place by proxy at Modena (where Amalia sojourned) on 15 January 1699 and in person at Vienna on 24 February 1699. Fully empowered and himself hopeful of male heirs, Joseph acceded to the imperial throne on 5 May 1705, the day of his father's death. Much to the chagrin of his devoutly religious mother, Eleonora Magdalena, Joseph persisted in his manner of living an extravagant life of partying and promiscuity even after his marriage to Amalia.

Several years before his accession, Joseph became involved as a military figure in the War of the Spanish Succession, a devastating conflict that dominated European political events for more than a decade at the beginning of the eighteenth century. At the close of the previous century it had become clear that the mentally deficient king of Spain, Charles II, would produce no male heirs and that the long line of Spanish Habsburgs would thus die out. Asserting rival claims to the Spanish throne, descendants of Leopold I and Louis XIV vied for the written support of the feeble Charles II. Leopold's second surviving son, Archduke Charles (1685–1740), became the Austrian claimant, while Philip, duke of Anjou, the second son of the dauphin of France, was advanced as the French candidate. Finally, shortly before his death in 1700, Charles II drew up a will in which he proclaimed that Philip was Charles's rightful successor. After Charles II's death Philip departed for Madrid, where he was tumultuously received as King Philip V of Spain.

However, the question of the Spanish succession was not to be resolved so easily. Louis XIV refused to give assurances that Philip would never inherit the French crown; a united France and Spain would have given preeminence to the French in both Europe and the New World, a prospect that worried most other European nations. As a result, war broke out in 1701; an alliance of the maritime nations, the Holy Roman Empire, and Brandenburg was pitted against France, Spain, and Bavaria.

During the early stages of the war, Joseph completely won the admiration of his own people by leading victorious forces in critical battles at Landau, a key city near the Alsatian border.[2] Defeating the French for the first time at Landau on 10 September 1702, Joseph returned to a hero's welcome in Vienna. However, following a French siege on 6 November 1703, the allies were forced to surrender Landau, and the threat to Austria in the ensuing months was especially grave. Marlborough's historic defeat of the French at Blenheim on 13 August 1704 preceded the recapture of Landau by Austrian troops on 23 November 1704; Joseph's presence during the fighting once again seems to have inspired the victory. After each of the two victories at Landau, Joseph's heroism was celebrated again and again in verse and music; the anonymous cantata *Cetre amiche,* for instance, was a special tribute to the archduke. Giovanni Bononcini glorified Joseph's heroism with three secular dramatic works: *Proteo sul Reno* (19 March 1703); *Il fiore delle eroine* (10 July 1704); and *Il ritorno di Giulio Cesare, vincitore della Mauritania* (December 1704?).[3]

In the meantime, Archduke Charles was making preparations to advance his claim as heir to the Spanish throne. On 12 September 1703 he was proclaimed king of Spain in Vienna; as Charles III, he traveled northward to Holland and England and then southward to Portugal before conquering Barcelona, where he established his court. In Vienna poets and composers continued to pay homage to Charles.

Although no records of an official appointment have come to light, Antonio Maria Bononcini appears to have held the post as Charles's Kapellmeister in Austria; among Bononcini's fairly numerous compositions dedicated to Charles is the grand cantata *La Fortuna, il Valore e la Giustitia*. Meanwhile, Charles attracted many artists and musicians to his court in Barcelona. Eventually, however, events in the War of the Spanish Succession turned the tide in favor of France (see chapter 13).[4]

The War of the Spanish Succession dominated political affairs during the reign of Joseph I, but the young emperor was faced with many other challenges. Heroic on the battlefield, he proved to be reasonable and shrewd in making peace. After ending a long Hungarian uprising led by Franz Rádóczi II, Joseph was largely responsible for a treaty—signed only days after his death—that promised to bring peace to the area for many years. As emperor, Joseph also augmented the Habsburg dominions by acquiring Sicily in 1707, Flanders in 1708, and, at various times, portions of the Italian peninsula traditionally viewed as critical to the empire's security.

Joseph I as Patron and Musician

Joseph I also proved to be a more forward-looking ruler than either his father or his brother. His liberal education and broad interests are often cited as early signs of the Enlightenment in Austria. Shortly after his accession Joseph founded the famous Akademie der Bildenden Künste, which opened officially on 6 December 1705. He oversaw plans for the new court theater, supported the initial stages of construction of Schönbrunn, endorsed the development of the suburb Josephstadt (named in his honor), and liberally patronized all the arts.[5]

Preoccupied with the War of the Spanish Succession and interested in history and politics as well as the arts, Joseph himself was less active as a musician than Leopold, for whom music was a principal avocation. Nevertheless, contemporary reports indicate that Joseph was an excellent musician and that he eagerly supported all forms of musical entertainment. Especially gifted as a dancer, he began to participate in ballets when he was only four years old, and he continued to join in courtly dancing at least until the beginning of the war. Although the question of who was responsible for Joseph's music education remains open, his most likely instructor appears to have been the court organist Ferdinand Tobias Richter (1651–1711).[6] According to E. G. Rinck, who published a biography of Joseph in the year following the emperor's death, Joseph played "ein vollkommenes clavecin, bliess die flöte, und tractierte noch viel andere instrumenta mit . . . annehmlichkeit."[7] Joseph is listed as one of the performers of the four cantatas by Carlo Badia for Leopold's name day in 1699; it seems likely that he participated as a flute player in the second and fourth cantatas.[8] He is also known to have played the flute in the autumn of 1702 at Schloss Mainberg, while Count Rudolf Franz Erwein von Schönborn played the cello and the count's brother Friedrich Karl played the violin.[9]

The rather small number of extant compositions by Joseph shows him to be a skilled technician who, according to Othmar Wessely, may have been influenced by Alessandro Scarlatti.[10] Perhaps Giovanni Bononcini, the highest paid and best-known composer during Joseph's reign, also influenced the emperor's style and taste. That Joseph admired the celebrated composer of the opera *Camilla* is most clearly reflected in the large number of commissions awarded Bononcini for dramatic works specifically honoring the young emperor and empress. Joseph's surviving works include the *Regina coeli* for soprano, two violins, viola, cello, and organ; an aria, "Alma ingrata," for a 1705 *sepolcro;* at least five arias inserted in operas by Giovanni Bononcini and Marc'Antonio Ziani; an aria for lute; and perhaps at least one cantata.[11]

CULTURAL GROWTH

During Leopold's last years and Joseph's brief reign, Italian artistic innovations exerted enormous influence upon cultural developments throughout the Habsburg lands.[12] Both the aging Leopold and Joseph imported large numbers of Italian architects, painters, sculptors, scenic designers, interior decorators, landscapers, poets, and musicians. The growing number of commissions came not only from the imperial family but also from members of the nobility and from the church. Although the aristocracy had lost much of its power, it retained considerable wealth, prestige, and tradition; noble families rivaled one another by building opulent winter palaces in Vienna and summer residences in the nearby countryside. The powerful church requested the construction of many magnificent monasteries. In most of these works an Italian influence remained prevalent. At the same time, an increasingly large number of native Austrian and German artists of all types began to receive important commissions and leading appointments.

In no field was this truer than in architecture, which received the greatest share of financial support. To be sure, Italians added richly to the extraordinary architectural transformation that was taking place in the late seventeenth and early eighteenth centuries. In Vienna, for example, Andrea dal Pozzo, Martinelli, and Carlo Carlone designed palaces for the nobility. But the highest achievements in Austrian baroque architecture belonged to three native artists: Johann Bernhard Fischer von Erlach (1656–1723); Lukas von Hildebrandt (1668–1745); and Jakob Prandtauer (1660–1726). Fischer von Erlach was a student of the renowned Bernini, and in fact, an Italian influence is dominant in the works of all three Austrian giants. However, a French influence is also significant, and it is noteworthy that Versailles was selected as the model for the luxurious Habsburg summer palace known as Schönbrunn. Together the three great men brought Austrian architecture to its zenith and created a characteristic baroque style for Vienna that dominates much of its profile even today.

During the late baroque era, theater construction and scenic design remained important supplements to the great achievements in Austrian architecture. The field of theater design, however, was entirely dominated by Italians; the three great court designers of the late seventeenth and early eighteenth centuries were Ludovico Ottavio Burnacini (1683–1707), Antonio Beduzzi (1675–1735), and Francesco Galli-Bibiena (1659–1739). Burnacini, who served the Habsburgs from 1652 to 1657 and from 1659 to 1707, designed the famous Theater auf der Cortina (razed during the Turkish Siege of 1683) and created all sets for sacred and secular dramatic works until his death in 1707.[13] However, it was Francesco Galli-Bibiena who oversaw the remodeling of the old Komödienhaus, beginning in 1698.[14] The emperor suspended large theatrical productions after 25 June 1702 because of the War of the Spanish Succession, and it was in the ensuing months that Giovanni Bononcini, Francesco Conti, and other Viennese artists found shelter at the court of Queen Sophie Charlotte in Berlin. Galli-Bibiena later designed an entirely new court theater that stood in the place of the razed Komödienhaus. After the death of Burnacini, Galli-Bibiena was retained but did not replace Burnacini as the first court-theater designer; that honor was given to the Bolognese architect Antonio Beduzzi, whose appointment officially began on 1 January 1708. Beduzzi had been in Vienna at least since the beginning of 1705. He was active not only as a theater architect but also as a fresco painter and an engraver; it was Beduzzi, in fact, who was responsible for the elaborate engravings in Carlo Agostino Badia's cantata collection entitled *Tributi armonici*, issued sometime between 1699 and the beginning of 1705. As an architect, Beduzzi's most important contribution was probably the Kärntnertortheater, Vienna's first specifically public theater.[15] Beduzzi held his post only until the accession of Charles VI, who dismissed him and Francesco Galli-Bibiena, replacing them with Francesco's brother, Ferdinando Galli-Bibiena (1656–1743), the renowned theater designer who had served Charles in Barcelona.[16]

Opera performances took place not only in Viennese theaters especially designed for this purpose but also in the summer pleasure palaces—the Neue Favorita, Schönbrunn, and Laxenburg—even before residences included the large theaters that were built in the middle of the eighteenth century. Performances were given in large halls and outdoors in the adjoining parks, sometimes on ponds that made ideal settings for spectacular baroque effects.[17]

During the early eighteenth century, native Austrian and German painters carried on the baroque tradition that they had learned from artists like Pietro da Cortona and Fra Andrea dal Pozzo. Hence, the Italian influence in the visual arts remained predominant. Among the Austrian painters active in the late baroque era were Martin Hohenberg (Altomonte, 1657–1745), Johann Michael Rottmayer von Rosenbrunn (1654–1730), Daniel Gran (1694–1757), and Paul Tröger (1698–1762). While native Austrians were rising to the forefront in the field of painting, Italian painters such as Chiarini, Beduzzi, and Carlo Carlone continued to receive commissions at the imperial court. Italian influence seems to have been less pervasive in sculpture than in architecture and painting, and a characteristic Austrian style is discernible already by the early eighteenth century. Important sculptors of the period include Steinl, Paul Strudel, Caspar, Matticelli, and the highly esteemed Rafael Donner (1692–1741).[18]

The principal duties of court poets in the early eighteenth century consisted of supplying librettos for large musical works that celebrated events in the lives of the Habsburgs. In this domain the Italians reigned supreme, receiving a constant flow of commissions for librettos of operas, serenatas, cantatas, oratorios, *sepolcri,* and a myriad of other dramatic works. An increasingly large number of scholarly works has richly augmented our knowledge of the late seventeenth- and early eighteenth-century libretto.[19]

After the active career of Nicolò Minato came to an end in 1698, Domenico Cupeda (ca. 1635–1704) was appointed first court poet; Cupeda had resided in Vienna since 1695. In 1701 the Arcadian Pietro Antonio Bernardoni (1672–1714) from Modena was named second court poet, and he succeeded Cupeda as first poet three years later. In 1706 Joseph I appointed the Roman librettist Silvio Stampiglia (1664–1725) as an additional court poet. The influential Giovanni Bononcini's most frequent collaborator, Stampiglia apparently held a post of equal rank with Bernardoni. All three poets—Cupeda, Bernardoni, and Stampiglia—are known to have written texts for Viennese cantatas.

HABSBURG MUSIC CHAPELS, 1700–1711

The constant growth of the Habsburg chapel that had taken place in the second half of the seventeenth century continued through the reign of Joseph I; much of this expansion was due to the development of instrumental music and the need for larger groups of players for the performances of lavish operas.[20] In the early years of Leopold's reign, the number of court musicians seems to have been about 60; by 1702 the total had increased to 102; and by the time of Joseph's death the figure had reached 107.[21] Musicians frequently did not receive their payments promptly, and during the years 1702–1703 the financial strain on the imperial treasury was so great that performances of large dramatic works were suspended. Many musicians left the court temporarily, but after the military danger to Austria subsided, most resumed their activities at the prestigious imperial court.

In the last years of the seventeenth century and the early years of the eighteenth century, the Habsburgs made three important changes in the structure and membership of the chapel. First, in 1694 Leopold created the post of court composer especially for the young Carlo Agostino Badia. Later composers to receive this important appointment included Johann Joseph Fux, Giovanni Bononcini, Pier Francesco Tosi, Francesco Conti, and Giuseppe Porsile. A second innovation was the admittance of women singers to the chapel for the first time in 1700. Although women such as Giulia Masotti sang solo roles in secular works from 1636, they were not admitted as regular members of the chapel until 1700.[22] Anna Maria "Lisi" Badia and Cunigonda Sutterin became the first prima donnas to join the chapel officially. The inclusion of these and other women singers probably suited the requirements for the satisfactory performance of contemporary dramatic music. The third change was the creation of the post of *Musik-Oberdirektor* in 1709; this position was usually held by a member of the lesser nobility, and the first man to serve was the Marchese Scipione Publicola di S. Croce. The *Musik-Oberdirektor* may have been a dilettante musician, but his duties were purely administrative; he was directly in charge of the organization of the chapel, and he served as a liaison between the Kapellmeister and the *Oberhofmeister* of the entire court.

Following the death of Draghi in 1700, the assistant Kapellmeister, Antonio Pancotti, received the appointment as Kapellmeister, and Marc'Antonio Ziani (ca. 1653–1715) was called from Venice to assume the duties of assistant Kapellmeister. Ziani became one of the leading composers at the Habsburg court. The number of important commissions that he received through the reign of Joseph was equaled only by the number given to each of the Bononcini brothers. Pancotti seems to have been a composer of minor importance; his number of extant works is surprisingly small, and he received few significant commissions. There is also no evidence that Pancotti composed cantatas. He may have been selected for his administrative rather than musical abilities; this conjecture is supported by the fact that the position of *Musik-Oberdirektor* was created shortly after Pancotti died on 11 June 1709.[23] No new Kapellmeister was selected until the reign of Charles VI. The dominant personality of the early eighteenth century, and perhaps the most famous Viennese musician of the entire period, was the Austrian Johann Joseph Fux (1660–1744). Fux rose gradually from court composer (1698) to assistant Kapellmeister (1711) to Kapellmeister (1715).

For the most part, a composer's nationality defined his duties after 1700, just as it had from the beginning of Leopold's reign. Thus, the vast majority of operas, serenatas, cantatas, oratorios, and *sepolcri* continued to be provided by the Italian faction, while the Austrians and Germans composed liturgical works, keyboard music, instrumental ensemble pieces, and ballet music. The lines of distinction, however, were not always strict. Fux, for example, wrote a large number of sacred and secular dramatic compositions with Italian librettos, but he did not receive a commission for an Italian opera until 1708, a fairly advanced date in his career. Like Pancotti, he does not seem to have composed any Italian cantatas. This genre remained almost exclusively the domain of the Italians until after 1715.

During the early eighteenth century the expenditures for the Habsburg chapel and for dramatic music rose to a new high. Ludwig Ritter von Köchel estimated that the total amount spent for the chapel personnel—including poets, dancers, and scenic designers—in an average year during the period 1708–38 was about 110,000 florins; for musicians alone the Habsburgs spent approximately 100,000 florins, a considerable increase over the amount expended in the late seventeenth century.[24] Individual "star" composers such as Giovanni Bononcini were promised enormous wages, though the Habsburgs never made good on all their extravagant promises. Several individual singers were also handsomely paid, and this trend continued through the reign of Charles VI. Musicians frequently had to wait many months or even years before receiving payments. During stressful times such as the military crisis of 1702–1703 and in the confused period following Joseph's death, payments seem to have halted almost entirely.

GENRE DESIGNATIONS

The genre designations for secular dramatic works given in Vienna at the turn of the eighteenth century vary greatly; they include terms such as *dramma musicale, dramma per musica, componimento drammatico per musica, favola pastorale, festa teatrale, servizio da camera, scherzo musicale,* and *operetta.*[25] These works range in length from full operas in three to five acts to small, one-act compositions of almost cantata-like proportions. Unlike the cantata, however, the smaller one-act opera, whatever its designation, included staging and costumes. In general, terms such as *dramma musicale, componimento, rappresentazione, trattenimento,* and *favola* were used for large works in several acts, while designations such as *festa teatrale, servizio da camera,* and *scherzo musicale* were reserved for the smaller one-act compositions. One term that appeared with greater frequency in the early eighteenth century was *cantata,* and this genre was to play a far greater role in the musical life of Vienna under Joseph I than it had under Leopold I.

OCCASIONS, PLACES OF PERFORMANCE, AND PERFORMERS

The cantata sources offer only fragmentary information about the occasions for which cantatas were commissioned during the ascendancy and reign of Joseph I. Badia prepared the four cantatas preserved in A-Wn, 16308, for Leopold's name day (15 November) in 1699. In addition, he was commissioned to compose two grand cantatas: *La Pace, e Marte supplicanti avanti al Trono della Gloria* for Joseph's name day (19 March) in 1701, and *Il sacrificio di Berenice* for the name day (19 November) of Elizabeth Christina (the wife of Charles VI) in 1712. At that time Elizabeth was still in Barcelona, upholding the Austrian claim to the Spanish throne even after her husband's departure.

Ziani composed *l'Ercole vincitor dell'invidia,* a *cantata per servizio di camera,* for Joseph's name day in 1706. At the time the court was still officially in mourning for Leopold; according to Franz Hadamowsky, the period of mourning was not over until 19 June 1706.[26] Large dramatic works were not staged during this period, so smaller pieces such as *l'Ercole* were evidently considered appropriate for important dates in the lives of the Habsburgs. Curiously, Joseph's name day in 1706 is also given as the occasion for Badia's cantata *Il tempo parta alla fama*. The information about the occasion in the sole surviving source (D-Dl, 2192/J/.1) was not entered by the main scribe (possibly Badia himself) but was added by a later hand:

Cantata
Nel Giorno del
Nome di
Giuseppe I.mo
Imperatore ecc.
Il Tempo Parta
alla Fama.
Musica del
Carlo Agostino
Badia
1706.

It seems very unlikely that two works were commissioned for Joseph's name day in 1706. Since the information about the occasion for Ziani's *l'Ercole* was entered in the archival copy by a Habsburg scribe, there seems to be little question about its accuracy. The details about the occasion added in the manuscript of Badia's *Il tempo parta alla fama* therefore appear to have no basis.[27]

Antonio Maria Bononcini's three-voiced grand cantata *La Fortuna, il Valore e la Giustitia* was written for the name day of Charles III of Spain (the future Emperor Charles VI) on 4 November 1706. In 1707 Giovanni Bononcini composed the hybrid work entitled *L'Oracolo d'Apollo;* it consists of three arias, each of which is followed by a substantial ballet. (Köchel misread the date in the manuscript as 1701, as did Joseph Mantuani.)[28] Köchel and Alexander von Weilen both state that the librettist was Silvio Stampiglia and that the work was composed for the birthday of Empress Amalia Wilhelmina (6 January).[29] Otto Erich Deutsch lists 6 January 1707 as the date of performance.[30] In the manuscript itself, however, there is no information about a librettist, an occasion, or a specific date of performance, and thus "no basis for their conjectures is known."[31] Moreover, 6 January is actually the birthday of the empress dowager Eleonora Magdalena, not Amalia Wilhelmina. Because *L'Oracolo d'Apollo* is a special work that is nowhere designated as a cantata, I have omitted it from the list of cantatas discussed in subsequent chapters.

The anonymous cantata with the text incipit *Cetre amiche* was written for the celebration of one of the Austrian victories at Landau during the War of the Spanish Succession. The victory was led by Joseph, the king of the Romans, who is identified in the text as the "gran figlio d'Augusto." Since Joseph's presence during the fighting at Landau inspired victories in both 1702 and 1704, the composition could have been a tribute to his heroism after either battle. In his catalog of manuscripts now at A-Wn, Mantuani suggested the year 1702, but there is nothing in the source or in the text to confirm this conjecture. Another anonymous cantata, *Alli giusti miei lamenti,* served a twofold purpose: it paid homage to Leopold shortly after his death on 5 May 1705, and it honored Joseph as the empire's heroic new leader.

At least four academic cantatas were composed by Ziani during Joseph's reign. These include two extant *accademie* from 1706 plus two from 1707 for which no scores seem to survive. The four Ziani *accademie* give evidence that the practice of composing academic cantatas, which had been initiated by Pederzuoli and Draghi, continued even after the death of Leopold. Composers who wrote *accademie* were evidently selected on the basis of rank in the imperial chapel; from their inception the Viennese academies had included only members of the Habsburg family, the aristocracy, and a leading circle of artists. Like Draghi and Pederzuoli before him, Ziani gained acceptance at academic meetings by virtue of his prestigious position.

From the sporadic information about occasions that comes down in cantata sources, we can conclude that a small number of cantatas were written for important dates in the lives of Habsburgs—a battle victory, a coronation, and several name days—and that at least four more were composed for academic sessions. In all, these pieces account for only slightly more than 10 percent of the cantatas prepared for Vienna between roughly 1699 and 1712. What, then, were the occasions for the other cantatas preserved in archival sources? Many cantatas may have served as pure entertainment for the Habsburgs and their guests during meals. Early evidence that Italian vocal chamber works provided entertainment during meals can be found in an inventory of music belonging to Archduke Leopold Wilhelm.[32] On folios 6v–10v the titles of 250 works are given under the rubric *Per servicio di tavola.* A rare piece of evidence that cantatas continued to function as table music well into the eighteenth century can be seen in a holograph by Antonio Caldara.[33] The Habsburgs' special affection for music and contemporary reports about the frequency of musical events at court make it plain that works were performed not only as tributes on festive days but also as part of the daily court routine. If cantatas were given on a regular basis during meals in the private chambers of the imperial family, there would have been little need to make notes of these facts in the manuscripts themselves. Caldara's fleeting reference to table music offers a rare but valuable insight into the practical use of Viennese cantatas.

Other cantatas may have given renowned visiting singers opportunities to be heard at court or possibly even served as audition pieces. The celebrated Francesco Pistocchi, for example, visited Vienna in 1700 during his return from Ansbach to Bologna. Still other cantatas may have preceded or accompanied related forms of entertainment, especially dance. Giovanni Bononcini's *L'Oracolo d'Apollo,* while, strictly speaking, not a cantata, may be indicative of a practice of embellishing dances during Carnival season with vocal chamber music.[34]

For intimate performances, a variety of summer and winter locations were available. The inner rooms of the several tracts of the Hofburg served as settings for vocal and instrumental chamber music. Hadamowsky inventories a sizable number of intimate vocal works from 1687 to 1701 that were performed in the "Kaisers quartier," "Kaiserin[s] quartier," "Königs Seiten," "im neuen Stock" (of the Leopold tract), "in un Gran Salone dell'Imp. Palazzo," and "auff geheimer Schaubühne." One very specific setting is named "1. Zimmer, wo man in den Neuen Stock [the Leopold tract] geht, neben der 1. Ante camera."[35] Other cantata performances may have taken place in elaborate banquet halls and in the courtyards and gardens of the summer residences.

Especially in the 1680s and 1690s aristocratic and Habsburg "family" performances had been quite common, and Leopold himself wrote several dramatic works for Carnival season that involved members of the nobility and the imperial household. With Leopold's advancing age, the marriages of his daughters, the entrance of Joseph and Charles into world politics, and the exigencies of the War of the Spanish Succession, the Habsburg family presentations seem to have become more rare after 1700. After this time Leopold also seems to have ended his activity as a composer.

Scant information comes down about the performers of cantatas from the last years of the seventeenth century through the end of Joseph's reign. The title page of A-Wn, 16308, which contains the four Badia cantatas performed on Leopold's name day in 1699, offers the following description: "Fatta dalla S.M.: del Re de' Romani Archiducca et Archiduchesse con cavalieri e Dame." The *Re de' Romani* would of course have been Joseph; the *Archiducca* would have been Charles; and the *Archiduchesse* would probably have been Leopold's daughters Elizabeth (1680–1741) and Maria Anna (1683–1754), the future wife of John V of Portugal. The manuscript provides no specific names of *cavalieri,* but a *Dama* is identified at the beginning of each of the first three cantatas. The first folio of the fourth cantata is missing, but it too probably named a specific court lady. The names of the ladies given in the manuscript for cantatas 1–3 are Contessa della Torre, Contessa Sousin, and Contessa Fünfkirchen, respectively. The vocal part of each cantata is scored for soprano solo throughout; thus it appears that each of the cantatas was sung by a single court lady. The vocal writing does not place unusual demands upon the individual singers in range or in coloratura passagework, and it is therefore appropriate for dilettante singers. If the cantatas were sung by four court ladies, how then did the king of the Romans, the archduke, the archduchesses, and the court gentlemen participate? The scores of Badia's cantatas include prominent instrumental parts for flutes, violins, and lutes, as well as continuo. Joseph is known to have been a competent flutist; the second and fourth cantatas of MS 16308 contain important flute solos.[36] Charles—at the time only fourteen years of age—studied keyboard instruments and may have participated as a continuo player. Perhaps the archduchesses and unnamed gentlemen of the court also played some of the instrumental parts. It is also possible that some members of the Habsburg family and the nobility participated in other forms of entertainment appended to the cantatas—either dramatic presentations or ballet. Hadamowsky indicates that Habsburgs frequently danced in court entertainments during the late seventeenth century.[37] The third cantata includes both an instrumental interlude and an *aria menuett* that could conceivably have accompanied dancing; ballet music by another composer could also have been inserted between the individual cantatas or after the singing. In any event, the manuscript of these cantatas supplies enough information to document the participation of a sizable group of dilettante performers who gathered to pay tribute to the head of the imperial establishment on his name day in 1699.[38]

Unfortunately, no other specific information about individual performers is preserved in cantata manuscripts. Since many of the cantatas may have been presented as table music or for a variety of informal occasions, the composers themselves may have participated. Giovanni Bononcini and Attilio Ariosti are known to have sung duets of Agostino Steffani during their stay at the court of Queen Sophie Charlotte, and Bononcini was unquestionably an important teacher of singers.[39]

Women singers such as the star soprano Giulia Masotti had flourished at the imperial court in the 1670s but apparently did not continue to take a prominent role in performances during the last decades of the seventeenth century. This was to change at the outset of the eighteenth century. The wives of composers may well have inspired the composition of numerous cantatas. The most celebrated of these during the years 1700–1711 would have been the Florentine soprano Anna Maria Elisabetta "Lisi" Nonetti Badia, who arrived in Vienna in 1700. She began to receive a monthly stipend of 120 florins on 1 July. The date of her marriage to Carlo Badia is unknown. In 1706 Carlo probably accompanied his wife to Venice, where she sang at the Teatro S. Giovanni Crisostomo. At Vienna she was featured in works not only by Badia but also by composers such as Fux and Giovanni Bononcini. Along with her husband, she was retained after the accession of Charles VI; she died on 7 January 1726. Giulia Masotti's daughter Theresia (1682–1711), who married the theorbist and composer Francesco Conti (1682–1732) in 1705, is also known to have been active as a singer at court.[40] A soprano who had received an appointment just three months earlier than Lisi Badia was Cunigonda Sutterin, who, according to Köchel, died in September 1711.[41] Was she perhaps a relative of Eleonora Suterin, the wife of Antonio Maria Bononcini?[42] Antonio's undated Viennese cantata *Ecco Amor che mi segue* contains some unusual vocal pyrotechnics, including a written-in "high C" (c3)—the only such instance from the cantata repertoire of this period. The remarkable vocal writing suggests that the composer was intimately familiar with the ability of a particular singer.

A third soprano engaged by Habsburgs early in the eighteenth century was "Kath. Kaplerin," who received an appointment on 1 January 1707 and continued in the emperor's service until 1713.[43] In 1707 she appeared in Giovanni Bononcini's *Etearco;* other details about her activity in Vienna remain to be documented. Only one other woman received an official appointment as a singer in Vienna before the reign of Charles VI. Lowell Lindgren has shown that the acclaimed soprano Maria Landini sang in Giovanni Bononcini's *Muzio Scevola* already on 30 June 1710.[44] She was to become Francesco Conti's second wife sometime between August 1714 and Carnival 1715 and enjoyed a career as one of the leading singers during the early reign of Charles VI. Her official appointment began on 1 January 1711, and she remained a prima donna at the imperial court until her death in 1722. Since she was active in Vienna almost a full year before the death of Joseph, it is entirely possible that some of the cantatas dating from 1710 to 1712 were composed for her. Yet another soprano who may have visited Vienna during the first decade of the eighteenth century was Regina Schoonjans, probably a singing student of Giovanni Bononcini's. She traveled to Berlin with the circle of artists who served Sophie Charlotte near the end of Leopold's reign, but her official appointment at Vienna did not come until 1717. Later she became the *seconda soprano* in many of Conti's operas. Her Viennese service may actually predate the reign of Charles. Lindgren's detailed lists of singers who performed in dramatic works by Giovanni and Antonio Maria Bononcini reveal that still other women appeared from time to time at Vienna, even if they did not receive enduring appointments.[45]

Köchel offered details about the many male singers active at the Habsburg court during the early years of the eighteenth century, and Lindgren's lists provide additional information.[46] Here it is necessary only to cite a handful of the most acclaimed singers for whom cantatas may have been written: the soprano castratos Giuseppe Galloni and Domenico Tollini; the alto castratos Francesco Ballerini, Antonio Bernacchi, and Gaetano Orsini; the tenors Giovanni Buzzoleni (Bucceleni), Carlo Costa, and Silvio Garghetti; and the bass Rainieri Borrini. The scarcity of cantatas written for tenor and bass leaves little doubt that the genre was principally the domain of high voices.[47] Since his service in Vienna began as early as 1699, Orsini may well be the alto for whom many cantatas from the period preceding the reign of Charles VI were intended.[48]

Two other renowned singers who may have sung cantatas during their visits to Vienna are Francesco Pistocchi and Pier Francesco Tosi. As indicated above, Pistocchi sojourned in Vienna in 1700 while he was en route from Ansbach to Bologna; his *trattenimento per musica* titled *Le risa di Democrito* was given at court during Carnival season of that year. Tosi held a position as court composer in Vienna from 1 July 1705 until 1711, although there are apparently no extant compositions by him dating from this period. Perhaps he was active during this time as a singer or a singing teacher; he may also have been busy drafting his *Opinioni,* first published at Bologna in 1723. The presence of exciting personalities like Pistocchi and Tosi in Vienna may have motivated other composers to write Italian cantatas.

Cantata sources provide even less specific information about the instrumentalists who participated in cantata performances at Vienna. Several composers may have played continuo parts for vocal chamber music. Attilio Ariosti was a skilled harpsichordist, and the painting of him now in Sophie Charlotte's writing room shows him composing while seated at the harpsichord. Marc'Antonio Ziani must also have been an excellent keyboard player. As for performers of bass lines, Giovanni Bononcini was described in 1709 as "indisputably the first" cellist of his day, and he probably played many of the ornamental basses of his own cantatas, which were lavishly praised by Francesco Gasparini in 1708.[49] Like his brother, Antonio Maria Bononcini had been a pupil of G. P. Colonna at Bologna and had played in the orchestra of Cardinal Pamphili while the latter was papal legate there in 1690–93. The florid obbligato cello part in Antonio's earliest known composition, a *laudate pueri* dated 19 February 1693, and a set of twelve cello sonatas from about the same time indicate that he too was a cello virtuoso.[50] The elaborate cello obbligato parts in the first and last arias of Antonio's cantata *Mentre al novo apparir* (A-Wn, 17607, no. 4), dated 1708, lend support to this conjecture.

We can only speculate about the identities of the other instrumentalists who took part in cantata performances. Ariosti was not only a keyboard player but also the leading viola d'amore virtuoso of his generation. One of his cantatas that was probably not composed for Vienna, *Pur alfin gentil viola,* contains an ornamental viola d'amore obbligato that is obviously alluded to in the text.[51] (Ariosti also wrote at least two sets of pieces specifically for the viola d'amore.) The second arias of two of Ariosti's Viennese cantatas, *Che mi giova esser Regina* (A-Wn, 17591, no. 2) and *Furie, che negl'abissi* (A-Wn, 17575, no. 5), have obbligato parts for an unspecified instrument; in each aria the part is written in soprano rather than treble clef, the usual clef for violin parts. These two arias may give further evidence of Ariosti's predilection for the viola d'amore, and he may have performed the obbligatos himself.

Elsewhere cantata composers called for various combinations of obbligato violins, violas, flutes, and lutes. Köchel gives the names of players who were employed by the Habsburgs during the period from roughly 1700 to 1711. Perhaps the most prominent violinist was Nicola Matteis, son of the Italian violinist of the same name who had settled in England in 1672. Matteis the younger began his service in Vienna on 1 July 1700 with a monthly salary of seventy-five florins, a sum higher than that earned by any other Viennese violinist of the period. He retained his post until his death on 23 October 1737. Matteis may have been the virtuoso who played some of the florid violin solos found in cantatas of the period.[52] Only two cantatas, Badia's *Quai lamenti improvisi* (1699) and Ziani's *l'Ercole vincitor dell'invidia* (1706), require *liuti.* At the time that Badia composed *Quai lamenti improvisi,* the Habsburgs employed at least two theorbo players (Orazio Clementi and Georg Reutter), as well as one lutenist (Andreas Boor). The position of theorbist was an important one in Vienna.

Clementi was a celebrated player, but he was probably eclipsed by the still more famous Francesco Bartolomeo Conti, who began his service in Vienna on 1 April 1701. Conti may have been the theorbist who played the arpeggiated interlude for lute and the obbligato part in one aria of *l'Ercole vincitor*. Many operas of the period 1700–1711 include arias with elaborate written-out lute accompaniments; although similar parts are seldom found in cantatas, it is certainly possible that Clementi, Conti, and other virtuosi participated in cantata performances as continuo players, with or without keyboard instruments. Many Conti cantatas that probably date from the reign of Charles VI actually include beautiful obbligato parts for lute or theorbo.[53]

The most puzzling question with regard to the instrumentalists concerns the flute parts found in cantatas by the Bononcinis and Badia. In Köchel's detailed list of musicians engaged by the emperors, no names of flutists are given. It is possible that some of the known wind players—oboists, bassoonists, cornetto players, or brass players—doubled as flutists and that therefore the names of flutists were not listed separately. Distinguished virtuosi may have visited Vienna from time to time, although the frequency of flute parts implies that players were hired on a regular basis. The emperor Joseph himself is known to have been a satisfactory flutist, and other members of the Habsburg family or of the aristocracy may have performed with him in cantatas that required more than one flute. Yet the sheer virtuosity of the parts—especially in the cantatas of Antonio Maria Bononcini—makes it seem unlikely that they could have been performed by dilettantes. Thus I believe that flute players were actually employed by the Habsburgs and that they may have doubled on other wind instruments or have been employed in some nonmusical capacity; in any case, their names have not yet come to light.

LIBRETTISTS AND LIBRETTOS

Cantata sources from 1700 to 1711 identify six librettists: Pier Maria Ruggieri, Donato Cupeda, Domenico Mazza, Paolo Antonio del Negro, G. D. Filippeschi, and Pietro Antonio Bernardoni. The Abate Ruggieri prepared texts for seven of Badia's *Tributi armonici* (nos. 2, 3, 6, and 9–12). Ruggieri is known otherwise only by his librettos for two oratorios, Badia's *La clemenza di Davide* (1703) and Fux's *La Regina Saba* (1705).[54] "Dottore" Mazza supplied the text for Ziani's *l'Ercole vincitor*, del Negro composed the libretto for Badia's *Il sacrificio di Berenice* (1712, the year of the interregnum), and Filippeschi wrote the verse for Badia's *La Pace, e Marte supplicanti*.

The two most important poets of this group are Cupeda and Bernardoni, each of whom held an important post at the imperial court. Donato Cupeda wrote the texts for the four Badia cantatas in A-Wn, 16308 (dated 1699). On 1 January 1694 he began to serve as a substitute at the side of Minato, whom he eventually succeeded as court poet in March 1698. From this time until his death at the end of 1704, Cupeda was the first court poet. Stylistically, he followed the lead of his renowned predecessor, preferring mythological and historical subjects embroidered freely with amorous and comic episodes. The Italian composers who set his librettos most often (M. A. Ziani, Draghi, Giovanni Bononcini, Badia, and Ariosti) all wrote cantatas for Vienna; it is certainly possible that some of the anonymous texts of their cantatas were in fact written by Cupeda.[55]

Another librettist who is known to have provided texts for cantatas is Pietro Antonio Bernardoni (1672–1714). Bernardoni is the author of Antonio Bononcini's *La Fortuna, il Valore, e la Giustitia* and the two academic texts set to music by Ziani in 1706. He is also the poet of three cantatas by Ariosti (*Che mi giova, l'Idol mio,* and *Pastor, pastore hai vinto*), as well as one by Badia (*Begl'occhi neri*). Born at Modena, Bernardoni began to write verse during his youth, and cantata texts have been identified among his earliest works.[56] He was deeply influenced by the Bolognese poet and scholar Lodovico Antonio Muratori (1672–1750), an outspoken critic of the Marinists. In 1691 Bernardoni joined the famed Accademia dell'Arcadia, assuming the name Cromiro Dianio. In July 1701 he received an appointment as second poet at the imperial court. He arrived at Vienna in September and was awarded an annual salary of two thousand florins. In October 1703 he received permission to visit Italy, but he had returned to Vienna by 1705, becoming the first poet following the death of Cupeda. Bernardoni's salary was increased by a thousand florins in 1706. Toward the middle of that year Joseph I engaged Silvio Stampiglia (1664–1725) as an additional court poet. A rivalry between the two librettists may have been responsible for Bernardoni's decisions to give up his prestigious appointment and to retire to Bologna with an imperial pension in 1710. Following a journey to Rome in 1711, Bernardoni was married in Bologna, where he died three years later. Besides some thirty-eight librettos for large sacred and secular dramatic works performed at Vienna during his tenure (1701–10), Bernardoni wrote a number of smaller poems that appeared in two separate volumes. The first was printed at Bologna in 1694; the second, dedicated to Joseph I, was published at Vienna in 1705. Bernardoni has been called a transitional figure whose poetry stood midway between the sonorous, pretentious style of writers such as Vincenzo da Filicaia (1642–1707) and Alessandro Guidi (1650–1712) and the simpler, more dignified style of the reformers, notably Metastasio.[57] His *Rime varie* of 1705 includes many cantata texts. According to one recent writer, the verse of this collection is "of scanty poetic worth, except for some *canzonettas* that seem to anticipate in their melodic qualities and ease of rhythm the perfect 'ariette' of the Metastasian melodrama."[58] Among the cantata texts in this volume are the four set to music by Ariosti and Badia. In view of Bernardoni's interest in the cantata and his nine-year association with the Viennese court, it seems plausible that he may have been the author of some of the anonymous cantata texts from the period.

TABLE 6.1. MINOR POETS OF DRAMATIC WORKS PERFORMED IN AUSTRIA, CA. 1697–1711

POET	NO. OF LIBRETTOS	COMPOSER
G. B. Ancioni	3	Badia (1709)
		Fux (2 works, 1710)
Lodovico Addimari	1	Pasticcio by court musicians (1702)
Francesco Ballerini	1	Conti (1711)
R. N. Batticassa	1	Badia (1698)
G. B. Lampugnani	1	R. Borrini? (1697)
Count Ottavio Malvezzi	1	Badia (1702)
G. F. Roberti	2	Badia (1699 and 1700)
Riccardo Rodiano	1	G. Bononcini (1701)
Rocco Maria Rossi	1	Anonymous (1710)
Giuseppe Spedazzi	3	Badia (1697, 1700, and 1706)
Nunzio Stampiglia	4	Badia (1708, 1709, and 1710)
		A. M. Bononcini (1711)

In all, only twenty-one cantata texts from 1700 to 1712 have attributions. While court appointees such as Cupeda and Bernardoni may have been responsible for some of the anonymous texts, cantata composers undoubtedly drew upon a large reservoir of verse by contemporary poets. After all, composers like Giovanni Bononcini and Attilio Ariosti traveled widely throughout their careers and collaborated with many librettists. The possibility that Ariosti himself wrote some of his own texts should not be overlooked. He had provided the libretto for Bononcini's *Polifemo,* performed at Sophie Charlotte's Berlin court in the summer of 1702. The poetry of Ariosti's cantatas does in fact contain some of the most elaborate metaphors and imaginative conceits found in the Viennese cantata texts. The more charming and vivid imagery found in the texts of Ariosti's cantatas may be a sign that some of the poems are indeed by him or simply a reflection that he, as a known poet, selected his texts with greater care.

It is probable of course that some of the anonymous poets never resided in Vienna. A perusal of lists of dramatic works compiled by Weilen, Hadamowsky, Ferrari, Lindgren, Bauer, Köchel, and the present writer reveals that court poets active in Vienna during the period 1700–1712—particularly Cupeda, Berardoni, and Stampiglia—certainly dominated the supply of librettos for imperial entertainments. Nevertheless, names of many other poets are cited. Among these are such well-known figures as Apostolo Zeno (1668–1750), Pietro Pariati (1665–1733), Francesco de Lemene (1634–1704), and Cardinal Pietro Ottoboni (1667–1740). Zeno and Pariati were of course court librettists during the reign of Charles VI. Lemene and Ottoboni were active as cantata librettists, but neither poet is known to have visited Vienna.

The list of other poets whose large dramatic texts were occasionally set to music by Viennese composers is fairly extensive, and it has not yet been possible to isolate precisely which ones resided in Austria. Table 6.1 lists the names of some of these minor poets, the number of librettos for dramatic works from ca. 1697 to 1711 by each poet, and the names of composers who set these texts.[59]

Among the poets listed above, Nunzio Stampiglia probably resided in Vienna during the period 1708–11. If he was accepted at Vienna, it was perhaps due to the favor extended to his more famous brother, Silvio, who in turn had probably received his appointment as court poet in 1706 because of the influence of Giovanni Bononcini. Silvio was Giovanni's frequent collaborator in Rome during the 1690s, and he provided the majority of librettos for Bononcini's large dramatic works during the reign of Joseph. He may also have written texts for the Viennese cantatas of Bononcini and other composers. The poetry of Francesco Conti's cantata *Gira per queste selve* (A-Wn, 17593, no. 6) is attributed to "Stampiglia." The date of the cantata is unknown. Silvio Stampiglia remained an imperial poet until his death, although he apparently requested release from his Viennese responsibilities in 1714.[60]

More and more during the late seventeenth century, the structure of cantata texts reflected the influence of the larger dramatic genres, that is, opera and oratorio.[61] David Burrows has indicated that this tendency can be found already in the cantatas of the Cesti generation: "The prestige of the larger form [opera] led the cantata to abandon its earlier musical and poetic forms and to assume an essentially dramatic shape."[62] In practice this meant that cantata texts are divided into sections of narrative and lyric content that are paralleled musically by passages of recitative and aria. In the cantatas of late seventeenth-century Vienna, a regular alternation of recitative and aria elements is not yet established. By the first decade of the eighteenth century, however, passages of recitative and aria alternate in frequently rigid patterns.

As in the earlier period, a text of the early eighteenth century is likely to portray a single, often unresolved situation with little or no plot development. Within this framework, the situation unfolds in a single setting, often unspecified. The verse may be delivered impersonally by a narrator or personally by one, frequently unnamed character. Ensemble cantatas, including the Badia chamber duets, are apt to have texts with named characters, usually shepherds and shepherdesses such as Filli and Clori, Tirsi and Aminta, or Elisa and Aquilio. In the ensemble *accademie* of Ziani, the tone is impersonal; the conflict lies not between characters in an unfolding drama but between unnamed individuals who debate general questions of life and love.

The various aspects of love are by far the most popular subjects for cantata texts in the period 1700–1711. Especially common are librettos dealing with a lover who suffers because of jealousy, inconstancy, or separation from his beloved. Thus, for example, one lover complains of his beloved's attempts to make him jealous: "Cruel Nice, why do you wish to distill in my breast the barbarous poison of jealousy? This soul and this heart sigh only for thee, but your new ardor redoubles my pain and my grief."[63] Another describes the anguish caused by a separation: "Who has ever experienced more barbarous suffering than that which a heart suffers because of separation? When one can experience it and not die, it is the miracle of Love and not of steadfastness."[64]

Many texts depict an almost helpless lover who is tyrannically oppressed by his beloved or by the god Amor (Cupid). Hence, in response to his cruel, unfaithful beloved, a lover vows to remain steadfast to the end: "My poor heart will die faithful and constant to your countenance; and then my miserable heart will go about saying that only for your eyes it was a martyr of love."[65]

The conflict between a lover's desire to remain obedient and his need to be freed from tyrannical Love becomes central in text after text. In one cantata text, a defiant character declares his determination to defeat the force of Love: "Hear me, oh cruel Love: you will take my life but not my liberty. My heart shall combat your arrogant right hand as long as it shall have breath."[66] Another lover declares the greater advantage of accepting servitude: "Obeying the will of the well-beloved is a comfort. That sole moment when one leaves off serving seems a century of pain."[67] Still another lover expresses the ambivalent feelings of pleasure and pain brought about by release from his beloved: "The pleasure of liberty is certainly sweet to a bound heart. But the bound heart no longer has such satisfaction."[68]

The subjects of the occasional cantatas were to some extent governed by the days or events that they honored. Some of the occasion texts are allegories that pay flattering tribute to members of the imperial family by comparing them with historical and mythological heroes and heroines. Of special interest are the texts of the two anonymous cantatas, one written after a battle victory at Landau and the other for the coronation of Joseph I. In both librettos the mood progresses from grief and anguish to joy and celebration. In *Cetre amiche,* an unidentified narrator—evidently a spokesman for the patriotic spirit of Austria—mourns the loss of liberty and the wounds inflicted by foreign tyrants, that is, the French. The narrator's laments give way to jubilation as he recounts the glory of the Austrian victory, inspired by Joseph, "the great son of Augustus [Leopold]." The librettist of *Alli giusti miei lamenti* uses an allegorical framework to express patriotic feelings about the accession of Joseph I. The three characters named in the libretto are Austria, the Protective Deity of Austria, and the Protective Deity of the Roman Empire. At the beginning of the text, Austria laments Leopold's death and the anguish caused by war. Austria's Protective Deity consoles Austria by offering a "successor Hercules," who is "Joseph the great, the wise, the pious, born to bear not only the burden of Austria, but also the world." Finally, the Protective Deity of the Roman Empire declares that Joseph will succeed in uniting an empire threatened internally by rebellions and externally by assaults of foreign powers.

The texts of the two extant academic cantatas by Ziani follow the method established in the texts of the *accademie* by Draghi and Pederzuoli. Thus, in Ziani's

Cieco fanciul, Amore and Speranza debate whether it is possible to find a love without hope, while in *Ahimè ch'io son piagato* (A-Wn, 17650), two lovers discuss which is more charming, a beautiful woman who weeps or a beautiful woman who sings.

Like the broad outlines of early eighteenth-century cantata texts, the internal structures show a greater degree of regularity than the verse forms found in texts of the previous generation. Least structured are the recitative texts, which are not organized into strophes. Nevertheless, even these narrative portions are almost entirely written in lines of seven and eleven syllables, and they include considerably more rhyming than the recitatives of the previous generation.[69] Perhaps significantly, the earliest cantatas from this period—the four by Badia from 1699—contain the fewest rhymes in recitatives. Elsewhere rhyming is not always used consistently throughout a recitative; nor does it occur in a very organized or predictable fashion, except at the end of a recitative, where there is almost invariably a rhymed couplet. This concluding couplet sometimes corresponds to a brief musical passage of arioso set in a definite tempo and meter. Occasionally the final line of a recitative rhymes with one of the lines that precedes the penultimate verse. Most of the recitative texts are not long, except for the extensive narrative sections of the anonymous cantatas that paid tribute to the battle victory at Landau and the coronation of Joseph I.

In general, most of the aria texts exemplify the characteristics of the *canzonetta,* a poetic form that became popular in the early seventeenth century and reached its zenith in the librettos of the Arcadian poet Paolo Rolli (1687–1765) and the reformers Apostolo Zeno (1668–1750) and Pietro Metastasio (1698–1782).[70] In the early eighteenth century, a *canzonetta* text usually consisted of a single strophe, varying in length from four to eleven lines. Individual verses contained between three and ten syllables. These lines were distributed in a fixed pattern. Within the broad limits of the *canzonetta* style, poets were able to achieve an enormous variety of metrical patterns.[71]

A perusal of aria texts also reveals a great deal of variety in the manner in which lines are distributed between the A and B sections of the da capo structure. Thus, for example, in a strophe of six lines, the verses might be divided 3 + 3, 4 + 2, or 2 + 4. In stanzas of greater length, lines are often divided into more irregular groupings. The A section of the first aria of Badia's *Begl'occhi neri,* for instance, contains only four lines, while the B section consists of seven lines. In the second aria of Badia's *Il sole,* the A section has only two lines, while the B section is made up of five verses. A great variety of rhyme schemes can also be seen in the aria texts of this period. Perhaps the most complex and irregular internal structures are found in the librettos of the Ziani *accademie* written by Pietro Antonio Bernardoni. The adventurous nature of these poems may reflect a heightened degree of virtuosity reserved for academic occasions.

Although some streamlining of poetic structure and simplification of rhetoric is evident in cantata texts of the early eighteenth century, especially in the nonacademic poetry of the Arcadian Bernardoni, the influence of the Marinists is still clearly perceptible. Many texts, notably the librettos for the battle victory and coronation cantatas, abound with hyperbolic language and outrageous metaphors. In the love texts, the librettists seem unusually preoccupied with the power of Amor, the god of Love, and with his arrows, darts, bow, torch, flames, and battlefield. Also described in great detail are the features of the beloved, especially the eyes and hair. For the eyes the librettists called upon a large variety of specific words such as *occhi, stelle, pupille, pupillette, lumi,* and *luci.* One lover's fascination with his beloved's tresses seems to foreshadow passages from Alexander Pope's *Rape of the Lock* (1714): "What insufferable torment it is to conceal the flame of Love and not be able to say, 'For you I die,' and to waste away little by little among the chains of a head of golden hair."[72]

While the texts of early eighteenth-century cantatas definitely cannot be defended as examples of great literature, their worth can be fully appreciated only in relationship to the music. And the very limitations of the cantata subjects, characters, verse forms, and rhetoric gave the composers a familiar framework that could be freely elaborated and enriched by their music. In short, "the cantata text was written to satisfy narrative and musical, not poetic, requirements."[73] To the conventions of the poetry the composer added his vocabulary of baroque rhetorical devices. Finally, to text and music the singer brought bel canto and improvisational art, which undoubtedly accounted for much of the cantata's popularity and effectiveness.

7

The Composers

In the waning years of the seventeenth century and the opening years of the eighteenth century, the Habsburg chapel at Vienna underwent a complete transformation. The period can be likened to the 1660s, a decade of rich innovation following years of status quo. In their turn, the 1660s were followed by the quarter-century dominated by Draghi. The remarkable influx of new musical talent at the end of the seventeenth century once again made Vienna one of Europe's most important centers of dramatic music. This talent included not only leading composers of the period but also virtuoso singers and instrumentalists.

The group of composers who served the aging Leopold and his heir received their training in northern Italian centers. From Bologna came Giovanni and Antonio Maria Bononcini, Pier Francesco Tosi, and Attilio Ariosti. Ariosti never became an official member of the chapel, but he prepared many dramatic works for court entertainments. Bologna also provided important artists such as the poet Pietro Antonio Bernardoni and the stage designer Antonio Beduzzi. From Verona the Habsburgs imported Carlo Agostino Badia, from Venice Marc'Antonio Ziani, and from Florence the theorbist Francesco Bartolomeo Conti. The importance of Rome must be considered too, for it was there that the Bononcini brothers first won recognition as opera composers. And Giovanni's influence at Vienna probably led to the appointment of the Roman librettist Silvio Stampiglia as court poet. Among the many important new composers who resided in Vienna during the period 1700–1711, at least five—Badia, the Bononcini brothers, Ziani, and Ariosti—made significant contributions to the cantata repertoire.

CARLO AGOSTINO BADIA

The first of the new wave of northern Italians to receive an appointment at Vienna was Carlo Agostino Badia (1672–1738), probably a native of Verona.[1] His earliest known work is the oratorio *La sete di Cristo in croce,* a *sepolcro* written for Innsbruck in 1691. At the beginning of 1692 he may have resided at Rome, where his two earliest secular dramatic works were produced.[2] One of the two works, *Amor che vince lo sdegno, ovvero Olimpia placata,* has a text by Amalteo Aureli, who had been active as a librettist at Innsbruck and Vienna in the 1660s. However, by the spring of 1692 Badia was definitely employed as court composer at Innsbruck. The youthful Badia won the enthusiastic patronage of Eleonora Maria (1653–97), widow of both King Michael Wisniowiecki of Poland and Duke Charles of Lorraine and stepsister of Emperor Leopold I. In addition to the 1691 oratorio, Badia composed for Innsbruck two operas in 1692, as well as two *sepolcri* for Holy Week in 1693.[3]

Eleonora Maria took up residence in Vienna toward the end of 1693. With her support and a recommendation from the king of Poland, Badia was appointed *Musik-Compositeur* at the imperial court on 1 July 1694.[4] He received an initial monthly salary of sixty florins, retroactive to 1 July 1693.[5] Badia thus became the first in a succession of distinguished musicians (including Fux, Giovanni Bononcini, Pier Francesco Tosi, Francesco Conti, and Giuseppe Porsile) who held the title of court composer at Vienna in the late baroque era.

After initial successes, Badia went to Rome, probably in 1695, to complete his musical studies, but because of a lack of funds, he returned to Vienna before the end of that year.[6] Until 1697 he seems to have composed only oratorios for Vienna. His first opera for the Habsburg court, *Bacco, vincitor dell'India,* was performed during Carnival season in 1697 and dedicated to Eleonora Maria. Increases in Badia's salary underscore his continued favor with the court. His initial monthly stipend of sixty florins was enlarged by thirty florins in 1699 and by an additional thirty in 1702, bringing his income to a level as high as any court musician except for the Kapellmeister Pancotti and the highly acclaimed composer Giovanni Bononcini. He appears to have become a favorite of the aging Leopold and during the early part of his career at Vienna was praised by Draghi as "ein gutter virtuoso."[7] Pancotti designated him as a man of "gar guttn Tallento vnd Vngemeiner prontezza."[8]

The date of Badia's marriage to the soprano who probably sang many of his cantatas, the Florentine prima donna Anna Maria Elisabetta "Lisi" Nonetti (ca. 1680–1726), is unknown. The soprano received an appointment at Vienna on 1 July 1700. In 1706 Badia probably accompanied her to Venice, where she appeared in two operas by Carlo Francesco Pollarolo at the Teatro S. Giovanni Crisostomo.[9] Badia's own operas and oratorios were performed in northern Italy, and his works were also presented in other parts of Europe. For example, the grand cantata *La Pace, e Marte supplicanti avanti al Trono della Gloria,* first performed at Vienna on 19 March 1701, was revived on 6 June 1709 during a visit to Dresden by the king of Denmark.[10] For the Danish king's entertainment, Badia was also commissioned to write the opera *Gli amori di Circe con Ulisse;* the performance took place on 20 June 1709. It seems unlikely that Badia himself traveled to Dresden for the performance, which was directed by Baron Francesco Ballerini, one of the most famous singers at the imperial court.

During approximately seventeen years of service at the courts of Leopold and Joseph (1694–1711), Badia enjoyed a period of remarkable creativity, producing at least thirty-four oratorios and twenty large secular dramatic works.[11] He also composed a substantial number of chamber cantatas and duets. Among the many cantata composers active at Vienna from 1690 to 1740, Badia appears to have been the only one to have had a collection engraved while in the service of the emperor. A volume of twelve cantatas dedicated to Leopold, *Tributi armonici*, was published by Weigl at Nuremberg probably between 1699 and 1704. Badia's productivity declined gradually during the reign of Joseph, who clearly favored the Bononcini brothers and Marc'Antonio Ziani. Nevertheless, Joseph frequently supplemented Badia's income with secret sums of money that apparently rescued the composer from persistent debts.[12]

Badia was not the most important composer of his generation at Vienna, but he holds the distinction of being the first to introduce the stylistic innovations of the late baroque era to the Habsburg court. As Egon Wellesz has demonstrated, Badia's style underwent a gradual maturing process.[13] The numerous early works are characterized by smooth melodic writing, lyric grace, and a lack of contrapuntal complexity. Badia can be credited with increasing the importance of idiomatic string writing at Vienna. The ritornellos and sinfonias of his operas, oratorios, and cantatas are longer than those of his predecessors, and he also calls for more varied vocal and instrumental combinations, as well as more frequent solo obbligatos. He appears to have been the first composer employed at Vienna to use concerto grosso contrasts. In the trio "Quanto e di grande" from *Le gare dei beni* (21 February 1700), for example, Badia calls for two opposing groups. He may have been influenced by Giuseppe Torelli, who visited Vienna from December 1699 until March 1700.[14]

Badia became a central figure in the development of the cantata at Vienna during the final years of Leopold's reign and the brief emperorship of Joseph. Between approximately 1699 and 1712 he composed approximately fifty-three chamber cantatas and two grand cantatas. Thus, as the new generation of talented Italian composers entered the service of the elderly emperor and his increasingly influential heir, Badia led the way in establishing the cantata as a popular, previously neglected genre.

GIOVANNI BONONCINI

Giovanni Bononcini (1670–1747) was one of the most popular and widely performed Italian composers of the early eighteenth century.[15] He was the son of the important composer of instrumental music and theorist Giovanni Maria Bononcini (1642–78).[16] G. M. Bononcini turned to vocal genres only late in his career, producing two sets of cantatas (opp. 10 and 13, Bologna, 1677–78), a volume of madrigals (op. 11, Bologna, 1678), and a *dramma da camera* entitled *I primi voli dell'aquila austriaca del soglio imperiale alla Gloria* (Modena, June 1677; only the libretto is extant). Perhaps the first composer to use the term *cantata per camera,* he dedicated the chamber opera and madrigals, as well as his *Musico prattico* (op. 8, Bologna, 1673), to Leopold I, which no doubt helped to prepare the way for the eventual engagement of both sons (by his first marriage) at the Habsburg court.

Giovanni was born on 18 July 1670 at Modena, one of several centers of instrumental music in late seventeenth-century Italy. After his father's death (18 November 1678), he moved to Bologna, where he studied with Giovanni Paolo Colonna. At the age of fifteen, the precocious composer published three sets of instrumental music (opp. 1–3, Bologna, 1685) and became a member of the prestigious Accademia Filarmonica. From January 1687 through May 1688 Bononcini held an appointment as a singer and instrumentalist at San Petronio. In the second half of 1687, he succeeded Giuseppe Felice Tosi as *maestro di cappella* at San Giovanni in Monte. Many lexicon articles indicate erroneously that it was Giovanni Maria who served at San Petronio in Bologna and at San Giovanni in Monte; other articles also incorrectly report that Giovanni Maria was a pupil of Colonna.[17] In the following years, Giovanni gave up this appointment, and by 1690 he was again in Modena, now for the performance of a Lenten oratorio commissioned by Duke Francesco II. Afterward he returned to Bologna, where he joined the orchestra of Cardinal Benedetto Pamphili, the papal legate at Bologna from 1690 to 1693.[18] At Bologna Giovanni also published ten vocal *duetti da camera* (op. 8, 1691, reissued in 1701), which he dedicated to Emperor Leopold. One of the manuscript copies of the *duetti,* A-Wn, 17579, is an oblong *Prachtband* in heavy leather binding that appears to be a dedicatory copy prepared for Leopold. The foliation is in modern pencil; on the first folio there is an inscription not in the main scribe's hand: "Per Sua M.^tà Ces.^a." The writing may be Bononcini's. In the exquisitely lettered dedication, he recalled his father and the works by Giovanni Maria dedicated to Leopold.[19]

Bononcini's career as an internationally acclaimed opera composer began in 1692 at Rome, where he was employed by Filippo and Lorenza Colonna and by Luigi della Cerda, the brother of Lorenza. During this time, Bononcini and the librettist Silvio Stampiglia began an artistic association that was to last, with interruptions, for thirty years. The two men collaborated on at least twelve dramatic works of varying length during Bononcini's first stay in Rome (1692–96). By far the most successful of these was the last, the celebrated *Il trionfo di Camilla,* first presented at the Neapolitan Teatro di San Bartolomeo on 27 December 1696, shortly after Luigi della Cerda had become viceroy at Naples. Bononcini also established himself as a leading composer of cantatas during this time.[20]

Following the death of Lorenza Colonna (20 August 1697), the newly famous Bononcini began to search for another appointment with the hope of finding one in a city more friendly to opera than Rome, where the Tor di Nona theater was demolished by papal decree in 1697. He received a recommendation to the Elector

Palatine Johann Wilhelm (d. 1716) from Cardinal Francesco Maria Medici, uncle of Anna Maria Luisa Medici, who had married Johann Wilhelm in 1691.[21] Actually, Bononcini probably never entered the service of Johann Wilhelm, for he had already received an appointment at the more prestigious court of Emperor Leopold I by the end of 1697.[22]

The exact date of Bononcini's arrival in Vienna is unknown, but it was probably not before the middle of 1698. In a claim for wages written sometime after he returned to Vienna near the end of his life, he cited 1 January 1698 as the initial date of his appointment; payments to artists beginning their service in Vienna were frequently made retroactively.[23] As for an official title, Bononcini's position changed several times during the first few years of his Viennese employment. At first, in three librettos of 1699, he designated himself simply as a member of the Bolognese Accademia Filarmonica. In the libretto for the single work of 1700, he is referred to as a "Virtuoso di S.M.C." Then on 7 January 1700 he became the third musician—after Badia and Fux—to be given the special title of court composer. His annual salary of 1,440 florins, equal to that of Badia or Fux, was paid retroactively to 1 July 1699. The new title, "Compositore di Musica in servizio di S.M.C.," began to appear in librettos of 1701.[24]

Almost from the outset of his service, Bononcini maintained a special relationship with Joseph I and his wife, Amalia Wilhelmina, the king and queen of the Romans; through the year 1705, nearly all of Bononcini's extant secular dramatic works bearing dedications were written for celebrations in honor of Joseph or Amalia. It was in recognition of this relationship that Joseph apparently made a pledge of two thousand florins, an amount to be added to three thousand florins from the court and private treasuries already promised by Leopold.[25] However, the Austrian treasuries were nearly depleted in the early years of the eighteenth century because of the extreme pressures from the War of the Spanish Succession, and the court musicians were left in dire circumstances.[26] Hence, the two thousand florins promised by Joseph were not paid by any treasury during the years 1698–1707.

The precise amounts that Bononcini, Fux, and other musicians received are difficult to document, since any sum above the salaries paid by the court treasury were in the nature of special bonuses. Until the death of Leopold (5 May 1705), Bononcini composed at least seven short secular dramatic works, three full-length operas, and one oratorio.[27] Because of the costly Italian campaign in the War of the Spanish Succession (beginning in the summer of 1701), both the funds and the appetite for dramatic entertainments at Vienna declined sharply. After the production of his *Gli affetti più grandi* (30 August 1701), Bononcini appears to have led a circle of musicians to Berlin, arriving sometime before 27 May 1702.[28] He was the dominant figure in a group of artists that included the singers Regina Schoonjans, Paulina Fridlin, and Antonio Tosi; the painter Anthoni Schoonjans (husband of Regina); the composers Attilio Ariosti and Antonio Maria Bononcini; and the instrumen-

FIG. 7.1. Portrait of Giovanni Bononcini by Antoni Schoonjans in Sophie Charlotte's writing room at Charlottenburg, Berlin. Courtesy of Stiftung Preussische Schlösser und Gärten Berlin-Brandenburg, photographer unknown.

FIG. 7.2. Portrait of Attilio Ariosti by Antoni Schoonjans in Sophie Charlotte's writing room at Charlottenburg, Berlin. Courtesy of Stiftung Preussische Schlösser und Gärten Berlin-Brandenburg, photographer unknown.

talists Francesco Conti and Giuseppe Maria Malagodi.[29] At Berlin Bononcini soon found favor with Queen Sophie Charlotte. Bononcini and Ariosti also participated as instrumentalists in performances, and Sophie Charlotte reported in a letter to Agostino Steffani that they sang his duets admirably.[30] The queen honored them by commissioning oil portraits of the two musicians (figures 7.1 and 7.2), probably by Anthoni Schoonjans.[31]

Bononcini and other musicians appear to have returned to Vienna by March 1703. During the period 1702–1704, Bononcini composed three works pertaining to the heroism of Joseph in the War of the Spanish Succession (see chapters 6 and 8). Following the death of Leopold, an edict was issued prohibiting all forms of entertainment for one year.[32] Little is known of Bononcini's activities during this period.

During the reign of Joseph I, Bononcini strengthened his position as the most favored court composer. At least ten dramatic compositions from the years 1705–11 are known.[33] Perhaps the clearest evidence of Bononcini's special relationship with Joseph is the fact that he composed only works for celebrations that glorified either the emperor or the empress, excluding entertainments for Carnival season. Bononcini collaborated almost exclusively with his friend the librettist Silvio Stampiglia, who had been summoned to Vienna sometime in late 1706. In all, during his first Viennese tenure (he was to return late in life), Bononcini composed at least twenty-one secular dramatic works, one oratorio, and a handful of cantatas. Like almost all music by Habsburg composers of the period, Bononcini's did not reach print. Thus, he did not continue to bring out sets of vocal and instrumental chamber music like the ones that had been published in Italy in the 1680s and 1690s. As owners of sources of all music performed at court, the Habsburgs preserved them in neatly copied archival manuscripts but evidently felt little need to make them more widely available in published versions.[34]

Certainly of Bononcini's compositions the opera *Camilla* must have been his most popular during his lifetime. Yet Bononcini composed many cantatas that were among the most widely admired examples of that genre in the entire eighteenth century. By 1702 Giovanni Mario de' Crescimbeni had named Bononcini, Carlo Cesarini, and Filippo Amadei as three "modern" cantata composers who were then active in Rome or had recently worked there.[35] In France he had long been the eye of a storm between partisans of French and Italian taste. The storm in France had begun in 1702, when François Raguenet published his *Paralele des Italiens et des François, en ce qui regarde la musique et les opera;* he had recently visited Italy and in the *Paralèle* meant to prove the general superiority of Italian music to French. In 1705 Raguenet rebutted attacks on his preference for Italian music with his *Défense du paralèle,* and for special praise he singled out Bononcini, claiming that by 1705 more than two hundred cantatas by Bononcini were known in Paris and that Bononcini's style had become "un model pour le gracieux."[36] His cantatas circulated in France not only in manuscript copies but also in print; a variety of arias and cantatas had been published in France by Ballard between 1704 and 1705.[37] In Italy, too, Bononcini's cantatas served as models: in his *L'armonico pratico al cimbalo* (Venice, 1708), Francesco Gasparini extolled Bononcini's inventiveness at composing ornamental basses: "Many such motifs, of various kinds, may be observed in the cantatas of many excellent composers—but especially in those cantatas by Giovanni Bononcini, most worthy Virtuoso of His Imperial Majesty. In these cantatas you will discern no little *bizzaria,* beauty, harmony, artful study, and fanciful invention, because of which they justly receive the applause of the whole world in admiration of his most delightful talent."[38]

Charles Burney's contention that Bononcini "was perhaps the most voluminous composer of cantatas, next to Alessandro Scarlatti, which Italy can boast" may indeed be valid.[39] A recent inventory of cantatas by Benedetto Marcello reveals that, based on extant sources, at least one other composer contends for the position as second most prolific cantata composer.[40] Bononcini was unquestionably among a handful of the most prolific composers of a genre that continued to enjoy enormous popularity throughout the first half of the eighteenth century. Of the more than three hundred cantatas and chamber duets known to me, a total of twenty-nine (seventeen solo cantatas and twelve duets) were published during Bononcini's lifetime; in addition, individual arias from selected cantatas were printed at Paris and London. The manuscripts of Bononcini's cantatas are widely disseminated today: more than two hundred manuscripts in approximately fifty European and American libraries preserve copies of his cantatas.[41] The large number of late seventeenth- and early eighteenth-century concordances give ample testimony to the widespread popularity and influence of Bononcini's cantata style.[42]

Only five cantatas can be identified as works that were definitely composed in Vienna during Bononcini's first residency there. These survive in two of the core Viennese cantata sources (see chapter 8). The core sources may not account for Bononcini's true significance as a cantata composer at Vienna, for it is highly possible that in 1698 he brought with him to his new home many favorite cantatas composed in Italy and that these works received performances at the Habsburg court. Some of the cantatas in a group of peripheral sources may eventually prove to be of Viennese origins, but their inclusion would not greatly alter the impression that Bononcini, one of the leading cantata masters of the entire baroque era, gave scant attention to the genre during his first fourteen years in Vienna. The evidence of extant sources leads to the conclusion that Bononcini composed almost all his cantatas before and after this period (1698–1712).

It seems paradoxical that so prolific and influential a cantata composer as Giovanni Bononcini should have written so few cantatas for Vienna precisely during years in which the court was giving fresh attention to the genre. His neglect was perhaps due to the steady stream of commissions for large dramatic works that paid homage to members of the ruling family, notably Joseph and Amalia.[43]

MARC'ANTONIO ZIANI

M. A. Ziani (ca. 1653–1715) was one of the most acclaimed and influential composers employed at Vienna in the early eighteenth century.[44] Born at Venice, he was a member of a large Ziani family that boasted several other musicians, including not only Marc'Antonio's renowned uncle Pietro Andrea but also the violinist Pietro Ziani. Theophil Antonicek has suggested that this Pietro Ziani may be the father of Marc'Antonio.[45]

Details that would throw light on the relationship of Pietro Andrea and Marc'-Antonio have not yet been uncovered. Marc'Antonio, who had begun his career as a singer at the Cathedral of Saint Mark's, tried unsuccessfully to succeed his uncle there in 1677. At the time of Pietro Andrea's death at Naples in 1684, both the pupil Cristoforo Caresana and an unnamed nephew were present; Antonicek has conjectured that this nephew might have been Marc'Antonio, but Saskia Maria Woyke maintains that Marc'Antonio's presence there has not been documented and that the unnamed nephew was probably Giovanni Battista Ziani.[46] On 28 September 1686 Marc'Antonio received the appointment as *maestro di cappella* of the Santa Barbara chapel of Duke Carlo IV Gonzaga at Mantua.[47] The duration of his tenure there remains unclear, but it seems possible that he continued to serve at Mantua until 1700, for he collaborated frequently with the Mantuan court poet, Francesco Silvani, throughout this period.

Although he failed to win a coveted appointment at Venice, Ziani maintained strong ties with the city's artistic circles. In 1687 he became one of the early members of the Sovvegno de' Signori Musici sotto l'invocazione di S. Cecilia Vergine, & Martire nella Chiesa di S. Martino, founded by Don G. D. Partenio.[48] His long career as a Venetian opera composer began in 1679. After initial successes, Ziani composed a steady stream of operas for Venice, producing an especially large number of dramatic works in the 1690s.[49]

When Leopold selected Antonio Pancotti to replace Draghi as Kapellmeister on 16 January 1700, Ziani was called to Vienna to succeed Pancotti as assistant Kapellmeister, receiving the official appointment on 1 April 1700.[50] Having already achieved wide recognition as a composer of dramatic music, Ziani had also established important ties with the imperial court in 1698 by dedicating the oratorio *Il giudizio di Salomone* to Leopold. His entrance into Viennese musical life in early 1700 was another milestone in the revitalization of the Habsburg chapel. His appointment followed Badia's by six years and Giovanni Bononcini's by only two years. Within a short time, Francesco Conti, Antonio Maria Bononcini, and Attilio Ariosti joined the circle of composers who established the late baroque style at Vienna and shaped the development of music there during the reign of Joseph I.[51]

During the years 1702–1703, the imperial court was unable to commission many new works because of the financial burdens of the War of the Spanish Succession. Unlike the Bononcini brothers, Conti, and other Viennese artists, Ziani appears to have remained in Vienna, probably because he held the second-ranking administrative post. Ziani's importance to the Habsburgs is further reflected by the fact that he was the only composer to match each of the Bononcini brothers in the number of commissions for large dramatic works performed during the reign of Joseph.[52] The *accademie* of 1706–1707 are evidence that he belonged to the select group of artists invited by the emperor to join the Viennese academy.

Ziani was a prolific composer of operas, oratorios, and sacred music. His excellence in writing counterpoint closely matched the style preferred by the Habsburgs, and he deftly exploited the vast vocal and instrumental resources found in Vienna. He does not appear to have devoted much attention to the cantata. Only a handful of chamber cantatas and one grand cantata are extant; of these, at least five were composed for Vienna. Perhaps Ziani wrote so few cantatas for the imperial court because of the demands of his administrative duties, first as assistant Kapellmeister and then, beginning in 1712, as Kapellmeister, and also because of the constant pressure of supplying large new works for church and theater.

ATTILIO ARIOSTI

One of the more shadowy figures of baroque music history, Attilio Ariosti (1666–1729) nevertheless played a significant role in the musical life of major courts in Italy, Prussia, Austria, and England.[53] Born at Bologna on 5 November 1666, he stemmed from an old and distinguished family. He may have studied along with the Bononcini brothers in the *scuola* of the Bolognese *maestro* G. P. Colonna; in any event, he was to become an early advocate of the viola d'amore and the instrument's leading virtuoso in the first half of the eighteenth century. Like Antonio Cesti, he combined ecclesiastical duties with professional musical activities, and his adventures as a composer of secular music resulted in conflicts with the church reminiscent of the ones that Cesti had experienced a half-century earlier.

During the weeks from 20 June to 25 July 1688, Ariosti was admitted to the Servite order at Bologna.[54] In 1692 he received major orders, assuming the name Fra Ottavio, and from as early as 1693 he served as organist at the church of Santa Maria dei Servi.[55] His earliest known compositions date from 1693 to 1695.[56] By the spring of 1696 Ariosti had obtained release from his order and was residing at Mantua; his first efforts as a composer of secular dramatic music probably date from this time.[57] At this time, both Ziani and Caldara were also active at the Mantuan court of Duke Carlo IV Gonzaga.

A settlement between Carlo IV and Sophie Charlotte, electress of Brandenburg and wife of the future king of Prussia, abruptly ended Ariosti's service at the Mantuan court. Drawn up without regard for Ariosti's personal wishes, the agreement was one of many made by various Italian noblemen with the Prussian monarch, who was keenly interested in developing a modern Italian chapel that could rival the music establishments of other European capitals. During the 1690s she was successful in bringing a number of important singers, instrumentalists, and composers to Berlin. For example, in 1696 two of Italy's most acclaimed performers, the singer Francesco Antonio Pistocchi and the violinist Giuseppe Torelli, both of whom sojourned in Vienna four years later, participated in court entertainments there.[58] Ariosti journeyed to Berlin via Vienna, where he became acquainted with the influential papal envoy Santa Croce, who attempted unsuccessfully to free the composer from his obligation to the Protestant northern German court. By September or October 1697, Ariosti had officially entered the service of the Brandenburgs.[59] Once he had settled at the Protestant Prussian court, Ariosti quickly became a favorite of Sophie Charlotte, an intelligent patroness of the arts and sciences.

In 1701 Frederick agreed to lend his support to the Habsburg cause in the War of the Spanish Succession in exchange for being elevated to the rank of king, a title that only the emperor could grant. In the late summer following his accession (18 January 1701), the circle of artists that included Giovanni Bononcini and Francesco Conti arrived from the imperial court. In the summer of 1702, Ariosti provided the libretto for Giovanni Bononcini's one-act opera *Polifemo*, but he failed on the whole to win a distinguished reputation as a poet.[60] As a composer in Berlin he contributed music for at least five secular dramatic entertainments, and it seems likely that he wrote cantatas for the frequent evenings of chamber music.[61] As a performer he sang and played the harpsichord.

Ariosti's religious vows ultimately prevented him from acquiring a permanent post at Berlin. Fearful of a Protestant hegemony in Germany, Sophie Charlotte herself attempted relentlessly to retain the Italian musician, but in the end the papal forces succeeded.[62] The queen demonstrated her great admiration for Ariosti by commissioning his portrait, which is now located in Sophie Charlotte's writing room at Charlottenburg.[63] Ariosti chose to return to Italy via Vienna. Perhaps with the aid of the influential Giovanni Bononcini, who had returned to Vienna already by March 1703, he was successful in gaining some recognition as a composer at the court of the aged Leopold. Ariosti probably arrived at Vienna in late October or early November 1703 and quickly received a commission for a small secular dramatic work (*La più gloriosa fatica d'Ercole*) that honored Leopold's name day (15 November). His first effort for Vienna was soon followed by two works composed in the early months of 1704, one for Carnival season and the other for Joseph's name day (19 March). Although he continued to compose sacred and secular dramatic works for Vienna, there is no evidence that Ariosti ever became a member of the imperial chapel.

Perhaps because of the uncertainty of his position at Vienna, Ariosti maintained ties with other cities, especially his native Bologna. Rumors about his personal life that had begun in Berlin persisted in Vienna.[64] On 15 April 1707 Ariosti wrote to the elector palatine, Johann Wilhelm, from Vienna that Joseph I was dispatching him to Italy as an agent-general, empowered to represent the emperor to "presso tutte le Corti e Principi d'Italia," and that he had also been granted a pension.[65] At least two secular dramatic works by Ariosti were performed at Vienna in the months of April and May 1707. The details of his travels after this time are not entirely clear; when he eventually arrived at Bologna on 28 May 1708, he was greeted with honor, absolved of alleged misconduct, and dressed in "veste da camera di broccato d'oro e gran berettone in testa" to meet visitors.[66] He evidently maintained ties with the imperial court because on 4 November 1708 his *dramma per musica* entitled *Amor tra nemici* was performed in honor of the name day of Joseph's brother, Charles III of Spain (the future Emperor Charles VI); Ariosti may even have returned to Vienna for preparations. It seems likely that Joseph satisfied his considerable appetite for fresh compositions from Italy in part by enlisting the help of Ariosti, who returned to Vienna from time to time. In a letter of 6 November 1709 to the Bolognese count Pirro Albergati, for example, Ariosti related that he had arrived at Vienna and had delivered the count's compositions to the emperor.[67] At least one secular dramatic work by Ariosti himself had been staged at Vienna during the summer of 1709.[68] He retained his post as agent-general until the end of Joseph's reign. According to the philosopher Gottfried Leibniz, after the emperor's death Ariosti received an appointment at the court of the infant duke of Anjou, the future King Louis XV of France, probably as a roving agent.[69]

Ariosti achieved fame in his own time both as a composer and as a performer. He not only excelled as a player of the viola d'amore but also contributed significantly to the instrument's early literature. His cantata *Pur alfin gentil viola* may be the first composition to include a written part for the viola d'amore. Vivaldi may well have written his eight concertos for viola d'amore specifically for Ariosti, the leading virtuoso of the age.[70] Frequently associated with Giovanni Bononcini because of his Bolognese background and his tendency to serve at courts and in cities where Bononcini was also active, Ariosti holds a somewhat more modest position in the history of the cantata than his renowned contemporary. Neither as prolific nor as popular as Bononcini, he nonetheless composed a substantial number of cantatas. Probably the best known are the six published at London in 1724; at least twenty-one copies of this collection, *Cantates and a Collection of Lessons,* survive in eighteen European and American libraries.[71] In addition, at least eighty-eight cantatas are preserved in manuscript copies in numerous European libraries.[72] The vast majority of these cantatas come down in libraries north of the Alps, reflecting Ariosti's significance in countries such as Austria, Prussia, and England. Twenty-three cantatas are found in two core manuscripts of Viennese origins.[73]

ANTONIO MARIA BONONCINI

Until rather late in his life—the year 1721—Antonio Maria Bononcini (1677–1726) closely patterned his career after that of his older and more celebrated brother Giovanni.[74] Little is known of his youth and early education, but by 1686 he and Giovanni were both members of G. P. Colonna's *scuola* at Bologna.[75] Like his brother, Antonio Maria played in the Bolognese orchestra of Cardinal Benedetto Pamphili, the Bolognese papal legate. That his principal instrument was the cello is suggested by the score of his earliest dated composition, a *laudate pueri* (19 February 1693) for soprano solo, continuo, and elaborate cello obbligato.[76] Antonio Maria appears to have moved to Rome sometime after his brother went there in 1692, but probably because of his youth, he did not receive the numerous commissions awarded to Giovanni. Both Bononcinis were active as cantata composers during the 1690s, but Antonio Maria seems to have written only one larger work, the brief, allegorical *La Fama eroica* (1698).[77] He may also have been the Bononcini who played in the orchestra for an oratorio performed in the Roman Chiesa Nuova in 1698.

After Giovanni received an appointment at Vienna, Antonio Maria again followed him, but the date of his arrival at the Habsburg capital and the extent of his activities there before 1705 remain unknown. He is not mentioned in archival studies that list musicians employed at Vienna through the reign of Leopold.[78] In his autobiography, Georg Philipp Telemann reported that he heard both Bononcinis play in the orchestra for Giovanni's *Polifemo,* performed at the Berlin court of Sophie Charlotte in 1702.[79] Thus, Antonio Maria must have accompanied his brother to Berlin, and "it is probable that he performed at Vienna as well as Berlin through the intervention of his brother GB."[80] Giovanni's great influence with Joseph undoubtedly was the key to the beginning of his brother's successful career as a composer of dramatic music. In all, Antonio Maria received commissions for at least eleven large works performed at Vienna from 1705 to 1711; the genres include one full-length opera, six shorter secular dramatic compositions (including the grand cantata *La Fortuna, il Valore e la Giustitia*), and four Lenten oratorios.[81] Of the secular dramatic works, three were dedicated to Charles, three paid homage to Joseph, and one honored Amalia Wilhelmina. Significantly, the performance of Antonio Maria's earliest known work for Vienna, the Lenten oratorio *La Maddalena* (1705), was dedicated to Charles, who had recently advanced his claim to the Spanish throne by conquering Barcelona, as indicated on the title page of the libretto: "La Maddalena. Oratorio, cantato nella Real Casa di Spagna per le Feste celebrate da S. Altezza il Marchese di Pescara, e del Vasto, Ambasciatore ordinario di Carlo Terzo, Re delle Spagne, in memoria de' glorioisi Riportati da Sua Maestà in Cattalogna, colla presa di Barcelona alli 14 di Ottobre passato."[82] Antonio Maria's frequent dedications to the Austrian heir to the Spanish throne, even from the outset of his activities as a composer at Vienna, support the suggestion made by Lindgren that he served, in effect, as Kapellmeister to Charles.[83] If so, Joseph may have created the post especially for Antonio Maria as a favor to Giovanni.

After Joseph's accession, Antonio Maria continued to be among the select group of composers most patronized by the court. Following Giovanni's *Endimione*, Antonio's *Arminio* was the second work presented during Joseph's reign. Moreover, only Giovanni and the Kapellmeister Marc'Antonio Ziani received a comparable number of commissions during Joseph's years as emperor. Antonio Maria must have received an appointment as court composer at some point during 1710, for the librettos for the second of two dramatic works dating from that year and for the single composition from 1711 specifically mention this title. In an 11 March 1720 statement of back pay due to musicians, Antonio Maria's yearly salary is listed as two thousand florins.[84] On at least two occasions, he also received sums of money from the private imperial treasury.[85]

In contrast to Giovanni, Antonio Maria was not a particularly prolific or influential cantata composer, although his works show great skill and attention to detail. At the time that he received his appointment from the emperor, he was still a young and little-known composer who had worked mainly in the shadow of his older brother. Still somewhat overshadowed by Giovanni during his Viennese tenure, he began to establish himself as an important composer of secular vocal music in his own right. Nevertheless, Antonio Maria never achieved the degree of international prestige enjoyed by Giovanni. Thus, for example, he published no collections of cantatas or duets. Of the approximately thirty-eight chamber cantatas, four chamber duets, and one grand cantata known to me, only about one-fifth come down in more than one copy, and only two cantatas survive in as many as three sources.[86] (Because of some conflicting attributions to Giovanni, the total should not be construed as fixed; it represents an estimate based upon current research.)[87] For Vienna, Antonio Maria composed at least thirteen chamber cantatas and one grand cantata; these works are preserved in four manuscripts at A-Wn.

COMPOSERS WHO MAY HAVE WRITTEN CANTATAS FOR VIENNA

Besides more than one hundred cantatas known to have been composed for Vienna by Badia, M. A. Ziani, Ariosti, and the Bononcini brothers, several other composers active in the imperial capital during Leopold's last years and Joseph's reign may have written cantatas. A gifted musician with a distinct preference for Italian style, Joseph himself definitely tried his hand at cantata composition, although no extant cantata can be ascribed to him with certainty. Joseph's activity as a cantata composer is confirmed by a letter of 19/30 July 1707 from Charles Montagu, 1st Earl of Halifax (1661–1715), to Charles Montagu, 1st Duke of Manchester (1662–1722). Manchester was an English ambassador to Vienna; his interest in music can be seen from his correspondence, which reveals that he sent fresh compositions by Vien-

nese composers to an eager Halifax and that he even attempted—unsuccessfully—
to entice Giovanni Bononcini into making a visit to England as early as 1707. In the
letter to Manchester, Halifax thanked him for supplying some scores, including a
cantata by the emperor: "I return your Lordship a thousand thanks for the songs
and the fine opera which you have sent me. The cantata of the Emperor's own making is so good we suppose Buononcini had a hand in it, and I'm afraid he [Joseph]
will excell his predecessor [Leopold] in music more than in politics."[88] The cantata
in question could possibly be *Presso allo stuol pomposo di mille fiori*, which is attributed to Joseph in D-Bsb, Mus. Ms. 30186. In this manuscript, a second early hand
has drawn a line through the name "Giuseppe" and has replaced it with "Leopoldo."
For several reasons, the attribution to Joseph seems more plausible. In the first
place, the style of the cantata is late rather than middle baroque. This is reflected by
the clear alternation of recitative and aria and by the use of the da capo aria, style
features that are not typical of the music of Leopold or of his favored Kapellmeister,
Draghi. Second, the contents of the manuscript date chiefly from the early years of
the eighteenth century, that is, from the very last years of Leopold's reign or from
the years immediately following his death. Most of the forty-six cantatas preserved
in MS 30186 were written by composers active in Vienna during this period: Attilio
Ariosti, Giovanni Bononcini, and Francesco Conti. The few remaining pieces are
by contemporaries such as Handel, Alessandro Scarlatti, Nicola Fago, and Francesco Pistocchi. MS 30186 belongs to a large group of sources at D-Bsb that once
formed part of the Sammlung Bokemeyer. The sources of this collection date from
approximately 1700, but their exact origins remain the subject of dispute.[89] Leopold's last dated compositions stem from the year 1697.[90] In any event, the contents of
MS 30186 belong to Leopold's declining years and thus to the years in which Joseph
was active as a composer. A third piece of evidence points to Joseph as the actual
composer: the anonymous text was also set by Giovanni Bononcini, Joseph's favorite composer and one who was primarily active in Joseph's service even before the
death of Leopold.[91] The attribution of the version of *Presso allo stuol pomposo* in MS
30186 cannot be made with certainty, therefore, but existing evidence suggests that
if either emperor composed this cantata, it was probably Joseph I.

A second composer who may have contributed cantatas to the Viennese repertoire during the early years of the eighteenth century is Francesco Bartolomeo
Conti (1681/82–1732).[92] Active as a theorbist from an early age in his native city of
Florence, Conti entered the emperor's service as a court theorbist on 12 July 1701.
He subsequently became one of Europe's most acclaimed virtuosos not only on the
theorbo but also on the mandolin. With Leopold's approval, Conti's initial monthly
salary of one hundred guilders was to be paid retroactively to 1 April 1701, but he
actually received no payment until October 1702; like many Viennese court musicians, he frequently went long periods without being paid. Because of the seriousness of the War of the Spanish Succession in 1701–1702, Conti joined the group

of Viennese artists who journeyed to the court of Sophie Charlotte in Berlin. In his autobiography, Georg Philipp Telemann reported that as a student at Leipzig University he had traveled to Berlin in 1702 and heard two operas there; Telemann identified Conti as one of the members of the orchestra for the performance of Giovanni Bononcini's *Polifemo*.[93]

The precise time of Conti's return to Vienna is unknown. Many nineteenth- and twentieth-century scholars have contended that he was absent from the imperial court again at the beginning of Joseph's reign; their argument rests upon Köchel's *Die kaislerliche Hof-Musikkapelle,* which indicates that Conti was not engaged during the period 1 October 1705 through 31 December 1707.[94] Recently, however, Hermine Williams has demonstrated that Conti was almost definitely employed as court theorbist from the time of his initial appointment in 1701 through the reign of Joseph and that he eventually received payment for all this time, with the exception of the brief period of 1 October 1706 to 30 June 1707, precisely the months when he visited London.[95] Conti resumed his position at Vienna in the summer of 1707 and was elected a member of the Bolognese Accademia Filarmonica in 1708.

Conti married three times. His first wife was Theresa Kugler, the mother of Ignazio Maria, who also became a theorbist and composer at Vienna. Theresa died on 15 April 1711, only two days before the death of Emperor Joseph I. Francesco's second and third wives were sopranos acclaimed in many European capitals. Some time between August 1714 and Carnival 1715 he married Maria Landini—"La Contini"— a prima donna in Vienna until her death in July 1722. Two years later he married Maria Anna Lorenzani, a leading diva at Charles's court until her husband's death. Each of these renowned sopranos received the salary of a star—4,000 florins annually. This stipend in addition to Conti's double salary of 2,880 florins enabled him to live much of his life as a wealthy man, residing in the company of noblemen.[96]

As a composer at Vienna, Conti began his career in early 1706 with the opera *Clotilde* and the oratorio *Il Gioseffo,* ostensibly a tribute to the new emperor. He does not seem to have written further dramatic works for Vienna until 1712, and the vast majority of his operas and oratorios date from his years of service under Charles VI. I have inventoried approximately eighty cantatas by Conti. Almost half of these come down in Viennese archival copies, and many other cantatas that survive in libraries such as D-Bsb and D-MEIr were certainly composed for Vienna. Only twenty-two cantatas by Conti can be dated with some precision; of these, perhaps the earliest are the three cantatas in A-Wn, 17567, a manuscript that I have dated 1712 (see chapter 13). None of the archival manuscripts can be assigned with certainty to Conti's first decade in Vienna, years in which he served Leopold I and Joseph I. Williams has suggested that a number of Conti's cantatas that feature the flute as an obbligato instrument, including one with a text by Silvio Stampiglia, may have been composed for Joseph I, an accomplished flute player, "with the express purpose of providing opportunities for the emperor to perform."[97] Lacking clear evidence of Conti's cantata activity before the reign of Charles VI, however, I will reserve discussion of his contribution to the Viennese cantata repertoire for chapter 13. Although future research may make it possible to identify specific Conti cantatas as products of his first years in Vienna, several clues certainly lead to the conclusion that he composed most of them after the death of Joseph I. First, among the many important composers active in Vienna during the first decade of the eighteenth century, Conti was the youngest; at the time of his appointment in 1701 he was only nineteen or twenty years old. Second, before the accession of Charles VI, Conti held only the appointment as court theorbist; he did not receive the official appointment as court composer until 1713 or the beginning of 1714. Although he wrote a few dramatic works for Vienna in the years 1706 and 1710–11, Conti did not enter the select circle of composers who regularly provided music for court activities until 1714. Certainly the period from that year until roughly 1725 represents the time of Conti's greatest productivity as a composer. Third, the evidence in the Conti archival manuscripts themselves lends weight to the theory that most of his cantatas were written after Joseph's reign: the bindings, watermarks, and scribes of most of the cantata manuscripts clearly associate them with the sources that form the music library of Charles VI, sources that include not only dated Conti manuscripts but also manuscripts of works by composers such as Caldara, who entered Charles's service in 1716. Finally, the lengthy dimensions, elaborate instrumentation, and advanced style of many Conti cantatas link them historically with the later generation. Some thirty cantatas have obbligato parts for three or more instruments, and at least fourteen could be described as grand cantatas.

A third composer who may have written cantatas for Vienna during the early part of the eighteenth century is Pier Francesco Tosi (1654–1732).[98] He was not the son of the prestigious Bolognese composer Giuseppe Felice Tosi. Assuming the priesthood before 1681, Pier Francesco nevertheless made an active career as a singer in Rome, Milan, Reggio Emilia, and Genoa before traveling in 1693 to London, where he enhanced his reputation as a performer and singing teacher.

Tosi began his association with the Habsburg court in 1701, traveling widely as a diplomatic and musical agent for the future emperor Joseph I. Then, on 1 July 1705 he received an appointment in Vienna as court composer, receiving a monthly salary of one hundred florins.[99] He continued to act as a diplomatic representative not only for the emperor but also for the Elector Palatine Johann Wilhelm, a nobleman who maintained close ties with the imperial court and befriended other Italian musicians such as Giovanni Bononcini and Attilio Ariosti.[100] Tosi retained his appointment in Vienna until the death of Joseph I (17 April 1711).

Tosi is best known for the *Opinioni de' cantori antichi e moderni* (1723), in which he defended the "pathetic" style of earlier opera composers and deplored the *cantar sempre allegro*, the avoidance of minor keys, and the excessive use of fermatas found in arias of more recent composers. The treatise and its various translations went through many editions and reprintings.[101] The number of extant compositions by Tosi is rather small. The manuscript A-Wn, 18843, contains his oratorio *Il martirio di Santa Caterina,* performed at Vienna in 1701, four years before his appointment. The oratorio may have been one factor that led to Tosi's employment at the Habsburg court. Otherwise, his known compositions comprise only about a dozen cantatas and arias in a handful of European libraries.[102] Burney also noted Tosi's activity as a cantata composer: "Tosi was, it seems, not only a very fine singer, but also a composer. Mr. Galliard relates, that after his voice had left him he composed sundry cantatas of an exquisite taste, especially in the recitatives, wherein he says the author excels, in the pathetic and expression, all others."[103] In his MGG article about Tosi, Luigi Ferdinando Tagliavini cites the cantata *Vibrò maligna stella* as an outstanding example of Tosi's art.[104]

Since Tosi achieved some recognition as a cantata composer, it is somewhat surprising that none of his cantatas comes down in a Viennese library. In fact, at present there is no concrete evidence that any of the extant cantatas was actually written for Vienna. Besides the 1701 oratorio, no other compositions by Tosi are known to have been performed at the imperial court. How, then, did Tosi come to hold the title of court composer for approximately six years? It is of course possible that compositions by him are now lost or have not yet been identified. Tosi may also have been occupied with activities as a teacher, a singer, and a diplomat. It is also plausible that he began work on the *Opinioni* during this period. Several of the extant cantatas may yet prove to be of Viennese origins, but at present Tosi's influence as a cantata composer in Vienna appears to have been negligible.

8

Repertoire and Sources

New Interest in the Cantata

The sudden growth of cantata activity at Vienna in the early years of the eighteenth century can be attributed largely to the advent of a new generation of Habsburg rulers and court musicians. Perhaps the single most important factor was the rise of Joseph's influence. Born in 1678, the heir to the throne was ready to assume a large personal and political role by the beginning of the next century. Lacking his father's strict ecclesiastical background, Joseph assumed the reins of power with natural ease. His heroism and high spirits created a confident new atmosphere in Austria, even in the face of the French assault. Thus, the more progressive and secular attitudes of the court probably contributed to the fresh interest in the cantata.

With the emergence of a new ruler, Vienna attracted many young and prestigious artists to its court. In no field was this more evident than in music. Although Joseph composed less frequently than his father, he was especially interested in nourishing the development of secular dramatic music in Vienna. While still king of the Romans he began to establish his own circle of prominent Italian composers. These men included some of the most talented opera composers of the period; as a result, expenditures for opera and the number of performances given annually increased significantly. To assist the new Kapellmeister, Antonio Pancotti, the Habsburgs sent for the influential Venetian Marc'Antonio Ziani, and several gifted court composers were added to the chapel, primarily to meet the constant demand for new dramatic works. Among the new group were several men who had already achieved acclaim in Italy as cantata composers. Not surprisingly, then, composers like Giovanni and Antonio Bononcini, Ariosti, and Ziani continued to write cantatas at the court of Joseph I, who perhaps tried his hand at the genre.

Besides the generational changes taking place within the ruling family and the chapel, several other conditions probably contributed indirectly to the increase in cantata composition. During the late seventeenth century Austria had withstood two menaces that at times seriously threatened Vienna itself. One menace had been the devastating plague of the late 1670s and the 1680s, which took the lives of tens of thousands and forced most of the court to flee. A second menace was the Turk-ish Siege of Vienna in 1683; although Austria emerged victorious, the damage to Vienna was inestimable. For the remainder of the century Austrian troops under Prince Eugene were preoccupied with pushing the Turks farther and farther from Habsburg lands. These two menaces were grim factors in the daily life of the court. It is not surprising that Leopold refrained from engaging a host of new composers to assist the overworked Draghi. As serious as the War of the Spanish Succession was to become, it was played out mainly in other parts of Europe and only briefly in 1703 threatened Vienna itself. Thus the court was able to proceed with its routine of splendid and expanded festivities, including many cantata performances.

Certainly also the increased prominence of star singers at the turn of the eighteenth century must have inspired the composition of many cantatas. The Habsburgs engaged not only some of Europe's leading castrati but also several cel-ebrated women. The cantata, always primarily the domain of the soprano voice, offered a perfect technical and expressive vehicle for these virtuosos. At least two of the prima donnas (Lisi Badia and Maria Landini Conti) were to marry major court composers, and the associations of other singers with composers like Giovanni Bononcini are well documented. It seems evident that cantatas were tailor-made for specific voices. The presence in Vienna of fluent cantata librettists like Pietro Antonio Bernardoni and Domenico Cupeda must also have added to the growth of the genre's popularity.

Interest in the cantata, therefore, reached a new peak at the beginning of the eighteenth century. The increased popularity of the genre raises many intriguing questions. How much cantata activity actually took place in early eighteenth-cen-tury Vienna? Were all the performances controlled by the Habsburgs, or were many cantatas sung on gala occasions in the residences of the aristocracy and intelligen-tsia? In the late baroque era the Viennese nobility built an astonishing number of new palaces and remodeled many older ones. Requiring no scenery or costumes, cantatas might have been performed often as *Hausmusik,* especially in salons that included good keyboard instruments. At present our knowledge of the cantata in Vienna is limited to sources and documents related exclusively to the imperial fam-ily. Italian composers and singers were, after all, appointed by the emperor, and the focus of their activities was to provide entertainment for the imperial family and its guests. Yet the possibility of informal readings and performances in the residences of the more musically minded nobility must be considered. A search through the correspondence and other documents of important noblemen may eventually shed some light on this question.

Finally, to what extent were cantatas by nonresident composers available in Vienna? Were there many performances of cantatas written by composers working in other parts of Europe? Did Vienna enjoy a vigorous music trade that included cantatas? With regard to these questions, there is some specific information that leads me to conclude that the actual level of cantata activity was far greater than the surviving sources of cantatas by Habsburg composers suggest. Many prominent imperial musicians traveled to Italy and other parts of Europe one or more times during their Viennese tenures, and a large number of other composers and dilettantes visited the Austrian capital. It seems reasonable to assume that many musicians brought to Vienna cantatas not only of their own but also of other composers. In a letter dated 6 November 1709 to the Bolognese count Pirro Albergati (1663–1735), Ariosti reported that he had arrived in Vienna and had submitted compositions by the count to Joseph; Albergati had dedicated his instrumental work *Pletro armonico*, op. 5, to Leopold in 1687, and he was also the composer of many cantatas, including a number of printed volumes of *cantate spirituali* and *cantate da camera*.[1]

The archives of A-Wn and A-Wgm contain many cantatas by late baroque composers who either visited Vienna briefly (e.g., Astorga, Caldara before his appointment, possibly Fiorè) or never resided in Austria (Steffani, Vivaldi [until the end of his life], Lotti, Benedetto Marcello, Alessandro Scarlatti). While some of these cantatas are preserved in Habsburg archival copies and were therefore definitely performed at court, many others come down in sources copied in other parts of Europe and may well have been brought to Vienna for performances. Composers like Antonio Lotti and Giovanni Bononcini (before his Viennese appointment) dedicated published cantata volumes to the elderly Leopold and to Joseph. Handsome handwritten copies of these collections were presented to the emperors; selected works were presumably performed at least informally and were then added to the Habsburg archives.[2] A-Wn, Supp. Mus. 2452 is an early handwritten catalog of the music library of Charles VI, and it contains an appendix of compositions performed during the reigns of Leopold I and Joseph I (or shortly after Joseph's death).[3] Among other items, the appendix includes a list of *componimenti da camera, e da teatro* that contains many references to cantatas. Some of the items are easily identifiable as volumes now in the music archive at A-Wn: no. 44, for example, is A-Wn, 17567; no. 45 is probably A-Wn, 17593; no. 48 is A-Wn, 17579; and so on. The composers whose cantatas were performed included not only court appointees like Giovanni Bononcini, Conti, and Caldara but also figures who never received positions, such as Benedetto Marcello, Porpora, Francesco Scarlatti, Astorga, and Fiorè. (At least three of these composers—Porpora, Astorga, and Scarlatti—visited Vienna early in the reign of Charles VI.) Two catalogs dated 1778 (Supp. Mus. 2454 and 2455) list additional works belonging to the imperial music library of the first half of the eighteenth century.[4] These inventories contain entries for many more cantata volumes, most of which date from the reign of Charles. In summary, it appears that the court collected or was given cantatas by many nonresident composers; this broad interest in the cantata clearly began already in the first years of the eighteenth century.

The amount of music trade in Vienna during the first decade of the century is difficult to determine. A 1714 inventory of printed music in stock at the store of the principal book dealer, Johann Michael Christophori (ca. 1660–1731), contains no references to Italian music.[5] Italian compositions circulated in Vienna for the most part in manuscript copies. By the third decade of the century, announcements concerning the sales of large manuscript collections of music began to appear in the leading German-language newspaper, the *Wienerisches Diarium*. Unfortunately, no records of such sales from the time of Joseph I have been uncovered, but it seems plausible that musicians and noblemen amassed such collections even before Charles's accession.

THE REPERTOIRE OF CANTATAS BY HABSBURG COMPOSERS

The numerous extant cantatas from roughly 1700 to 1711 give evidence of a vigorous amount of cantata activity at Vienna in the early eighteenth century. I have identified 104 cantatas by composers in the service of the Habsburgs during the last years of Leopold I and the reign of Joseph I. The criteria for identifying the cantatas composed specifically for Vienna during the period 1658–1700 obtain also for the period 1700–1711. Only composers who were appointed members of the Habsburg chapel (Carlo Badia, Marc'Antonio Ziani, Giovanni and Antonio Bononcini) or who resided in Vienna for an extended period (Attilio Ariosti) are included. Their cantatas come down in twenty-three core sources: twenty-two manuscripts and one print that are clearly of Viennese origin and dated or assignable to the approximate period 1700–1711 on the basis of internal evidence. The manuscripts include a pair of holographs, nineteen archival copies, and a single source now at D-Dl. Professional scribes prepared the archival copies on sturdy imperial paper. These manuscripts are preserved in bindings with imprints that confirm Habsburg ownership.

The dates 1700 and 1711 should be understood as guidelines and not as absolute boundaries. At least four Badia cantatas date from 1699, but these compositions obviously belong stylistically and historically with the period under consideration. Likewise, a small number of cantatas preserved in the core sources were composed shortly after 1711. The years 1712–16 were transitional ones in which the entire chapel was reorganized under the supervision of the *Musik-Oberdirektor,* Count Molard. A list of members was posted at the beginning of 1713, but significant changes occurred as late as 1716. A few cantatas by the earlier generation of composers date from the interregnum year, 1712. These include three chamber cantatas by Giovanni Bononcini and one grand cantata by Badia.

Table 8.1 presents a summary of cantatas by Badia, Giovanni Bononcini, Antonio Maria Bononcini, Ziani, Ariosti, and anonymous masters.[6] For each composer I have indicated totals for all extant cantatas known to me from the composer's entire career and the number of cantatas in core Viennese sources.

TABLE 8.1. TOTAL EXTANT CANTATAS AND CANTATAS IN CORE VIENNESE SOURCES

COMPOSER	TOTAL EXTANT CANTATAS	CANTATAS IN CORE SOURCES
Badia	61	55
G. Bononcini	nearly 300	5
A. M. Bononcini	at least 42	14
Ziani	at least 8	5
Ariosti	94	23
Anonymous masters	—	2

TABLE 8.2. CORE SOURCES CONTAINING CANTATAS BY BADIA

SOURCE	DATE	NUMBER OF BADIA CANTATAS
Tributi armonici	between 1699 & 1704	12
A-Wn, 16308	1699	4
A-Wn, 17725	1701	1
A-Wn, 17574	1704	15
A-Wn, 18794	before 1706	4
D-Dl, Mus. ms. 2192/J/1	1706	1
A-Wn, 17734	between 1706 and 1712	10
A-Wn, 17721	between 1706 and 1712	7
A-Wn, 17675	1712	1

Of the sixty-one cantatas by Carlo Agostino Badia, at least fifty-five were definitely written for Vienna.[7] (The origins of six cantatas now at F-Pn have not been documented, but the copyist is clearly not Viennese.) Owing to his youthful facility and his favor with Leopold, Badia composed the majority of his cantatas during the early part of his career. At least thirty-two works date from the five-year period 1699–1704. Among these early cantatas are the twelve *Tributi armonici* published by Johann Christoph Weigel at Nuremberg some time between 1699 and 1704.[8] The grand cantata *Il sacrificio di Berenice* was composed in 1712. Table 8.2 lists the core sources containing Badia cantatas, the date or approximate date of each source, and the number of Badia cantatas in each.

In his catalog of manuscripts now at A-Wn, Josef Mantuani indicated that the Badia and Bononcini compositions in A-Wn, 17721 are all arias, but they are actually cantatas. Mantuani also reported that MS 16308 contains only three cantatas, but a closer examination of the source reveals that it includes a fourth cantata for which the opening music is lost. Mantuani assumed that folios 81–101v are a continuation of the third cantata (folios 65–80). (The foliation is written in modern pencil.) It is clear that between folios 80 and 81 an original folio has been torn out. Musically and textually the third cantata ends on folio 80; the tonality, instrumentation, and text on folio 81 are unrelated to the contents of folio 80. Moreover, folio 80v has blank staves only; folios of blank staves do not occur within other cantatas of MS 16308. Thus, the missing folio probably contained the opening music for a fourth cantata. This conclusion is borne out by one additional piece of evidence: at the beginning of the third cantata (folio 65), "Cantata terza" has been written over the words "Cantata Quarta," which are almost entirely deleted. The fourth cantata was probably inscribed in a manner similar to the opening folios of cantatas 1–3, identifying the title, the name of the court lady for whom the cantata was composed, and the number of the cantata in the manuscript. Although the beginning music is missing, the first words of the opening aria are evidently *Dea loquace,* the first line of the A section of a da capo aria. Fortunately, it is possible to reconstruct the entire aria, for the da capo is written out. However, it is possible that this cantata, like the first three in MS 16308, began with a recitative.

For MS 17734 Mantuani gave only nine text incipits. Jakob Torbé maintained that the volume actually contains eleven cantatas.[9] For folios 11–19v Mantuani listed only one text incipit, and for folios 25–32v he also inventoried only one. Torbé claimed that each of these groups of folios really consists of two separate cantatas. With regard to folios 25–32v, I concur with Torbé and believe that a new composition begins on folio 29. Not only is there an abrupt tonal shift at this point (from F to G), but, as Torbé points out, the name of the beloved referred to in the text changes from Eurilla to Clori. Torbé's case for dividing folios 11–19v, with a new piece beginning on 16, is less persuasive. There are no obvious textual details, such as the names of lovers, to support his conclusion. Moreover, the aria text beginning on folio 16 is a logical continuation of the text on folio 15v, and the remaining text (folios 16v–19v) provides some resolution of the stated problem. The tonality of the music on folio 16, D major, is the same as the end of folio 15v. Finally, the scribe of MS 17734 seems to separate individual cantatas by leaving at least a partial folio of blank staves between the end of one piece and the beginning of another; there are no blank staves before folio 16. While the failure of the scribe to provide an attribution at the beginning of each cantata and the rather general topics of the texts leave open the question of how many cantatas are preserved in folios 11–19v, I believe that Mantuani was correct in his assumption that this section of MS 17734 contains only one cantata.

Apart from the twelve *Tributi armonici,* each Badia cantata survives in one core source only for which there are no concordances. Hence, there are no conflicting attributions. However, the anonymous texts of *Già tra l'onde* (A-Wn, 17574, no. 3), *Augellin vago e canoro* (A-Wn, 17721, no. 1), and *Sapesse il core almen* (A-Wn, 17734, no. 8) were set by a variety of other composers.[10] *I sospiri dell'aure,* the sixth cantata in A-Wn, 17721, is actually anonymous in the source. Cantatas 1–5 and 7 in this manuscript are all attributed to Badia, and the remaining two pieces are ascribed to Giovanni Bononcini. Because the cantata occurs within a cluster attributed to Badia, because it opens with a bipartite instrumental movement similar to other Badia introductions, and because of other stylistic details, I have assigned it to Badia.

TABLE 8.3. CORE SOURCES CONTAINING CANTATAS BY GIOVANNI BONONCINI

SOURCE	DATE	NUMBER OF CANTATAS
A-Wn, 17721	between 1706 and 1712	2
A-Wn, 17567	ca. 1712	3

If Raguenet was correct in his statement that by 1705 more than two hundred cantatas by Giovanni Bononcini were known in France (or even if he exaggerated somewhat), then it seems likely that Bononcini composed the vast majority of these cantatas in the years preceding his arrival at Vienna. Only five cantatas can be assigned to the Viennese period (1698–1712) with comparative certainty, representing a tiny fraction of his enormous output.

Table 8.3 lists the core sources with Bononcini cantatas, the approximate date of each manuscript, and the number by him in each source.[11] With one exception, these two manuscripts preserve the only complete copies of the cantatas composed for Vienna. The exception is *Clori, svenar mi sento* (A-Wn, 17721, no. 8), which is also preserved in F-Pn, Rés Vma 967, a manuscript prepared by musician and copyist Charles Babel.[12] The Habsburg policy with regard to ownership of music sources seems to have been so strict that even the cantatas of the much admired and widely imitated Giovanni Bononcini did not circulate much beyond the imperial capital.

Other sources at A-Wn with Bononcini cantatas (the MSS 17576, 17579, 17748, E.M. 161, E.M. 168, SA.67.A.25, Supp. Mus. 2403, Supp. Mus. 5188, Supp. Mus. 22123, and Supp. Mus. 22124 as well as the prints MS 5280 and SA.67.B.94) are not of Viennese origin from the period under consideration here. The Bononcini cantatas in E.M. 161 and 168 are part of the Este music collection that was brought from Padua to Vienna in 1803.[13] The MS A-Wn, SA.67.A.25, is Viennese, but it dates from considerably after 1711, perhaps during the time of Giovanni's second Austrian residence (1736–47). Each of the three fragments that constitute A-Wgm, VI 15497 (Q 4563) contains one Bononcini cantata; these cantatas and three preserved in separate manuscript fragments at A-Wgm—VI 15496 (Q 4562), VI 15498 (Q 4564), and VI 15499 (Q 4565)—were perhaps copied for early eighteenth-century Viennese performances, but their numerous Italian concordances suggest that they were composed before Giovanni arrived at Vienna.[14]

Four core sources contain fourteen cantatas composed by Antonio Maria Bononcini for Vienna. Each source is devoted exclusively to his cantatas. Table 8.4 gives details of manuscript numbers, dating, and the number of cantatas in each source.[15] Individual parts for the twelve cantatas in MSS 17587 and 17607 are preserved in MS 15931. This source contains three instrumental parts (flutes 1–2 and bassoon) for the cantatas in MS 17587 as well as six instrumental parts (violins 1–2 *di concerto*, violins 1–2 *di concerto grosso*, cello *di concerto*, and double bass *di concerto grosso*) for the cantatas in MS 17607. Mantuani cataloged MS 15931 as if it preserved parts

TABLE 8.4. CORE SOURCES CONTAINING CANTATAS BY A. M. BONONCINI

SOURCE	DATE	NUMBER OF CANTATAS
A-Wn, 17586	1706	1
A-Wn, 17587	1708	6
A-Wn, 17607	1708	6
A-Wn, 17637	before 1713	1

TABLE 8.5. CORE SOURCES CONTAINING CANTATAS BY M. A. ZIANI

SOURCE	DATE	NUMBER OF CANTATAS
A-Wgm, VI 13378 (A 407)	between 1700 and 1715	1
A-Wn, 17635	1706	1 (*accademia*)
A-Wn, 17650	1706	1 (*accademia*)
A-Wn, 17570	1706	1
D-Bsb, M Mus. Ms. Autogr. Ziani, Ant. 1	between 1700 and 1715	1

for six entirely different cantatas by Antonio Maria, for which no complete scores remain. He noticed that a few Italian words had been written in before each movement, requiring separately copied instrumental parts, and he assumed that these words represented titles of cantatas. Actually, they are the final words of recitatives and other movements without separate parts; they evidently served as cues for the various instrumentalists who had only parts in front of them during the performances.

All fourteen cantatas by Antonio Maria in core sources are unica.[16] The anonymous text of *Sul margine adorato* (A-Wn, 17607, no. 1) was also set by Giovanni del Violone (Lulier).[17] In MS 17587 only the second and sixth cantatas are specifically attributed to Antonio; the other four cantatas are anonymous within the source. However, the entire volume is assigned to him on the front binding ("CANTATE CON FLAUTI DI ANTONIO BONONCINI") and in the partbooks ("Di Anto:° Bononcini").

I have examined only eight extant cantatas by Marc'Antonio Ziani.[18] No sources have been identified for two related works that he is known to have composed.[19] Of the eight extant works, at least five were prepared for Viennese entertainments.[20] Table 8.5 summarizes the locations of core manuscripts with Ziani cantatas and their dates. Each of the five cantatas listed in table 8.5 survives in one core source only.

Twenty-three cantatas by Attilio Ariosti come down in two manuscripts definitely of early eighteenth-century Viennese origins. The cantatas in MS 17591 are all attributed to "P. Attilio Ariosti" on the title page (folio 1). In MS 17575, however, only the first cantata bears an attribution ("Di P. Attilio Ariosti"); cantatas 2–11 are anonymous within the source. Concordances identifying Ariosti as the composer have been located for nos. 1, 4, and 9; no. 11 is also anonymous in a manuscript at

TABLE 8.6. CORE SOURCES CONTAINING CANTATAS BY ARIOSTI

SOURCE	APPROXIMATE DATE	NUMBER OF CANTATAS
A-Wn, 17575	between 1706 and 1712	11
A-Wn, 17591	between 1706 and 1712	12

TABLE 8.7. CONCORDANCES OF ARIOSTI CANTATAS IN CORE SOURCES

SOURCE	NO.	TITLE	CONCORDANCES
A-Wn, 17575	1	*Oh miseria d'amante core*	D-Bsb, 30188; D-SHs, Mus B.1:3
A-Wn, 17575	4	*È pur dolce a un cor*	A-Wn, E.M.178
A-Wn, 17575	9	*Mi convien soffrir in pace*	D-Bsb, 30074
A-Wn, 17575	11	*Sia con me Fillide irata*	D-Bsb, 30197 (anonymous)
A-Wn, 17591	1	*Genio che amar volea*	D-Bsb, 30182
A-Wn, 17591	6	*Belle stille che grondate*	D-Bsb, 30094
A-Wn, 17591	8	*Cieco Nume alato Arciero*	D-Bsb, 30212
A-Wn, 17591	10	*Tante e tante del ciel*	D-DS, Mus.Ms.46

D-Dsb.[21] Mus. ms. 17575 was copied by a single Habsburg scribe. All eleven cantatas are of approximately the same length, are scored for alto and continuo, and share many other stylistic details. For these reasons, and because of the concordances with ascriptions to Ariosti, I have tentatively assigned the entire volume to him.

A total of eight Ariosti cantatas in the two core sources (four in MS 17575 and four in MS 17591) have concordances; the remaining fifteen cantatas appear to be unica. Table 8.7 gives a summary of manuscripts with concordances.[22] Of all the cantatas in core Viennese manuscripts, only these eight by Ariosti seem to have circulated somewhat beyond the emperor's orbit. Thus far it has not been possible to determine whether some of the concordances actually predate the copies in the core sources, although I believe that the copies in D-Bsb are slightly later. It may be that the emperor exercised less control over Ariosti's cantatas because they were composed by a musician who did not hold an official post at the court chapel.

In the concordant copies of *Mi convien soffrir in pace* and *Tante e tante del ciel*, the cantatas are transcribed up a perfect fifth and a major second, respectively, for soprano (see the entries for these two cantatas in appendix A, an index of cantata text incipits and sources). The anonymous cantata text *Genio che amar volea* was also set by Giovanni Bononcini.[23]

The music of at least two anonymous cantatas also belongs to the period 1700–1711; these cantatas are the compositions in honor of the battle victory at Landau (1702 or 1704) and the coronation of Emperor Joseph I (1705). The 1702 cantata is preserved in MS 18758 at A-Wn, and the 1705 composition comes down in MS 18513.[24] Lindgren speculates: "Bononcini might have also composed the two anonymous cantatas that respectively celebrate Joseph's military exploits and accession to the imperial throne."[25]

TABLE 8.8. LIBRARIES CONTAINING CORE CANTATA SOURCES

LIBRARY	NO. OF CORE SOURCES
A-Wgm	1
A-Wn	20
B-Bc	1
D-Bsb	1
D-Dl	2
D-W	1
GB-Lbl	1
I-Bc	1
I-Rsc	1

THE SOURCES

The following discussion of Viennese cantata sources for the period 1700–1711 includes information not only about the core sources but also about a number of peripheral sources, some manuscripts falsely attributed to Viennese origin, and several lost cantata sources.

THE CORE SOURCES

These twenty-two manuscripts and one print contain the cantatas that I believe are definitely Viennese and date from ca. 1700 to ca. 1712. The core sources survive in nine European libraries. Table 8.8 lists the individual libraries that contain core sources, both manuscripts and copies of the print, and the number in each library.[26]

The second part of appendix B, a catalogue raisonné of all the cantatas composed during the period 1658–1712, includes the twenty-three core cantata sources from 1700 to 1712. The observations given here summarize some of the most important features of the core sources, which have been divided into four categories: holographs, the print, dated and undated archival copies, and one nonarchival core manuscript.

Holographs

The MSS A-Wgm, VI 13378 (A 407) and D-Bsb, M Mus. ms. Autogr. Ziani, Ant.1 are holographs, probably the only such sources pertinent to this chapter.[27] Each manuscript contains a single Ziani cantata, and each is possibly a fragment from a larger collection.

Of special interest is the cantata *Troppo conosco, o Filli,* found in the holograph at D-Bsb. According to an early handwritten catalog of sources at A-Wgm, *Troppo conosco* was once preserved in a holograph belonging to that collection.[28]

In the numbering system of this early catalog, it is listed as MS VI 13377; therefore, it was probably a companion manuscript to the holograph of *Filli mi disse un di* (titled *Rotta fede*), now at A-Wgm in MS VI 13378 (A 407). Were there actually two holographs of *Troppo conosco,* one now in Berlin and one formerly in Vienna but now lost? Or is the holograph reportedly once owned by A-Wgm the source now at D-Bsb? Some tangential evidence can be marshaled to advance the latter possibility. Each of the two extant cantatas, one in Vienna, the other now in Berlin, comes down in an unbound fragment of four unnumbered folios; each is oblong in format, with ten staves per folio. The watermark of the holograph at D-Bsb has the three-crescent design commonly found in Viennese papers; unfortunately, no watermark in the source at A-Wgm could be discerned. Each cantata is signed with the same simple autograph: "M. A. Ziani."

On folio 1 of the holograph at A-Wgm, Eusebius Mandyczewski, the archivist at the turn of the twentieth century, has designated the source an original autograph; however, there is no hint of an early owner. On the other hand, a modern librarian has indicated that the holograph at D-Bsb once belonged to the vast autograph collection of the Viennese scholar Aloys Fuchs (1799–1853). Richard Schaal does not include either manuscript in his basic list of autographs that originally were part of Fuchs's collection.[29] Schaal points out, however, that Fuchs was also very active as a broker of manuscripts for other collectors and that his library was richly augmented by subsequent owners before it was dispersed to various European libraries. The exact details of ownership, therefore, remain clouded. Nevertheless, it seems quite likely that only one holograph of the cantata *Troppo conosco* existed, that it belonged temporarily to A-Wgm (probably at the end of the nineteenth century), and that it eventually became part of the music collection at D-Bsb.

The Badia Print

The single printed volume relevant to this study is Badia's *Tributi armonici,* published at Nuremberg some time between 1699 and 1704. Copies are preserved in at least seven European libraries.[30] The collection was engraved by Johann Christoph Weigel (1661–1726), a member of the distinguished family of printers and engravers who settled at Nuremberg toward the end of the seventeenth century.[31] It contains a set of beautiful ornamental engravings by Antonio Beduzzi (Beducci), who was active at Vienna at least from 1705 and succeeded Ottavio Burnacini there as theater designer and architect on 1 January 1708.[32] At the beginning of Badia's volume is a full-page Beduzzi engraving depicting Leopold and the Muses providing the inspiration for the composition of the cantatas. Twelve smaller engravings decorate the first letters of the cantata texts. Figures 8.1, 8.2, and 8.3 are reproductions of the title page, dedication, and initial engraving from the exemplar D-W, 9 Musica div.

TRIBUTI ARMONICI
Dedicati
ALLA SAGRA CESAREA REAL MAESTÀ
DI LEOPOLDO PRIMO IMPERATORE
DE ROMANI
Da
Carlo Agostino Badia Compositor di Musica
della Maestà Sua.
Joh. Christoph Weigel, excudit

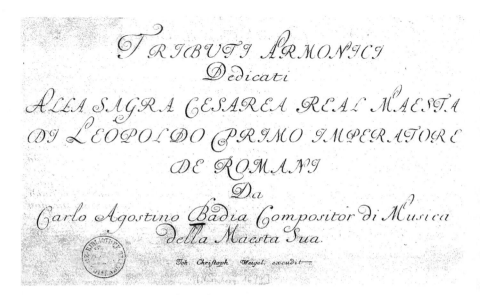

FIG. 8.1. Title page of Carlo Badia's *Tributi armonici* (Nuremberg, between 1699 and 1704). Courtesy of Herzog August Bibliothek Wolfenbüttel: 9 Musica div.

Sagra Cesarea Reale Maestà

Nel riflettere, che li Principi della Terra sono vere imagini de' Numi del Cielo, e che quelli nell' vso della bontà, e della Clemenza prendono le norme da questi, trouo motiuo per lusingare con felici speranze la superbia di quell' ossequioso rispetto, che mi hà dato l'impulso a consagrare a V.ra M.tà Ces. gli annessi musicali componimenti. Sò, che ad una mente tanto eleuata, e ad vn genio così delicato, e gentile, qual è quello di V.ra Ces. M.tà, dourebbersi note più uirtuose, ed armoniche di quelle, che ardisco presentarle; Non dimeno soffrir non sò, che la conoscenza del mio debol talento mi tolga la fortuna di porgere alla Ces. M.tà V.ra gli omaggi della mia profonda venerazione. Si degni dunque la sua Cesarea magnanimità felicitare le mie diuote brame, con accordare un generoso gradimento al tributo d'umiltà ossequiosa, che le consagro, e segnerò con candida pietra quel giorno, che mi abilitò alla sorte di potermi palesare, qual sono, con tutta la diuozione, che deuo

Di V.ra M.tà Ces.

Umiliss.mo Diuot.mo et Ossequios.mo Seruitore
Carlo Agostino Badia

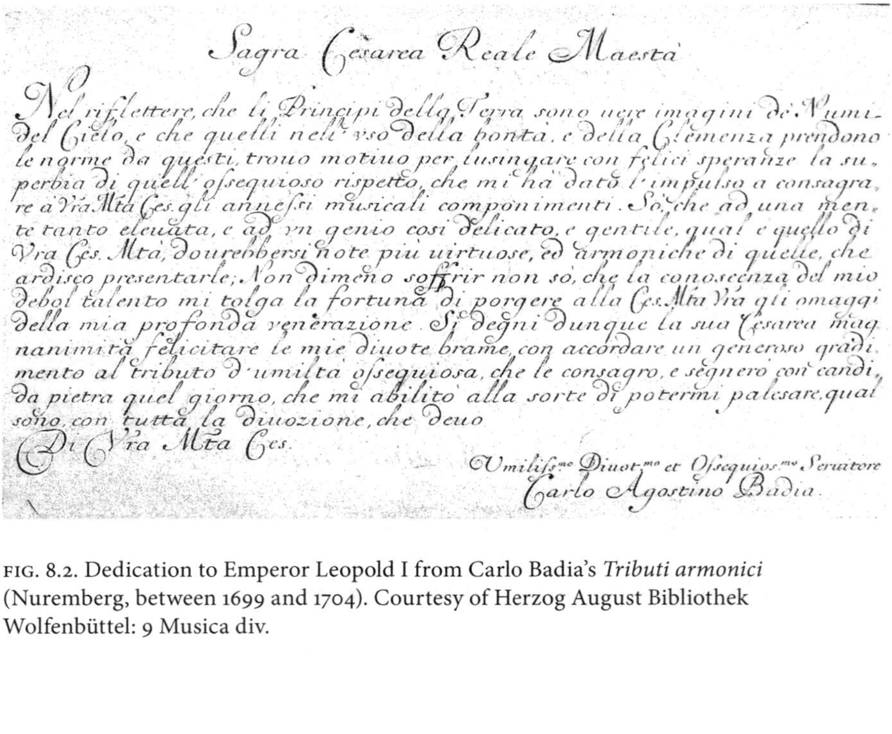

FIG. 8.2. Dedication to Emperor Leopold I from Carlo Badia's *Tributi armonici* (Nuremberg, between 1699 and 1704). Courtesy of Herzog August Bibliothek Wolfenbüttel: 9 Musica div.

FIG. 8.3. Engraving by Antonio Beduzzi, preceding the first page of music in Carlo Badia's *Tributi armonici* (Nuremberg, between 1699 and 1704). Courtesy of Herzog August Bibliothek Wolfenbüttel: 9 Musica div.

Badia's cantata print contains no date or specific information that enables us to identify with certainty the year in which it was published. Without providing documentation, several recent lexicographers have offered the year "1699" or "probably 1699."[33] Earlier biographers, including Walther, Gerber, Fétis, Eitner, and Schmidl, either avoid giving a date or indicate that the *Tributi armonici* are undated. The new edition of Emil Vogel's chronology of Italian secular vocal music of the sixteenth and seventeenth centuries offers the date "1699."[34] The more recent RISM entry (1971) does not specify a date. In an earlier article on the Weigel family, Franz Krautwurst cautiously dates the volume "*c.*1700," a reasonable deduction based upon historical evidence.[35]

By composing these "tributes" for Leopold, Badia was probably offering the emperor a formal gift of thanks for sending him to Rome to complete his musical studies near the end of the seventeenth century. The earliest year in which the cantatas could have been published is 1699, for Weigel did not begin his career at Nuremberg until that time. Because the *Tributi armonici* are dedicated to Leopold, we can assume that they date no later than 1705. Since the emperor died on 5 May of that year, it seems plausible that the cantatas were composed and that preparations for the collection, if not the actual engraving, took place before 1705. Therefore, Badia's print dates from sometime between 1699 and 1704, precisely the years in which he was most active as a cantata composer.

The Archival Copies (Dated and Undated)

Nineteen sources at A-Wn constitute the total number of extant archival copies. These manuscripts contain 89 of the 104 core cantatas from 1700 to 1711; of these 89 compositions, 80 are unica. The following summary provides some general observations about the formats, bindings, watermarks, and scribes of the archival copies.

On the whole, these beautiful archival copies remain in unusually good condition. The manuscripts were not used for performances but were meticulously prepared for the libraries of the emperors Leopold I and Joseph I after the occasions for which the music was commissioned. Today the manuscripts belong to the Musiksammlung at A-Wn and are thus housed in the Palais Mollard on Herrengasse in the first district. The appearance of the archival copies is much neater and the physical condition far better than most cantata manuscripts of this period. Moreover, these copies are remarkably rich in details such as dates, occasions, dedications, and poets. Four archival sources dating from 1699 to 1704 belong to the Biblioteca Leopoldina; these copies contain a total of twenty-one cantatas. Thirteen sources from Joseph's library preserve sixty-four core cantatas. Badia's *Il sacrificio di Berenice* and probably the three cantatas by Giovanni Bononcini in MS 17567 date from 1712, the year of the interregnum.

The archival copies come down in either standard upright format or oblong format. Two manuscripts from the Biblioteca Leopoldina are in upright format, the type usually found in Habsburg music manuscripts of the late seventeenth century. Upright format is found in only one other archival source pertinent to this chapter; this manuscript (18513) preserves the cantata for the 1705 coronation of Joseph and is thus chronologically very close to the group of sources from the reign of Leopold. Two archival copies from the Biblioteca Leopoldina, twelve of thirteen sources from Joseph's library, and the two manuscripts that date from the interregnum are oblong, the shape used almost exclusively for music manuscripts after the death of Leopold.

All the archival copies are cropped manuscripts. The three sources in upright format (16308, 18513, and 18758) are similar in size—roughly 20 by 30 cm—and appearance, each source having ten staves per folio. The sixteen manuscripts in oblong format likewise have similar dimensions, ranging from 20.5 by 29 cm to 25 by 31 cm, and layout, half of the sources having eight staves per folio and the other half ten. In all but two manuscripts (17574 and 17721), the original foliation or pagination has been cropped; in sixteen manuscripts, foliation has been added in modern pencil.

Of the nineteen archival copies, seventeen retain their original bindings. Generally in excellent condition, many of the bindings have elaborate gold imprints confirming Habsburg ownership. The materials of the bindings are of three basic types: (1) white parchment; (2) red paper over cardboard; or (3) rich red, reddish-brown, dark-brown, or black leather. White parchment was the characteristic material used for bindings of the Biblioteca Leopoldina; only MSS 16308 (dated 1699) and 18794 (undated) have parchment bindings. MSS 17725 and 18513 are bound in red paper over cardboard. The red-paper bindings also belong to the earlier period: MSS 17725 and 18513 were copied in 1701 and 1705, respectively. The remaining thirteen archival sources have leather bindings; only one of these manuscripts, 17574 (dated 1704), contains cantatas composed before the reign of Joseph. Leather bindings predominate almost to the exclusion of all other types after the death of Leopold.

Various ornamental designs, coats of arms, and other Habsburg insignia are imprinted on the bindings either in plain black or with gold. In the majority of the archival copies, the pages are also gilt-edged. Manuscripts with cantatas by Ariosti and Antonio Maria Bononcini have the least elaborate imprints, possibly because these two composers did not hold official titles through the first decade of the eighteenth century. Thus, of the four sources with cantatas by Antonio Maria (17586, 17587, 17607, and 17637), two have no imprints at all, while the other two have only the musical genre and the composer's name on the front binding. One of the Ariosti volumes, MS 17575, has no designs but only dark lines along the edges of the binding. The other Ariosti collection, MS 17591, is edged with gold lines and has a simple gold design in each corner of the front and back. Similarly, unpretentious patterns are found on the bindings of several manuscripts with cantatas by Badia (17574, 17675, and 17734) and Ziani (17570).

The bindings of five archival copies display much more ostentatious imprints that clearly associate them with Habsburg patronage. MS 17721 has not only gilt trimming around the edges but also an imprint of the Habsburg coat of arms with the Aquila, the two-headed eagle representing the two fundamental aspects of imperial power (Holy Roman emperor and king of the Romans). Variants of this basic Habsburg imprint appear on the bindings of MSS 17567, 18513, and 18794, where the coat of arms and the two-headed eagle are further embellished by symbols such as the scepter, the crown, and the apple. The red-paper binding of MS 18513 is also ornamented by a gilt pattern of swirls, birds, and flowers; this highly ornate manuscript is the one that preserves the cantata for the coronation of Joseph. The earliest of all the archival copies, MS 16308 (dated 1699), has an imprint of the likeness of Leopold on the front of the binding, as well as the Habsburg seal with double-headed eagle and crown on the back, imprints similar to those found on the bindings of manuscripts from the previous generation.

The papers of the nineteen archival manuscripts are also in generally excellent condition. Cream-colored or slightly yellow from age, the papers are predominantly of medium weight and of good to superior quality. The watermarks found in most of the archival manuscripts are variants of a basic three-crescent design that was used extensively by Venetian paper mills by the end of the seventeenth century. Venice continued to be a major exporter of sturdy papers with three crescents

TABLE 8.9. CHRONOLOGY OF ARCHIVAL CANTATA SOURCES AT A-WN

SOURCE	DATE OR APPROXIMATE DATE	NUMBER OF CORE CANTATAS
16308	1699	4
17725	1701	1
18758	1702	1
17574	1704	15
18513	1705	1
18794	before 1706	4
17570	1706	1
17586	1706	1
17635	1706	1
17650	1706	1
17587	1708	6
17607	1708	6
17734	between 1706 and 1712	10
17721	between 1706 and 1712	9
17575	between 1706 and 1712	11
17591	between 1706 and 1712	12
17637	before 1713	1
17675	1712	1
17567	ca. 1712	3 (of 12)

throughout the eighteenth century. Other watermarks found in papers of archival cantatas include the coat of arms, fleur-de-lis, monogram, eagle, and anchor. Viennese mills seem to have manufactured very little of the paper, if any.

The scribes who copied the nineteen sources at A-Wn were professionals hired by the Habsburgs to prepare archival manuscripts of music composed for court activities. The two main scribes of the period were Johann Salchi (pensioned 1711, d. 1722) and Killian Reinhardt (d. 1729), but there may have been others.[36] Any attempt to disentangle the family of scribes who copied the archival manuscripts must be based upon a study of all Habsburg music manuscripts from the period 1700–1711.

Ten archival manuscripts bear specific dates ranging from 1699 to 1712. On the basis of their occasions, the cantatas in two additional sources (18758 and 18513) have been dated. I have assigned approximate dates to the remaining seven manuscripts, using evidence such as imprints, bindings, formats, watermarks, the contents of the individual manuscripts, and the years in which composers are known to have been active at Vienna. Table 8.9 summarizes the chronology of all nineteen archival copies.

One Nonarchival Core Manuscript

In addition to the two holographs, the print of Badia's *Tributi armonici,* and the nineteen archival copies, one other source contains a cantata that clearly dates from the period under consideration. This source is the manuscript D-Dl, Mus. 2192/J/1, which preserves a single Badia cantata. The work, beginning with the verse "Scesa dal ciel superno messagiera di giorno" and entitled *Il tempo parta alla fama*, was not copied by one of the professional Habsburg scribes. The hasty appearance of the handwriting lends support to the claim made by EitnerQ that the manuscript is an autograph score, but further investigation is required to confirm this conclusion. At the right of the first folio of the manuscript, a later hand has indicated that this cantata was composed for Joseph's name day (19 March) in 1706, but for reasons offered in chapter 6, I do not believe that the dating is accurate.

THE PERIPHERAL SOURCES

In the course of cataloging cantatas for the present study, I also located a number of cantatas by Badia, the Bononcini brothers, Ziani, and Ariosti that may be of Viennese origin and perhaps date from the period 1700–1711.[37] These compositions survive in what I designate as peripheral sources. At the present stage of inquiry, however, the evidence about dating and provenance is inconclusive.

Prominent among the peripheral sources is a group of three manuscripts in the library of the Schlossmuseum in Sondershausen, Germany: D-SHs, Mus. B.1:1, B.1:2, and B.1:3.[38] According to Ernst Ludwig Gerber, these treasures were brought as part of a group of twenty manuscripts, all the work of a single scribe, from England to Sondershausen about 1720.[39] The forty works in the three cantata sources were beautifully copied in a style closely resembling that of Viennese professional scribes of the early eighteenth century.[40] A Modenese collection, I-MOe, Mus. F 99, was also prepared by the scribe of the Sondershausen manuscripts. It contains twenty-three of Giovanni Bononcini's popular, widely disseminated cantatas, six of which are also found in Viennese libraries.[41] At first glance, the style of the Sondershausen and Modenese scribe appears so similar to the Viennese practice that it would be easy to conclude that the copies were actually written by a Viennese court copyist. Yet a closer scrutiny of these manuscripts and a comparison with some sixty contemporary cantata sources at A-Wn reveals no exact match. While the Sondershausen copyist may well have honed his technique in Vienna, there is clear evidence that he was not one of the professional scribes employed by the Habsburgs.

Nevertheless, the contents of the Sondershausen manuscripts reveal early eighteenth-century connections to Vienna. Among the composers represented are five who were actually employed in Vienna: Giovanni Bononcini is represented by twelve cantatas, Badia by eleven, Ariosti by eight, Conti by four, Antonio Maria Bononcini by two, and Caldara by one. B.1:1 contains a single cantata by Astorga, who spent part of the year 1712 in Vienna, and one work by Fiorè, whose contacts with the Habsburg court are well documented. Yet rather surprisingly, only two of all these cantatas can be found in core Viennese copies of the period: Conti's *Pastorelle gioite* (in A-Wn, 17601) and Ariosti's *Oh miseria d'amante core* (in A-Wn, 17575). The eleven cantatas by Badia were obviously copied from the composer's *Tributi armonici,* which, judging from the seven known extant copies, circulated rather widely. The single cantata by Caldara, *In mille guise Amor,* belongs to the set of the composer's cantatas published at Venice in 1699. Four cantatas by Giovanni Bononcini and both cantatas by Antonio Maria appear to be unique to the Sondershausen manuscripts. The remaining cantatas by Giovanni, like those in the Modenese collection, circulated rather widely and cannot at this time be traced with any certainty to Viennese origins.[42] The only cantata by Astorga in Sondershausen, *Palpitar già sento il core,* can be found in at least five additional manuscripts, none in Austria.[43] The cantata by Fiorè may well be an unicum.

Three manuscripts purchased by Duke Anton Ulrich von Meiningen may contain cantatas composed for Vienna during the period 1700–1712. These manuscripts (D-MEIr, Ed 82, Ed 109i = 82c, and Ed 123m = 82d) were copied well before the duke arrived in Vienna in 1725; they preserve cantatas by Ariosti, Astorga, Badia, possibly Giovanni Bononcini, Caldara, Colombani, Fago, Fiorè, Handel, Leporati, Mancini, Alessandro Scarlatti, and anonymous composers. The seven Badia examples in Ed 123m = 82d are concordances for cantatas in core archival copies at A-Wn. The cantatas by Ariosti and Astorga, both of whom are known to have resided in Vienna, have not turned up in Habsburg archival copies, but that does not preclude the possibility that one or more of them were composed in Vienna. *Amor che far degg'io,* a cantata attributed to Bononcini (Giovanni or Antonio Maria) in Ed 109i = 82c, is assigned to "Astorgas" in the table of contents at the end of the manuscript.[44] No Viennese concordances have been found for any of the fifteen anonymous cantatas of these manuscripts. Current research indicates that all the other composers named in these anthologies never visited or resided in Vienna.[45]

SOME SOURCES FALSELY ATTRIBUTED TO VIENNESE ORIGINS

In his study of the cantata in Vienna during the late seventeenth and early eighteenth centuries, Jakob Torbé included two collections at A-Wn that are actually not of Viennese origins: MSS 17576 and 17748. Each volume contains a total of twenty cantatas. MS 17576 preserves thirteen cantatas by Francesco Mancini, five by Giovanni Bononcini, and one each by Giuseppe Giacomo Saratelli and Gaetano Carpani. MS 17748 contains seventeen cantatas by Giovanni Bononcini and three by Handel. Torbé discusses only the cantatas by Bononcini and Mancini.

I believe that MSS 17576 and 17748 were copied in England. The coupling of Bononcini and Handel in 17748 is at least a hint of this manuscript's English origins. The combination of Bononcini and Mancini in 17576 is less helpful for establishing the manuscript's origins; however, Mancini's dramatic music enjoyed success at London as early as 1710, shortly after Bononcini's initial successes there. More conclusive evidence can be found in the sources themselves: (1) the bindings have no imprints or other evidence of Habsburg ownership; (2) the neat scribes do not belong to the familiar group of Habsburg copyists; and (3) the watermarks are of the Dutch-English types used in the early eighteenth century. A check of recent thematic indices of cantatas by Bononcini and Mancini gives details about concordances.[46] Many cantatas in 17576 and 17748 come down also in Italian manuscripts, some of which predate the English copies. In summary, then, I believe that few of the cantatas in MSS 17576 and 17748, if any, were composed for Vienna.

Torbé's tendency to include cantatas by composers such as Mancini, Lotti (A-Wn, 17638), Fiorè (A-Wn, 17567), and Gasparini (A-Wgm, VI 12322) is misleading. Documentation is lacking to support the conclusion that any of these composers resided in Vienna. Torbé points out accurately that Lotti dedicated the ornate manuscript of his *Duetti, terzetti, e madrigali a più voci* (Venice, 1703) to Leopold I.[47] He also notes that works by Mancini, Fiorè, and Gasparini were performed at Vienna in the early part of the eighteenth century. As much can be said of a host of other composers of the same generation, including Handel, Scarlatti, Pollarolo, Pistocchi, and Carlo Grossi.[48] In short, an extraordinary number of compositions of all types were dedicated to Leopold and Joseph by composers who were not active in Vienna, and the Habsburgs imported many works for performances at the imperial court. To include cantatas by composers whose main centers of activity were cities such as Venice, Mantua, and Naples in a study of the Italian cantata at Vienna ultimately weakens the effort to isolate the Viennese repertoire and to understand its significance to the evolution of the baroque cantata in general.

THE LOST SOURCES

Several libraries owned copies of early eighteenth-century Viennese cantatas that are now missing. Exemplars of Badia's *Tributi armonici* once preserved at A-Wm and D-Bsb appear to be lost. Ziani is known to have composed two *accademie* in 1707 for which no sources have been located.[49] Finally, as noted earlier in this chapter, the autograph of Ziani's *Troppo conosco, o Filli* is missing from the shelves at A-Wgm, but the copy at D-Bsb may well be the source once housed at A-Wgm.[50]

9

Style Overview

The Style Transition

The new infusion of Italian talent at the beginning of the eighteenth century completely revitalized the imperial chapel and sustained its position as one of Europe's leading centers of dramatic music.[1] For nearly forty years Antonio Draghi, Leopold's faithful servant and favored composer, had controlled the development of dramatic music, turning out works of conservative but consistent quality for countless court occasions. But Draghi's style underwent so little change that by the end of the seventeenth century Vienna had fallen behind the innovations of Venice, Rome, Naples, and other opera centers in Italy. Thus the works of the newcomers who received commissions at the turn of the eighteenth century (Badia, Ziani, the Bononcini brothers, Ariosti, and Conti) departed radically from the middle baroque style that had become so firmly rooted in Austria. In comparing the dramatic music of the earliest of the newcomers, Carlo Agostino Badia, with the late operas of Draghi, Egon Wellesz observed that it is difficult to believe that the two men were actually contemporaries.[2] In Vienna there was not really an evolution to late baroque style, there was simply a sudden break with the older tradition.

Draghi's age and waning productivity were certainly reasons for the importation of new talent, but the growing number of occasions honored with performances of dramatic music and the rising influence of the archdukes Joseph and Charles were equally important factors. Beginning in 1659 the birthdays of the emperor and empress dowager were celebrated annually with performances. In 1678 these occasions were supplemented with the name days of the emperor, empress, and empress dowager. Ten years later performances were added for the birthdays of the empress and the archduke Joseph.[3] Gradually other dates in the lives of Habsburgs (Joseph's name day, the birthday and name day of the empress, Amalia Wilhelmina, and the birthdays and name days of the future emperor and empress, Charles and Elizabeth Christina) were included in the list of occasions honored annually. The Habsburgs also commissioned works for special events such as betrothals, marriages, the celebration of an Austrian military victory, and the return of an emperor from a journey.

Although the new group of Italian composers was to some extent influenced by developments in Venice, it is more appropriate to speak of a "northern Italian circle of composers working in Vienna" than a strictly Venetian contingent. Secular dramatic music in Vienna served exclusively as entertainment for the imperial court and the aristocracy. In this respect, operas composed for Vienna more closely resembled dramatic works written for courts in Mantua, Modena, and Rome than those produced in Venice, where a general audience attended performances in public opera houses. A composer in Vienna was commissioned to write an opera for the celebration of a specific occasion, and his work paid homage to a member of the Habsburg family. Thus, an opera performed in Vienna often contained hidden references to members of the court and always concluded with a *licenza*, which specifically paid tribute to the honored person. This practice corresponded to the tradition of northern Italian courts, from which the Habsburgs drew most of their composers until the end of the baroque era. In matters of style, however, Venice remained most influential. This is apparent in the operas of Viennese composers at the turn of the eighteenth century from their use of more varied instrumentation, the clear division of recitative and aria, the role of the bass line, and the structural details of the aria. Many features that had already become established in Venice by the 1680s did not appear regularly in Viennese dramatic music until after 1700.

In comparing secular dramatic music of the first decade of the eighteenth century with Draghi's oeuvre, perhaps the most immediately noticeable advances can be found in the increased importance and variety of the orchestration. The younger composers call for many more specific instruments, write more idiomatically for strings and winds, provide written-out ritornellos, give more details of dynamics and phrasing, and enrich their works with a variety of special effects. Concertino/ripieno and solo/tutti contrasts first appear in Badia's opera *Le gare dei beni* (25 July 1700), and they remained popular devices throughout the reign of Joseph. Giuseppe Torelli sojourned in Vienna from December 1699 until March 1700 and may have influenced Badia and other Viennese composers with regard to concerto contrasts, but these contrasts were already familiar to Modenese and Bolognese composers such as the Bononcini brothers and Ariosti. The contrasts are used in instrumental movements and aria accompaniments not only of operas and oratorios but also of cantatas, especially those by Antonio Maria Bononcini. After 1700 a far greater number of opera and cantata arias include obbligato and concertizing instrumental parts. Usually the obbligato parts and the bass line have a clear thematic relationship with the vocal part, a characteristic of late baroque Venetian opera. Imitation and echo devices become regular features of part writing.

Structurally, the late baroque Viennese operas and cantatas incorporate the clear division of recitative and aria that had already become established in northern

Italy by the last decades of the seventeenth century. The da capo aria, with clear tonal relationships, reigns supreme in Vienna after 1700. The use of a *Devise* at the beginning of the A section of a da capo aria occurs less frequently than in arias by contemporary Venetian composers.[4]

A careful scrutiny of cantatas by Badia, Ziani, Ariosti, and the Bononcini brothers reveals many differences in the five composers' styles. To speak, therefore, of a unified "Viennese cantata style" or of a "Viennese school" greatly oversimplifies the complex musical scene that existed in Vienna at the turn of the eighteenth century. Composers who wrote cantatas for the Habsburg court came from diverse centers such as Venice, Modena, Bologna, and Rome. In this chapter, references to the "Viennese composers" or the "Viennese cantata" should not be construed to mean that a circle of composers developed a style unique to Vienna. Perhaps the single characteristic that most distinguishes cantatas in Vienna from cantatas written elsewhere in Europe is the tendency to include obbligato instruments more frequently and to use larger groups of instruments in general.[5] This feature may be attributed in part to the unusually large number of players available to Habsburg court composers. Thus I have used terms such as the "Viennese cantata composers" as conveniences to describe a group of men working in the same location during the same years.

If few indigenous Viennese traits can be isolated in them, the general characteristics of the 104 works pertinent to this study can nevertheless be summarized. In the following overview, I deal only with basic features such as the broad structural plans, the selection of voices and instruments, and the recitative style. In chapters 10 through 12 I discuss in detail several aspects of the cantata that provide insight into the styles of the individual composers. In the captions for music examples, the cantata numbers refer to the serial numbers given in appendix A, while the roman numerals designate arias or vocal ensembles within cantatas.

Broad Structural Plans

The cantatas of the Draghi generation consisted of a free intermingling of recitative, arioso, and aria. In the first decade of the eighteenth century, the structure of the cantata evolved into a fixed pattern of alternating recitatives and arias.[6] The first movement of a cantata may be either a recitative or an aria. Of the 104 cantatas analyzed here, 56 begin with an aria, while the remaining 48 open with a recitative. No cantata concludes with a recitative. The number of arias usually varies from two to four, though seven exceptionally long cantatas contain between six and sixteen arias. Table 9.1 summarizes the patterns of recitative and aria found in ninety-seven of the early eighteenth-century Viennese cantatas.

The placement of two arias in succession can be found in only four cantatas (including Ziani's *L'Ercole vincitor,* discussed below). Of these, the cantata written

TABLE 9.1. PATTERNS OF RECITATIVE AND ARIA

PATTERN	BADIA	ZIANI	ARIONTI	G. BONONCINI	A. M. BONONCINI	ANON.	TOTAL
A–R–A	17	0	16	1	3	0	37
R–A–R–A	14	0	6	3	3	0	26
A–R–A–R–A	8	1	0	1	1	1	12
R–A–R–A–R–A	9	1	1	0	4	0	15
A–R–A–R–A–R–A	1	0	0	0	0	0	1
R–A–R–A–R–A–R–A	3	0	0	0	1	0	4
A–R–A–R–A–R–A–R–A–R–A	0	1	0	0	0	0	1
R–A–R–A–R–A–R–A–R–A–R–A	0	1	0	0	0	0	1

TABLE 9.2. UNUSUAL PATTERNS OF RECITATIVE AND ARIA

PATTERN	TITLE	COMPOSER
A–A–R–A	*Vorrei, pupille belle*	A. M. Bononcini
A–R–A–A–R–A	*S'una volta io potrò*	Badia
A–R–A–A–R–A–R–A–R–A–A–R–A–R–A–R–A–A	*Alli giusti miei lamenti*	Anon.

for the accession of Joseph I, *Alli giusti miei lamenti,* is special not only because of the juxtaposition of arias but also because of its unusual length.

For the opening movement of *Vorrei, pupille belle,* Antonio Bononcini constructed a highly unusual design. It unfolds much like a da capo aria, but the central section consists entirely of *recitativo semplice.* The outer sections proceed in a strict meter ($\frac{3}{4}$) and tempo (largo) with the accompaniment of two violins and continuo. The use of recitative within this piece softens the subsequent effect of juxtaposing two arias. The two successive arias at the center of Badia's *S'una volta io potrò* contrast sharply in tempo and meter. The most unconventional overall scheme occurs in the anonymous cantata *Alli giusti miei lamenti,* written for the coronation of Joseph I. Here the first aria (da capo) is repeated in its entirety after a recitative; only a ritornello separates the repetition from the next new aria (also da capo), which also recurs after an intervening recitative. (The two arias thus account for the first four arias in the diagram given in table 9.2.) The composer inserted only an instrumental ritornello between arias 6 and 7; likewise, arias 10 and 11 are divided by a brief instrumental passage, not by a recitative. Another special feature of this cantata is the concluding chorus (thirty-six measures), one of only two examples found in the Viennese cantatas of this generation.

The formal plans of four grand cantatas composed for the name days of members of the Habsburg family merit special consideration. Except for a single ritornello, Badia's brilliant showpiece *La Pace, e Marte supplicanti* (for Archduke Joseph, 1701) includes no independent instrumental music and is comprised of six arias and a final duet interspersed with recitatives in the pattern A–R–A–R–A–R–A–R–A–R–A–R–Duet. Antonio Bononcini's *La Fortuna, il Valore, e la Giustitia* (for Charles III, 1706) is only slightly more complex; after an *ouverture*, it consists of seven arias and a final trio arranged in the comprehensive scheme R–A–R–A–R–A–R–A–R–A–R–A–R–A–R–Trio. Rather more complex patterns are found in Ziani's *L'Ercole vincitor* (for Joseph I, 1706) and Badia's *Il sacrificio di Berenice* (for Elizabeth Christina, 1712). Ziani's homage to Joseph opens with a sinfonia, followed by sixteen arias and three duets, alternating in the following configuration: A–R–A–R–Duet–R–A–A–R–A–R–A–R–Duet–R–A–A–R–A–R–A–R–A–R–A–R–Duet–A–R–A–R–A–R–A. The eighth aria consists of two strophes, with binary ritornellos at the beginning and after each strophe. Badia also introduces *Il sacrificio di Berenice* with a sinfonia, then proceeds with a combination of fifteen arias and a final four-part chorus: R–A–R–A–R–A–R–A–R–A–R–A–R–A–R–A–R–A–R–A–R–A–R–A–R–A–R–A–Chorus. The ninth aria is actually a series of five strophes sung in succession by soprano (Arsinoe), alto (Tolomeo), soprano (Berenice), tenor (Conone), and soprano (Arsinoe) in the formal design ABACA; the first and final strophes have identical words and music. The thirteenth aria draws upon minuet form; it begins with a ritornello followed by the same music with text, which is repeated *piano;* the second half of the minuet includes no ritornello but provides the expected repeat. The ensuing purely instrumental minuet adheres to the basic binary structure.

Independent instrumental movements contribute to the broad outlines of twenty cantatas. (The patterns of recitative and aria shown above do not take these instrumental pieces into account.) Of the five composers, only Ariosti never includes separate instrumental music in his cantatas. Not surprisingly, the instrumental movements always occur in cantatas with obbligato or concertizing parts. They consist of introductions—brief or fairly extended—and of ritornellos inserted between vocal movements.

Ten cantatas begin with instrumental introductions, for which the composers use terms such as *sinfonia* (the anonymous *Cetre amiche,* Badia's *Il sacrificio di Berenice,* Ziani's *Ahimè, ch'io son piagato,* and the same composer's *L'Ercole vincitor*); *preludio* (Giovanni Bononcini's *Clori, svenar mi sento* and Antonio Bononcini's *Ecco Amor*); *ouverture* (Antonio Bononcini's *La Fortuna, il Valore, e la Giustitia*); and *entré* (Badia's *Qui fra l'ombre*). The manuscripts for two cantatas (Badia's *Scesa dal ciel* and Ziani's *Cieco fanciul*) do not provide genre designations for the instrumental openings.

The designs of the introductions vary considerably. Instrumental pieces in only one movement initiate two cantatas by Badia and one by Antonio Bononcini. The opening of Badia's *Qui fra l'ombre* uses homophonic texture and a binary structure, while his introduction to *Scesa dal ciel* and Antonio's *preludio* for *Ecco Amor* are imitative and through-composed. The instrumental openings of five cantatas are divided into two movements, probably showing the influence of the French overture. The anonymous *Cetre amiche* begins with a movement in cut time that has many phrase repetitions but no conventional design; it continues with an imitative section in $\frac{3}{4}$ that is repeated. Ziani's *Ahimè, ch'io son piagato* starts with a binary Andante in $\frac{4}{4}$ and concludes with an imitative Allegro in the same meter. The introduction to Giovanni Bononcini's *Clori, svenar mi sento* consists of two binary movements, a stately Largo with frequent dotted notes and a dance-like Presto in $\frac{3}{8}$. Antonio Bononcini's *La Fortuna, il Valore, e la Giustitia* begins with a Largo in cut time and continues with a movement in *tempo giusto* and common time. Curiously, the sinfonia at the beginning of Badia's *Il sacrificio di Berenice* reverses the usual format of the French overture; the opening imitative movement in common time and marked Allegro, e presto is followed by an Adagio with dotted rhythms. Of all the cantata composers of this generation, only Ziani chooses three-movement introductions, namely, for *Cieco fanciul* and for *L'Ercole vincitor*. The three-movement introduction to *Cieco fanciul* opens with a binary Allegro in $\frac{4}{4}$, proceeds with a Larghetto cantabile also in $\frac{4}{4}$, and closes with a ternary (ABA) Allegro in $\frac{3}{8}$. The sinfonia of *L'Ercole vincitor* commences with a binary Allegro, continues with a highly ornamental Grave, and concludes with a fugal Allegro in four parts.

Brief instrumental ritornellos, separated from surrounding vocal movements by double bars, occur in nineteen cantatas by Badia, Ziani, Antonio Bononcini, and the two anonymous composers. These ritornellos make use of the full instrumental ensembles. In eleven cantatas (six by Antonio, four by Badia, and one by an anonymous composer), instrumental ritornellos appear only once. Antonio particularly prefers positioning this tutti ritornello just before the final recitative and aria. Badia favors a single tutti ritornello at the center or end of a long cantata. In two works he introduces separate instrumental ritornellos twice, using two different plans: (1) A–R–A–Rit.–R–A–Rit.; and (2) Rit.–R–A–R–A–R–A–Rit. The two *accademie* by Ziani, Antonio Bononcini's *La Fortuna, il Valore, e la Giustitia*, Badia's *Il sacrificio di Berenice*, and the anonymous *Alli giusti miei lamenti* include from four to nine ritornellos inserted at points throughout the cantatas. Ziani provides no fewer than thirteen independent ritornellos for the lengthy grand cantata *L'Ercole vincitor*. He also calls for an independent passage of lute arpeggios over a bass line with detailed figuration, a unique example in the cantata repertoire of this period. Thematic material of a separate ritornello is almost always derived from the preceding aria. The fuller instrumentation of the ritornello often contrasts with the simpler continuo accompaniment of the aria. If the aria itself contains a recurring continuo ritornello, this may be omitted at the conclusion and replaced by the tutti ritornello.

TABLE 9.3. VOCAL RANGES OF CANTATAS FOR VIENNA

RANGES	NO. OF CANTATAS	BADIA	ZIANI	ARIOSTI	G. BONONCINI	A. M. BONONCINI	ANON.
S	68	43	2	12	4	7	0
A	23	5	0	11	1	6	0
T	2	1	0	0	0	0	1
SS	5	41	0	0	0	0	
TB	1	1	0	0	0	0	0
SSA	1	1	0	0	0	0	0
SST	1	0	0	0	0	0	1
SAB	1	0	0	0	0	1	0
SSAT	1	1	0	0	0	0	0
SSATB	1	0	1	0	0	0	0

TABLE 9.4. CANTATAS WITH OBBLIGATO INSTRUMENTS

COMPOSER	NO. OF CANTATAS	NO. WITH OBBLIGATI	% WITH OBBLIGATI
Badia	55	15	27
Ariosti	23	2	9
A. M. Bononcini	14	14	100
G. Bononcini	5	1	20
Ziani	5	3	60
Anonymous	2	2	100

SELECTION OF VOICES

Ninety-three of the 104 cantatas from this period are written for solo voice; six works require two singers, three compositions call for three, one requires four, and one expands the number of singers to five. In addition, *Alli giusti miei lamenti,* the three-voiced cantata written for the accession of Joseph I in 1705, concludes with a five-part chorus. As in Italy, the selection of voices at Vienna reveals a great preference for high ranges, particularly soprano. Table 9.3 provides details about the voices used in these 104 cantatas written for Vienna.

INSTRUMENTATION

The accompaniments for 67 of the 104 cantatas consist of continuo only. Thus, more than a third of the cantatas include parts for one or more obbligato instruments. Not all the composers consistently require additional instruments. Antonio Bononcini, for example, always writes obbligato parts, while Ariosti requests an additional instrumental line for only two arias from two individual cantatas. Table 9.4 reviews the number of cantatas by each composer and indicates the percentage with obbligato instruments.

TABLE 9.5. OBBLIGATO INSTRUMENTS OF CANTATAS FOR VIENNA

OBBLIGATO INSTRUMENTS	NO. OF CANTATAS	BADIA	ZIANI	ARIOSTI	G. BONONCINI	A. M. BONONCINI	ANON.
fl 1–2	12	5	0	0	1	6	0
vl 1–2	6	3	0	0	0	5	0
vl 1–2, vla	3	1	0	0	0	1	1
fl 1–2, vl 1–2	2	2	0	0	0	0	0
instrument in soprano clef (vla d'amore?)	2	0	0	2	0	0	0
vl 1–2, vla, ob 1–2, bn	2	0	1	0	0	1	0
vl 1–2, vla, bn	1	0	1	0	0	0	0
vl 1–2, vla, ob 1–2, bn, lute	1	0	1	0	0	0	0
vl 1–2, vla, tr	1	1	0	0	0	0	0
instrument in treble clef (fl?)	1	1	0	0	0	0	0
vlc?	1	1	0	0	0	0	0
unison vl	1	0	0	0	0	0	1
unison lutes	1	1	0	0	0	0	0
2 treble instruments	1	1	0	0	0	0	0
vl 1–2, vlc	1	0	0	0	0	1	0
2 instruments in soprano clef, 1 in alto clef	1	1	0	0	0	0	0

Making use of the broad assortment of players at the Habsburg court, the composers scored the cantatas for a colorful variety of instruments. Table 9.5 specifies the types of obbligato instruments, the number of cantatas in which each combination appears, and the composers who used each combination.

For the first movement of *Un guardo solo, o bella*, Badia divides the bass line between a simple part and a more elaborate one evidently intended for cello obbligato. The unspecified treble parts in Badia's *Scesa dal ciel* may be either for two flutes or for two violins, the paired obbligati favored by the composer elsewhere. The absence of clearly idiomatic figurations for flute or violin makes it difficult to determine the exact instrumentation. Badia also fails to stipulate which instruments he wishes to play the treble line in the *entré* [sic] of *Qui fra l'ombre* or the three upper parts (two in treble clef, one in alto) in *I sospiri dell'aure*, two of seven cantatas by the composer in A-Wn, 17721. The emphasis on flutes in other cantatas of this manuscript gives some weight to the conjecture that flutes also participated in *Qui fra l'ombre* and *I sospiri dell'aure*. Paired violins and viola could also have been used for the latter cantata, providing a homogeneous sonority; string and woodwind doublings were also common.

Ariosti also does not designate the instrument for the single obbligato line in *Furie che negl'abissi* or in *Che mi giova esser regina*. Curiously, in each cantata he notates the obbligato in soprano clef and places it below the vocal line, adding the rubric "si suona" for the second aria of *Furie che negl'abissi*. These procedures are unique in the Viennese cantata repertoire, and they suggest that the obbligati were not intended for one of the standard treble instruments—violin, flute, or oboe. The composer may well have written these parts for the viola d'amore, an instrument on which he excelled as a player himself. (For this instrument he definitely composed the obbligato line in *Pur alfin gentil viola*, a cantata not written for Vienna.) The obbligato lines in the two Viennese cantatas largely lack idiomatic figurations that would help to identify the instruments, though the line in *Furie che negl'abissi* includes many melodic sixths that suggest string crossings. The range extends from f♯[1] to g[2] in *Che mi giova* and from a[1] to g[2] in *Furie che negl'abissi;* thus its lower limit remains well within the normal compass of the viola d'amore, whose lower strings were seldom used by eighteenth-century composers. Especially unusual, however, is the use of the soprano clef; composers customarily notate viola d'amore parts in alto clef. Yet the composer's long association with the instrument and the inclusion of viola d'amore obbligati in at least two contemporary Viennese operas (Fux's *Gli ossequi della notte*, 1709, and Ariosti's own *Marte placato*, 1707) support the conclusion that he intended viola d'amore also in the cantatas.[7]

The manuscript of Giovanni Bononcini's *Clori, svenar mi sento* likewise leaves some questions about what instruments should play the upper parts. For the two treble lines of the *preludio* the composer designates no instruments. However, he specifies *flauto solo* for the obbligato of the first aria. Like the *preludio,* the second aria requires two upper parts, but Bononcini again does not indicate what instruments are to play them. At two points during this aria, the lower obbligato line drops out while the upper line (marked "solo") continues; when the second line resumes, the parts are labeled "tutti." By tutti Bononcini may simply have wished to draw attention to the resumption of both lines. It is also plausible that violins doubled flutes and that the solo passages were to be performed by the flute soloist of the first aria.

If a cantata begins with an instrumental introduction, the noncontinuo instruments almost always reappear as obbligati in arias and sometimes also in tutti ritornellos. The exception to this practice is Badia's *Qui fra l'ombre;* here the instrumental opening calls for one treble instrument and continuo, but throughout the remainder of the cantata no obbligato line occurs. Perhaps the instrumentalist of the introduction improvised obbligati above the bass-line ritornellos of the arias. The exceptionally rudimentary bass lines of these ritornellos make the addition of obbligati likely. Only a few years earlier, during the last years of Draghi's tenure, scribes frequently wrote out only the bass lines of ritornellos, indicating that obbligato parts should be filled in. Moreover, the preceding cantata in A-Wn, 17721 (*I sospiri dell'aure,* for alto, three unspecified instruments, and continuo, probably by

Badia) concludes with just such a bass ritornello, entirely separated from the final aria and inviting obbligato as well as continuo realization.

The most sumptuous orchestral accompaniments occur in works by Ziani and Antonio Bononcini, as well as the two grand cantatas by Badia. For the *prima accademia* of 1706, *Cieco fanciul,* Ziani uses first and second violins, viola, oboes, bassoon, and continuo. In the first and third movements of the introduction, he assigns the bassoon a separate part, only slightly more elaborate than the bass line. Elsewhere the bassoonist probably doubled the bass line. The oboes play an independent line only in the fifth aria. The marking "senza hautbois" for the obbligati of the first aria implies that the oboes doubled the violins in most other places. For the grand cantata *L'Ercole vincitor,* also 1706, Ziani expands the instrumental palette of *Cieco fanciul* by adding lute. Here too the composer indicates when the oboes are silent and when they double the violins. By the late baroque era, doublings by oboes and bassoons had certainly become common procedures. The sinfonia of *L'Ercole vincitor* also creates a special effect with the use of *tasto solo.* For the *seconda accademia* Ziani asks for only a slightly smaller ensemble: first and second violins, viola, bassoons, and continuo. He again provides a separate line for the bassoons, a slightly modified version of the continuo line, only in the sinfonia. The possibility that oboes doubled the violins even though they are not specified in the score cannot be excluded.

Antonio's most elaborate orchestration can be seen in *La Fortuna, il Valore, e la Giustitia* and in *Mentre al novo apparir.* Scored for first and second violins, viola, first and second oboes, unison bassoons, and *bassi,* the grand cantata demonstrates Antonio's usual attention to detail by providing numerous contrasts between "violini soli" and "tutti" (i.e., with oboes) and indicating clearly when only bassoons play the bass line. The third aria reverses the usual doubling procedure by indicating "Hautbois soli" as the obbligato instruments and "tutti" for passages to be doubled by the violins. He scores *Mentre al novo apparir* for a slightly smaller ensemble: first and second violins, cello, and continuo, specifically designated for "contrabasso e cembalo" in the opening aria with cello obbligato. An isolated example in the Viennese repertoire, Bononcini's specific reference to the double bass gives fascinating evidence of baroque continuo practices; it also suggests that the double bass may have been used in other cantatas scored for fairly large instrumental ensembles.

For the two celebratory grand cantatas, *La Pace, e Marte supplicanti* (1701) and *Il sacrificio di Berenice* (1712), Badia draws on the core string group of divided violins and violas. However, in the virtuosic earlier work he achieves a brilliant effect with the rare addition of trumpet.[8] The interplay of trumpet and vocal trills, scales, and sustained tones is especially effective in the third aria.

Solo/tutti contrasts in seven cantatas confirm the orchestral nature of the instrumentation. For example, the title page of Antonio Bononcini's *Ecco Amor* in-

TABLE 9.6. BROAD INSTRUMENTAL CONTRASTS IN THREE CANTATAS

LÀ NELL'ARABE SELVE (BADIA)

Aria 1:	fl 1–2, vl 1–2, bc
Aria 2:	solo fl, bc
Aria 3:	solo vl, bc
Aria 4:	fl 1–2, vl 1–2, bc

MENTRE AL NOVO APPARIR (A. M. BONONCINI)

Aria 1:	vl 1–2 (solo/tutti), vlc obbl, bc (cb, hpcd)
Aria 2:	bc
Rit.:	tutti
Aria 3:	vl 1–2 (4 solo vl/tutti), bc
Aria 4:	unison vl (4 solo vl/tutti), vlc obbligato, bc

CIECO FANCIUL (ZIANI)

Introduction:

	Allegro:	vl 1–2 (doubled by ob 1–2), vla, bn, bc
	Larghetto cantabile:	vl 1 (2 soloists), vl 2 (2 soloists), vla, bc
	Allegro:	vl 1–2 (ob 1–2), vla, bn, bc
Aria 1:	unison vl (without ob), vla, bc	
Rit.:	vl 1–2 (ob 1–2), vla, bc	
Aria 2:	bc	
Rit.:	vl 1–2 (ob 1–2), vla, bc	
Aria 3:	bc	
Rit.:	vl 1–2 (ob 1–2), vla, bc	
Aria 4:	bc	
Rit.:	vl 1–2 (ob 1–2), vla, bc	
Aria 5:	unison vl, unison ob, vla, bc	
Aria 6:	bc	
Rit.:	vl 1–2 (ob 1–2), vla, bc	

cludes the description "In Soprano Concertata con Violini e concerto grosso," and throughout the composition solo and tutti groupings are opposed. The composer exploits similar contrasts in the first and third arias of *Troppo rigore, Clori,* and in the third and fourth arias of *Mentre al novo apparir* he gives even more specific directions, asking for "soli quattro violini" at times during the vocal sections and "tutti" elsewhere. Ziani also specifies the precise number of violins in the middle movement of the introduction to *Cieco fanciul;* for this passage he requests two first violins and two second violins, reserving the full complement for the outer movements. For the aria accompaniments, however, he does not supply such detailed instructions. The anonymous composer of *Cetre amiche,* a cantata scored for first and second violins, viola, and continuo, contrasts "tutti" with "concertino" throughout the work. The same opposing forces are required in Badia's *Il sacrificio di Berenice.* Even more specific is the instruction found in the Adagio second movement of this grand cantata, where the composer pits a solo violin against unison tutti violins.

In the cantatas with medium or large instrumental ensembles, the composers achieve variety not only by using solo/tutti contrasts but also by changing the instrumentation from movement to movement. Badia's *Là nell'arabe selve,* Antonio Bononcini's *Mentre al novo apparir,* and Ziani's *Cieco fanciul* exemplify this type of broad instrumental contrast. (Always accompanied by continuo only, recitatives have been excluded from table 9.6.)

Idiomatic instrumental writing plays a consistently significant role only in the cantatas of Antonio Bononcini. For string obbligati such as the violin solo of *Sul margine adorato* (II) or the cello solos of *Mentre al novo apparir* (I and IV), he requires rapid string crossings, large leaps, and double stops. Badia also exploits string crossings in both grand cantatas. Trills and rapid figuration idiomatic to the flute can be seen in cantatas such as Antonio's *Tutta fiamme e tutta ardore* (II). Characteristic flute trills and scales occur, though less often, in works by Badia (*Rusignol che tempri il canto,* I) and by Giovanni Bononcini (*Clori, svenar mi sento,* II). In the third aria of *La Pace, e Marte supplicanti,* Badia clearly revels in the high range and technical potential of the trumpet. Ariosti includes oscillating patterns indicative of string crossings in the unspecified obbligato part of *Furie che negl'abissi* (II).

Antonio Bononcini also supplies markings for phrasing and articulation more frequently than his contemporaries, combining terms such as *staccato, battuto,* and *cantabile* with tempo indications. The rare designation *battuto* (strictly measured) appears twice, once at the beginning of the *preludio* for *Ecco Amor* and again for the second aria of *Sul margine adorato.* The vertical lines used often to indicate staccato in cantatas of the next generation are found here and there already in Antonio's *La Fortuna, il Valore, e la Giustitia.* At the end of the first section of the introductory Allegro of *L'Ercole vincitor,* Ziani indicates "lunga l'arcata" for the final note, and for the Grave violin figuration he suggests "arcate distese."

DYNAMICS

With few exceptions, the composers reserve dynamics for arias and vocal ensembles. The frequency and choice of markings depend upon the individual composer. Giovanni Bononcini, for example, uses no dynamics in his five Viennese cantatas, while Ariosti introduces only one *forte/piano* echo in a single cantata (*Ne spatiosi campi,* II). Ziani draws upon dynamic contrasts only slightly more often than Ariosti, and he too relies primarily upon simple echo effects. Badia especially favors the *piano* repetition of a phrase or group of phrases at the end of the A section of a da capo aria. He includes the device in at least twenty-five arias, so often, in fact, that it may be considered a hallmark of the composer's style. Occasionally he repeats the effect in the closing ritornello of an aria. Outside of echo phrases, however, dynamic shadings seldom appear in Badia's scores. An exception occurs in the first aria of *Scesa dal ciel,* where the composer designates *piano* for the obbligato instruments during fragments of the ritornello and when the tenor first enters. The sinfonia of the anonymous *Cetre amiche* contains several *pianissimo/forte* contrasts.

Virtually every cantata by Antonio Bononcini displays some dynamic shading. The composer only rarely employs the straightforward echo devices commonly found in scores of Badia or Ziani; instead, he prefers dynamic markings for structural reasons or for expressive word painting. He often sets apart the final phrase of a large vocal section by making it *piano.* Frequently the A and B sections of a da capo aria conclude with similar thematic material, and the use of a *piano* dynamic at both places subtly underscores the symmetry. Antonio sometimes varies this technique by applying it to the penultimate phrases of A and B. Cantatas with solo/tutti passages are apt to include numerous *forte/piano* markings, but the instrumental and dynamic contrasts are not necessarily coordinated. The composer often selects ritornello fragments or entire ritornellos for dynamic shadings; thus, for example, in the middle of the B section of the aria "Quanto più cara, quanto più bella" (*Mentre al novo apparir,* III) he inserts a sudden *forte,* tutti ritornello. Antonio occasionally prescribes the more extreme *pianissimo* in response to a simple *forte.* He achieves perhaps the most refined effect of the entire Viennese cantata repertoire in the initial aria of *Vorrei pupille belle.* As in many other arias, he concludes the A section with a *piano* phrase; however, he marks the beginning of the written-out da capo *piano,* saving *pianissimo* for the final phrase.

RECITATIVE AND ARIOSO

The recitatives of the Viennese cantatas exhibit the familiar traits of late baroque *recitativo semplice.*[9] Accompanied by continuo only, the vocal lines unfold in short, speech-like, syllabic phrases over largely static bass lines. A group of phrases concludes with a typical V–I or I $^6_4$–V–I formula in a new key, the continuo part cadencing immediately after the vocal line. The final group of phrases ends in a key related to the tonality of the ensuing aria, though usually not its tonic or dominant. Recitatives rarely exceed twenty bars in length. Fragments or entire sections of arioso may be interpolated or appended according to the taste of the individual composer.

Harmonically, the *recitativo semplice* features unstable chords that produce a continuous sense of forward motion toward a new cadential formula. Thus, first-inversion chords outnumber triads in root position, and dominant sevenths in first and, more especially, in third inversion are common. Typically, a recitative opens with a long tonic pedal over which the dominant seventh, its inversions, and the leading-tone triad are sounded. The composers thus delight in the dissonant effect of the leading tone against the tonic. Melodically, the vocal line proceeds mostly by step and small skips, with occasional affective leaps such as the diminished fourth and the diminished seventh.

To these general observations some specific remarks about the recitatives of each composer can be added. Ariosti's rarely depart from the conventional style. He consistently begins an initial recitative with V^7/I and often introduces an interior recitative with a first-inversion chord. Modulations using $V\,{}^4_2$ chords occur so frequently that they become clichés; somewhat fewer examples of $V\,{}^6_5$ can be found. Ariosti includes expressive melodic diminished fourths but seldom exploits melodic sevenths. Equally rare are chromatic bass lines.

Badia elicits all the stock harmonic techniques, favoring the $V\,{}^4_2$ and diminished-seventh chords. He writes very slow-moving bass lines that frequently settle on a single tone for four or five bars. The key rhythm also tends to proceed slowly. He includes some daring melodic leaps, especially ascending minor ninths and major sevenths that create emphatic dissonances with the bass line.

Ziani prefers more stable harmonies than his contemporaries. He chooses more plain, root-position triads and writes fewer $V\,{}^4_2$ chords. When using the dominant seventh, he customarily places it in root position or first inversion. He tends also to be more conservative melodically; affective intervals occur sparsely, though a rare descending diminished seventh occurs in at least one recitative.

Giovanni Bononcini often opens with a stable, root-position triad but thereafter favors quick harmonic changes and key rhythm. He writes long, directional bass lines, especially in ascending patterns. The composer often achieves forward motion by writing modulations that ascend by steps—from c minor to d minor, for example, or from D major to E major. Giovanni also draws upon coloristic chords like the Neapolitan sixth and the diminished seventh. Affective leaps encompass not only the customary diminished fourth and diminished seventh but also more unusual intervals like the diminished third.

Antonio Bononcini's recitatives contain many of the conventional formulas, though he notates fewer dominant sevenths over tonic pedals than Ariosti, for example. A common progression consists of the dominant seventh followed immediately by the dominant seventh (or its inversion) of the relative key. Descending modulations using a series of $V\,{}^4_2$–I^6 chords often lead rapidly from one tonality to another. The composer also explores some more adventurous harmonic routes. In the *recitativo semplice* that forms the B section of the opening aria of *Vorrei, pupille belle,* he shifts abruptly from f minor to e minor. In the final six bars of the second recitative of *Sopra l'orme d'Irene,* he moves rapidly through a succession of seven keys: D major, G major, A major, D major, f♯ minor, b minor, and C major. Antonio's harmonic vocabulary also embraces unexpected resolutions of the diminished-seventh chord.

TABLE 9.7. MAJOR KEYS USED IN CANTATA ARIAS

COMPOSER	TOTAL ARIAS	NO. IN MAJOR	E♭	B♭	F	C	G	D	A	E
Badia	155	96	0	16	15	12	17	15	19	2
Ariosti	48	23	0	3	9	1	2	4	4	0
A. M. Bononcini	41	19	0	6	6	1	2	1	3	0
Ziani	33	21	1	4	2	4	2	4	4	0
G. Bononcini	11	4	0	2	0	0	0	0	2	0
Anonymous	12	8	0	2	0	2	1	1	2	0
Totals	300	171	1	33	32	20	24	25	34	2

To varying degrees the composers insert arioso passages within their recitatives. Giovanni Bononcini includes no ariosi, and his brother mostly, though not entirely, avoids this style. Ziani appends an arioso in strict tempo to only one recitative. Badia composes ariosi more often than Ziani or Antonio Bononcini, but Ariosti is the only composer who uses them regularly. His ariosi also tend to be more elaborate and florid than those of his contemporaries.

The dimensions and complexity of the ariosi also vary considerably. They range from entire separate movements to brief cadential flourishes. In general, the ariosi can be classified under five headings:

1. Complete, self-contained movements

   These are distinct from actual arias because they are shorter and not cast in da capo, binary, strophic, or another conventional design. A clear example occurs just before the final (second) aria of Ariosti's *È pur dolce a un cor legato.* The composer actually designates the fifteen-bar passage as an "aria," but it consists only of a brief sequential statement in two segments. A similar nineteen-bar arioso, in $\frac{3}{2}$, follows the first recitative of Ariosti's *L'idol mio de' pianti miei,* though here the composer does not use the term *aria.* The seventh cantata in Badia's print, *Un guardo solo, o bella,* begins with an eleven-measure arioso marked "affettuoso"; after a short *recitativo semplice* the composer reintroduces the arioso, an exact duplicate of the original. (The entire movement resembles the opening of Antonio Bononcini's *Vorrei, pupille belle;* in each example the passages in strict tempo frame a *recitativo semplice,* creating a da capo–like design. However, Badia's ariosi and recitative are much shorter than the corresponding passages by Antonio.) Badia's chamber duet *Chi brama d'amar* includes a movement for two sopranos beginning in *semplice* style but gradually becoming stricter in tempo, with florid vocal patterns and a melodic bass line.

2. Long ariosi appended to *recitativi semplici*

   The change from *semplice* style to arioso may be made clear by a specific tempo marking, a change of meter, the use of the term *a rigore,* or simply by an obvious shift to more melodic writing in both vocal and bass lines. The initial recitative of Antonio Bononcini's *Occhi, voi che mirate,* for instance, concludes with an expressive twenty-four-measure Largo in $\frac{3}{4}$. Here as elsewhere, the composer excels in chromatic harmony and melody, using them to paint the word *piangete.* The first recitative of *Se avessi in mezzo al petto* also ends with a Largo arioso, but in $\frac{4}{4}$; Antonio uses affective harmony and imitation between vocal and bass lines, but he avoids ostentatious vocal flourishes. Badia adds a nineteen-measure arioso in $\frac{3}{8}$ at the conclusion of the first recitative of *A Clori, che fra l'erbe.* To clarify the change from *semplice* style to arioso at the end of the third recitative of *Ahimè, ch'io son piagato,* Ziani instructs the performers to execute the final fifteen measures *a rigore.* The passage opens with a two-measure, bass-line ritornello; it includes imitation involving two motives but is not especially florid. Applying a similar technique at the ends of recitatives from the cantatas *Ne' spatiosi campi* and *Mi convien soffrir,* Ariosti uses the term *a tempo* to signal the beginnings of ariosi.[10]

3. Brief cadential passages in strict tempos at the ends of *semplice* sections

   These conclude many recitatives by Ariosti and Badia, especially those in the manuscripts A-Wn, 17574, 17591, and 17721. Less frequently, they occur in the final measures of recitatives by Antonio Bononcini. These final ariosi seldom last more than four or five measures, but the composers invest them with surprisingly chromatic harmony, bits of imitation, expressive leaps, and—especially Ariosti—exceedingly florid vocal patterns.

4. Brief ariosi interpolated throughout *semplice* recitatives, particularly at cadences

   The tendency to vacillate between *semplice* and arioso styles can be seen in cantatas like Ariosti's *Tante e tante del ciel* and Badia's *D'amica selva.* Ariosti again tends to incorporate more elaborate coloratura figures.

5. Melodic flourishes used primarily for word painting

   Not restricted to cadences, these ornamental figures add color and variety to the recitatives of Badia, Ariosti, and Antonio Bononcini. The long melisma on the third syllable of *gorgheggiano* in the first recitative of Badia's *Uno spirito galante* illustrates the exploitation of an obvious effect suggested by the text.

ARIA KEYS

Tables 9.7 and 9.8 summarize the keys used in arias from the Viennese cantatas. Not surprisingly, the composers neglect key signatures with dense numbers of sharps or flats. Only the single aria in E major (by Badia) is written in a key exceeding three sharps or flats. None of the arias in major keys contains a signature with more than two flats. Minor arias with signatures of one to three flats are common, but minor

TABLE 9.8. MINOR KEYS USED IN CANTATA ARIAS

COMPOSER	TOTAL ARIAS	NO. IN MINOR	C	G	D	A	E	B	F#
Badia	155	59	12	14	17	15	1	0	0
Ariosti	48	25	4	7	7	3	2	2	0
A. M. Bononcini	41	22	2	7	4	6	2	0	1
Ziani	33	12	2	2	2	1	0	5	0
G. Bononcini	11	7	0	5	2	0	0	0	0
Anonymous	12	3	0	1	0	1	1	0	0
Totals	300	128	20	36	32	26	6	7	1

TABLE 9.9. INCIDENCE OF ARIA KEYS

KEY	INCIDENCE	% OF TOTAL ARIAS	% OF INDIVIDUAL COMPOSERS' OUTPUTS					
			ARIOSTI	BADIA	ZIANI	G. BONONCINI	A. M. BONONCINI	ANON.
g minor	36	12.0	15	9	6	45	17	8
A major	34	11.4	8	12	12	18	7	17
B♭ major	33	11.0	6	10	12	18	15	17
d minor	32	10.7	15	11	6	18	10	0
F major	32	10.7	9	10	6	0	15	0
a minor	27	9.0	6	10	3	0	15	17
D major	25	8.4	8	10	12	0	2	8
G major	24	8.0	4	11	6	0	5	8
c minor	20	6.7	8	8	6	0	5	0
C major	20	6.7	2	8	12	0	2	17
b minor	7	2.3	4	0	15	0	0	0
e minor	6	2.0	4	.7	0	0	5	8
E major	2	.6	0	.1	0	0	0	0
f# minor	1	.4	0	0	0	0	2	0
E♭ major	1	.4	0	0	3	0	0	0

arias with sharp signatures occur infrequently. The keys with no sharps or flats (C major and a minor) appear noticeably less often than tonalities such as g minor, d minor, F major, A major, and B♭ major. Antonio Bononcini composed the only aria in f# minor, a rather unusual key in the early eighteenth century.

Table 9.9 lists the keys in order of the number of occurrences in the cantata repertoire. Major arias outnumber minor arias by 171 (57 percent) to 129 (43 percent). Nevertheless, the composers frequently draw upon keys such as g minor and d minor. The Bononcini brothers particularly favor g minor. In the 1742 translation (*Observations on the Florid Song*) of Pier Francesco Tosi's *Opinioni de' cantori antichi e moderni* (1723), J. E. Galliard cited "Bononcini," along with Scarlatti, Gaspa-

TABLE 9.10. TEMPO MARKINGS USED FOR ARIAS

TEMPO	ARIOSTI	BADIA	ZIANI	G. BONONCINI	A. M. BONONCINI	ANON.	TOTAL	% OF 300 ARIAS
[none]	28	92	7	3	2	11	143	47.8
Allegro	2	26	16	0	2	1	47	15.7
Andante	1	6	3	0	9	0	19	6.4
Largo/larghetto	10	4	2	0	2	0	18	6
Adagio	3	11	0	2	0	0	16	5.3
Vivace	3	0	2	2	7	0	14	4.7
Affettuoso	0	5	0	1	5	0	11	3.7
Spiritoso/con spirito	0	0	1	2	7	0	10	3.3
Presto	1	3	2	1	0	0	7	2.3
Cantabile	0	1	0	0	5	0	6	2
Non presto/non troppo presto	0	4	0	0	0	0	4	1.3
Tempo giusto	0	0	1	0	2	0	3	1
Alla francese	0	1	0	0	0	0	1	.3
Minuet	0	1	0	0	0	0	1	.3

rini, and Mancini, as one of the composers intended by Tosi when the Italian writer spoke of "the best that [are] now living."[11] During the years 1705–11, Tosi worked at the Habsburg court with the Bononcini brothers, and he was undoubtedly well acquainted with their music. In his 1723 treatise he deplored the more recent trend of "the moderns" to avoid arias in minor keys (those that "have not the *Sharp* third"), in slow tempos, and in "pathetick" style.[12] These features can be found in a high percentage of arias by the Bononcinis and may well account for Tosi's admiration for the music of "Bononcini."

CONTINUUM (TEMPO/METER)

The cantata composers use a rich variety of tempos and meters.[13] Table 9.10 inventories the tempo markings given for arias, but does not include those for ariosi and instrumental movements. The list does not account for all slight modifications of basic tempo markings; these have been included in the totals for the standard terms. If a tempo consists of two common designations (e.g., andante e allegro; affettuoso e adagio), then I have recorded it under the first. Antonio Bononcini likes to combine a tempo indication with an instruction for articulation, using pairings such as affettuoso e staccato, andante e staccato, and spiritoso e battuto. To strengthen a particular tempo marking, Ariosti sometimes presents it twice at the beginning of an aria—for example, largo largo and adagio adagio to mean very

TABLE 9.11. METERS USED FOR ARIAS

METER	ARIOSTI	BADIA	ZIANI	G. BONONCINI	A. M. BONONCINI	ANON.	TOTAL	% OF 300 ARIAS
$\frac{4}{4}$	24	76	17	6	22	6	151	50.5
$\frac{3}{4}$	9	38	7	3	9	2	68	22.7
$\frac{3}{8}$	5	18	7	2	3	1	36	12
$\frac{12}{8}$	3	7	2	0	4	0	16	5.3
$\frac{6}{8}$	2	8	0	0	1	2	13	4.3
$\frac{2}{2}$	3	2	1	0	1	0	7	2.3
$\frac{2}{4}$	0	5	0	0	1	0	6	2
$\frac{3}{2}$	2	0	0	0	0	1	3	1

broad and very slow, respectively. For a similar purpose, Badia and the anonymous composer of *Cetre amiche* add assai after allegro in four arias. Composers also occasionally qualify a familiar tempo with a negative description such as non molto allegro (Ziani), allegro ma non presto (Badia), andante e non presto (Badia), and non troppo presto (Badia). Antonio Bononcini is the only composer to invoke the terms *cantabile* and *tempo giusto*. Unique in the cantata repertoire, Badia's isolated use of the term *alla francese* presents an interesting conundrum. In chapter 6, I noted French influence in Vienna, especially with regard to ballet music, the preference for the French overture, and the occasional use of choruses in large dramatic works. The term *air en rondeau* also appears rarely in operas written for Vienna—in Ariosti's *Marte placato* (1707), for example. However, the second aria of Badia's cantata *Non so se più mi piace,* marked "alla francese," does not differ structurally or stylistically from the composer's other da capo arias. His use of alla francese may refer to an aspect of performance practice, but for the present, the composer's precise intention remains unclear.

A survey of meter used in arias is given in table 9.11. Already noted with respect to the cantatas of the late seventeenth century, the trend toward choosing the quarter note rather than the half note as the basic value for the beat becomes even more decisive in the first decade of the eighteenth century. Old-fashioned by the turn of the century, meters like $\frac{3}{2}$ appear in only a tiny portion of the arias. Nearly three-fourths of all the arias involve standard modern meters such as $\frac{4}{4}$ and $\frac{3}{4}$, though composers seldom select $\frac{2}{4}$. Increasingly popular are quick arias with the eighth note representing one beat.

Only six of the three hundred arias include sudden changes of tempo and/or meter. Giovanni Bononcini contrasts the $\frac{4}{4}$ A section of the second aria of *Or nel bosco* with a B section in $\frac{3}{8}$. In the first aria of *Sento dentro del petto,* he uses the same two meters, coordinating them with the tempo markings adagio and vivace. Ariosti contrasts an opening vivace in $\frac{3}{4}$ with a central adagio in $\frac{3}{2}$ during the first aria of *Quando Nice era fida.* The second aria of his *Ne spatiosi campi,* not a da capo,

TABLE 9.12. THE USE OF THE *DEVISE* IN VIENNESE ARIAS

COMPOSER	TOTAL ARIAS	NO. WITH *DEVISEN*	% WITH *DEVISEN*
Ariosti	48	31	65
Badia	155	23	15
A. M. Bononcini	41	2	5
G. Bononcini	11	0	0
Ziani	33	7	21
Anonymous	12	7	58

contains a central two-measure phrase in adagio with the same thematic material found in the longer, surrounding presto sections. In the final aria of *Per te sola, Filli mia,* Badia applies a similar procedure but to a standard da capo design: an A section marked "no[n] presto" leads to an adagio B section constructed of the thematic ideas set forth in A. Badia varies both the meters and the themes between sections of the third aria of *Scesa dal ciel;* the A in $\frac{4}{4}$ is followed by a B section in $\frac{3}{8}$.

THE USE OF *DEVISEN*

None of the Viennese composers consistently includes a *Devise* at the beginning of the first vocal section of A, although Ariosti does use the device in nearly two-thirds of his arias. *Devisen* had become standard in arias by Italian composers of the late seventeenth century. Table 9.12 provides details about the percentages of arias containing *Devisen*.[14]

ARIA DESIGNS

Table 9.13 reviews the types of designs found in Viennese arias. The da capo aria, together with its variants (the modified, expanded, and miniature da capo), completely overshadows all other types.[15] In the strict da capo, the return of A simply duplicates the opening section except for the expected improvised ornaments; the da capo may or may not be written out in the manuscript. The modified da capo retains the essential ABA structure but includes either some small written-in alterations in the da capo (the omission or abbreviation of a ritornello or the condensation of a vocal section) or the replacement of an entire B section with *recitativo semplice.* Still another modification can be seen in the final aria of Giovanni Bononcini's *Or nel bosco,* which adheres to the fundamental design but involves repetition of each large section, resulting in the scheme AABBAA. The miniature da capo also displays the familiar three-part plan, but the dimensions of each section are limited to only a few measures. Occurring most often in the works of Ziani, the expanded da capo adds one or more components to the usual three sections. Ziani creates structures such as ABA¹Coda, ABA¹C, ABCA¹Coda, and ABCA¹A²Coda.

TABLE 9.13. VIENNESE ARIA DESIGNS

DESIGN	ARIOSTI	BADIA	ZIANI	G. BONONCINI	A. M. BONONCINI	ANON.	TOTAL	% OF 300 ARIAS
Da capo	41	140	26	10	38	8	263	87.7
Modified da capo	2	2	0	1	1	1	7	2.3
Two-part (AB or AA^1), no repeats	3	2	0	0	0	2	7	2.3
Two-part (AB) with repeats	0	7	1	0	0	0	8	2.7
Expanded da capo	0	0	5	0	0	0	5	1.7
Miniature da capo	0	0	1	0	2	0	3	1
Strophic/modified strophic	2	0	0	0	0	0	2	.7
Strophic; each strophe two-part, with repeats	0	1	0	0	0	0	1	.3
ABCC	0	1	0	0	0	0	1	.3
ABACA	0	1	0	0	0	0	1	.3
AABBCC^1	0	1	0	0	0	0	1	.3
Through-composed	0	0	0	0	0	1	1	.3

Strict binary arias (AB) with repeats appear only eight times and nearly always in cantatas by Badia. Two-part arias (AA^1 or AB) without repeats occur only slightly less often, in cantatas by Ariosti, Badia, and one of the anonymous composers. Three-part arias (AABBCC^1 or ABCC) not specifically related to the da capo structure can be seen in two cantatas by Badia. The strophic aria, the most popular type during the Draghi generation, nearly disappears in the first decade of the eighteenth century; Ariosti uses it, but only twice. In addition, Badia experiments once with combining the strophic principle and binary structure; each of two strophes unfolds in a clear two-part pattern with repeats. Finally, by assigning five strophes to several singers in *Il sacrificio di Berenice,* Badia creates a rounded ABACA structure.

10

Aspects of Form

In chapters 10–12 I examine in detail the style of twenty-five representative arias from Viennese chamber cantatas from the early eighteenth century.[1] The discussion focuses upon aspects of form (chapter 10); melody, harmony, and rhythm (chapter 11); and the relationship of text and music (chapter 12). The twenty-five arias represent approximately 8.5 percent of the total (three hundred) and include nine by Antonio Bononcini, five by Ariosti, five by Badia, three by Giovanni Bononcini, and three by Ziani (see table 10.1). The number by each composer reflects to a limited degree his output of cantatas for Vienna, but it is also indicative of his breadth and variety of styles. Thus, Antonio Bononcini covers a far wider range of styles and techniques in only 34 arias than Badia does in 134. The complete aria texts can be found in appendix C.

The Conventional Da Capo Design

The universal popularity of the basic da capo (ABA) plan gives the Viennese aria—as indeed the late baroque aria in general—the semblance of a stereotyped mold into which composers merely poured their ideas. However, a closer look at works by the Bononcini brothers and Ziani, for example, reveals a striking degree of originality in the treatment of the component parts of the da capo scheme. Compositional aspects such as unity, variety, scope, balance, and the coordination of structure and tonality are handled with great diversity. Nevertheless, it is possible to summarize the most basic features of the conventional, early eighteenth-century da capo aria. Among the Viennese composers, Badia tends to conform to the conventional design most often, and for this reason I have selected one of his arias ("Gelosia, furia d'Alletto" from the cantata *Qual in mar la navicella*) as a model for discussion here (see example 10.1).

"Gelosia" conveniently telescopes all the usual ingredients of the da capo aria. Clear, emphatic articulations at the ends of the A and B sections delineate the familiar ternary shape. The motivic ideas of A supply the material for development

TABLE 10.1. 1700–1712: ARIAS SELECTED FOR DETAILED ANALYSIS

COMPOSER	ARIA TEXT INCIPIT	CANTATA TEXT INCIPIT	SERIAL NO. (APP. A, CHAMBER CANTATAS)	ARIA NO. WITHIN THE CANTATA
A. M. Bononcini	"Al tuo bel volto"	Troppo rigore, Clori	98	II
	"Amore ingannatore"	Amore ingannatore	8	I
	"Benché m'abbia la cruda saetta"	Sul margine adorato	91	II
	"Men crudele e men severo"	Occhi, voi che mirate l'ardor	56	I
	"Per non arder più d'Amor"	Occhi, voi che mirate l'ardor	56	II
	"Più barbaro martire"	Mentre al novo apparir	45	I
	"Sentimi, crudo Amore"	Ecco Amor che mi segue	28	I
	"S'io ritorno a innamorarvi"	Amore ingannatore	8	II
	"Un cor più tormentato"	Tutta fiamma e tutta ardore	99	II
Ariosti	"Al voler del bene amato"	Al voler del bene amato	6	I
	"Cangi Amore sua face"	Quando Nice era fida	65	I
	"È pur dolce"	È pur dolce	29	I
	"Insoffribile tormento"	Insoffribile tormento	39	I
	"Nice crudel, perché"	O miseria d'amante core	57	I
Badia	"Basti per mio contento"	Scrive a chi la tradì	75	III
	"Gelosia, furia d'Alletto"	Qual in mar la navicella	64	II
	"Ombra del mio bel sol"	Allor che rimirava	4	II
	"Se sarai mio, io tua sarò"	A Clori, che fra l'erbe	1	III
	"Sì vaga e sì vezzosa"	Sì vaga e sì vezzosa	86	I
G. Bononcini	"Dio d'Amor, deh, mi rispondi"	Clori, svenar mi sento	22	I
	"Dolce amor che sei mia vita"	Sento dentro nel petto	82	I
	"Pena e soffri, o fido core"	Non ardisco pregarti	51	I
Ziani	"Brami e speri un vile affetto"	Cieco fanciul che in traccia	18	VI
	"Navicella che paventa"	Cieco fanciul che in traccia	18	V
	"Se infelice, se giamai"	Ahimè, ch'io son ferito/ piagato	2	II

EX. 10.1. Badia, Cantata 64/II: complete aria. Conventional da capo design.

in B, and the continuum remains the same throughout both sections.[2] The modest dimensions of the aria—a total of fifty-seven measures, including the da capo—are typical of the Viennese repertoire, and the proportions of A (twenty-four measures) and B (nine measures) reflect the general practice of giving greater weight to the opening section. Also representative of the Viennese aria is the broad tonal plan:

EX. 10.1. continued (*above and facing*)

TABLE 10.2. SYMBOLS FOR ANALYSIS

A, B, A^1	The opening section, middle section, and varied repeat of the opening of a da capo aria
1A, 2A	The first and second vocal sections of the A of a da capo aria
1B, 2B	The first and second vocal sections of the B of a da capo aria
R, R^1, R^2	The initial ritornello, its first and second variants
P	Principal thematic material
T	Transitional material
S	Secondary material
K	Closing material
N	New material
a–e	Melodic phrases
x, y, z, w	Significant melodic motives
m	Additional motive, not as important as x, y, z, or w
(a)	Derived material (indicated in parentheses)
r	Rhythm of a motive
↑ ↓	Inversions
x$^{1-2}$	Sequence (the nos. 1–2 indicating pitch variants of the original motive)
eeeee	Coloratura
vvvvv	*Fortspinnung*
L	Verse line
L1a, 1b	The first and second parts of a line
3 4	No separation in the setting of the two lines

A begins in the tonic (B♭), cadences briefly on the dominant (F) at the midpoint (measure 12), returns immediately to the tonic, and remains there until the conclusion of the section.[3] B opens in a closely related key (g, the relative minor), moves sequentially through other tonalities, settles in a second related key (c minor, the supertonic) approximately halfway through (measure 29), and continues in this key until the final cadence.

Thus the internal designs of both A and B are roughly two-part, and this binary approach is underscored not only by the tonal plan but also by the distribution of the text. In A (lines 1–2), Badia sets the first line twice at the beginning but does not return to it until the main melodic motive recurs in the tonic immediately after the central cadence on the dominant. In B (lines 3–4), the third line comes only at the beginning and again at the midpoint, where the tonality of c minor first becomes established. On the whole, the initial line of A or B is apt to be set fewer times than subsequent lines.

A few other details of the internal structure of A are also typical of many Viennese arias. A brief, four-measure ritornello at the beginning and end frames the vocal portion of the section. (In contrast, B contains no purely instrumental passages.) After the introductory ritornello, the soprano begins with a *Devise*, a single phrase separated from the singer's next entry by an abbreviated, two-measure ritor-nello. There are no further ritornellos until the concluding one, an exact duplicate of the opening statement.

The most important symbols for the discussion of variants from the conventional design and articulation of form are given in table 10.2.[4]

VARIANTS FROM THE CONVENTIONAL DESIGN

The cantata composers of the early eighteenth century created many fascinating variants from the conventional design found in Badia's "Gelosia, furia d'Alletto." The frequency and extent of the alterations vary considerably from composer to composer. Modifications include (1) expansion or compression of the usual scope; (2) departures from the customary degree of complexity; (3) large-scale changes of the da capo pattern; (4) unusual balances between A and B sections; (5) unusual modulation schemes; (6) unexpected resolutions at important structural points; (7) written-out da capos that contain more elaborate changes than the anticipated, informal vocal ornamentation; (8) special uses, modifications, or omissions of the ritornello; (9) the alteration or omission of the *Devise;* (10) the introduction of new motives in B; and (11) the tendency to use some specialized motives with, for example, transitional or closing functions.

1. Expansion or compression of the usual scope

The most prevalent change from the conventional design of the da capo aria involves its overall scope. Expansion or compression of the basic plan occurs when-ever component parts are added or subtracted. Thus, for example, Antonio Bononcini often uses a profusion of ritornellos, including them not only at the beginning and end of A but also between 1A and 2A, between 1B and 2B, and occasionally at other points. On the other hand, Ariosti sometimes omits ritornellos altogether. Frequently Antonio also writes longer vocal sections than his Viennese contemporaries; Ariosti and Badia are usually concise.

Each of the Viennese cantata composers is capable of sustaining an aria that is considerably longer than the average length of sixty to eighty measures. Giovanni Bononcini's "Pena e soffri," for example, consists of 176 measures, of which the A section alone requires 70 measures. He achieves extra length not by inserting additional ritornellos but by fleshing out the 1A and 2A sections with varied phrase repetitions and extensive roulades. He uses the same technique in the thirty-six-measure B section, where one lengthy phrase stretches to nineteen measures, culminating in a sustained f^2. From the procedures he uses for enlarging the conventional aria, Bononcini reveals his primary interest in the voice, which is evident from the extended vocal passages that account for the added length.

Ariosti seldom attempts an aria of more than 60 measures, and his 132-measure "Cangi Amore" therefore affords an interesting exception. The composer concentrates mainly upon lengthening A, which consists of fifty-nine measures. He also gives greater prominence to ritornellos than in most of his arias: the initial eight-measure ritornello is only slightly shortened in later statements, one between the *Devise* and the remainder of 1A and another at the conclusion of A. Moreover, like Giovanni Bononcini, Ariosti draws upon florid vocal writing to augment his aria; virtually every phrase in the A section of "Cangi Amore" is ornamented with sequential coloratura patterns.

Although "Cangi Amore" demonstrates Ariosti's ability to compose a piece of extended length, the vast majority of his arias display his predilection for concise, economic arias. In some instances this tendency results in arias that are considerably shorter than the conventional ones. For example, "Nice, crudel" is a tight miniature with an A containing eleven measures and a B consisting of only five. Ariosti discards all unessential or ornamental material: there are no ritornellos (except for a brief cadential figure after the *Devise* and at the end of A), and vocal coloratura is held to a minimum. He further compresses the conventional design by shortening the usual 2A and 2B sections; the customary return of line 1 at the beginning of 2A is omitted, and, similarly, the first line of B does not return to signal the beginning of a 2B section.

Like Ariosti, Badia rarely composes arias of great length, but he also does not write diminutive examples, which seem to be Ariosti's specialty. In "Se sarai mio," Badia ventures into a much longer plan than usual. The 166-measure aria is divided into a 58-measure A and a 50-measure B. Badia creates a more spacious composition by placing greater emphasis on the purely instrumental components; this approach contrasts with Giovanni Bononcini's greater stress on the vocal portions. The opening seventeen-measure ritornello is repeated in its entirety at the end of A, and an additional fifteen-measure ritornello is inserted between 1B and 2B. In all, the soprano sings in only seventy-five measures—less than half of the total.

In Ziani's "Navicella che paventa," added emphasis upon instrumental writing only partly accounts for the aria's unusual length (166 measures). Substantial ritornellos at the beginning and end of A, between 1A and 2A, and in the middle of B certainly contribute to the broader plan of the piece. Undoubtedly another factor is the aria text, a nine-line canzonetta; most aria texts consist of only four to seven lines. Ziani does not overload his melodies with coloratura patterns, but his treatment of the text is also not as syllabic as settings such as Ariosti's "Nice, crudel." The constant integration of florid passages into the vocal line increases the lengths of many phrases and thereby extends the overall dimensions of the aria.

In the cantatas of Ziani, Ariosti, Badia, and Giovanni Bononcini, long arias turn up only rarely, but in the cantatas of Antonio Bononcini, they are the norm. The continuo aria "Al tuo bel volto," for example, consists of no fewer than 218 measures in an andante tempo; if we include the separate but thematically related orchestral ritornello that follows the aria, the piece totals 237 measures, a length

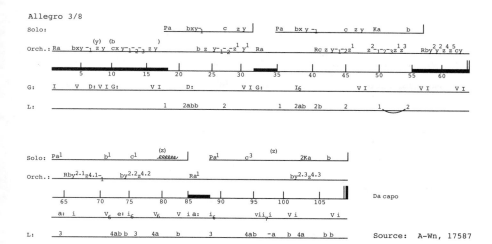

DIAGRAM 10.1. A. M. Bononcini, Cantata 95/II. An expanded da capo aria, with coda-like extensions (K) at the ends of A and B; additional ritornellos between 1A and 1B and between 1B and 2B; and a comprehensive tensional tonal plan.

that simply dwarfs many Ariosti and Badia arias. Although "Al tuo bel volto" is the longest of all the arias analyzed for this study, it is by no means an isolated example from Antonio's cantatas: "S'io ritorno innamorarvi" stretches for 194 measures, "Men crudele" for 187, and "Un cor più tormentato" for 171. In fact, arias of fewer than one hundred measures are quite rare in Antonio's cantatas.

Antonio consistently accomplishes broader dimensions than his Viennese contemporaries by using a more ambitious and sophisticated structural plan, one that approaches the grand da capo scheme of the next generation. While not all the ingredients of this design can be found in every aria, they occur with such frequency and consistency that a basic plan emerges. In its most elaborate phase, the plan considerably amplifies the conventional Viennese design through the addition of ritornellos separating 1A from 2A and 1B from 2B and of coda-like extensions at the ends of 2A and 2B.

Perhaps the clearest example of Antonio's basic structural and tonal plan is the aria "Un cor più tormentato," which includes all these elements (diagram 10.1). Particularly admirable are the clarity and balance that pervade the composer's work. The shape of the B section closely resembles the A section, excluding the opening and closing ritornellos of A. Internally, the phrase structure and other details of 2A parallel 1A, and the contours of 2B similarly correspond to 1B. Antonio reinforces the symmetry of his aria with a clear tonal plan. A modulation to the dominant (D) at the end of 1A is followed by a return to the tonic (G) in the middle ritornello of A; beginning in the supertonic (a minor), 1B moves to its dominant (e minor), then

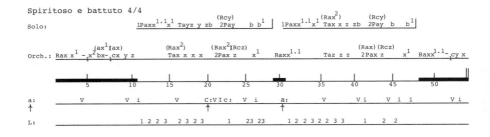

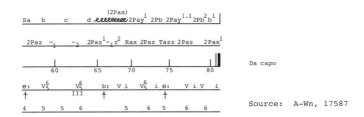

DIAGRAM 10.2. A. M. Bononcini, Cantata 56/II. A polythematic da capo aria with a tensional tonal plan in both A and B.

returns to a minor during the central ritornello. The tonality remains in this key for the rest of B. (Alternately, the first key used in B moves to its dominant but then is not heard again after 1B; instead, the composer moves on to other related keys for the remainder of B.)

Antonio subtly changes his basic design from aria to aria so that he avoids stereotypes (diagram 10.2). In the a-minor aria "Per non arder," for instance, he includes no codas at the ends of 2A and 2B, perhaps because these sections—like 1A and 1B—conclude with varied phrase repetitions that provide sufficient closing material. He also omits the ritornello between 1B and 2B. The tonal scheme of "Per non arder" closely resembles the plan used in "Un cor più tormentato," featuring a modulation to the dominant of the initial key in both A and B. Another interesting feature of "Per non arder" is the eight-measure section in C major/c minor at the end of 1A. Not only has the composer modulated here to the relative major, but he continues in the new tonality (together with its parallel minor) long enough to establish another tonal area where important motivic material is stated. This feature, which becomes standard in the grand da capo aria of the next generation, shows that Antonio was searching for a broader structural plan in which contrasting thematic material could be coordinated with opposing tonic/dominant (or relative major/minor) tonalities.

Antonio uses a similar procedure in the lengthy "Al tuo bel volto," also in a minor. Here the establishment of a new tonal area is carried out even more convincingly. In 1A, following a C-major cadence (measure 20), he writes a ten-measure ascending sequence, transitional in character and ending with another cadence in C (measure 30); a thirteen-measure passage in c minor with an important new melody follows, concluding the 1A section with a Picardy-third cadence. Extensive passages like this one give further evidence of Antonio's attempt to coordinate a broad structure with a tensional tonal plan.

In most arias Antonio is able to sustain interest because of his fertile harmonic imagination and melodic inventiveness. In "Al tuo bel volto," however, the leisurely andante tempo plus Antonio's insistence upon preserving all components of the full symmetrical scheme given in diagram 10.1 cause the aria to sprawl to extraordinary dimensions. Eventually monotony sets in: the languid opening melody returns so often that the listener's interest diminishes even before the da capo begins. Yet the aria contains many fascinating structural details. By bringing back the opening theme in the tonic key (a minor) in the middle of B (measure 112), Antonio momentarily produces a sense of false recapitulation; here the repeat of the B text clarifies the situation, and an alert listener soon realizes that the da capo has not yet begun.

2. Departures from the customary degree of complexity

Antonio Bononcini's arias surpass all other Viennese composers' not simply because of their dimensions but also because of their greater complexity, especially in their intricate motivic development, sophisticated contrapuntal techniques, rich harmonic details, and interplay of vocal and instrumental lines. Particularly fascinating is the proliferation of differential motives that are constantly varied and developed. In many arias Antonio creates a web of motives that permeate the vocal and instrumental lines; no other Viennese composer attempts such a detailed motivic fabric. His rich imagination can be seen in arias such as "S'io ritorno a innarmorarvi" (example 10.2). Here the ritornello alone contains four motives that recur throughout the aria. Antonio uses several variants of each motive. Alterations include changes in both surface rhythm and melodic profile.

In general, much of the complexity in Antonio's arias derives from the composer's greater attention to instrumental writing. His arias contain more numerous and substantial ritornellos than those of his contemporaries. Moreover, he is the only Viennese composer to include at least one obbligato instrument in every cantata. During the 1690s Antonio had played cello in orchestras in Bologna and Rome; his awareness of contemporary developments in instrumental music probably accounts for his keen interest in concertato effects. In arias like "Sentimi, crudo Amore" and "Più barbaro martire," to name only two, Antonio provides detailed indications for soli and tutti. In "Sentimi, crudo Amore," the soprano is accompanied by continuo and four-part strings (violins 1–2, viola, and cello), which are frequently divided into groups of soli and tutti; the precise instrumental markings are often coupled with specific dynamic indications, mostly *piano/forte* contrasts.

EX. 10.2. A. M. Bononcini, Cantata 8/II, mm. 1–10. The use of four distinct motives (*Pax, y, z,* and *w*) in an opening R.

In "Più barbaro martire," the accompaniment for the alto soloist consists of first and second violins (each part, solo/tutti), cello obbligato, and continuo (including double bass). Here Antonio enriches the instrumental palette not only by the basic solo/tutti contrasts he often prefers but by the addition of an elaborate cello obbligato, a further indication of concerto influence upon his style. Throughout the aria, the cello retains an independent, virtuosic motive that clearly delineates its obbligato function. The composer himself may have performed the obbligato part.

Antonio achieves greater complexity, therefore, by writing more numerous and longer ritornellos, by using solo/tutti contrasts, and by occasionally combining these procedures with an elaborate obbligato part. But the complexity stems not only from the purely instrumental sections but also from the intricate interplay of vocal and instrumental lines. In many Badia arias with obbligato instruments, the obbligati play very little during the vocal sections, or they simply echo or alternate with the voice. In most of Antonio's arias, the interrelationship of vocal and instrumental parts (including the bass line) is far more complex. For instance, in "S'io ritorno a innamorarvi," he creates a detailed concertato between alto and flute; the two parts act as equal partners, having many combinations and exchanges of motivic material.

At times the importance of the instrumental obbligato seems to overbalance the vocal line. In "Benché m'abbia la cruda saetta" the highly expressive and elaborate solo violin obbligato largely overshadows the simpler, conjunct soprano melody. Antonio's sensitivity to idiomatic string writing is abundantly clear from the sixteenth-note figuration with its frequent leaps requiring string crossings.

In other style categories, Antonio's arias also prove to be more complex than his contemporaries'. His harmonic vocabulary, for example, is the richest and most adventurous. Details of Antonio's harmony will be discussed in chapters 11 and 12. Suffice it here to point out the composer's mastery of a wide range of seventh and ninth chords, secondary dominants, borrowed chords, inversions, and suspensions in passages from arias such as "Sentimi, crudo Amore."

3. Large-scale changes of the da capo pattern

The vast majority of arias from Viennese cantatas adhere to the da capo format. Occasionally, however, a composer adjusts or discards the basic three-part shape and invents a special plan. Ariosti's "Insoffribile tormento" consists of only two large sections in the scheme AA¹. A (measures 1–22) unfolds much like the first section of a da capo aria, having an introductory and final ritornello and ending in the tonic (e minor). Beginning in D major, A¹ (measures 23–32) continues with statements of the main melody in various keys, then settles in the tonic again in measure 27 before concluding with an abbreviated ritornello. Ariosti clearly does not intend a return to the A section; I have found no examples in the Viennese repertoire of arias in which the B section ends in the tonic. Besides, the words "da capo" do not appear at the end of measure 32, and no fermata occurs at the end of A; the scribe of MS 17591 uses these signs consistently for Ariosti's da capo arias. Finally, the distribution of the text confirms the unusualness of Ariosti's plan. He uses lines 1–3 of the five-line canzonetta in the A section; he then begins A¹ with lines 4–5 but returns to lines 1–2 shortly before he reestablishes the tonic key. Structurally and harmonically, then, "Insoffribile tormento" is a two-part aria, but Ariosti retains at least a trace of da capo influence by bringing back the initial lines of text in the second half of A¹.

Antonio Bononcini composes da capo arias almost exclusively. One exception is "Benché m'abbia la cruda saetta," a g-minor aria that consists of a single section with a three-part harmonic plan (diagram 10.3). Because of its ternary design, this brief aria superficially resembles a miniature da capo. However, no major articulations occur at the ends of the first and second subsections. Furthermore, the first subsection concludes in the relative major, not the tonic. The text distribution is also unusual.

In his "Se infelice, se giammai," for bass and continuo, Ziani uses a broad ternary structure reminiscent of the da capo design yet different in several important respects. The A section concludes in the dominant rather than the tonic, and it moves directly into the B section. In A¹ Ziani keeps the modulation to the dominant; in order to reestablish the tonic, he appends a nine-measure coda, creating a design that foreshadows the first movement of the classic concerto (diagram 10.4). After the final cadence of the aria, Ziani adds a separate eighteen-measure orchestral ritornello for first and second violins, viola, and continuo; this ritornello consists of material from the A section in a four-part, densely contrapuntal texture.

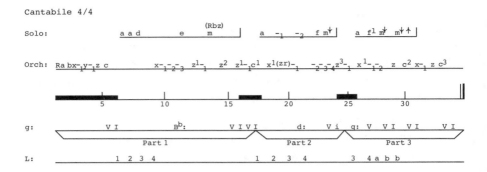

DIAGRAM 10.3. A. M. Bononcini, Cantata 88/II. A brief aria in one section, with a three-part harmonic plan.

In the aria "Brami e speri," for two sopranos and continuo, Ziani devises a still more unusual variant of the customary da capo design. Between the initial A and its return he inserts not one but two contrasting sections (B and C). As in "Se infelice, se giammai," a modulation to the dominant at the end of A is retained in A¹, and, similarly, a brief coda at the end of the aria is used to confirm the original tonality of G major. Although this aria is scored for two sopranos, it is not really a duet but rather a dialogue between Amore and Speranza (diagram 10.5). Like "Se infelice, se giammai," the aria "Brami e speri" is followed by a separate four-part orchestral ritornello.

4. Unusual proportions between A and B

Viennese composers of the early eighteenth century show a remarkable unanimity in their approach to the question of balancing A and B sections of the da capo aria. Composers of this generation obviously felt that a short B section, between one-third and two-thirds the length of A, could provide a sufficient amount of contrast. Partly, of course, the disparity in lengths can be attributed to the ritornellos that frame most A sections, while B sections tend to contain more activity, particularly in rate of motivic change and modulation. In general, composers did not like to digress too long before reestablishing the central tonality. Table 10.3 summarizes the proportions of A and B sections in nineteen Viennese da capo arias.

In two arias, "Sì vaga e sì vezzosa" and "Basti per mio contento," Badia greatly exaggerates the length of A in comparison to B, so that the proportions are approximately 4 to 1. In complete performances of these arias, therefore, B actually accounts for only one-ninth of the total performing time, resulting in an overall structural plan that seems rather imbalanced. An aria in which B is actually longer

Andante 3/4

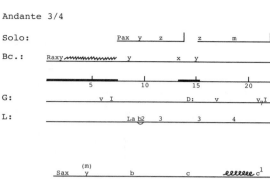

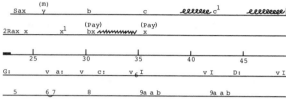

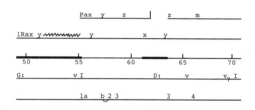

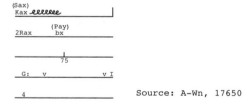

Source: A–Wn, 17650

DIAGRAM 10.4. Ziani, Cantata 2/II. A variant of da capo design (ABA¹–Coda).

than A is extremely rare. Of the arias analyzed for the present study, Badia's "Se sarai mio" exhibits A and B sections of the almost equal proportions of fifty-eight and
fifty measures. It is especially surprising to find these dimensions in an aria by Badia, a composer who seldom writes a B that is more than one-third the length of A.
The text distribution partly accounts for the unusual proportions: Badia uses only
the first two verses of the seven-line text in A, saving the remaining five lines for B.
In "Se sarai mio" he also expands B by inserting a lengthy ritornello in the middle

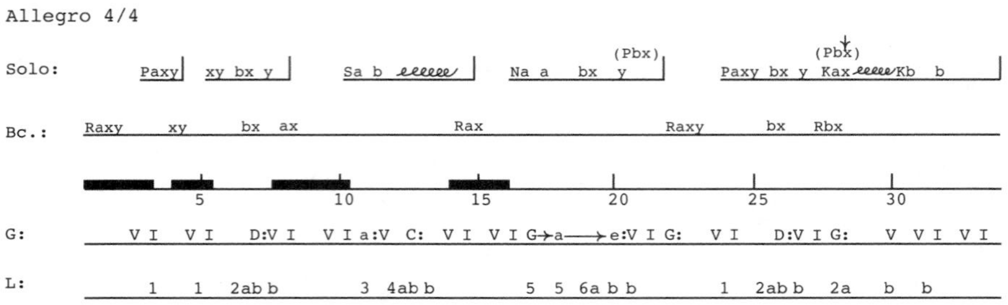

```
Allegro 4/4
                                                          (Pbx)              (Pbx)
Solo:      Paxy  xy bx y       Sa b ееееее   Na a  bx  y          Paxy bx y  Kax ееееее Kb  b

Bc.:   Raxy   xy    bx  ax           Rax              Raxy     bx   Rbx

                          5            10         15        20        25        30
G:          V I   V I   D:V I   V I a:V  C:  V I  V I G→a──→e:V I G:   V I   D:V I G:   V  V I  V I

L:          1    1   2ab b       3  4ab b     5  5  6a b b      1   2ab b   2a    b    b
```

Source: A-Wn, 17635

DIAGRAM 10.5. Ziani, Cantata 18/VI. Another variant of da capo design (ABCA^1–Coda).

TABLE 10.3. THE PROPORTIONS OF A AND B SECTIONS IN VIENNESE DA CAPO ARIAS

COMPOSER	ARIA	A	B	B's % OF TOTAL
Badia	"Sì vaga e sì vezzosa"	35	9	11.4
Badia	"Basti per mio contento"	34	9	11.6
Ariosti	"Al voler del bene amato"	16	5	13.5
Ariosti	"È pur dolce"	15	5	14.3
Badia	"Gelosia, furia d'Alletto"	24	9	15.8
A. M. Bononcini	"Al tuo bel volto"	94	38	16.8
G. Bononcini	"Dio d Amor"	58	25	17.7
Ariosti	"Nice, crudel"	11	5	19.2
Ziani	"Navicella che paventa"	70	34	19.5
Badia	"Ombra del mio bel sol"	26	13	20.0
A. M. Bononcini	"Per non arder"	54	27	20.0
G. Bononcini	"Pena e soffri"	70	36	20.4
A. M. Bononcini	"Amore ingannatore"	36	19	20.9
A. M. Bononcini	"Men crudele"	73	41	21.9
A. M. Bononcini	"S'io ritorno"	75	44	22.7
A. M. Bononcini	"Più barbaro martire"	41	25	23.4
A. M. Bononcini	"Sentimi, crudo Amore"	46	32	25.8
A. M. Bononcini	"Un cor più tormentato"	63	45	26.3
Badia	"Se sarai mio"	58	50	30.1

(measures 75–88). Motivic material from this ritornello reappears over a long vocal pedal near the end of the section, further delaying the return of A.

Like Badia, Ariosti favors a short B section, seldom exceeding half of A. Giovanni Bononcini often writes a B section approximately half as long as A. The balance and flow of component parts in his arias seem carefully calculated. In "Pena

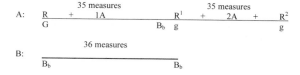

DIAGRAM 10.6. The structural plan of Giovanni Bononcini's
Pena e soffri.

e soffri," for example, the symmetry of the structural and tonal plan contributes to
the aria's stability in general. B is only half as long as A; moreover, the clear division
of A into two equal parts results in a neatly balanced five-part scheme using only
two tonalities (diagram 10.6). A similar plan, though not as perfectly symmetrical,
unfolds in Giovanni's "Dio d'Amor." Also preferring B sections that last about half
as long as A sections, Ziani uses these proportions in his strict da capo arias. Even
in his arias with variant designs, he constructs a series of brief, approximately equal
sections (see diagrams 10.4 and 10.5).

Of all the Viennese composers, Antonio Bononcini consistently composes the
longest B sections. Only in "Al tuo bel volto" does he contrast A with a central
section that is half as long. Here B is probably shorter than usual because of the
slow tempo and the aria's spacious dimensions in general. Mostly, however, Antonio writes arias in which B ranges from half to nearly three-fourths of A, and the
long middle sections account for the greater lengths of many of his arias. They also
illustrate his fondness for fuller and more detailed designs.

The most radical contrasts of sectional lengths occur in the two arias with
changes in continuum, Ariosti's "Cangi Amore" and Giovanni Bononcini's "Dolce
amor." (Neither aria is included in table 10.3.) In "Cangi Amore" the driving mo-
tion of the opening vivace in $\frac{3}{4}$ is suspended during the middle adagio in $\frac{3}{2}$. Ariosti
achieves contrast not only by the abrupt changes in tempo and meter but also by
a drastic reduction in the density of rhythmic activity and by the exploitation of
the soprano's dark lower range in B. In "Dolce amor" Giovanni counterbalances
an opening adagio in common time with a Vivace in $\frac{3}{8}$. Here too rhythmic density
plays a role: B is much more active not simply because of its vigorous sixteenth-note
motion but also because of the frequent incisive and imitative entries between bass
and soprano. In "Cangi Amore" the A section consists of fifty-nine measures, while
B contains only twelve measures. In "Dolce amor" the proportions are reversed: an
eight-measure A contrasts with a thirty-measure B. In each aria the seeming disparity is offset by the changes in tempo and meter. Trial performances revealed that
in actual duration the B of each aria consumes about half as much time as the A.
Thus, consciously or intuitively, Ariosti and Bononcini adhere even in these arias
to the balance favored by composers of their generation.

Only two of the twenty-five arias analyzed here have abrupt changes in continuum and motivic material, and such arias are exceptional in early eighteenth-century Viennese cantatas in general. Contrasts in arias like "Cangi Amore" and "Dolce amor" are text-related and reflect the composers' attempts to vividly delineate the affects of A and B.

5. Unusual modulation schemes

In several arias the key schemes do not conform to the conventional plan, which emphasizes a modulation to the dominant or relative major in the middle of A, an immediate return to the tonic, and then a series of modulations to closely related keys in B. In Badia's "Sì vaga e sì vezzosa" and Giovanni Bononcini's "Dolce amor," for example, the A section contains no modulation to the dominant at all but remains in the tonic throughout. Badia contrasts a long, tonally static A section in D major with a B that quickly explores a succession of related keys—the relative minor, dominant, mediant, and supertonic—as well as the tonic itself. Using a simpler method, Bononcini balances an A entirely in g minor with a B completely in the relative major, B♭.

In Ariosti's "Al voler del bene amato," the modulatory goal of A becomes the mediant rather than the dominant. This elegant aria begins in A major and modulates to c♯ minor in measures 7–9, approximately halfway through the A section. By starting B also in c♯, Ariosti strengthens the substitute polarity of tonic and mediant; the B section concludes in the dominant minor (e), another unusual choice. In fact, Ariosti uses fewer directional and more migrant modulations than any of his Viennese contemporaries, and at least in this style category his arias seem archaic. In the brief g-minor aria "Nice, crudel" for instance, he does not use the standard modulation to the relative major but chooses instead movement to the key of F major (♭VII). After a hint of d minor, the aria returns to the tonic for the rest of A. The itinerant nature of the modulations continues in B: in only five measures the tonality fluctuates from the dominant minor (d) to the relative major (B♭) to the subdominant major (C), finally settling again in the dominant minor. In Giovanni Bononcini's "Dio d'Amor," also in g minor, the tonality vacillates constantly between the tonic, the dominant minor (d), and the relative major (B♭) throughout the first thirty-one measures of the A section, providing yet another instance of an aria from the Viennese repertoire that lacks a clear tensional modulation.

The fifty-measure B section of Badia's "Se sarai mio" winds through an especially large number of modulations. The key scheme is particularly unusual because it begins in the submediant (E♭) and ends a half-step lower, in the dominant minor (d).

On the whole, Antonio Bononcini composes the arias with the most advanced and carefully planned tonal organizations. Virtually all his A sections include strong directional modulations to the dominant or relative major. In arias like

"Per non arder" and "Al tuo bel volto" Antonio remains in the relative major (or its parallel minor) long enough to firmly establish a new tonal area. While these arias belong to a minority in Antonio's work, they are indicative of his search for a broader form coordinated with a clear tonal plan. His willingness to experiment with tonality and structure can also be seen in the F-major aria "Sentimi, crudo Amore"; following the orthodox modulation to the dominant (C) and the usual return to the tonic, Antonio inserts a six-measure section strongly inflected by the subdominant (Bb, measures 22–28). The digression to Bb major is reinforced by a stable area in this tonality in the middle of the B section (measures 61–64). In general, however, departures from the strongest tonal relationships within A sections are rare in Antonio's arias. Moreover, the modulations of his B sections are often less migrant and more directional than those of his contemporaries. He frequently begins in a closely related key, modulates to the dominant of that key, and returns to the first key; in this manner, B closely corresponds to A in its tonal plan. With such symmetry and tonal organization in mind, Antonio is capable of sustaining longer B sections with far fewer modulations than most other Viennese composers.

6. Unexpected resolutions at important structural points

In the g-minor aria "Dolce amor," Giovanni Bononcini avoids the anticipated harmonic resolutions at two important structural points. A concludes with a Phrygian cadence on the dominant chord, setting up a typically late baroque bifocal tonal situation: the dominant chord resolves directly to the relative major at the beginning of B.[5] In A[1] the vocal section also ends with an unexpected and expressive effect; the cadencing vocal line is underpinned by a deceptive cadence in the bass line, which then completes the aria with a brief cadential figure. A surprising conclusion to the opening ritornello of the written-out A[1] section of Bononcini's "Pena e soffri" appears to be an amusing scribal error; in the last two measures of the ritornello, the tonality shifts suddenly from the tonic (g minor) to the supertonic (a minor). The tonality returns to the tonic immediately at the beginning of 1A. Since the momentary key change does not occur at the corresponding place in A, it is almost certainly unintended.

7. Changes in written-out da capos

In at least one written-out da capo, Bononcini does incorporate several changes that are obviously intended. The alterations occur in A[1] of "Dolce amor." Although the aria belongs to a large number of Viennese cantata arias with written-out da capos, it appears to be the only one with structural alterations from the A section, basic changes from the original version quite apart from the informal ornaments that performers were expected to execute. The first change occurs in the introductory ritornello, which Bononcini shortens in A[1] from three measures to one measure so that it includes only the initial melodic module. He lengthens the vocal section of A¹ by expanding the expressive melisma on the word *pietà* from one and one-half measures to three measures; the final line of A is also enriched in A¹ by an additional one and one-half measures (example 10.3a–b). Bononcini also modifies the conclusion of A; he varies the last cadence for voice and continuo and adds an instrumental cadential figure.

8. Special treatment of the ritornello

Among the Viennese composers, Ariosti and Badia tend to be the most literal in their treatment of the ritornello. In arias such as Ariosti's "Al voler del bene amato" and Badia's "Basti per mio contento," the closing ritornello simply duplicates the opening one. The tendency to abbreviate or omit ritornellos is most pronounced in arias by Ariosti. In "Nice, crudel," for example, there is no opening ritornello at all, and only a one-measure cadential figure comes at the end of A. Using similarly obvious techniques, Giovanni Bononcini sometimes abbreviates the final instrumental statement; he shortens the original version by omitting the first measure or two or by compressing the remainder of the ritornello. In "Dolce amor," Bononcini treats the ritornello with more freedom. It appears in its complete three-measure version only at the beginning of the aria. At the end of A Bononcini omits the ritornello altogether, and at the outset of the da capo he includes only the first melodic module (one measure). Finally, the aria ends with a simple cadential pattern like the one that concludes the initial ritornello.

Additional ritornellos often occur in arias by Antonio Bononcini but also occasionally in pieces by Badia and Ziani. Antonio interpolates ritornellos between 1A and 2A, between 1B and 2B, and, less frequently, before the coda-like extensions of 2A and 2B. Badia's "Se sarai mio" includes far more instrumental writing than most of his arias. The initial ritornello is unusually long (seventeen measures), and it recurs almost literally at the end of A; throughout this section Badia introduces bits of the ritornello between vocal phrases. However, the most interesting feature of this aria is the long, fourteen-measure ritornello in the middle of B, a section where Badia scarcely ever interrupts the continuity of the vocal writing. In this passage Badia avoids simply duplicating the opening ritornello and instead borrows only selected subsidiary motives (measures 8–11) from it to provide the material for the entirely new ritornello (example 10.4a–b).

In the A-major aria "Navicella che paventa," Ziani includes ritornellos not only at the beginning and end of A but, like Antonio Bononcini, also between 1A and 2A and between 1B and 2B. In the A section the interior ritornello (measures 29–37) is an abridged version of the introductory one (measures 1–13). In a typical Viennese aria that includes a ritornello between 1A and 2A, it usually follows a modulation to the dominant or relative major; the interior ritornello then reestablishes the tonic and cadences firmly in the tonic just before 2A. Ziani proceeds somewhat differently. Following the standard modulation to the dominant (E) at the end of

EX. 10.3a–b. G. Bononcini, Cantata 82/I, mm. 6–7 and 43–46. Comparison of melismas on the word *pietà* in A and A^1.

1A, Ziani returns to the tonic (A), but he repeats the modulation to the dominant, cadencing there at the end of the central ritornello. In the measure that leads into the 2A section, a descending bass line soon restores a sense of the original tonality, but even in the ensuing section Ziani continues to allude to E major by stressing V-of-V. In B the brief ritornello between 1B and 2B (measures 79–83) borrows motives first heard in measures 5–6 of the opening. For the final ritornello Ziani uses two versions, one for A and another for A^1. He writes the complete ritornellos out only once, but at the end of A he indicates by means of a sign (:S:) that the instrumentalists should skip from measure 63 directly to measure 70 for the tonic cadence before beginning B. The extension at the end of A^1 (measures 64–70) avoids the reference to the dominant of E major heard in the first part of the ritornello and thus provides a firmer conclusion in the tonic. The use of such an extension is extremely rare, and it is all the more remarkable because its motive is not related to material heard previously (example 10.5).

Ritornellos that begin and end in different keys occur sparsely in Viennese cantatas. The internal ritornello of the A section of Ziani's *Navicella che paventa* is one example, moving from A to E. Slightly more common are initial ritornellos that end with cadences in the dominant instead of the tonic. In Giovanni Bononcini's "Dio d'Amor," for example, the tonality moves from the tonic (G) through the relative major (B♭), returns to the tonic, and concludes with a cadence in the dominant minor (d). The ritornello at the end of A almost duplicates the initial one, but Bononcini writes a slightly longer conclusion that supplies the essential cadence in the tonic. Motion toward the dominant within the introductory ritornello can also be found in works by Antonio Bononcini; for instance, the aria "S'io ritorno a in-namorarvi" ends on an implied dominant, and the unaccompanied triplets played by the flute prepare the return of the opening motive, now sung by the alto.

EX. 10.4a–b. (*above and facing*) Badia, Cantata 1/III, mm. 8–10 and 74–88. Use of subsidiary motives from the opening R (10.4a) to build a long R in B (10.4b).

Initial ritornellos that end on the dominant are exceptional, even in arias by Antonio Bononcini, but almost as a standard technique he does include a modulation to the dominant (or relative major) in the middle of the introductory ritornello, reaffirming the tonic in the second half. In a sense, then, the opening ritornello forecasts the modulatory plan of the A section. This concept is carried out neatly in arias like "Per non arder," "Un cor più tormentato," "Men crudele," and "Amore ingannatore." In each of these arias, Bononcini omits the modulation to the dominant in the closing ritornello, thus providing a more stable conclusion.

As his music clearly shows, Antonio dislikes literal repetitions of ritornellos in general. He modifies the instrumental passages not simply by abbreviating them, extending them, or adding modulations to the dominant but by frequently varying and developing the motivic material. Because of his flexible and varied approach, the ritornellos in most of Antonio's arias never sound the same twice. In the closing ritornello of the A section of "Un cor più tormentato," for example, he introduces a new rhythmic variant of prominent triplet motives (*Pay* and *z*) first heard in the introduction; this variant subsequently serves as the most important instrumental idea in the first half of B (example 10.6a–b).

Most introductions in Antonio's arias begin by announcing the principal motive to be sung by the voice, but they usually continue with three or four motives reserved especially for the instruments. In arias like "Benché m'abbia la cruda saetta," Antonio embroiders the purely instrumental motives and their variants around the smooth vocal melody. Often the vocal and instrumental lines do not cadence together, but the obbligato violin enters and leaves freely, forming elaborate filigree with the soprano melody. Sometimes, too, Antonio begins an internal or closing ritornello even before the voice reaches its final cadence. In "Benché m'abbia" he also creates a new motive from two earlier ones. In measures 21–22 and 26–27 he blends the prominent descending melodic sevenths heard in motive *y* of the introduction with the characteristic triplet sixteenths of *w* (example 10.7a–c).

EX. 10.5. (*above and facing*) Ziani, Cantata 18/V, mm. 57–70. Variant version of the closing R.

EX. 10.6a–b. A. M. Bononcini, Cantata 99/II, mm. 5–9 and 57–70. The motives *Pay* and *z* from the opening R; a variant used in the closing R of A and the beginning of B, based on this variant.

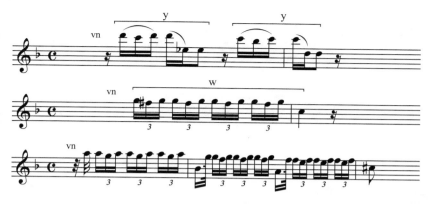

EX. 10.7a–c. A. M. Bononcini, Cantata 91/I: mm. 2–3 (the motive *Pay*),
4–5 (*Paw*), and 21–22 (a combination of *y* and *w*).

In "Più barbaro martire," the ritornello motives similarly decorate the vocal
line. Antonio cleverly varies the concluding ritornello by having the violins enter
an octave lower with a point of imitation instead of together; moreover, they are accompanied by a bass line that was lacking in the introduction. The simple half-step
motion at the end of motive *x* becomes the seed for development in measures 49–51
of the B section.

As an alternative procedure Antonio occasionally has the singer participate in
all the important motives of the ritornello, not just the head-motive. In "Sentimi,
crudo Amore," the virtuoso soprano part acts as an equal partner with the three
obbligato instruments (violins 1–2 and viola) and the bass line; Antonio distributes
the important motives among all the parts. In "Men crudele," three of the six motives from the ritornello are purely instrumental, while the other three are sung
by the soprano either literally or with slight modifications. The head-motive *x* and
the fragments *w* and *m* are heard in the vocal line (example 10.8a–c). In B of "Men
crudele," slightly modified fragments of *m* are heard in alternation between first
and second violins.

Antonio's fertile imagination in varying a motive throughout an aria can be
seen from his treatment of a triplet figure from the opening ritornello of "S'io
ritorno a innamorarvi" (see example 10.2). Variation techniques include rhythmic
changes, inversions, and other melodic alterations.

9. Special treatment of the *Devise*

As in their handling of many other elements of the da capo design, Badia and
Ariosti are the most consistent and conventional in their use of the *Devise*. Ariosti
in particular almost always includes one at the beginning of 1A. On the other hand,
a *Devise* seldom occurs in the Viennese arias by the Bononcini brothers.

EX. 10.8a–c. A. M. Bononcini, Cantata 56/I. Comparison of instrumental and vocal versions of *Pax, w,* and *m.*

The vocal motive of arias with *Devisen* is quite short, usually only one or two measures, and the *Devise* itself is followed by a truncated or abbreviated ritornello. Thus, in Ariosti's "Insoffribile tormento" or in Badia's "Gelosia, furia d'Alletto," two beats are cut from the beginning of the introductory ritornello. The same method is used by Ariosti in "Cangi Amore," but in this aria both the initial ritornello (measures 1–8) and the *Devise* (measures 9–12) are substantially longer. Sometimes a composer includes only a tiny fragment of the ritornello after a *Devise* (Badia's "Se sarai mio") or, ignoring the ritornello altogether, writes only a short cadential figure for continuo (Ariosti's "Al voler del bene amato"). Following the brief *Devise* in "Sì vaga e sì vezzosa," Badia gives a somewhat compressed version (measures 13–21)

EX. 10.9. Ariosti, Cantata 29/I, mm. 3–6. Comparison of the *Devise* with the second vocal entrance.

of the long opening ritornello (measures 1–11). On a rather smaller scale, this tendency to condense the ritornello in the statement between the *Devise* and the rest of 1A occurs in Ziani's "Brami e speri." Here the beginning of the ritornello is left intact, while most of the second half is omitted.

In "Amore ingannatore," one of the few arias by Antonio Bononcini that includes a *Devise,* the composer follows it with only the final measure of the opening ritornello. His partiality for recurrent design features is evident even in this dimension, for he includes the *Devise* not only at the beginning of 1A but also at the outset of 2A.

Perhaps the most fascinating example of a *Devise* comes at the beginning of Ariosti's "È pur dolce a un cor legato." In this aria he embellishes the vocal line with an extraordinary number of complex ornaments. After the introductory ritornello and the *Devise* followed by an instrumental cadential figure, the alto part resumes with a melody similar to the *Devise* but overlaid with richer ornamentation (example 10.9). Since in general any varying of the *Devise* is highly unusual, perhaps the question of performance practice deserves consideration here, for the difficult and irregular scales and roulades suggest the type of improvised ornaments intended for a da capo. The da capo of "È pur dolce" is not written out; the scribe of MS 17575 chose not to write out any da capo. Possibly we have here an example of an aria in which the composer felt it was important to specify the da capo ornaments, and as a consequence the scribe decided to write them directly into the A section. If so, then the vocal line may have been much simpler in the original A, and this may ac-

EX. 10.10. Ariosti, Cantata 29/I, A section complete (alto line only). Comparison of
the ornamental melody from A-Wn, 17575, with a hypothetical simplified version.

count for the varied repetition of the *Devise*. By observing the changes between the
original *Devise* and the ornamental overlay, we may add to the store of knowledge
concerning appropriate ornamentation (example 10.10).[6]

10. The use of new motives in B

Apart from the two arias with obvious contrasts in continuum and thematic material (Giovanni Bononcini's "Dolce amor" and Ariosti's "Cangi Amore"), the technique of introducing completely new motives in B seems to have played a very small role in the arias of Viennese cantatas. The composers obviously felt that developing motives from A—especially through repetition and sequence, the baroque stock-in-trade—was an essential ingredient for achieving unity in their compositions. At times, as at the beginning of the B section of Badia's "Se sarai mio," the melodic profile of an important idea is changed to the extent that it almost seems new; even here, however, the rhythmic patterning shows that the B melody derives from the principal A idea. Somewhat exceptionally, then, the B section of Badia's "Ombra del mio bel sol" begins with a sawtooth melody unrelated to motives from A; a similar phrase concludes B. Some motivic variants in the B sections of Antonio Bononcini's arias also appear new, but a more careful examination reveals an overwhelming preference for derivative material.

11. The use of specialized motives

Arias by Viennese cantata composers of this generation do not display the kind of thematic specialization found in works of the late eighteenth century. Yet an occasional aria suggests that a composer was attempting to create a broader, more detailed design than usual, to coordinate particular motives with specific tonal areas, or otherwise to differentiate the functions of individual themes. As mentioned earlier in this chapter, Antonio Bononcini composed several arias that not only include the standard modulations to the dominant or relative major but remain there long enough to establish firmly the new tonality with its own motives. In the expansive aria "Al tuo bel volto," Antonio actually approaches a plan in which primary, transitional, and secondary functions are differentiated. After the instrumental introduction, the voice enters in the tonic (a minor) with the head-motive of the ritornello, the main melody of the entire aria, that is, the primary theme. Spun out in a long arch, the cantabile melody (measures 10–20) is entirely in the tonic except for the concluding cadence in the relative major (C). A new ten-measure section consisting of a long ascending sequence with descending scales in the bass line contains the usual characteristics of a transition: an unstable, modulatory passage leading to a new tonality. The modulatory goal turns out to be C major again, so the effect of the transition is somewhat diluted, but it nevertheless serves as an active bridge between two areas that are more stable. After establishing C major, Antonio shifts to c minor (the parallel) for the secondary thematic area (measures 31–44), and the key remains c minor except for the Picardy-third cadence at measure 44. This secondary area has its own languid, descending motive and is expressively inflected by the Neapolitan sixth in measure 41. After measure 44 the tonality shifts immediately back to a minor, and the 2A section begins.

Though still only nascent, Antonio's tendency to delineate thematic functions shows him to be a more progressive composer than his contemporaries. In most of his arias this tendency is not as advanced as in "Al tuo bel volto." For example, in several arias a particular passage may not serve specifically as a transition between two tonally stable areas, but it may instead act as a preparation for the statement of important thematic material. Such a passage occurs in "S'io ritorno a innamorarvi." The triplet motive at the end of the ritornello does not bring the instrumental introduction to a solid conclusion with a cadence in the tonic; instead, it tapers off in the unaccompanied solo violin, ending with an implied dominant that prepares the return of the head-motive and the beginning of 1A. Throughout the aria the triplet figuration continues to serve a preparatory function, announcing the arrival of each significant idea.

Although arias by other Viennese composers do not contain the type of incipient transitional or secondary thematic specialization found in Antonio's, at least one aria by Badia and one by Giovanni Bononcini include passages that clearly function as closing material. Thus, at the end of 2A in "Gelosia, furia d'Alletto," Badia incorporates one and one-half measures of cadential figuration, consisting of a repeated whirling pattern in the soprano and constant reiteration of tonic–dominant in the bass. The special closing nature of the passage is confirmed by the text. In a typical 2A section, the first line comes only at the beginning, but in "Gelosia" the first line recurs not only at the beginning of 2A but also at the point where the closing material begins. A similar approach occurs near the end of the long A section of Giovanni Bononcini's "Pena e soffri"; here the composer arrests the movement of the aria by using repeated octave leaps in the bass and by having the soprano sing a sawtooth figure that alternates between the fifth and sixth scale degrees of g minor. As in Badia's aria, the special return of the first line of text underlines the function of the passage. Early eighteenth-century composers like the Bononcini brothers and Badia thus experimented occasionally with thematic specialization and, much more rarely, with the coordination of structure and tonality.

ARTICULATION OF FORM

The formal design of an eighteenth-century aria is closely related to the process of articulation. The locations of change and the amounts of stress assigned to the various large- and middle-dimensional articulations basically determine the shape of an aria. Except in a few works by Antonio Bononcini, articulation is less meaningful than in arias of later periods, partly because the motivic material of late baroque compositions usually does not change significantly.

Longer note values and rests confirm the large-dimensional punctuations at the conclusion of A and B. The A section also concludes with a decisive cadence in the tonic key. Composers may combine these techniques with homorhythm and, in triple-meter arias, with hemiola at the cadence. Hemiola serves both as a cadence signal and, because of the tactus speedup, as a terminal drive effect. Interior nodes such as the conclusions of the initial ritornello, 1A, and 2A often receive special emphasis. Giovanni and Antonio Bononcini sometimes stress the penultimate cadence of 2A. Ziani, on the other hand, prefers to disguise middle-dimensional articulations, marking only the most important structural joints with complete caesuras and forceful cadences.

To clarify the comprehensive outline and the internal design of an aria, a composer may subtly vary the weights of articulation by altering the intensity of one or more style elements. In longer, more elaborate arias, these articulations may be carefully adjusted so that emphatic cadences underline major structural divisions, slightly less prominent breaks delineate the end of subsections like 1A and 1B, and simpler effects conclude shorter vocal segments and ritornellos. Differentiations of this sort can be compared to punctuation such as the period, semicolon, and comma. A composer may signal a structural hiatus in the flow of an aria with an acceleration of chord rhythm, a change in surface-rhythmic activity, an important melodic peak, a shift from conjunct to disjunct motion, or an increase of harmonic tension. Changes in dynamics as well as phrase repetitions, responses, and echoes also mark the conclusions of some sections.

The extent of coordination of style ingredients at important cadences can serve as one index in evaluating the degree of a composer's stylistic control. In the more sophisticated arias, a hierarchy of articulation emerges. The coalescence of several elements at a single cadence may result in a highly effective concinnity. Another source of control is cadential rhyme—the recurrence of a particular formula at corresponding points such as the final phrases of 1A and 2A or the conclusions of 2A and 2B—lending unity and symmetry to an aria. In addition, some specialized types of articulation and other devices may effectively conceal outlines at times and prevent a structure from becoming overarticulated. Each of the five Viennese composers approaches the question of articulation differently, and the solutions reveal much about individual styles.

ZIANI

Few traces of a hierarchy of articulation can be seen in Ziani's arias. The composer consistently avoids full breaks except at the conclusions of A and B. His tendency to disguise the interior nodes of a design is most evident in the two arias not in conventional da capo structure, "Se infelice" and "Brami e speri." In "Se infelice," the bass line continues to move melodically through all final cadences of ritornellos and vocal sections, with little emphasis except for the universally popular technique of hemiola plus a slight acceleration of surface rhythm in the last phrase of the aria. One clearly coordinated cadence, comparable to the conclusion of the

B section of a da capo aria, helps to clarify the five-part design of "Brami e speri"; a half note followed by a half rest in both lines separates C from A[1] and prepares for the varied da capo and coda. Elsewhere Ziani does not divide sections with rests; at the end of the ritornello after A, the bass line cadences clearly before B begins, but not before C, where it continues directly by moving in steady eighths. The composer nearly always elides a ritornello with the beginning or end of a vocal section. Occasionally, as in measure 4, the end of a vocal phrase overlaps with the beginning of a ritornello. The only evidence of an effort to emphasize one cadence more than another occurs in the last vocal phrase of B, where the soprano line rises to the peak g^2 before leaping down by a minor sixth. The syncopated formula in measure 16 recurs at the end of C. Ziani underscores the conclusion of the aria by composing a slightly modified version of the penultimate phrase.

In Ziani's da capo aria "Navicella che paventa," the principal coordinated articulation takes place at the end of B. Here homorhythm, a longer note value, and an eighth rest prepare the return of A. Melodically, the leap of an ascending fifth to a peak of $g\sharp^2$ makes this the most intense cadence of the aria. Otherwise Ziani does not vary the weights of articulation perceptibly. As in "Brami e speri" he veils the design with elisions.

ARIOSTI

In a similarly continuous, late baroque manner, Ariosti also prefers to conceal both the large- and middle-dimensional seams of the da capo structure. In arias like "Nice, crudel" and "È pur dolce," the constant eighth-note motion of the bass line disguises all articulations except the end of B; even the final ritornello of A is elided with the beginning of the middle section. Cliché V–I or I$^6_4$–V–I harmonies combined with a descending octave in the bass line provide an elementary source of unity at cadences in "È pur dolce." The tendency to conclude large vocal sections and subsections with the same formula can also be seen in "Insoffribile tormento." First used at the end of 1A, the dotted figure ♩. ♫ returns at the conclusion of 2A and A[1]. Ariosti enhances the rhythm of the final vocal phrase by including an additional affective figure ♩ ♬♬ ♩. ♫ for the word *foco.*

More emphatic structural cadences complete the vocal sections of Ariosti's "Al voler del bene amato" and "Cangi Amore." These pieces also feature typically active bass lines that mask most caesuras. Yet Ariosti focuses some attention upon the terminal cadences of vocal sections. Thus, in "Al voler" the gradually rising line in the final phrase of 2A reaches a climax of a^2, then drops an octave just before the cadence. The second highest peak occurs in the penultimate bar of B; the top pitches $f\sharp^2$ and g^2 are approached by an ascending fifth and followed by an affective rhythm, Ariosti's favorite device at important cadences (example 10.11). Other phrase endings, such as the conclusion of the opening ritornello or of 1A, do not receive special

EX. 10.11. Ariosti, Cantata 6/I, mm. 19–22. An important peak and
an affective rhythm at the end of B.

emphasis. The B section of "Cangi Amore" shows careful planning of a melody
that rises gradually from d¹ to a peak of f² in the penultimate phrase. The composer
coordinates the melodic highpoint with increased harmonic intensity: a 7–8 suspension overlapping bars 69–70 and a melodic anticipation plus a dramatic octave
descent embellish the expressive Phrygian cadence. Moreover, the effect is followed
by a full articulation (a whole note in the bass line and a half note plus rest in the
soprano), rare in Ariosti's work. An echo of the Phrygian cadence a fifth lower, now
without the octave leap, brings the section to a quiet close.

BADIA

Badia similarly splices many phrases at structural joints. In "Se sarai mio," for example, he conceals articulations between A and B, between 1A and 2A, and between
ritornellos and vocal sections. By dovetailing the beginnings and endings of aria
segments, the composer creates a seamless fabric articulated mainly by the simple
alternation of vocal and instrumental timbres. The most pronounced cadence occurs at the end of B, where the combination of homorhythm, a longer note value,
and the terminal effect of hemiola clearly defines the boundary between the middle
section and the da capo. Fragments from the head-motive of the ritornello punctuate many phrases; these too tend to cover the margins of vocal subsections. In B the
dialogue between soprano and first flute results in some overlap. Although a real
hierarchy of articulations does not emerge in "Se sarai mio," the recurrent Corelli
clashes in the final bars of ritornellos intensify several instrumental cadences and
provide a bit of unity. In the ritornellos that frame 1A and 2A the composer coordi-

EX. 10.12. Badia, Cantata 75/III, mm. 16–20. Overlap between the end of a
vocal phrase and the beginning of a bass-line motive.

nates the dissonant effect with hemiola, a speedup of chord rhythm, and a melodic
peak.

Badia's approach to questions of middle- and large-dimensional articulation is
clearly illustrated by continuo arias like "Gelosia, furia d'Alletto," "Ombra del mio
bel sol," and "Basti per mio contento." The main features of his blueprint include (1)
a full break at the end of B; (2) a less emphatic articulation between A and B, often
disguised by continuous bass-line motion; (3) elided articulations between 1A and
2A and between ritornellos and vocal sections; and (4) placement of the greatest
weight at the final cadence of 2A through the intensification of one or more style
characteristics. In "Gelosia" a major ninth ascending to a peak of g^2 brings the 2A
subsection to an impressive conclusion, and in "Ombra" a rising diminished seventh coincides with faster chord rhythm. The composer emphasizes the end of 2A
in "Basti" by repeating the penultimate phrase of four and one-half bars in a *piano*
dynamic; both phrases include contrary motion, a melodic climb to a peak of g^2, a
subsequent leap of a minor sixth to a dissonant chord (iv^7), and hemiola. The same
aria contains an excellent example of overlap. The beginnings of bass-line phrases

EX. 10.13. Badia, Cantata 4/II, mm. 1–7. An elision of an opening ritornello with 1A in which the bass line continues with motivic material while the voice sustains.

consisting of sixteenth-note figuration derived from the ritornello usually coincide with new vocal phrases, but in measure 18 the motive begins one-half measure early while the soprano is still completing a phrase (example 10.12).

Badia uses a special technique at the ends of the opening ritornellos of "Gelosia" and "Ombra." As usual he elides the introduction and 1A, but one of the lines sustains a tone while the other continues immediately with thematic material. In "Gelosia" the bass line holds the final note of the ritornello while the soprano begins with motivic material, but in "Ombra" the reverse and more unusual procedure obtains (example 10.13).

"Sì vaga e sì vezzosa" represents an anomaly not only in Badia's work but also in the Viennese repertoire in general. The aria consists of a long succession of meticulously articulated phrases, each unit separated from the next by an eighth rest in all parts. The introduction alone includes eight caesuras, and the vocal sections continue in the same manner. With so many coordinated articulations, the principal structural cadences do not sound any more emphatic than those at subphrases, particularly since Badia does not heighten them with specific melodic, harmonic, or rhythmic details.

EX. 10.14. G. Bononcini, Cantata 51/I, mm. 97–102. A full articulation at the end of the penultimate phrase of B, signaling a cadenza.

GIOVANNI BONONCINI

Of the five Viennese composers, Giovanni Bononcini tends to make the design of an aria clearest by using fully coordinated articulations at important points. Thus, in many arias a full break occurs not only at the end of B but also between A and B, at the end of the opening ritornello, and between the penultimate and final phrases of B. In the lengthy aria "Pena e soffri," for example, the instrumental introduction concludes with a firm cadence in the tonic followed by two beats of rest before the soprano enters. Bononcini avoids another complete articulation until the end of A; perhaps desiring to prevent the structure from seeming too obvious, he elides 1A and 2A and the end of 2A with the concluding ritornello. In "Dio d'Amor" he articulates at the same points but adds one between 2A and the ritornello. An aria like "Dolce amor" or "Pena e soffri" also includes an emphatic half or deceptive cadence at the end of the penultimate phrase of A[1] or B, a clear signal for the improvisation of a cadenza by the singer (example 10.14).

The arias by Giovanni also show more control over the subtleties of differential articulation than those by most of his contemporaries. In "Pena e soffri," the composer places the most stress on cadences at the end of 2A and 2B, underlines the nodes between 1A and 2A and between 1B and 2B somewhat less, and heightens the conclusions of ritornellos least. In addition, the ends of the penultimate phrases of 2A and 2B precede and prepare the most climactic moments of the aria. Bononcini therefore establishes a parallel relationship between the conclusions of vocal sections. Functioning mainly as a frame for 1A and 2A, the ritornello concludes with little special cadential emphasis other than a rising line and slight acceleration of chord rhythm. At the end of 1A the composer combines hemiola, a peak of g^2, and a more jagged vocal line with leaps of a minor sixth, a minor seventh, and a tritone. An almost identical formula concludes the penultimate phrase of 2A, which cadences in the tonic (g minor) instead of the relative major; as a result, the melody reaches a secondary peak of $E\flat^2$. The final cadence surpasses the intensity of the earlier ones; a melodic high point of g^2, a soprano line with two tritones, and expressive harmonies, including vii^6-of-V, a chord often used by Bononcini to increase the tension at a concluding phrase. A comparable cadence occurs at the end of 2B. Here the hemiola correlates with a subpeak of f^2 as well as with leaps of an ascending fifth and a descending minor seventh. As in the earlier structural cadences, in the final measures of 2B the repetitious bass-line motive disappears, and the texture becomes largely homorhythmic. The use of sevenths and other large leaps at important cadences is a feature often found in the music of Handel, but it applies equally to the arias of Bononcini. The deceptive penultimate cadence of 2B, ending with the progression i^6–V $^4_2$, is certainly similar in spirit to many comparable places in arias by Handel.[7]

A rather clear hierarchy of specialized articulations thus contributes to the structural clarity of "Pena e soffri." A similar pattern, though less methodically conceived, unfolds in "Dio d'Amor." In this aria an isolated melodic climax of d^3 in the flute strengthens the final cadence of 2A. The flute moves in contrary motion with the bass through five measures in the penultimate phrase of 2B, reaching a secondary peak of c^3. Forming an echo-like response to the flute, the concluding phrase for soprano and continuo alone includes a high point for the singer followed by a descending minor sixth. In the shorter aria "Dolce amor," a cadence with a rising fifth and a falling minor seventh underscores the end of the contrasting B section. The same aria contains a laminated effect with rhythmic imitation near the end of A.

Antonio Bononcini

The number and placement of coordinated articulations followed by rests vary greatly in the arias of Antonio Bononcini, making it more difficult to generalize about his style. Probably the most typical procedure can be seen in arias like "Men crudele," "Un cor più tormentato," and "Sentimi, crudo Amore." Complete breaks occur only at the two most important structural hinges in the da capo structure, the conclusions of A and B. In "Men crudele," Antonio disguises articulations like the ones between the introduction and 1A and between 1A and the internal ritornello by simply keeping the bass line in motion. At all other points he elides the end of one section with the beginning of another.

The miniature three-part aria "Benché m'abbia" (not in the conventional da capo design) contains several emphatic cadences, but they are not followed by rests;

EX. 10.15. A. M. Bononcini, Cantata 8/I, mm. 54–57. A highly unusual
elision between B and the beginning of the da capo.

the flow of the aria continues from the beginning until the end. The da capo aria
"Amore ingannatore" includes a highly unusual connection between the end of B
and the beginning of A¹; a measure of motivic material in the bass line leads directly from one section to the next. Curiously, it is the only measure in which the
bass line abandons its supporting role and becomes thematic (example 10.15).

In several arias Antonio provides clear articulations with rests not only at the
principal structural joints but also at one or more internal cadences. The most common location for such an articulation is the end of the opening ritornello, as in "S'io
ritorno," "Per non arder," and "Più barbaro martire." Less frequently he inserts a
full break between 1A and the internal ritornello. Often the composer also empha-

sizes the head-motive of an aria by setting it apart with rests. One location where he virtually always uses an elision or overlap is the juncture between 2A and the concluding ritornello. Having achieved a climax near the end of the vocal section, he apparently wishes to continue the momentum of an aria until the end. Thus, for example, the end of 2A in "Più barbaro martire" overlaps with the beginning of the ritornello.

A large number of coordinated articulations with rests occur throughout "Al tuo bel volto." These can be seen at the conclusions of ritornellos, 1A and 2A, 1B and 2B, penultimate phrases, and elsewhere. The numerous pauses produce a heavy, deliberate effect that matches the serious mood of the text. Unlike Badia's "Sì vaga e sì vezzosa," however, the frequent articulations do not cause "Al tuo bel volto" to become static; long rising and falling phrases, differentiated rhythms, and directional harmonies contribute to the flow of the aria.

As in many other facets of his work, in the use and distribution of differential articulations Antonio's arias vary greatly. He rarely exploits the systematically weighted cadences found in Giovanni's "Pena e soffri." The reasons appear to be twofold. First, he often places the main climax approximately two-thirds to three-fourths of the way through a section rather than at the concluding cadence. Second, Antonio's arias are filled with so many interesting melodic, harmonic, and rhythmic details that individual structural cadences do not necessarily stand out. "Benché m'abbia," for example, includes admirable details such as idiomatic string writing, expressive harmonies, and beautiful embroidery of the obbligato line about the simpler vocal melody but not specialized or especially emphatic articulations. Often, however, Antonio stresses a specific cadence more than any other. In arias like "Un cor più tormentato," "Più barbaro martire," and "Men crudele," he draws special attention to the conclusion of 2A, the location also favored by Giovanni. At the end of 2A in "Un cor più tormentato" the composer coordinates hemiola with simultaneous descending melodic sevenths in soprano and bass lines. A more dramatic effect heightens the conclusion of 2A in "Più barbaro martire." The final phrase combines quicker chord rhythm with larger and larger melodic leaps for the alto, peaking on d^2. The last measures of 2A in "Men crudele" include a vocal line that rises gradually from f^1 to g^2, then concludes with an exposed cadence for soprano and continuo without obbligato instruments, highlighted by an increase in the number of leaps in both parts and the usual broadening effect of hemiola (example 10.16).

In "Sentimi, crudo Amore," Antonio heightens the intensity noticeably at the end of B. The penultimate phrase, performed by soprano and violins without continuo, incorporates an ascending major seventh, a reference to the augmented mediant triad of d minor, and a firm cadence in that key. Reentering just as the upper parts cadence, the bass line outlines first the tonic chord of d minor and then the

EX. 10.16. A. M. Bononcini, Cantata 56/I, mm. 173–79. A climactic phrase
at the end of 2A.

supertonic of the dominant minor (a), while the soprano maintains a long trill on d^2. On the first beat of measure 76 the soprano drops out, the bass line descends to $G\sharp^1$, and the chord changes to vii^7-of-v; the emphasis upon this unstable chord invites a spontaneous embellishment or cadenza, especially in light of the brilliant high c^3 and virtuosic coloratura earlier in this aria (example 10.17).[8]

In "Amore ingannatore," Antonio places the greatest emphasis near the end of the ritornello. Syncopated rhythms, contrary motion, a melodic peak of $e\flat^3$, and dissonant harmonies produce concinnity in measures 6–7; at the cadence the harmony and rhythm become simpler. The cadence with the most stress in "S'io ritorno" comes near the end of the penultimate phrase of 2A, where the composer again creates concinnity by combining contrary motion, intense harmony, and alto and flute lines that ascend to peaks of d^2 and d^3, respectively. Written in a lower range, with a *piano* dynamic, and without flute obbligato, the final vocal phrase is an echo response to the penultimate one. With his sharpened sense of symmetry, Antonio uses precisely the same procedure at the end of B: the climax occurs in the penultimate phrase, and the last segment concludes the section softly. This type of large-dimensional cadential rhyme can be found in several arias by Antonio.

At times Antonio avoids a full articulation where expected by extending a phrase in one or more lines while the others pause. For example, in measure 74 of "Un cor più tormentato," the flute enters first above the bass line, followed by the soprano in measure 75. After the half cadence (V^6 of e minor) in measures 76–78, the bass drops out and then the soprano, but the flute moves ahead. The expected tonic chord is cleverly delayed until the beginning of measure 80, and the entire phrase is stretched until measure 84.

"S'io ritorno" offers several examples of delicate elisions and special articulations. In measure 20 the composer creates a delightful elision by means of an isolated d^1; the alto ends a phrase with d^1 just as the bass begins a new segment with the same pitch. Similar interlocking phrases occur throughout the aria, sometimes by means of an octave instead of a unison. One of the three lines may overlap while the other two elide; thus, in measure 26, the bass cadences on the first beat, the flute begins on beat 1, and the alto continues through beat 2. (Overlap occurs often in more contrapuntal arias like "Men crudele" and "Più barbaro martire.") A finely honed articulation concludes the ritornello of "S'io ritorno"; after cadencing, the bass line stops in measure 8, but the flute continues unaccompanied another two measures, ending on the dominant pitch. A full break prepares the beginning of 1A in the tonic. Special articulations in which the bass line drops out can also be seen in arias like "Per non arder" and "Sentimi, crudo Amore." As in many other style categories, in variety of articulation Antonio's works demonstrate that he is one of the best craftsmen among the Italians of his generation.

EX. 10.17. (*above and facing*) A.M. Bononcini, Cantata 28/I: mm. 72–78.
An emphatic penultimate cadence of B followed by a change from the
tonic chord of d minor to vii7-of-V, signaling a cadenza and concluding
with a firm cadence in the tonic.

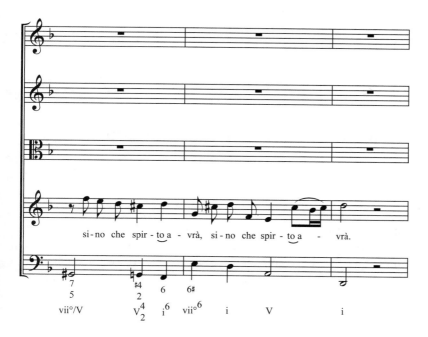

11

Melody, Harmony, and Rhythm

A study of melody, harmony, and rhythm in arias by secular cantata composers working in Vienna in the early eighteenth century greatly deepens our understanding of their individual styles. The composers use these basic style elements not only to enrich the content but also as sources that contribute to forward movement.

MELODY

MELODIC MOTION: PEAKS AND LOWS

The degree of activity within an aria is partly determined by the long-range placement of melodic peaks and lows as well as the shapes and patterns of individual lines. The distribution of high and low points may contribute to the broad sweep of an aria. In many works the placement of melodic climaxes seems largely haphazard, but in the arias of several composers, peaks are more carefully and consistently arranged.

Total range obviously influences the amount of movement generated by an individual vocal or instrumental line, the highest and lowest pitches often serving as significant extremes. Figure 11.1 summarizes the vocal ranges of the arias. The chart reveals many fifth-degree/tonic relationships in the vocal parts of the Viennese arias.

Ariosti is often content to restrict the vocal line to a fairly small compass. Thus the soprano lines of "È pur dolce" and "Al voler del bene amato" span only an octave and a minor ninth, respectively. While the pitch a^2 in "Al voler" does exceed the normal upper limit of a typical Ariosti aria, the total range remains rather limited because the vocal line never sinks below $g\sharp^1$. Working within these restricted ranges, the composer also shows little control over the distribution of peaks and lows. Only in an occasional A or B does he seem to plan the high point of a section. In "Cangi Amore," for example, the soprano rises gradually from d^1 at the beginning of B (measure 60) to a dramatic f^2 in the penultimate phrase (measure 70). Equally impressive is the handling of the peak in "Al voler del bene amato." Here Ariosti reserves the climax for the final phrase of A; the soprano line winds slowly

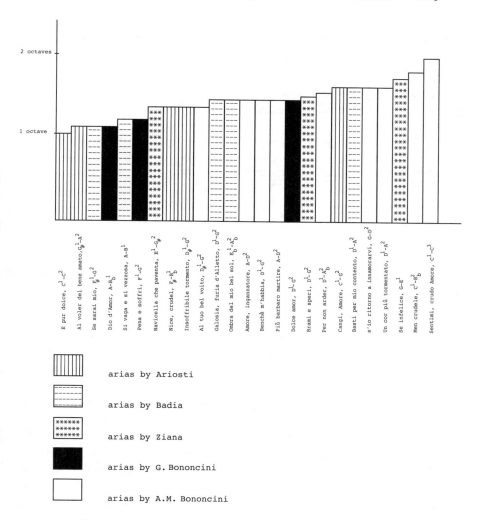

FIG. 11.1. Vocal ranges in selected arias by Viennese cantata composers.

upward from b1 through a long florid sequence until it crests on a2; Ariosti stresses the top pitch by approaching it with a fresh surge of coloratura and by placing it on an accented beat (see example 11.15).

Moderate vocal ranges between a minor ninth and a twelfth predominate in arias by Badia. Like Ariosti, he saves an important melodic climax for the final phrase of A in a few arias. However, this peak does not necessarily exceed other high points in an aria; in "Basti per mio contento," for example, the line rising to g2 at the end of A provides a forceful conclusion, but the same pitch occurs at several other points in the section and is immediately surpassed by a2 in the opening

EX. 11.1. Ziani, Cantata 18/V, mm. 99–104. The placement of the highest peak at the end of B.

phrase of B. Similarly, the top pitch (g^2) at the end of A in "Gelosia, furia d'Alletto" is not an isolated peak, though the leap of an ascending ninth gives it special prominence (see example 10.1). In other arias, Badia seems to have no special plan for organizing melodic climaxes.

Ziani also favors comfortable ranges, though the compass of the bass aria "Se infelice" extends a full octave and a major sixth. The pinnacles of his melodies consistently occur in B. He seems to use melodic peaks more for the purpose of heightening a particular word than for emphasizing an important cadence. Thus, the top e1 in B of "Se infelice" highlights the key word *crudo*. The highest peak in "Navicella che paventa" ($g\sharp^2$) comes twice near the end of B; the second time it initiates the hemiola cadence and gives special emphasis to the repetition of the word *torna* (example 11.1).

Giovanni Bononcini also prefers moderate vocal ranges. In pieces like "Pena e soffri," he never forces the voice into unusual stratospheres; yet he keeps the tessitura high, focusing mainly on the area from $b\flat^1$ to f^2, where the soprano voice can be heard to best advantage. Few early eighteenth-century composers possess the older Bononcini's instinct for idiomatic and ingratiating vocal writing. Like Ziani, Giovanni sometimes places the melodic high point of an aria in B. In "Dolce amor" the peak g^2 occurs several times, notably on the downbeat of measure 31, where the soprano line leaps to the high point from a minor seventh below. Moreover, the general rising motion of the coloratura, reaching higher and higher pitches on the first beats of four consecutive measures, draws special attention to the peak in measure 31 (example 11.2). In general, however, Bononcini prefers a melodic climax

EX. 11.2 G. Bononcini, Cantata 82/I, mm. 27–33. Emphatic approach to an important peak in B.

in the penultimate or final phrase of 1A or 2A. For example, the highest point in the soprano line of "Pena e soffri" is g^2; it occurs several times in both A and B but receives most emphatic treatment in the final measures of 1A and 2A. This tendency to reserve climaxes for concluding phrases is sometimes applied to an obbligato line. In "Dio d'Amor" Bononcini saves the top pitch (d^3) of the flute part for the end of A2; a secondary peak (c^3) comes in the penultimate phrase of B.

With regard to range, Antonio Bononcini generally makes the greatest demands upon the singer. None of the arias analyzed has a span of less than a diminished eleventh. In two arias Antonio calls for exceptional technique: the range of "Men crudele" extends from c^1 to $b\flat^2$, and the compass of "Sentimi, crudo Amore" covers a full two octaves, from c^1 to c^3. Records documenting the names of singers who performed specific cantatas at the Viennese court before the 1720s have not been uncovered. Antonio may have written these arias for one of the prima donnas newly added to the imperial chapel or for one of the soprano castratos.[1] This virtuoso aspect derives not only from the unusual summits but also from the use of the voice's sustaining power in a high tessitura. Thus, the $b\flat^2$ of "Men crudele" is preceded by an a^2 held for more than three quarter-note beats. The two high pitches crown the top of a long nine-bar phrase that requires extraordinary breath control. No other Viennese cantata composer makes such brilliant use of the soprano's upper range.

Antonio Bononcini often places the highest vocal peak about two-thirds to three-fourths of the way through A, reserving a secondary high point for the final phrase. This plan can be seen in arias like "Amore ingannatore," "Men crudele," and "Sentimi, crudo Amore." Thus, in "Men crudele" the crest of a^2–$b\flat^2$ caps the dramatic second phrase of 2A, and a subordinate peak of g^2 climaxes the long final

EX. 11.3. A. M. Bononcini, Cantata 45/I, mm. 33–34. Placement of a peak in the final phrase of 2A.

phrase. "Sentimi, crudo Amore" contains the highest vocal peak reached in any Viennese aria; the soaring high c^3 in measure 35 is an isolated example in the whole repertoire (see example 11.19).[2] Future research may demonstrate that it is one of the earliest notated examples in music history. Bononcini interpolates the peak about three-fourths of the way through A, using f^2 as a subpeak three times in the final phrases of 2A. With his customary fondness for symmetry, he uses the same plan in B: the highest pitch (a^2) occurs approximately three-fourths of the way through B (measure 72).

As an alternative procedure, Antonio delays the most prominent peak until the penultimate or final phrase of 2A. Hence, the outstanding effect achieved by the contrary motion in the penultimate phrase of "S'io ritorno" (see example 11.30) is coordinated with high points for both the alto (d^2) and flute (d^3). In B the climax for the alto (d^2) correspondingly belongs to the penultimate phrase. Antonio postpones the peak of "Più barbaro martire" until the last phrase of 2A. As in measures 48–51 of "Amore ingannatore," he creates a melody on two planes: from the middle of its range (the pitches d^1 and c^1) the alto line springs upward to higher and higher peaks, reaching the only d^2 of the aria in the final bar (example 11.3).

The ritornellos of several arias by Antonio also show careful planning. For example, he saves the top d^3 of the flute obbligato in the long opening ritornello (measures 1–17) of "Un cor più tormentato" for the arch of the final phrase. And in "Amore ingannatore" the combination of contrary motion, syncopated surface rhythms, harmonic tension, and melodic peak (eb^3) produces concinnity near the end of the initial ritornello (see example 11.30).

In two arias by Antonio the vocal line drops to a low pitch at the conclusion of B. Thus, the soprano descends to $d\sharp^1$ on the word *pace* at the conclusion of B in "Per non arder"; the use of a melodic valley and a *piano* dynamic aptly enhances the text. At the end of B in "Al tuo bel volto" the soprano line descending to e^1 also seems completely appropriate to the text ("fu martire d'Amor").

Fewer specific remarks can be made about the ranges of bass lines. The largest range occurs in Giovanni Bononcini's "Dolce amor," in which the bass stretches from low C^2 to g^1, a compass of two octaves and a fifth. Bass ranges of two octaves and a fourth can be found in three arias by Antonio Bononcini and in one aria by Ariosti. (Antonio uses the same span for the elaborate cello obbligato in "Più barbaro martire.") The Bononcini brothers' tendency to exploit large bass ranges may be a reflection of their own interest in the cello; both excelled as string players, and they may well have participated in the initial performances of their works. Elsewhere, a span of approximately two octaves is common.

Since Antonio writes more obbligato parts than any of his contemporaries, it is difficult to draw comparisons about the ranges of these instruments. However, on the basis of the arias analyzed, he consistently uses the widest ranges for obbligato instruments. None of the arias by Badia, Ziani, or Giovanni Bononcini includes a flute, violin, or oboe part with a range exceeding an octave and a minor sixth. A pair of arias by Antonio ("Più barbaro martire" and "Sentimi, crudo Amore") contain violin parts extending from g^1 to d^3. His flute parts regularly rise to peaks of e^3 or eb^3. With its bass line descending to low C^2 and its violin obbligato soaring to d^3, "Sentimi, crudo Amore" has the largest total range of all Viennese arias.

Two composers, Badia and Ziani, effectively use wide range within a single phrase and abrupt shifts. In particular, Badia does not hesitate to explore more than an octave within a phrase. For example, he begins 2A of "Basti per mio contento" with a line that leaps up an octave from g^1 to g^2, then slides gradually down an octave and a fourth to d^1. Typically, too, Badia shifts ranges between phrases; the initial phrase of 2A is followed by one beginning a minor ninth higher, on eb^2. The opening of B in his "Gelosia, furia d'Alletto" demonstrates the composer's ability to keep a line moving forward by using frequent shifts of range (see example 10.1, measures 25–29).

Sudden changes of range and wide compasses within a phrase are less common in arias by Ariosti and the Bononcini brothers. Ariosti reaches peaks and valleys very gradually, sometimes over an entire section or subsection. In contrast, the lines of Ziani's arias often move quickly up and down, exploring the full vocal range. A single phrase frequently includes many leaps. The opening vocal melody of "Navicella che paventa" shows his predilection for broad undulating patterns; it also illustrates his tendency to end a long phrase up in the air (example 11.4). Often he ends a phrase with a vigorous upsurge by coordinating a large leap with quicker surface rhythm.

MELODIC SHAPES

More often than any of the other Viennese composers, Ariosti writes long conjunct melodies with gradual climbs and descents. He especially favors melodies that as-

EX. 11.4. Ziani, Cantata 18/V, mm. 14–23. A wide-ranging vocal line.

cend slowly through several measures to important peaks. Though he may inflect the beginning of a vocal theme with a striking interval, such as the descending minor sixth in "Al voler del bene amato" or the ascending tritone in "Insoffribile tormento," he usually continues with simple diatonic motion consisting predominantly of steps and small skips. In arias like "Nice, crudel" he achieves some variety by contrasting wave-form melodies with rapid descents. Phrases of mostly level activity can be found in B sections, where the composer depends upon simple, repeated-note patterns in sequential repetition. Beginning and ending on the same pitch, the opening theme of "Cangi Amore" attests to Ariosti's ability to create an elegant arch (example 11.5).

Smooth descending lines, shapely curves, and wave forms dominate the melodic activity of Badia's arias. He consistently reveals his affinity for falling lines that begin in middle or high range. Since so many phrases start on middle or high pitches, extended curves tend to be of the reverse or concave type. Occasionally Badia shifts the direction at the end of a reverse curve so that a long S-shape unfolds. At the outset of "Ombra del mio bel sol," for example, he produces a long conjunct S-curve; beginning on d^2, the melody moves downward by steps to $f\sharp^1$, then rises gently again to d^2. Instead of ending the phrase at this point, however, the composer uses an $e\flat^2$ passing tone to extend it directly into the next phrase, which begins from a new peak (f^2) heard in relationship to the initial pitch. A systematically undulating pattern occurs just before the conclusion of 2A in "Gelosia, furia d'Alletto" (see example 10.1). Some less regular wave forms in the same aria and in "Sì vaga e sì vezzosa" add variety.

Giovanni Bononcini also prefers conjunct curves and wave forms. He specializes in cantabile melodies that move mainly by step but include skips that do not disrupt the basic curves. Passages with many short phrases, such as the opening of B in "Dolce amor," consist of a series of miniature arches. Extended coloratura lines take on highly patterned shapes, also moving chiefly by steps and small skips. These lines offer singers attractive opportunities for vocal display without overtaxing technical abilities (see example 11.2). Frequently the composer uses intervals like the minor seventh and the tritone at important structural cadences. Level pla-

EX. 11.5. Ariosti, Cantata 65/I, mm. 8–12. An opening theme designed as a broad arch.

teaus sometimes occur at peaks of phrases; in B of "Pena e soffri," for example, the line twice rises to a sustained f^2, bringing the voice into a brilliant tessitura without pushing it into virtuosic heights. Gently undulating figures turn up in virtually every aria. Arias like "Pena e soffri" and "Dio d'Amor" contain many less regular wave patterns, but even these lines proceed largely by steps and small skips.

The most fascinating aspect of Ziani's melodies stems from his often deliberate avoidance of symmetrical curves and predictable patterns. Gradually rising and falling lines are also rare. Instead, he includes many skips and large leaps in phrases that follow irregular zigzag routes. Several long lines leave a breathless, nonstop impression because of their continuous rhythmic activity and constantly twisting shapes. Successions of fourths and fifths in sawtooth patterns contribute a degree of regularity to some phrases, but Ziani usually interpolates these figures within long meandering lines.

The widest spectrum of melodic shapes can be found in arias by Antonio Bononcini. These include gradual rises and falls ("Al tuo bel volto"), level plateaus ("Men crudele"), sawtooth patterns ("Amore ingannatore"), elegant arches ("Benché m'abbia"), and more irregular shapes ("S'io ritorno"). Arias such as "Al tuo bel volto" and "Un cor più tormentato" contain some exceptionally long ascending phrases in stepwise motion, reminiscent of several passages by Ariosti (compare example 11.25a–b and example 11.15). Antonio may vary the long ascent of a line by using a succession of rising and falling skips that do not contradict its general direction. The occasional leaps in arias such as "Amore ingannatore" are carefully adapted to the declamatory word rhythms. As a special effect in "Mentre al novo apparir" the composer uses wider and wider leaps to reach a particularly impressive peak (see example 11.3). Sometimes within a single phrase he contrasts stepwise and leaping motion. The lengthy opening melody of "S'io ritorno a innamorarvi" contains unusually variegated contours consisting of rising and falling, conjunct and disjunct patterns.

Antonio's treatment of obbligato melodies is also extremely varied. Whereas his contemporaries scarcely differentiate between the vocal and obbligato lines, the younger Bononcini writes instrumental parts that demonstrate his command of

EX. 11.6a–c. A. M. Bononcini, Cantata 45/I, mm. 68–71, and idiomatic string writing in the motives *Ray, z,* and *w.*

idiomatic techniques such as string crossings and rapid, skipping figurations. The motives *Ray, z,* and *w* of "Più barbaro martire" exemplify his flare for idiomatic string writing (example 11.6a–c).

HARMONY

THE ROLE OF THE BASS LINE

One of the most varied aspects of the cantata arias from the early eighteenth century is the relationship of the bass line to the upper parts. As the term *basso continuo* implies, the bass line characteristically assumes a prominent role in providing unity, at other times becomes the essential ingredient of variety, and occasionally combines both functions.

In the manuscripts the amount of continuo figuration varies considerably. Badia and Ariosti, for example, frequently provide no figures at all. Although Ariosti adds more figuration than usual in the ritornellos of two arias, "Al voler del bene amato" and "Insoffribile tormento," because of the chromatic harmonies, during the remainder of each aria he includes details only sparsely. In general Giovanni Bononcini uses a modest amount of figuration. The most specific figures can be found in scores by Ziani and Antonio Bononcini, especially the latter. Like other

EX. 11.7. Ariosti, Cantata 29/I, mm. 1–7. A quasi-ostinato walking bass.

facets of his work, the figured basses of Antonio's cantatas demonstrate meticulous attention to detail.

Many bass lines remain largely independent from the upper parts throughout an aria. In some arias, for example, the bass line functions only as harmonic support and does not share in significant melodic and motivic material. More rarely, a composer assigns a sharply defined motive to the bass, keeping it consistently separate and independent from melodies heard in the vocal and/or obbligato lines. Far more frequently, however, bass and treble lines are clearly integrated, so that the bass often announces the primary vocal motive in the introductory ritornello. It may also participate in imitation with one or more of the upper parts. Finally, a more complex relationship combines several treatments in many arias, so that the function of the bass line constantly changes. It may share one or more motives with the vocal line while retaining its own independent material, or it may alternate between thematic sharing and pure harmonic support. In general, the arias without obbligato parts—that is, the continuo arias—have more active and interesting bass lines; however, Antonio Bononcini excels at assimilating the bass into the total texture of arias with obbligati.

All of the Viennese composers occasionally write arias with bass lines that lack distinctive motives and serve mainly as foundations. In the majority of these pieces, the bass line consists of simple walking patterns in eighths or quarters. Ariosti especially favors undifferentiated eighth-note basses. In arias like his "È pur dolce a un cor legato" the regularity of the rhythmic and melodic patterning lends a quasi-ostinato shape to the bass line. However, none of the Viennese composers builds an entire aria upon a strict ostinato (example 11.7).

In two arias with obbligati, "Se sarai mio" and "Sì vaga e sì vezzosa," Badia chooses not to include the bass line in the motivic web but gives it a purely supporting function. In the triple-meter aria "Se sarai mio," the bass moves mostly in groups of eighths or alternating eighths and quarters. The composer uses its continuous motion to disguise many articulations, and in general his tendency to elide phrases is characteristic of late baroque style. A notable exception occurs in the aria "Sì vaga e sì vezzosa"; here Badia repeatedly interrupts the walking patterns so

EX. 11.8. A. M. Bononcini, Cantata 56/II, mm. 15–19. Division of the bass line.

that the bass confirms the phrase and subphrase articulations of the upper parts. In this aria he seems to anticipate one of the basic characteristics of early classic style.

Because the vast majority of his arias contain important obbligati, Antonio Bononcini also writes a few nonmotivic walking basses. A good example occurs in "Amore ingannatore," but even here the younger Bononcini includes interesting details lacking in walking-bass arias by other composers. At the beginning of the aria, for instance, the bass line shares rhythmically, if not melodically, in the imitative texture. Antonio also pairs it frequently with the alto in concertato opposition to the two flutes. In "Benché m'abbia la cruda saetta" he composes a more conventional, sequential walking bass that serves as a constant support for the legato vocal line and ornamental violin obbligato.

In four other arias with obbligati, Antonio mixes the principal role of the bass as harmonic foundation with other functions. The predominantly walking bass

of "Per non arder," for example, sometimes shares one of the most important mo-
tives (♩ ♫ ♫ | ♩ 𝄾), which it plays homorhythmically with the unison flutes or
with the soprano. Curiously, at all points where this occurs the composer actually
notates two separate bass lines, one for the continuo and one for a quasi-obbligato
bass part that plays the motive. In the manuscript the scribe uses an additional
staff, blank except for the places where the obbligato bass branches off from the
continuo. The divided bass line in "Per non arder" is one of the most interesting
aspects of performance practice in the Viennese cantata repertoire. The lines may
have been performed by two cellos, by cello and bassoon, or perhaps by double
bass and obbligato cello, the instruments specified by the composer in the cantata
"Mentre al novo apparir" (A-Wn, 17607, no. 4). In any event, the divided bass line
of "Per non arder" once again demonstrates Antonio's persistent concern for detail
(example 11.8).

In "S'io ritorno a innamorarvi" Antonio writes a bass line that is rhythmically
and melodically more varied than most conventional walking basses; though it
functions chiefly as harmonic support for the flute and/or alto, now and then it also
participates in the motivic process. He reserves the most striking motives (x and y)
for the flutist and singer, but the bass enters subtly into the development of z and especially w; moreover, measures 20–23 and similar passages are rhythmically related
to x, a further unifying device. (For the four motives of this aria, see example 10.2.)

In the arias "Men crudele" and "Un cor più tormentato," Antonio provides
some relief from the prevailing polarity of melody and bass by including the bass
in occasional points of imitation. "Un cor più tormentato" contains widely spaced
hints of imitation involving the bass line at points such as measures 9–10 and 71–75.
In "Men crudele," however, the imitation occurs more frequently. In the opening
ritornello and at several points in the 1A section, the bass imitates the head-motive
played by one of the upper parts. Antonio expands the imitation of the head-motive
in the 2A section, giving it in succession to the flutes, the voice, the bass, and again
to the voice.

In an aria with flute obbligato, "Dio d'Amor," Giovanni Bononcini tends to ex-
clude motivic material from the bass line. Only one tiny fragment (𝄾 ♪ ♫ ♩. 𝄾| ♪)
appears from time to time in the bass line as a unifying device. However, Giovanni
does not depend solely upon the stereotyped patterns found in arias like Ariosti's
"Nice, crudel." In rhythmic variety the bass of "Dio d'Amor" is more equal to the
upper lines and integrated into the total texture.

The ambitious continuo aria by the older Bononcini, "Pena e soffri," is dominated throughout by an independent driving bass motive first heard in the opening
ritornello (example 11.9). This ritornello neatly exemplifies the kind of ornamental
bass for which Giovanni was lavishly praised by Gasparini. Characterized by a descending octave leap and the surface rhythm ♫ ♩ ♫ ♩ ♫♫, the basic one-measure
motive continues in the bass line relentlessly through the entire aria, vocal as well

EX. 11.9. G. Bononcini, Cantata 51/I, mm. 1–9. A ritornello generated out of a bass motive kept largely independent from the vocal line.

EX. 11.10. G. Bononcini, Cantata 51/I, mm. 125–35. Integration of an independent bass motive into vocal coloratura.

as instrumental sections. The composer interrupts the incessant repetitions of the motive only to underpin the most important structural cadences, such as those at the ends of 1A, 2A, and 2B. The soprano takes up the instrumental motive only in a few places, during long coloratura passages appended to the purely vocal melodies. Giovanni alters the vocal version of the instrumental motive slightly to avoid the octave leaps, but in other details of rhythmic and melodic profile the motive

EX. 11.11. G. Bononcini, Cantata 82/I, mm. 1–4. A ritornello with a
bass line that states the primary vocal melody.

is clearly related. Invariably the vocal statements alternate with those in the bass
(example 11.10).

"Pena e soffri" is the only aria offered for analysis in this study that contains
a bass line made up entirely of a pervasive but independent motive, without reference to the vocal line. Such arias are indeed unusual in early eighteenth-century
Viennese cantatas. Far more frequently, the Viennese composers introduce an
important idea in the opening ritornello that serves as the head-motive in the 1A
section and as the germ for development throughout the aria. In Giovanni Bononcini's "Dolce amor," for example, the initial ritornello spins a languid melody
subsequently sung by the soprano; it consists of a two-beat motive—reduced to one
beat in measure 2—that is extended by repetition and sequence and dominates both
A and A^1 (example 11.11). Bononcini writes economically, using only one important
motive in the ritornello. As the soprano begins to sing, the bass line falls into the
background, providing simple harmonic support and returning to the principal
motive only briefly in the interpolated sequential roulade of A^1 (measures 44–46).
Bononcini therefore differentiates two bass functions, one as the germinator of the
main motive, and another as harmonic support.

Ariosti uses a similar procedure in "Cangi Amore." The introductory ritornello generates the most important motive of the aria, and this two-measure ker-
nel dominates all of A and A^1. However, the voice sings only the nub (♩ ♫) of the
instrumental motive, and Ariosti continues to distinguish between the two lines
in this manner. As in Bononcini's "Dolce amor," the role of the bass in "Cangi
Amore" becomes almost completely supporting during the long vocal sections,

EX. 11.12. Ariosti, Cantata 39/I, mm. 17–19. The use of simple surface rhythm as a device for integrating the vocal and bass lines.

and Ariosti falls back upon the type of walking bass found in so many of his brief arias.

The technique of beginning the ritornello and 1A with the same motive only to continue each differently seems to be an Ariosti trademark. In "Al voler del bene amato" the ritornello once again contains the seed of the initial vocal melody, but the two proceed differently after only one and one-half beats. Here Ariosti suggests the primary theme in the ritornello but saves the complete phrase for the voice. As in "Cangi Amore," however, the bass line reverts to stereotyped patterns while supporting the vocal line.

For "Insoffribile tormento" Ariosti only slightly varies his customary approach to the relationship of bass and vocal lines. As usual, the ritornello begins with the head-motive of 1A and soon branches off in an independent direction. During the vocal sections, however, the bass not only functions as harmonic background but also participates in the total motivic matrix. After the *Devise* and the ensuing abridged ritornello, the bass repeats the principal motive frequently in inversion; the surface rhythm (♪♫♩) remains unchanged. Thereafter Ariosti uses the motive again and again in the bass, either in inversion or unaltered. Many sections of the aria consist of repetitions of the basic pattern alternating between soprano and bass; only the surface rhythm remains constant (example 11.12). "Insoffribile tormento" thus represents an interesting exception to most of the composer's work; the bass becomes an actual partner in a texture that is more complex than usual.

In a few Ziani arias the treatment of the bass line is as uncomplicated as most of Ariosti's. In "Brami e speri," for instance, Ziani previews the primary vocal idea in the initial ritornello, but, unlike Ariosti, he gives a complete phrase (five beats), not just the head-motive. By alternately assigning the phrase to the voice in the *Devise*, the bass in the subsequent ritornello, and the voice again, the composer creates a simple point of imitation; for the remainder of the aria, however, the bass proceeds in a conventional walking manner, with fragments from the ritornello only sparsely interwoven. The bass line of "Se infelice" unfolds similarly but with an opening ritornello of two main ideas instead of only one. The second motive, with its characteristic ascending fourth and descending fifth, recurs often in the bass line throughout the aria, and a new motive consisting of descending thirds (measure 22) also becomes important. In general, the thread of motives in Ziani bass lines is less obvious than in those of his contemporaries, partly because he prefers to define his ideas by melodic intervals rather than by sharply differentiated surface rhythms. In fact, a page from the manuscript of "Se infelice" appears at first to consist of straight quarter-note motion with little profile; a closer look uncovers lines in which motives are subtly intertwined.

In many Viennese arias, imitation between the bass and vocal lines becomes a preeminent source of unity. Like the ritornello of Ziani's "Se infelice," the introduction of Badia's "Ombra del mio bel sol" includes two important motives. Each motive is used in imitation with the voice. The initial instrumental idea serves as the primary vocal motive, but Badia refreshingly modifies the vocal entrance by having the singer sustain the first tone while the bass line plays the motive again in its original octave. The second motive appears in sequential and modulating sections like the ones that close 1A, 2A, and B. Badia uses the two motives extensively in imitation both in A and in B, making the bass line a more consistently equal partner than it is in most of Ariosti's arias.

Equality of bass line and upper parts can be seen clearly in Antonio Bononcini's "Sentimi, crudo Amore." In this aria the bass line shares fully in the detailed motivic process, having a role equal to the two violins, viola, and soprano. Antonio includes the bass in the statement of two of the three principal motives in the ritornello; during the vocal sections he distributes the three motives among all five lines, using many combinations and permutations. Moreover, imitation is a basic feature of the style, not just an accessory. Antonio particularly likes to toss the first motive (♫♫) among all the parts; the piling up of entries of this simple motoric pattern accounts for much of the rhythmic vitality. The refinement of Antonio's imagination is evident in the B section, where the bass line repeats an obscure variant of *x* first heard in the viola in measures 18–24.

The bass line of Antonio's "Al tuo bel volto amante" combines two separate techniques: (1) generating the main vocal melody at the beginning of the ritornello as well as a prominent independent motive, the second idea of the ritornello; and (2) treating the bass line as an equal partner in imitative passages. The younger Bononcini sometimes favors surprisingly long points of imitation. First played in

EX. 11.13. Badia, Cantata 75/III, mm. 1–8. The use of the bass line to announce the primary vocal theme and an independent figuration.

measures 4–7, the independent motive consists of a descending scale in sixteenths; during the aria Antonio uses it often to contrast with sustained pitches in the soprano part.

The statement of both the primary vocal theme and an independent instrumental motive in the introductory ritornello is found also in two arias by Badia. In "Basti per mio contento" he keeps the functions of the two motives completely distinct. The opening conjunct idea becomes the principal vocal melody, and it dominates both A and B. The independent bass motive consists of a sequential sixteenth-note pattern with idiomatic instrumental leaps (example 11.13). Like Antonio, Badia sets the jagged instrumental figuration in relief against a slow-moving vocal line. While the soprano sings phrases derived from the head-motive, the bass typically provides simple harmonic support.

In "Gelosia, furia d'Alletto" the ritornello again introduces both the primary vocal melody and an independent sixteenth-note figuration. In this ritornello the two motives are rhythmically less differentiated, and they are not separated by the half-cadence that articulates the motives of "Basti per mio contento" (see example 10.1, measures 1–4). Badia unifies bass and vocal parts by weaving bits of the instrumental motive into the vocal melody, sometimes in inversion, as at the end of 2A. During the vocal passages the role of the bass alternates between harmonic support and sequential patterns derived from the independent motive.

The tendency to interlace the motives of various lines is most pronounced in arias by Ziani. Of the several rhythmic patterns that appear throughout "Navicella che paventa," the bass especially shares the figure ♩ ♫♫ with the other parts. The pattern appears in a myriad of melodic contours. Sometimes the bass plays it ho-morhythmically with one or more of the upper parts; at other times the bass carries the motive alone. At the beginning of 1A, for instance, the bass plays the motive while the soprano announces a new melody. Before long, however, Ziani inserts the bass rhythm into the soprano line. Thus, in his arias, motives are frequently treated as cells that can be integrated into any line at the beginning, in the middle, or at the end of a phrase. In this way he produces a motivic quilt. In "Navicella" the simple bass rhythm also serves to link phrases in a typically baroque manner that disguises articulations.

Antonio Bononcini's "Più barbaro martire" contains a bass line with a con-stantly changing function. The score includes an elaborate cello obbligato; the separate bass line is designated for "Contrabasso e Cembalo." In many phrases the bass doubles the ornamental obbligato, usually playing simplified versions but also frequently playing an octave lower than the cello part. The bass also acts as pure harmonic support, shares important motivic material, and takes part in imitation. Both the motives x and y, first played by the violins in the ritornello, are used in the bass line. Antonio particularly likes to redistribute motives among various lines, creating frequent part exchange (example 11.14a–b).

The Viennese composers seldom change the function of the bass line estab-lished in an A section to a new role in the B section. The only arias in which this ac-tually occurs are Ariosti's "Cangi Amore" and Giovanni Bononcini's "Dolce amor," the two pieces with sharp contrasts in continuum and motivic material. In the A of "Cangi Amore," the bass line includes important vocal motives and moves pre-dominantly in quarters; in B it serves simply as harmonic foundation and moves much more slowly, in dotted halves. The contrast is even sharper in "Dolce amor"; the bass line turns from a mainly supporting role in A to an equal partnership in the imitative texture of B.

Much more common than broad contrasts between A and B are arias in which composers differentiate between the melodic and/or rhythmic profiles of the bass and vocal lines. Of course, many arias do not include such differentiations. For ex-ample, in Badia's "Sì vaga e sì vezzosa" the bass dutifully parallels the obbligato line or soprano in tenths or thirds, moves largely in strict homorhythm with the upper parts, and always articulates with the obbligato player (flute or violin) or singer at the ends of sections. In most Ariosti arias, on the other hand, the rigid walking basses contrast with the more rhythmically diverse and melodically ornamental vocal lines (example 11.15). The distinct rhythmic densities of bass and vocal lines in Giovanni Bononcini's "Pena e soffri" also produce a layered effect. The older Bononcini coordinates homorhythm and melodic motion to underline important cadences.

Patterning also contributes to the structural role of many bass lines. Sequen-tial patterns tend to be most regular and unbroken in arias by Badia, for whom

EX. 11.14a–b. (*above and facing*) A. M. Bononcini, Cantata 45/I, mm. 1–4 and 85–88. Redistribution of the motives *x, y,* and *z.*

b

sequence is the indispensable means of extending ideas. Within a passage Badia sometimes uses as many as seven units of a basic module. But he is not alone in relying upon the hackneyed device. Highly patterned bass lines can also be found in arias by Ariosti and Giovanni Bononcini. The patterns are almost always derived from ritornello motives, and they become most regular during florid vocal lines. In

EX. 11.15. Ariosti, Cantata 6/I, mm. 10–14. Sharply differentiated vocal and bass lines.

the B section of Bononcini's "Pena e soffri," patterning occurs in three dimensions. One-measure repetitions of the basic instrumental motive are played beneath a sustained f^2 in the soprano; the motives are grouped into pairs so that two-bar units are superposed. After the two-bar unit occurs twice, the pedal shifts from the voice to the bass, and the vocal line descends chromatically (example 11.16). The soprano then rises again to a sustained f^2; now, however, the two-measure pattern occurs only once. Similarly, the bass pedal is reduced to two measures; the authentic cadence at the end of the first long phrase (measure 92) is replaced by an unusually effective deceptive cadence (I $^6_4$ to V $^4_3$-of-V) at the end of the second phrase (measure 101). By abbreviating the large unit and substituting the abrupt deceptive cadence for the expected authentic one, Bononcini halts the rhythmic momentum that had continued unabated from the beginning of the long aria.

Although Ariosti also depends heavily upon sequence for expanding phrases, he often avoids more than one repetition of a pattern. In phrases with several units, he likes to add modifications in order to dilute the rigidity of sequential patterning. Even less predictable are patterns used in arias by Ziani and Antonio Bononcini. Ziani frequently rolls a basic rhythmic fragment over again and again, yet with-

EX. 11.16. G. Bononcini, Cantata 51/I, mm. 84–92. Bass-line patterning beneath a vocal pedal.

out building a strict melodic sequence with it. On the whole the construction of Ziani's lines is rather elusive; there is an individuality to his approach that separates his work from his contemporaries'. Antonio occasionally builds conventional sequential bass lines, especially under roulades of arias like "Sentimi, crudo Amore." But more frequently he avoids cliché patterns. The bass lines of arias such as "Men crudele" and "Amore ingannatore" provide strong harmonic direction, but they lack extended sequences and usually tend to disguise the regularity of patterning in the upper parts.

In several arias, a particular melodic interval saturates the bass line so completely that it acts as a unifying device. Ziani especially likes perfect fourths and fifths, and he uses them extensively in arias like "Brami e speri" and "Se infelice." The affective augmented fourths in Ariosti's "Insoffribile tormento," the drooping descending sixths in Antonio Bononcini's "Al tuo bel volto," and the insistent octaves in Giovanni Bononcini's "Pena e soffri" certainly contribute to the motivic unity of these arias. In Bononcini's "Dolce amor" the prominence of the descending seventh seems to have more than a casual influence on the shape of the aria. The interval first appears twice in the opening ritornello (see example 11.11). In the B section, each segment of a three-part sequence begins with the outlining of a descending seventh in the soprano; curiously, the same sequence reappears—in a different rhythm and meter—in A¹, but here it is the bass that outlines the sevenths (example 11.17a–b). Elsewhere, as in measures 7, 46, and 48, Bononcini fills in descending sevenths with scale passages.

EX. 11.17a–b. G. Bononcini, Cantata 82/I, mm. 20–26 and 44–46. The use of descending melodic sevenths as a unifying device.

The range of the bass line sometimes plays a subtle role in its relationship with the other parts. In Giovanni Bononcini's "Dio d'Amor" the bass at the beginning of the ritornello returns an octave lower when the voice enters; with the octave displacement Bononcini avoids unwanted voice crossing and the crowding of bass and alto lines too close together. In "Nice, crudel" Ariosti occasionally permits the alto to cross below the bass, but the harmonies remain clear. The bass line also sometimes crosses above the voice, as in Ziani's "Se infelice," but here the singer is a bass, and the closeness of the two low parts lends a special dark quality to the entire aria. In the B section of "Cangi Amore" Ariosti exploits low range for coloristic reasons, providing a somber quality appropriate to the text. The widest range occurs in Antonio Bononcini's "Al tuo bel volto," where the bass spans two and one-half octaves, from D^2 to g^1.

From time to time Giovanni Bononcini leaves out the bass line for a measure or two to achieve a coloristic effect. In the aria "Dio d'Amor," he sets up a continuous musical dialogue between the alto (a questioning lover) and the flute (the god of love). Near the end of the A section the sudden omission of the bass line underscores this dialogue.

Antonio also allows the bass line to drop out briefly in many arias and thereby achieves some delightful coloristic and dramatic effects. He especially likes to begin a ritornello with only the obbligato instruments, having the bass enter in imitation one or two measures later. In subsequent ritornellos he may vary the technique by having one obbligato instrument begin alone and by pairing the second obbligato line with the bass in the staggered entrance. Similarly, at the beginning of 1A or 1B, Antonio frequently prefers to focus attention on the unaccompanied voice by

EX. 11.18. A. M. Bononcini, Cantata 45/I, mm. 15–16. Omission of the bass line, leaving a vocal pedal as the lowest pitch.

delaying the bass for a bar or two. The lower part may then respond with imitation or with a completely different motive (see example 11.14b).

Sometimes in the younger Bononcini's arias one of the upper instrumental lines or the voice momentarily assumes the role of the bass. In measure 11 of "Più barbaro martire," unison violins in parallel thirds with the alto briefly function as the lowest line.[3] In measures 15–16 the bass line again drops out, and a sustained a^1 sung by the alto becomes the bottom pitch (example 11.18). At times, the bass simply punctuates the beginning of each measure of a phrase, allowing the listener to focus principal attention upon the motivic upper lines. With many details such as these, Antonio greatly enriches the textural variety of his music.

The younger Bononcini also draws upon more dramatic effects. In measures 24–25 of "Per non arder," for example, the bass and soprano stop exactly at the point where the flute descends a minor seventh, leaving the instrument completely alone on the low pitch. The soprano continues immediately on the next beat, beginning one octave higher than the flute. Thus by isolating the particular colors of voices or instruments at climactic moments, Antonio achieves many expressive and dramatic details. Perhaps the most extraordinary example occurs in the aria "Sentimi, crudo Amore." The remarkably florid soprano phrase in measures 33–35 concludes with a brilliant high c (c^3), a rare instance in early eighteenth-century vocal music in general. Just here Antonio cuts off the bass and obbligati one and a half beats before the climactic peak, allowing the singer to reap the full benefit of the virtuoso passage (example 11.19).

la li - ber-tà

EX. 11.19. A. M. Bononcini, Cantata 28/I, mm. 33–35. Omission of the bass line and obbligato lines to expose the peak of a florid vocal phrase.

THE BROAD MODULATORY PLAN

Two important aspects of harmonic motion on a broad scale entail the overall modulatory scheme and the key rhythm (the rate at which modulations occur). A composer may consistently draw upon strong modulations between closely related keys to give direction to the movement in his arias. Tensional modulations such as tonic/dominant or minor/relative major occur frequently within A sections but also occasionally between sections or even within B sections. In several arias, however, composers do not exploit the polarity of keys; an individual A or B may contain no modulations at all or be dominated by migrant motion to a variety of keys without establishing a strong sense of direction.

Within the da capo framework composers usually place the strongest directional modulation near the midpoint of A, that is, at the end of 1A. The customary tensional poles of tonic/dominant and minor/relative major occur frequently. Of the eight da capo arias in major keys, five (three by Antonio Bononcini, one by Ziani, and one by Ariosti) contain the standard modulation to the dominant midway through A. In arias like Ziani's "Navicella che paventa" and Antonio's "Un cor più tormentato," a suggestion of the modulation to the dominant takes place already in the opening ritornello. Of the thirteen da capo arias in minor keys, nine (three by Antonio Bononcini and two each by Badia, Ariosti, and Giovanni Bononcini) move to the relative major at the end of 1A.

Antonio Bononcini uses goal-oriented modulations as a strong source of directional motion in A more consistently than any other Viennese composer. In two minor arias ("Per non arder" and "Al tuo bel volto") he achieves color and variety by treating the relative major and its parallel as ambivalent goals; in each aria a modulation to the relative major is followed by several phrases in its parallel. In the a-minor "Al tuo bel volto" Antonio strengthens the effect of the c-minor passage at the end of 1A by beginning B also in c minor. Apart from the three arias with modulations to the relative major in A, he composed two g-minor arias ("Più barbaro martire" and "S'io ritorno a innamorarvi") in which he substitutes the minor dominant as the modulatory goal of A. Thus, for Antonio the minor dominant is an important and satisfactory alternative to the relative major.

Ariosti uses more modally inflected substitutes in two arias, "Al voler del bene amato" and "Nice, crudel." In the A-major "Al voler" he replaces movement to the dominant (E) with a modulation to the mediant (c♯ minor). Somewhat like Antonio in "Al tuo bel volto," Ariosti underscores the unusualness of the mediant minor by recalling it at the beginning of B. "Nice, crudel" modulates from the tonic (g minor) to ♭VII (F), then passes briefly through the minor dominant (d minor) before settling in the tonic for the second half of A.

In "Dio d'Amor" Giovanni Bononcini dilutes the strength of the tonic minor/relative major opposition by constantly fluctuating between tonic, relative major, and dominant minor throughout the first half of A. The modulatory goal of Ariosti's d-minor "È pur dolce" is also unsettled; the composer moves first toward the subdominant (g minor) before establishing the relative major (F). No modulations at all occur in the A sections of four da capo arias, Badia's "Gelosia, furia d'Alletto" and "Sì vaga e sì vezzosa" and Giovanni Bononcini's "Dolce amor" and "Pena e soffri." In "Gelosia," however, Badia defines the end of 1A with an emphatic cadence on the dominant.

Strong modulations also lend directional movement to the four Viennese arias that are not cast in the da capo pattern. In both G-major arias by Ziani ("Brami e speri" and "Se infelice") the tonality shifts to the dominant at the end of the first section. In the e-minor "Insoffribile tormento," Ariosti selects G major as the modulatory goal, but the vacillation between G major and a minor in the center of the A section somewhat weakens the polarity of tonic minor and relative major. In the brief aria "Benché m'abbia la cruda saetta," Antonio Bononcini exploits both the relative major and the dominant minor in a neat three-part plan that foreshadows the modulatory plan of sonata form, though not the repetition scheme (diagram 11.1).

A tensional modulation occurs much more frequently within A than between the end of A and the beginning of B. Since the opening of B normally provides a fresh tonal outlook, the concept of polarity is less important at this structural joint than a quick smooth shift to new tonal ground. Of the eight arias in major, the B sections of five begin in the most closely related key, the relative minor, rather than

Part 1	Part II					Part III
g	B♭ B♭ (c)		(D)	d		g

DIAGRAM 11.1. The modulatory plan of A. M. Bononcini's *Benché m'abbia*.

the dominant. In two arias by Antonio Bononcini, "Un cor più tormentato" and "Men crudele," the tonality rises to the supertonic at the outset of B. Since in each aria 1B begins with the same material as A, the listener perceives the long-range relationship of the two sections as an ascending sequence. The B of Ariosti's "Al voler del bene amato" opens in the mediant minor, the tonality used already as the modulatory goal of A.

Of the thirteen da capo arias in minor, six move from the tonic at the end of A to the relative major at the beginning of B, two proceed to the dominant minor, two others to the submediant, one to the supertonic, one to ♭VII, and one to the mediant minor (the parallel of the relative major). The B sections of all three arias by Giovanni Bononcini open in the relative major; he generally prefers a small number of uncomplicated modulations. In his three minor arias, Badia, on the other hand, never modulates directly to the relative major between A and B; two of the B sections begin in the submediant, while the third sets out in the dominant minor. As an alternative to the relative major, Antonio Bononcini uses the supertonic in "Più barbaro martire"; here, as in "Men crudele" and "Un cor più tormentato," the repetition of the 1A theme up a step produces a large-dimensional sequence, moving the aria forward with the effect of a large stride. As still another choice, the mediant minor occurs at the beginning of B in "Al tuo bel volto"; its reappearance here after extensive use in A contributes to the aria's unity. The only aria in which the B section continues in the tonic is Ariosti's "Nice, crudel," but the tonality swerves toward the dominant by the end of the initial measure. For an aria not in the conventional da capo design, "Insoffribile tormento," Ariosti chooses ♭VII as the initial tonality of B.

In general, therefore, the B sections of both major and minor arias open immediately in new tonal areas, the relative keys being the most popular choices. Almost as much consistency can be seen in the relationship between the end of B and the return of A, especially in minor arias. In five arias in minor keys, the B section concludes in the relative major, and in six arias B ends in the minor dominant. The Viennese composers evidently felt that the strongest preparation for the da capo could be achieved by cadencing firmly in one of the most closely related keys at the end of the middle section. The principle applies less frequently to arias in major keys; however, the B sections of three arias do end in the relative minor. Other choices include the supertonic and the mediant. Conspicuously absent are major arias with B sections that finish in the dominant; composers consistently reserve the special tensional relationship of tonic/dominant for the central modulation of A. In fact,

A:	I		V	I		I
B:	ii		vi	ii		ii

DIAGRAM 11.2. Large-scale modulatory scheme of A. M. Bononcini's *Un cor più tormentato* (G major).

Per non arder					*Amore ingannatore*			
A:	i	Ill	i	i		i	III	i	i
B:	v	ii	v	v		III	^{b}VII	v	v

DIAGRAM 11.3. Modulatory schemes of A. M. Bononcini's *Per non arder* and *Amore ingannatore*.

only one of the arias in major keys contains any reference at all to the major dominant in B, and this aria, Badia's "Sì vaga e sì vezzosa," passes only fleetingly through the dominant near the beginning of the B section. The polarity of tonic/dominant as a style ingredient in the A section seems to have become so important by 1700 that composers wished to avoid diminishing its impact by additional references to the dominant in B. Curiously, Ariosti concludes the middle section of the A-major aria "Al voler del bene amato" in e minor. His choice of the minor dominant does not supply the kind of tensional relationship that might have been provided by concluding B in E major. Ariosti's modulations in general indicate that he is one of the more old-fashioned composers of the early eighteenth-century Viennese circle. Lingering traces of modality and bifocal tonality are evident from his greater emphasis on the mediant in major keys and ♭VII in minor keys. A further indication of bifocal tonality can be seen in the B section of the F-major aria "Cangi Amore," which closes with a Phrygian cadence in d minor; the dominant of d then resolves directly to F major.

The modulations of most B sections follow a more itinerant and less predictable course than the key changes of A sections. All A sections begin and end in the same key; about one-third of the B sections are also unified in this manner, but the internal modulations are rarely tensional. Several of the B sections that begin in the relative keys proceed upward by the circle of fifths one or two tonalities before exploring more varied directions. In arias like Ariosti's "È pur dolce" and "Nice, crudel," an ascending or descending sequential modulatory plan gives some direction and shape to B. However, the clearest and most directional key schemes occur in the B sections of Antonio Bononcini's arias. He uses several plans. The most tensional modulations can be seen in arias like "Un cor più tormentato"; beginning a step higher than A, the key changes of B actually mirror the pattern and pace of A (diagram 11.2). The modulatory routes of the B sections of "Per non arder" and "Amore ingannatore" show similar planning, having strong goals and designs influenced by the A sections (diagram 11.3). In "Amore ingannatore" Antonio begins B in the relative major but after the midpoint modulation shifts to the dominant minor. From the frequent interchange of the two keys it seems clear that he considers them as almost equal poles of opposition to the tonic.

Not all B sections of da capo arias by Antonio mirror the modulatory designs of the A sections, but nearly all have some kind of directional motion. In "S'io ritorno a innamorarvi," for example, the tonality spirals gradually upward by the circle of fifths, progressing from the relative major to ♭VII to the subdominant. In the F-major aria "Men crudele" the movement is predominantly upward by step; the B section opens in the supertonic and then proceeds at first to the subdominant, then to the minor dominant, and finally to the relative minor. A similar plan occurs in the g-minor aria "Più barbaro martire," but Antonio stops the ascending modulations on the minor dominant.

In a more typically late baroque style, the B sections of arias by Badia and Ariosti dart about from key to key without a specific plan. Giovanni Bononcini, however, prefers little or no modulatory activity within an individual B.

KEY RHYTHM

Closely related to the broad modulatory scheme of an aria is its key rhythm, the frequency and speed of the modulations. The Viennese composers show a surprising degree of individuality in their treatment of key rhythm, although a basic pattern emerges in many arias, particularly those by Ariosti and Antonio Bononcini. In Arisoti's "Al voler del bene amato" or Antonio's "Amore ingannatore," for example, the key rhythm of A is slow, with a tensional midpoint modulation followed by an immediate return to the tonic for the remainder of the section; the pace of modulations moves much more quickly during the first half to two-thirds of B but stabilizes during the last part of this section. According to this stereotypical plan, therefore, the greatest amount of activity and tonal variety occurs in the center of A and in the first part of B.

More than half of the Viennese arias do not conform in all details to this stereotype. Thus, Giovanni Bononcini prefers much slower key rhythm. In "Dolce amor," for instance, he uses only two tonalities, the tonic (g minor) for the entire A section and its relative (B♭ major) throughout B. In a rather brief aria like "Dolce amor," the use of one key per section is not surprising, but Bononcini's penchant for stable tonal areas is evident even in long arias like "Pena e soffri." Here the customary modulation from the tonic minor to the relative major takes place approximately halfway through A; returning to the relative major at the beginning of B, the composer does not change the tonality for the entire thirty-six-measure section. In the g-minor aria "Dio d'Amor," the principal modulation of A again occurs near the midpoint, although the constantly alternating cadences in the dominant minor and the relative major throughout the first half of A give this aria an unsettled flavor uncharacteristic of most of Bononcini's music. In B, however, the key rhythm becomes typically slow: the section begins and ends with phrases in the relative major that frame a longer central passage in the subdominant. Generally more concerned with shapely melodic curves and expressive harmonic details, Bononcini dislikes fussy modulatory plans.

Badia too writes arias with only one or two keys per section. The A sections of two arias in minor, "Ombra del mio bel sol" and "Basti per mio contento," contain the expected movement to the relative major. The B section of each aria likewise includes only one modulation; in the early measures of B in "Ombra del mio bel sol," the tonality shifts from the submediant to the subdominant, and in B of "Basti per mio contento," Badia uses only the minor dominant and the relative major. As an alternative plan, he contrasts a stable A with a B containing numerous migrant modulations. In each of the arias "Gelosia, furia d'Alletto" and "Sì vaga e sì vezzosa," the A lacks the usual motion to the dominant; B, on the other hand, skips through five or six keys in a random order. Badia achieves the greatest amount of contrast of key rhythm in the long g-minor aria "Se sarai mio." With its midpoint modulation to the relative major, A follows the normal pattern. However, B cadences in no fewer than ten keys; the modulations begin early in B and continue until its final cadence.

The key rhythms of several arias by Antonio Bononcini demonstrate special planning of modulatory motion. In arias like "Un cor più tormentato" and "Per non arder," the modulatory pace in B actually duplicates the rate in A. In "Più barbaro matire," "S'io ritorno a innamorarvi," and "Men crudele," Antonio uses midpoint modulations in A, but in B he creates a succession of tonal plateaus. In such B sections only three or four key changes take place; the modulations are evenly distributed throughout B, and modulatory routes are quick and direct, so that the section consists of a series of stable tonal areas. Like his brother, therefore, Antonio generally rejects overactive or complex modulatory schemes.

CHORD RHYTHM

While a basic pattern of key rhythm emerges in many Viennese arias, in an even larger number a more varied treatment unfolds. A comparable amount of variety can be found in the Viennese composers' handling of small-dimensional harmonic movement. Of course, many arias contain the kind of fast, beat-marking chord rhythm typical of late baroque style. Particularly in the works of Ariosti, a quick harmonic pace adds to the generally nervous motion. In arias like "È pur dolce," "Al voler del bene amato," "Nice, crudel," and "Insoffribile tormento," the chords proceed in regular patterns of eighths and quarters, with only a very limited control over chord rhythm. In "Nice, crudel," for example, the quick harmonic changes continue almost unabated, except for temporarily slower motion at the beginning of B (diagram 11.4). Ziani also uses mostly fast, undifferentiated chord rhythm that often corresponds closely to the surface rhythm of the walking basses (diagram 11.5).

DIAGRAM 11.4. Quick chord rhythm in Ariosti's *Nice, crudel*.

DIAGRAM 11.5. Coordination of bass-line surface rhythm and chord rhythm in Ziani's *Se infelice*, mm. 1–22.

Another composer who uses predominantly fast, regular chord motion is Antonio Bononcini. In triple-meter arias like "S'io ritorno," the chord rhythm moves in steady patterns of ♩ ♩ or ♩ ♩, with little differentiation even at cadences. The consistent rocking motion of such patterns adds to the serenity of slow legato arias like "Al tuo bel volto"; no jerky harmonic passages disturb the smooth flow and *costante* affect of this long aria. At some points the chord rhythm slows to only one change per measure (♩.). Slow, steady chord rhythm also contributes to the subdued mood of Badia's "Ombra del mio bel sol," an aria in common meter. Proceeding mostly by half and quarter notes, the chord changes move considerably

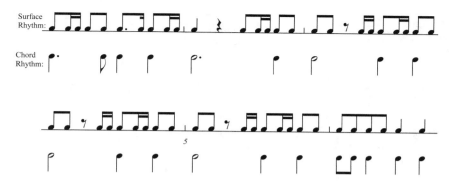

DIAGRAM 11.6. Contrast of bass-line surface rhythm and chord rhythm in Badia's *Ombra del mio bel sol,* mm. 1–6.

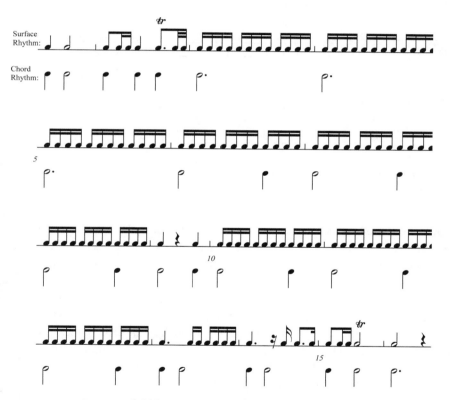

DIAGRAM 11.7. Contrast of obbligato surface rhythm and chord rhythm in A. M. Bononcini's *Men crudele,* mm. 1–16.

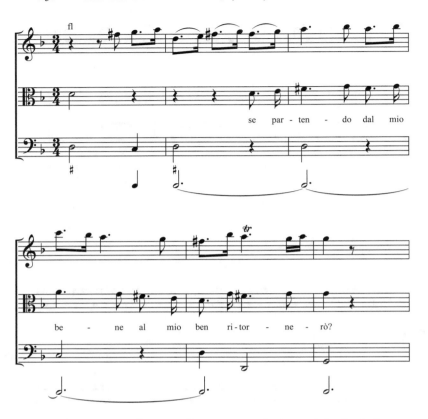

EX. 11.20. G. Bononcini, Cantata 22/I, mm. 40–44. Static chord rhythm before an important cadence.

slower than the surface rhythms (diagram 11.6). Similarly, Antonio differentiates between active, ornamental surface rhythm and slower, steady chord rhythm in "Men crudele." Here, too, he does not vary the rate of chord changes much, even at structural cadences (diagram 11.7).

Not all arias by Antonio contain completely uninflected chord rhythm. In "Sentimi, crudo Amore" he establishes a basic quarter-note harmonic motion in the opening ritornello, and this pace dominates much of the aria. In measures 56–57, however, the chord rhythm changes suddenly to eighths. The momentary acceleration occurs precisely at the point of greatest harmonic stress; it also underscores an important melodic peak of B. Through the coalescence of these three factors (a quickening of chord rhythm, an increased density of dissonance, and a melodic peak), Antonio achieves another marvelous concinnous effect.

Giovanni Bononcini also knows how to combine quicker chord rhythm with increased harmonic intensity to create a climactic moment. In the penultimate phrase of B in the triple-meter aria "Pena e soffri," the abrupt change in chord movement from steady dotted halves (measures 94–99) to quarters (measure 100) coincides with a switch from simple diatonic harmonies to affective chromatic ones.

Giovanni does in fact draw upon more specialized uses of chord rhythm than any other Viennese composer. One technique he favors before an important cadence is static or very regular chord rhythm. In "Dio d'Amor" the chord rhythm of the first twenty-four measures of A moves in diverse patterns of quarters, halves, and dotted halves. In measures 25–28 Bononcini largely suspends the aria's motion by coordinating a long inverted pedal in the flute, a smoothly undulating alto line, and simple, repetitious chord rhythm ($\downarrow$ $\downarrow$) consisting of tonic–dominant oscillation. The suspension of activity ends in bars 29–30: the flute moves downward from its pedal, the voice abandons its wave pattern by leaping to a peak of b♭', and the harmonic rhythm breaks away from the half-quarter swing by reinforcing the cadential hemiola. In measures 34–39 the composer repeats the effect in c minor, the subdominant, but instead of using the hemiola cadence at the end of the phrase, he shifts directly upward to the dominant triad (D major). At this point he completely arrests the harmonic motion, using various forms of the dominant triad and seventh throughout measures 40–43 before finally supplying the expected authentic cadence (example 11.20).

Not only in Giovanni's works but also in arias by all the Viennese composers, fluctuations in established patterns of chord rhythm are apt to occur most frequently at cadences. In triple-meter or compound duple arias, composers often alter patterned chord rhythm at phrase endings to underline broad hemiola effects. In the $\frac{6}{8}$ aria "Basti per mio contento" by Badia, the chord changes clarify the intended hemiola even at cadences where the surface rhythm of the bass line continues to emphasize the conventional metric accents. Here the surface rhythm of the soprano line reinforces the hemiola, creating the delightful kind of conflict between duple and triple meter characteristic of baroque music from the time of Monteverdi's *Scherzi musicali* (1607).

Giovanni Bononcini successfully uses such conflicts not only at cadences but also throughout an extended phrase or group of subphrases. At the beginning of 1A in "Pena e soffri," for example, the harmonic motion consists of only one chord per measure of $\frac{3}{4}$ and thus reinforces the metrical accents; during the first nine bars of 1A he seems to group the bass line into two-measure units above which the soprano line moves predominantly in $\frac{3}{2}$. At the first important cadence the chord rhythm and bass-line surface rhythm finally confirm the $\frac{3}{2}$ groupings that dominate the soprano line (example 11.21).

In many Viennese arias, quicker chord rhythm at the end of a phrase or subsection is one ingredient in the typical late baroque "drive to the cadence." In Badia's "Ombra del mio bel sol" the stable half-note chord rhythm changes to eighth-note motion at virtually every cadence in A (example 11.22). Accelerated chord rhythm

EX. 11.21. G. Bononcini, Cantata 51/I, mm. 10–18. Conflicting accents between soprano and bass lines.

in the approach to the cadence also occurs in many duple-meter arias by Giovanni and Antonio Bononcini (example 11.23a–b).

The treatment of chord rhythm is more varied than usual in Ziani's "Navicella che paventa" and in two arias by Badia. In the Ziani aria, harmonies often move slowly during the heads of themes or beginnings of phrases but progress more quickly during the internal parts of phrases and at cadences. Ziani varies the basic triple meter throughout the aria by constantly incorporating bits of hemiola within phrases and at cadences. Badia uses diverse chord rhythms in "Gelosia, furia d'Alletto" and "Sì vaga e sì vezzosa." In "Gelosia" chord rhythms vary from slow at the beginnings of sections, to slightly faster but regular during long sequential passages, to quick at cadences (see example 10.1). The shifting speeds of chord rhythm in "Sì vaga e sì vezzosa" tend to underline the irregular phrase structure and changing surface rhythms.

EX. 11.22. Badia, Cantata 4/II, mm. 20–23. Quicker chord rhythm at the end of a subsection.

EX. 11.23a–b. G. Bononcini, Cantata 82/I, mm. 1–3, and A. M. Bononcini, Cantata 91/I, mm. 4–6. Accelerated chord rhythm at a cadence.

SEQUENCE

By far the most common resource for middle- and small-dimensional movement in the arias of the Viennese composers is sequence, the stock device of the baroque era. All five composers rely upon sequential motion both for extending ideas and for modulatory purposes. Melodic, harmonic, and rhythmic sequences occur with great frequency. Yet a close examination of sequential passages in Viennese arias reveals a fascinating amount of diversity in the use of this commonplace technique. The distribution, types, and routes of sequential motion vary considerably. Moreover, some composers depend far more heavily upon this convention than others, and at least one composer consistently avoids literal harmonic and sequential patterning. The present discussion focuses chiefly upon sequence as an element of harmonic motion.

In more than two-thirds of the arias analyzed, sequence contributes significantly to the flow of both the A and B sections. However, Ziani generally dislikes strict sequential motion, and in two arias by Badia ("Se sarai mio" and "Sì vaga e sì vezzosa") and one by Antonio Bononcini ("Amore ingannatore"), sequence is reserved mainly for B. Particularly in the A of "Sì vaga e sì vezzosa" Badia refrains from using sequential patterns. The thirty-five-measure section lacks the usual midpoint modulation, and sequence is therefore not needed for reaching a directional harmonic goal. Instead, Badia extends his ideas with constant phrase repetitions that are treated literally, expanded, or slightly modified. The complete absence of sequential and modulatory motion gives this rather long A a static quality that is not overcome by other types of energy such as varied surface rhythms, leaping melodic lines, or occasional dissonant harmonies. These style characteristics do play important roles in the A of Antonio's "Amore ingannatore," which, much like Badia's "Sì vaga e sì vezzosa," contains very little sequence. Moreover, Bononcini's aria includes the internal tensional modulation.

Both modulating and nonmodulating sequences permeate the Viennese repertoire. Of course modulating sequences occur in areas with quick key rhythm, especially B, where composers usually explore a variety of keys. The opening measures of B in Antonio's "Sentimi, crudo Amore" exemplify the typical use of a modulating sequence at the beginning of a B section. The basic module consists of two measures and passes from d minor to g minor to c minor; Antonio cleverly extends the third unit by linking it to a new faster-moving sequence made up of half-measure units. A particularly expressive modulating sequence consisting of two four-measure units in d minor and c minor comes at the beginning of B in Ariosti's "Cangi Amore"; combined with a slow tempo and a descending bass line in a low range, the passage produces a somber striding effect (example 11.24). The midpoint tensional modulation of A also invites sequential treatment, though modulating sequences here are less common than in B. Badia uses such a sequence to move from g minor to Bb major at the end of 1A in "Basti per mio contento." In "Per non arder" Antonio Bon-

EX. 11.24. Ariosti, Cantata 65/I, mm. 60–67. An affective modulating sequence at
the beginning of B.

oncini overcomes the monotonous effect of sequential patterning by inserting varied
vocal material between more regular instrumental repetitions (see example 11.8). An
excellent example of a modulating sequence in an A section occurs in his "Al tuo bel
volto." After a cadence in the relative major (C) the tonality spirals upward through
G major and a minor, then continues in a nonmodulatory manner to a plateau on b
before cadencing again in C major. In B Antonio composes a marvelous chromatic
variant of the original sequence (example 11.25a–b). The use of extensive modulating
sequences like these in both A and B is a feature found almost exclusively in his arias.

More common is the nonmodulating sequence, a type of local activity found in
many arias but especially in pieces with slow key rhythm, such as Giovanni Bononcini's "Pena e soffri" and "Dolce amor." In the latter aria ascending sequences at the
beginning of 1A and 1B provide a limited amount of forward motion, while a descending sequence near the end of A¹ gives a sinking effect appropriate to the text.

Badia repeatedly resorts to nonmodulating sequential patterns as a fundamental means for expanding his material. His ritornellos usually contain at least one
important motive extended by sequence. After introducing *Ray* in the ritornello
of "Ombra del mio bel sol," for example, he continues with a three-part sequence

EX. 11.25a–b. A. M. Bononcini, Cantata 98/II, mm. 21–30 and 99–105. A modulating sequence in 1A and its chromatically altered version in B.

moving downward by scale degrees. The basic module appears again and again in sequence throughout the vocal subsections, often in imitation between voice and bass but with few modifications of the surface rhythm or melodic contour. The sequences always proceed downward by step. This type of movement turns up so often in Badia's arias that it can be cited as a specific trademark of his style (example 11.22). Near the end of the B section in the same aria, he uses *y* in a sequence consisting of two segments; then, taking only the conclusion of the second segment, he reduces the unit from four beats to two and finally to only one beat. The gradual shortening of the basic unit (implied acceleration) adds an additional thrust toward the penultimate cadence of B. Subtleties of this type do not appear often in Badia's arias, but they give evidence of his ability to approach sequence in a freer and more creative fashion.

Badia's preference for descending sequences contrasts with Ariosti's predilection for ascending patterns. In Ariosti's compositions, movement in general and sequence in particular are characterized by long gradual climbs with few sudden bursts of activity or leaps into fresh tonal territory. Whether rising or falling, sequences move by scale degrees, stressing clear diatonic harmonies. Passages like the excerpt from "Al voler del bene amato" in example 11.15 and the extremely sequential A of "Cangi Amore" illustrate the gradualism typical of most of Ariosti's music. The same type of moderate rising-and-falling motion, resembling a ride over a terrain made up of gently rolling hillocks, can be seen in "Insoffribile tormento." With its melodic tritones and secondary dominants, the initial idea is actually one of Ariosti's most daring inventions, but he is unable to sustain the intensity of this impulse. Recurring again and again in an endless stream of rigid sequential repetitions, even this striking theme eventually sounds trite and ordinary.

To summarize: all the Viennese cantata composers use sequence, but their handling of the device reveals much about their individual styles. Most dependent upon this type of activity are Ariosti and Badia; for them, sequence is the indispensable method for extending ideas. Ariosti scarcely ever proceeds more than a few bars without having recourse to sequential patterns. He frequently prefers small units—sometimes only one beat—and favors gradually ascending motion, achieving some variety in a few arias by slightly varying the repetitions of a module. Badia depends upon sequence almost as much as Ariosti, but he especially likes descending motion; he seldom alters a basic unit from one repetition to the next. Both Ariosti and Badia use far more nonmodulating than modulating sequences.

Giovanni and Antonio Bononcini also use a considerable amount of sequence, but their treatment is often less literal and their dependence definitely less than seen in arias by Badia. In Giovanni's arias, sequence is mainly a source of local activity. Antonio writes both extended modulating and nonmodulating sequences. For advancing his ideas, sequence is only one of several options that include variation and development techniques, part exchange, imitation, fragmentation, and strict repetition. In several sequences, the cyclic motion with seventh chords on every scale degree is reminiscent of similar passages by Corelli (example 11.26). Bononcini, who had recently arrived from Rome, may well have been familiar with the music of his great contemporary. Sometimes Antonio uses sequence in only two parts of a four-part texture. In "Amore ingannatore" he achieves a vigorous, cascading effect by writing a sequential canon between the two flutes; simultaneously, alto and bass proceed with nonsequential lines.

EX. 11.26. (*above and facing*) A. M. Bononcini, Cantata 28/I, mm. 1–9.
Seventh chords, inversions, and suspensions.

Of all the Viennese composers, Ziani turns least often to harmonic and me-lodic sequence, though he often uses rhythmic sequence as a unifying device. He seems almost deliberately to avoid obvious sequential motion in favor of freer, more meandering lines. Florid vocal passages contain fewer sequences than similar phrases in arias by his contemporaries; even Ziani, however, occasionally draws upon more regular patterning.

DISSONANCE

In varying degrees, dissonance provides small-dimensional movement and expression in arias by all the Viennese composers. However, an examination of the density, types (ornamental or structural), and functions (text related, cadential, or contributing to the general harmonic flow) uncovers diverse approaches to this expressive style element. In the majority of arias by Badia, Ariosti, and Ziani, the prevailingly consonant harmony partly accounts for the stable, often placid impression left by their music. Giovanni Bononcini experiments with biting, unprepared dissonance, but only rarely, to achieve a special effect. By far the greatest density of dissonance occurs in arias by Antonio Bononcini; as seen in example 11.26, many of his works are filled with suspensions, sevenths and ninths, unprepared dissonances, and even unusual clusters. Antonio's richer chord vocabulary and fondness for dissonance add considerably to the excitement and vigor of his music. In his arias, dissonance is not merely more pervasive, it is more radical and intense.

All five composers use dissonance for specific textual reasons. Details of affective, word-related harmonies will be considered in chapter 12. The present discussion concentrates upon the types and the functions not specifically related to the text.

Viennese arias contain numerous examples of ornamental dissonance of all types: passing tones, auxiliaries, anticipations, échappées, cambiatas, appoggiaturas, and suspensions. Structural dissonances other than the dominant-seventh chord turn up less frequently; Antonio is the only composer who consistently exploits seventh chords on all scale degrees.

In most arias by Badia, Ariosti, and Ziani, ornamental tones occur so fleetingly that they represent only dissonant flecks in a prevailingly consonant landscape. Badia occasionally writes an expressive sequential pattern in which he tangibly increases the frequency and intensity of dissonance. In a sequence from "Basti per mio contento," he incorporates structural seventh chords on the seventh, sixth, fifth, and fourth scale degrees of g minor. He uses a descending sequence consisting of three segments in the common-meter aria "Ombra del mio bel sol"; a 9–8 suspension, also ornamented melodically, occurs on the third beat of each unit (see example 11.22). Badia heightens the tension of this passage by adding a structural seventh chord on the second beat of each segment, by including auxiliary and passing tones, and by tingeing the harmony in the approach to the cadence with the dominant-ninth chord. Though brief, the impact of the ninth is especially telling here because the soprano line leaps to it from a diminished seventh below. Similar patterns can be found in other Badia arias, but very few contain dissonance that is as concentrated. Indeed, he seldom ventures outside the realm of stable diatonic harmonies. His smooth treatment of paired violins largely moving in parallel thirds in "Se sarai mio" contrasts sharply with the ruggedly dissonant handling of the same instruments in Antonio's "Amore ingannatore." Only at important cadences does Badia break away from the cliché triads. At the end of the ritornello that separates

EX. 11.27. Badia, Cantata 1/III, mm. 29–31. The Corelli clash at an important cadence.

the *Devise* from the rest of 1A, for instance, he uses a standard seventeenth-century cadence formula, the so-called Corelli clash. With the simultaneous resolution of a suspension and an anticipation, the cadence concludes with the characteristically dissonant parallel seconds (example 11.27).

Dissonance plays an even smaller role in arias by Ziani. In "Se infelice," the frequent suspensions between the two bass lines preserve the sense of continuous quarter-note harmonic movement even when the chord rhythm is actually slower. Unprepared and structural dissonance (other than the dominant seventh) are extremely rare. In arias by Ariosti, too, dissonance is primarily restricted to simple ornamental tones that help to generate the quick harmonic motion typical of his music. Nevertheless, he writes a few isolated passages in which he rather consciously experiments with structural dissonance. The intense opening of "Insoffribile tormento," for example, includes secondary dominants in first and third inversions and the full diminished-seventh chord. The surprise and freshness of the progression are soon lost, however, because Ariosti repeats the same harmonies again and again, never varying them or enriching them with additional structural dissonance.

Giovanni Bononcini exploits dissonance mainly for affective, text-related purposes. His harmonic language encompasses many ornamental and structural clashes, including the diminished seventh, secondary dominants in inversions, and the dominant-ninth chord. Bits of unprepared dissonance often inflect important structural cadences such as the end of B in "Dio d'Amor." A few measures earlier Bononcini embellishes a routine 9–8 suspension by having the dissonant line dip down to the seventh scale degree before resolving to the consonant octave.

Not surprisingly, the most far-reaching uses of dissonance can be observed in arias by Antonio Bononcini. Of course not all his music contains extreme concentrations of dissonance; in arias like "Al tuo bel volto," "Per non arder," and "Un cor più tormentato," the prevailingly consonant harmonies contribute to the overall sense of serenity or stability. Yet Antonio weaves some striking details into the

EX. 11.28. A. M. Bononcini, Cantata 91/I, mm. 1–4. Leaping from and to a dissonance.

harmony of even these arias. One of his favorite devices is the intertwining of obbligato and vocal lines within a small range. In measure 76 of "Un cor più tormentato," soprano and flute have the same three pitches (e^2, $f\sharp^2$, and g^2), but the soprano sings in descending eighths while the flute ornaments in groups of ascending triplet sixteenths.

Of the various types of ornamental tones, Antonio particularly delights in long chains of suspensions. In a descending sequence from "Men crudele," 9–8, 7–6, and 4–3 suspensions in the violins are also ornamented melodically, while the soprano moves in more varied patterns of rising and falling sixteenths. In the elaborate aria "Più barbaro martire," suspensions become an unusually important factor in propelling the forward motion. For the harmony of the motive x, used throughout the aria, Antonio builds suspensions on the first and third beats of measures 2–4 (see example 11.14a). He achieves additional intensity by alternating the suspensions with large melodic leaps in the violins on beats 2 and 4, producing syncopation. At the beginning of measure 4, violin 2 skips up to $e\flat^2$, forming a major seventh with violin 1 and causing a momentary c–d–$e\flat$ clash. Few arias in the entire Viennese repertoire match the fierce, relentless activity of "Più barbaro martire."

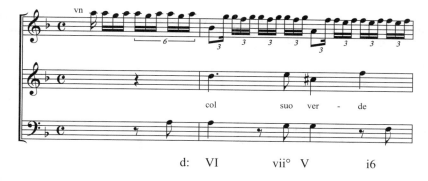

EX. 11.29. A. M. Bononcini, Cantata 91/I, mm. 21–22. The use of VI and V of d minor.

At times, Antonio combines chains of suspensions with series of seventh chords. In "Sentimi, crudo Amore," the piquancy of the progression at the end of the ritornello (see example 11.26) results partly from the spiral of Corellian sevenths on all beats and partly from the superposed suspensions on beat 3 of measure 6 and beats 1 and 3 of measure 7. On beat 4 of the following measure, Antonio uses a cambiata in the soprano over a dominant-seventh chord, a combination that recurs often. He is also partial to third-inversion seventh chords; in a descending sequence beginning in measure 12, he alternates $\frac{4}{2}$ chords on the sixth, fifth, fourth, and third degrees of F major with $\frac{6}{5}$ chords on the second, first, seventh, and sixth degrees.

Antonio writes many phrases in which one line leaps to or from a dissonance rather than proceeding in more orthodox, conjunct motion. Such leaps provide much of the expressiveness in the initial ritornello of "Benché m'abbia la cruda saetta." In measures 2–3 the obbligato violin twice leaps down a seventh from a chord in which it forms a ninth above the bass line. In the second half of measure 3 and the first half of measure 4, Antonio reverses the procedure: the violin leaps up a seventh from a consonant pitch to a ninth above the bass (example 11.28). Surely one of the most expressive moments in the whole repertoire occurs in measure 22, where the violin descends again by sevenths, this time to form $\frac{4}{2}$ chords on the sixth and fifth degrees of d minor (example 11.29).

Antonio's boldness with unprepared dissonance and unusual clashes results in occasional thorny passages such as measures 4–8 of the g-minor aria "Amore ingannatore." Especially noteworthy here are the échappée in the bass line, conflicting with the outlining of ii $\frac{6}{5}$ in violin 1 (measure 4, beat 2); the biting minor seconds between violins (measure 4, beat 4; measure 7, beat 3); the use of structurally dissonant chords such as V $\frac{4}{2}$ of ♭VII (measure 6, beat 2) and vii[07] (measure 6, beat 4); and the strident interlacing of the flutes at the end of measure 6 and the beginning of measure 7. By using the two forms of the sixth degree of melodic minor in

EX. 11.30. A. M. Bononcini, Cantata 8/I, mm. 4–8. Dissonant treatment of paired flutes.

the progression iv⁷–ii (of major), Antonio enriches the harmonic vocabulary and produces a striking cross-relation (example 11.30).

Perhaps Antonio's most adventurous use of dissonance occurs in "S'io ritorno a innamorarvi." In measures 21–24 and in similar passages, expressive dissonance gives a thrust of forward motion on the first beat of each measure. By combining $\frac{4}{2}$ chords with appoggiaturas, Antonio creates some four-tone clusters, for example, $b\flat^1$–c^1–d^1–$e\flat^1$. The resolution on beat 2 of each measure is usually to a $\frac{6}{3}$ chord. The dissonance in measure 24, beat 1 is also particularly stinging, even though Antonio no longer uses the $\frac{4}{2}$ chord, because the alto leaps down a major seventh to form a minor second with the bass.

CONTRARY MOTION

In the arias of several Viennese composers, contrary motion contributes to the general flow. At important cadences in continuo arias, Badia especially likes to have the two lines gradually expand away from one another or contract. In "Se sarai mio" he includes the obbligato flutes in the total process of outward expansion. Giovanni

EX. 11.31. G. Bononcini, Cantata 22/I, mm. 76–81. Contrary motion on a broad scale.

Bononcini uses the same technique in the penultimate phrase of B in "Dio d'Amor" but on an even broader scale (example 11.31).

The only composer who utilizes contrary motion on a regular basis is Antonio Bononcini. A bit of intervallic expansion between two obbligato instruments may bring a long phrase to a vigorous conclusion, as at the end of the ritornello in "Sentimi, crudo Amore" (see example 11.26). Contrary motion between the two violins at the beginning of "Più barbaro martire" gives an immediate burst of energy (see example 11.14a). Antonio uses oblique motion in "Al tuo bel volto"; the predominantly level soprano line contrasts with the rapidly descending scales in the bass (see example 11.25a). Contrary motion permeates "Amore ingannatore" and contributes to the agitated motion that pervades the entire aria. The device helps to highlight melodic peaks in the opening ritornellos and in many emphatic vocal phrases of several arias. Sometimes the syncopated alto and bass lines of "Amore ingannatore" begin in the same range and open out to a full two octaves. While omitting the syncopation, Antonio broadens the effect from one measure to two in measures 48–51 of B. As usual, the bass line proceeds downward mostly by steps, but the alto line now moves on two levels, rising repeatedly from the pitch a^1 to higher and higher peaks until the two-octave distance between parts is reached.

In measures 59–62 of "S'io ritorno a innamorarvi," contrary motion involves all three lines, each part rising and falling to form its own arch. The simultaneous use of both forms of melodic minor in measure 59 causes a direct false relation. Antonio also uses intervallic expansion effectively on a smaller scale. In passages like measures 20–22, alto and bass begin with a unison and open gradually up to a minor second, a minor third, a fourth, and eventually an octave.

SURFACE RHYTHM

Because of the late baroque tendencies to emphasize metrical accents and to build entire pieces from one or two short motives, surface rhythm represents one of the least varied aspects of movement in the early eighteenth-century arias. True, the cumulative effect of relentless repetitions of motoric germ cells like ♩. ♪, ♪ ♫, and ♫♫ can be one of raw energy and excitement, particularly in allegro and vivace arias. To achieve an impressive climax, the piling up of motives may be coordinated with other style features, such as the rising line in the opening ritornello of Antonio Bononcini's "Men crudele." Often, however, the insistent repetitions and undifferentiated rhythms produce a static or monotonous effect.

Ziani in particular uses a limited variety of note values and combinations. For example, continuous quarter-note motion dominates the entire aria "Se infelice"; four motives are differentiated largely by simple changes in melodic profile. Because of the homogeneous rhythms and absence of sharp articulations between modules, the listener is hardly aware that the composer has woven several motives into the fabric of the aria. Ziani varies the surface rhythms of "Brami e speri" and "Navicella che paventa" only slightly more than those of "Se infelice." The unending stream of eighths and sixteenths in "Brami e speri" does not contribute much to the shapes of individual motives. By constantly integrating bits of hemiola into the long phrases of the ³⁄₈ aria "Navicella che paventa," the composer provides some relief from the prevailing sixteenth-note motion (see example 11.4).

The arias of Badia also lack distinctive surface rhythms. Beat-marking and motoric patterns saturate the duple-meter arias "Gelosia, furia d'Alletto," "Ombra del mio bel sol," and "Sì vaga e sì vezzosa." The rhythms of the obbligato and bass lines in the initial ritornello of "Sì vaga e sì vezzosa" illustrate the composer's dependence upon only a few note values organized into a succession of short phrases. The many coordinated articulations between the two lines persist throughout A. Conspicuously lacking modulatory or other types of strong directional motion, the endless series of short phrases eventually produces a stuttering effect, impeding rather than advancing the flow of the aria. In the ⁶⁄₈ "Basti per mio contento" and the ³⁄₈ "Se sarai mio," Badia relies upon simple figures such as ♫♫♫, ♪ ♫♫, and ♩. ♪ ♩, scarcely ever varying them to stimulate greater activity.

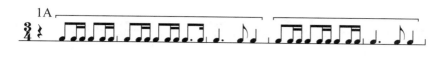

DIAGRAM 11.8. The surface rhythm of the opening soprano lines in 1A and 1B of Ariosti's *Cangi Amore*.

Syncopation plays a small role in a few Badia arias, but the dimension involved is usually the phrase or subphrase rather than the motive. Thus, in bars 10–12 of "Gelosia," two statements of a short phrase stressing beats 1 and 3 are followed by a new phrase beginning on beat 4. The technique of starting a phrase on a weak beat after one or two modules emphasizing metrical accents also occurs in "Ombra del mio bel sol," resulting in a more varied and asymmetrical phrase structure than usual.

Ariosti too seems largely dependent upon brief, repetitive motives. Once he establishes a rhythmic cell such as ♩ ♫ ("Insoffribile tormento"), he rarely modifies it during an entire aria. A limited amount of variety derives from his tendency to differentiate between the surface rhythms of bass and vocal lines, each proceeding with its own beat-marking pattern, as in "Nice, crudel." Occasionally the rhythm becomes faster or slower toward the end of an extended phrase. For obvious word-painting reasons, in two pieces ("Al voler del bene amato" and "È pur dolce") Ariosti introduces complex coloratura passages of thirty-seconds and sixty-fourths within a vocal line that moves characteristically in eighths and sixteenths; the sudden shifts between prevailing note values create, in a sense, terraced surface rhythms. The smaller note values appear more often in his works than in arias by other Viennese composers; perhaps foreshadowing the gallant style of the next generation, he composes many light and frivolous flourishes that ornament fundamentally simple melodic lines. At times, contrasting longer and shorter values within a single phrase produces more unusual surface rhythms. Improvised ornaments undoubtedly contribute to melodic and rhythmic variety; superimposed upon established motives, however, they do not alter the basic outlines of an aria.

At times, Giovanni Bononcini falls into the routine of using insistent motives throughout a section or an entire aria. In "Dolce amor" the common pattern ♩ ♫ dominates most of A and A[1], while the slightly longer unit ♫♫♫ | ♫ ⁊ | occurs repeatedly in B. The long strands of coloratura in the contrasting vivace

e   l'ec - ces-so de   le   pe - ne mi   sa   dir ch'io mo - ri - rò

EX. 11.32. G. Bononcini, Cantata 22/I, mm. 66–70. A conflict of accents between flute and alto.

section consist of unbroken successions of sixteenths. "Dio d'Amor" opens with more varied and active surface rhythms. Bononcini groups the differentiated values of the initial theme into a pair of two-bar phrases; the second unit modulates to the relative major, providing a logical answer to the first. (In typically baroque fashion, the moving bass line disguises the articulation between the two segments.) The syncopated stresses on beat 2, adapted to the alliterative text "Dio d'Amor," continue throughout the aria. In B a conflict between syncopations in the vocal lines and regular metrical accents in the flute obbligato produces a delightful interplay between the two lines (example 11.32). Evidently fond of this device, Bononcini uses it also in "Pena e soffri." The bass line consists of relentless reiterations of a one-measure motive, more active than many similar figures because of the octave leaps (see example 11.9). In coloratura passages the composer does not vary the note values.

As in many other style categories, in surface rhythm the works of Antonio Bononcini display the greatest variety and attention to detail. He, too, occasionally fashions a whole piece from one or two short motives. The simple patterns ♩♫ and ♫♩ permeate the vocal and instrumental writing of "Sentimi, crudo Amore"; however, the persistent imitative entries, vigorous octave leaps, and luxuriant harmonies make this one of Antonio's most successful compositions. "Per non arder" also lacks strikingly differentiated surface rhythms, though the beat-marking bass line contrasts with the more varied soprano and flute parts.

Like his brother, Antonio nearly always includes a prominent motive accenting beat 2 in a triple-meter aria. The initial three-measure theme of "Un cor più tormentato" contains stresses on beat 2 in both the second and third measures. A subtle relationship between measures 1–2 and measure 3 provides a bit of unification. Melodically, measure 3 follows the pattern established in measure 1 and the beginning of measure 2, but rhythmically it is a diminution. Syncopation constantly generates rhythmic activity in this aria. The frequent repetitions of the word *no* occur on weak beats. A lively variant of *Pay* (♬ ♩. ♫) includes not only the usual emphasis on beat 2 but also an additional "spring" effect because the end of

DIAGRAM 11.9. The motives *x*, *y*, and *z* of A. M. Bononcini's *Al tuo bel volto* used in linear combinations in 1A, mm. 21–30.

each measure is tied into the beginning of the next one: ♪ ♩ | ♫ ♩ ♩ ♫ ♫ ♫. Sequential syncopated patterns combined with rising melodic lines activate the duple-meter aria "Amore ingannatore" (see example 11.30). In "Più barbaro martire," large leaps alternating between first and second violins produce chains of syncopation throughout the aria.

More often Antonio bases the rhythmic material of an aria upon several sharply delineated motives introduced in the opening ritornello. "Men crudele" and "S'io ritorno" exemplify this procedure. The four ideas of the $\frac{3}{4}$ aria "S'io ritorno" are varied not only in surface rhythms but also in melodic contours: *x* contains a characteristic stress on beat 2 and moves mostly by steps; *y* consists of a leaping sequential pattern emphasizing beat 1; *z* is distinguished by its double-dotted rhythm; and *w* unfolds in ascending scales organized in triplets (see example 10.2). After their initial appearances, motives often recur in combinations. In "Al tuo bel volto" the ritornello announces three separate ideas (♩ ♩ ♩♩ ♩. ♬, and ♩. ♫ ♫♫♫) that return in linear combinations during 1A.

In several ritornellos, Antonio gradually accelerates the surface rhythms. A set of triplet sixteenths first appears in measure 3 of "Un cor più tormentato," recurs once in measure 5 and again in measure 6, then returns three times in measure 7. Perhaps the most effective use of gradually accelerating surface rhythms can be seen in the opening of "Benché m'abbia la cruda saetta." Here the note values change from eighths (measure 1) to groups of sixteenths punctuated by rests (measure 2), to patterns of continuous sixteenths (measures 3–4), and finally to a series of triplet sixteenths (end of measure 4). At the end of the phrase the surface rhythm stabilizes.

In other ways, however, movement in this ritornello follows a reverse pattern. Chord rhythm, for instance, begins in eighths, slows to quarters in measure 2, and changes to a half and two quarters in measure 4, precisely at the point of greatest surface-rhythmic intensity. Likewise, the leaping melodic contours suddenly become level during the half-measure of triplet sixteenths. The result is a brief lull; a clear articulation in the obbligato line on the second beat of measure 5 precedes the resumption of quicker chord rhythms and a rising melody at the cadence.

CHANGES IN TIMBRE

Reinforcing harmonic, melodic, and rhythmic changes, fluctuations in tone color contribute to movement. The anticipated alternation of instrumental ritornellos and vocal sections provides a kind of simple middle-dimensional rhythm; the addition or omission of a ritornello breaks the expected pattern and changes the flow of the conventional da capo scheme.

In pieces with the most varied colors—the arias with one or more obbligato instruments—changes in timbre influence movement most. However, activity in Badia's arias with obbligato instruments does not differ substantially from motion in continuo arias. In "Sì vaga e sì vezzosa," for example, the texture remains two-part throughout; the composer pairs the continuo line either with the single obbligato part *or* with the voice, never bringing the three lines together in a more complex relationship. Occasionally, fragments of the ritornello separate vocal phrases and add a bit of variety. In "Se sarai mio" long stretches of instrumental writing for two violins and continuo alternate with shorter vocal passages. Here too Badia keeps the vocal and obbligato roles distinct. Only near the end of B does he combine all four lines; an uncharacteristic point of imitation between first violin and soprano precedes the final cadence. Ziani also prefers to alternate rather than integrate vocal and obbligato colors. "Navicella che paventa" illustrates this tendency, though he tends to disguise the antiphonal effect a bit by overlapping the ends of vocal and instrumental phrases.

Giovanni Bononcini varies the relationship of vocal, obbligato, and continuo lines more than Badia or Ziani. In "Dio d'Amor" he alternates vocal and instrumental timbres, combines three independent lines, and includes points of imitation and part exchange. During approximately the first third of A, flute and alto simply trade material. The motion accelerates in measures 21–25 because the vocal and instrumental entrances become progressively closer; at first three beats apart, the two lines echo one another on each beat in measures 24–25. For the remainder of A until the ritornello (measures 26–47), three-part writing predominates, though Bononcini alternates many vocal and instrumental entries to enrich the texture and enhance the flow of the aria. In measures 26–28 and 34–37, flute and alto exchange parts: the pedal played by the flute in the earlier phrase moves to the alto line, and the undulating vocal melody shifts to the flute. A similar pattern of timbre changes occurs in B: flute and alto alternate for a few phrases, then proceed together in more complex interchanges until the da capo.

The most varied combinations and fluctuations of tone color can be found in arias by Antonio Bononcini. Obbligato instruments are not relegated to ritornellos; nor do vocal and instrumental lines simply alternate in a manner that keeps their colors distinct. Instead, the composer frequently writes vocal and obbligato parts of equal interest and intensity so that a full partnership or concertato competition emerges. Obbligato lines are equally active in A and B sections. The constant interplay of parts gives the music an increased flexibility, freeing it from the rigid alternation of vocal and instrumental entries so common in the da capo aria. Often an obbligato line at the end of a vocal section overlaps directly into the ensuing ritornello. However, to clarify the structure Antonio usually omits the obbligato briefly at two points, the beginning of 1A and the end of B.

"Per non arder" unfolds a continuing dialogue between unison flutes and soprano. After the long instrumental opening, fragments from the ritornello punctuate many short soprano entrances. During a longer vocal phrase, the flutes tend to enter in the middle, usually with different material. In corresponding passages from 1A and 2A, the relationship between obbligato and instrumental lines varies; thus in 1A the singer and continuo carry the first few phrases alone, but in 2A the same phrases are accompanied by a contrasting line for flute. In B Antonio gradually speeds up the alternations between the two parts, much like Giovanni in "Dio d'Amor" but over a more extended passage (measures 55–68). The quicker surface rhythms of the obbligato finally invade the soprano line at the point where the two lines no longer alternate but intertwine.

Several of these techniques can be cited as hallmarks of Antonio's style: the full partnership of vocal and instrumental lines; the tendency to vary the relationship of the two lines from 1A to 2A, usually resulting in increased activity in 2A; the avoidance of synchronized obbligato/vocal phrase entrances and endings; and the coalescence of the two lines at a climactic moment, often near the end of 2A or B. The constant staggering of vocal and instrumental phrases can be seen in arias like "Men crudele." At times, the two flutes move together in opposition to the voice. Elsewhere they enter and exit separately; even the phrase structure of the bass line shows some independence from the other parts. Another sign of flexibility is the continuation of the internal ritornello of A directly into the initial vocal phrase of 2A.

The numerous imitative entries in the arias with more than two obbligato instruments ("Più barbaro martire" and "Sentimi, crudo Amore") provide a constant source of activity. Antonio occasionally introduces solo/tutti and *forte/piano* contrasts. In "Più barbaro martire" the brilliant figurations for violins and cello almost overshadow the vocal part. Because the instruments play almost continuously, the texture of this aria is unusually dense. For a special effect Antonio suspends activity

EX. 11.33. A. M. Bononcini, Cantata 28/I, mm. 20–24. The combination of four
distinct motives.

briefly by appending an unaccompanied vocal pedal to the end of a long coloratura
passage; activity resumes with imitative entrances of the obbligato instruments (see
example 11.18). (Coloratura plays a slightly larger role in Antonio's work than in
most of the arias of his contemporaries but does not yet have the significance it was
to take on in the succeeding generation at Vienna.)

In "Sentimi, crudo Amore" a simple motive (♩ ♫ ♪♩) constantly tossed from one part to another propels the motion. Here again Antonio uses the technique of bringing instrumental entrances closer and closer. In measures 10–12 of 1A, six beats separate the initial statement of the motive from its next appearance; the entrances then occur after every two beats and finally on every beat. As in "Più barbaro martire," the instruments often drop out during virtuoso coloratura passages. In measures 20–24 the composer creates a fascinating four-part texture, giving paired violins, viola, soprano, and bass each a distinctive figure (example 11.33). The fertility of Antonio's imagination in texture as in other style categories leads me to hope that future investigations of his large secular dramatic works, sacred music, and instrumental pieces will be forthcoming.

12

The Relationship of
Text and Music

One of the most subtle and complex aspects of the cantata repertoire concerns the relationship of text and music. The twenty-five arias discussed here reveal a fascinating amount of variety in the interaction of textual and musical design, in the coordination of poetry with melody and rhythm, and in the musical realization of the affective poetic content.

With regard to structure, the distribution of lines often determines not only the broad scheme of an aria but also the internal design of an individual A or B section. Thus, a particular line signals the beginning of a section (1A or 1B), and its return usually marks the start of a subsection (2A or 2B). Within subsections, the composers arrange verses more freely. They extend the overall dimensions of an aria by emphatically repeating an individual line or word and achieve variety by combining, reordering, or shortening verses.

The poetic meter often influences the melodic shapes and surface rhythms. While the numerous trochaic and iambic texts result in some mechanical formulas, Antonio Bononcini in particular attempts to disguise the basic meter and avoid patterns too obviously derived from the words.

The composers draw upon a wide variety of stylistic details to enhance the content of texts. A few arias contain charming pictorial or descriptive effects suggested by specific words such as *lungi* and *lontananza*. More frequently, composers underscore complete lines or individual words with affective harmony, melody, or rhythm. In addition, specific timbres and dynamics may be selected to evoke particular moods. Not all the composers exploit style features for expressive purposes; Ziani in particular relies upon broader characteristics such as tempo and mode to achieve general affects. In two arias, Ariosti's "Cangi Amore" and Giovanni Bononcini's "Dolce amor," abrupt changes in tempo and meter create contrasting affects between A and B.

THE TEXT AND ITS INFLUENCE UPON THE MUSICAL DESIGN

The poetic canzonetta form found in arias of the early eighteenth century consists of a single strophe of four or more lines. Texts of the twenty-five arias vary in length from four to nine lines, with stanzas of six lines, used in eleven arias, most common. The dimensions of an aria do not always correspond to the length of the text. Hence, Ariosti's "Nice, crudel" contains one of the longest poems (nine lines) but only twenty-seven measures of music (including the da capo). By contrast, Antonio Bononcini's setting of the four-line strophe "Un cor più tormentato" stretches to 171 bars. His more melismatic treatment of the text, frequent line repetitions, and numerous instrumental passages account for the greater length.

The number of syllables per line also varies considerably, ranging from three to ten. In a few arias (Ariosti's "Insoffribile tormento," Ziani's "Brami e speri," and Antonio Bononcini's "Benché m'abbia"), all lines contain an equal number of syllables. More often, the poets write verses with contrasting or alternating numbers of syllables. The contrast may derive simply from masculine and feminine endings, but in a few texts the lengths of lines vary considerably.

In strophes with an even number of verses, the composers usually distribute the lines equally between the A and B sections of the da capo scheme. Thus, in ten of the eleven arias with six-line stanzas, the A section provides music for verses 1–3, while B continues with verses 4–6. The composers frequently divide texts with an odd number of lines so that B includes one more line than A. For example, the A of Ariosti's "Al voler" contains the first two verses of the five-line text, while B encompasses the remaining three. The texts of da capo arias are not always apportioned so obviously. Badia uses only two lines in the A of "Se sarai mio," saving the last five for B. Proportionally, the B section of "Se sarai mio" is the longest found in any of the Viennese da capo arias, and its unusual length can be attributed partly to the division of the text.

Greater freedom in the distribution of lines can be seen in the arias not in the conventional da capo design. All four lines of Antonio Bononcini's "Benché m'abbia," a miniature three-part aria, appear in both the opening and middle sections, but only lines 3–4 recur in the varied da capo. Ziani divides the six lines of "Brami e speri" into three pairs corresponding to the first three musical sections (A, B, and C). The return of the first couplet coincides with the varied da capo (A1); in the brief coda, only line 2 recurs. In "Se infelice," a setting of a nine-line canzonetta, the composer uses lines 1–4 in A and 5–9 in B; the first four lines are heard again in A1, and line 4 is repeated in the coda. The most unusual text distribution can be found in Ariosti's "Insoffribile tormento," a two-part aria (AA1) with a five-line strophe. Verses 1–3 serve as the text for the opening section; lines 4–5 come only at the beginning of the short A1 section, which concludes with the return of lines

1–2, each repeated. Though the aria is not a da capo musically, the return of the first two lines of text preserves at least one element of the customary three-part scheme.

The apportionment of text may also clarify the interior design of an individual A or B. Frequently, composers use the initial line of a section only at important structural points to signal the beginnings of sections and subsections. Thus, in a typical setting of a six-line canzonetta, line 1 occurs once at the opening of 1A but not again until 2A; line 4 is heard at the outset of 1B and again at the beginning of 2B. Lines 2–3 and 5–6 ordinarily receive many more repetitions than lines 1 and 4, which serve chiefly as structural signposts. This plan unfolds clearly in three arias by Antonio Bononcini ("Men crudele," "Sentimi, crudo Amore," and "S'io ritorno"). The composer applies the same technique to the eight-line strophe of "Più barbaro martire," coordinating lines 1 and 5 with the sections and subsections of the musical design.

These familiar distributions of text may be modified in one or more ways. An aria with a *Devise* at the beginning of 1A will include two opening statements of line 1, usually separated by a fragment of ritornello. With his customary instinct for symmetry, Antonio inserts a *Devise* not only at the outset of 1A of "Amore ingannatore" but also at the beginning of 2A, giving additional prominence to the initial line. The first verse may also return near the end of 2A to demarcate a closing passage or coda-like extension. The closing material of Giovanni Bononcini's "Pena e soffri" or Badia's "Gelosia" is underlined by the recurrence of the initial line. Similarly, the return of line 1 signals the coda of A in Antonio's "Un cor più tormentato." (As a variant, Antonio sometimes combines the beginning of the coda with the reappearance of line 2.) In "Per non arder" he brings the initial line back near the end of 1A for an unusual structural purpose. Here it coincides with the establishment of a new tonal area and fresh motivic material. Infrequently, as in Badia's "Ombra del mio bel sol," line 1 occurs four or more times within A. Badia's tendency to group lines 1–3 in long melodic phrases accounts for the unusual recurrences of the first verse.

The distribution of lines sometimes clarifies the internal scheme of the A section only. With its midpoint modulation to a closely related key, the A splits naturally into two subsections, usually confirmed by the text. The modulations of B often unfold less systematically, and the initial line of the section does not always reappear. This procedure can be seen in arias like Ziani's "Navicella che paventa," Badia's "Basti per mio contento," and Ariosti's "Al voler del bene amato." In only four arias (Ariosti's "Nice, crudel," Badia's "Sì vaga e sì vezzosa," and Giovanni Bononcini's "Dolce amor" and "Dio d'Amor"), the composers do not correlate the interior design of A or B with the allotment of text.

Apart from using initial lines to indicate the beginnings of sections and subsections, the composers arrange the verses with considerable variety. They frequently extend sections by repeating individual lines, parts of verses, or even particular words. Of the five Viennese composers, Ziani depends upon text repetition least often. He treats the long nine-line strophes of "Navicella che paventa" and "Se infelice" rather economically, never setting an individual line more than twice in succession. For emphasis at the end of a section, as in "Brami e speri," he repeats only the second half of the final line. Repetition plays a much greater role in the arias of Giovanni Bononcini, who usually skips rapidly through the opening lines of a stanza but then runs over the concluding one again and again. For example, he devotes approximately two-thirds of the A section of "Dolce amor" to verse 3 of the six-line text and allots two-thirds of B to line 6. Badia also favors repetitions of final lines. Ariosti, however, never repeats a line more than twice, preferring instead to restate groups of lines; the succession of verses in A of "Nice, crudel" illustrates this technique:

1-1-2-3-4-3-4-2-3-4-3-4

The arias of Antonio Bononcini involve the most varied treatment of text repetition. The composer sometimes stresses a specific line by stating it several times, or, like Ariosti, he may repeat pairs or entire groups of lines. Often he isolates only part of a verse or even an individual word for emphatic repetitions. Thus, in "Benché m'abbia" he rounds off the end of the last section by repeating the second half of the final line. Less frequently, he reveals only the first part of a line before setting all of it. Antonio may extend a melodic phrase by reiterating an individual word or a pair of words (example 12.1). He may also build a remarkably long phrase from a single word; the second line of "Al tuo bel volto" begins with the key word *morrà*, which Antonio sets in a rising line stretching to ten bars (see example 11.25a). The

EX.12.1. A. M. Bononcini, Cantata 99/II, mm. 93–108. The use of word repetitions to extend a musical line.

S'io ri - tor - no a in - na - mo - - - rar - vi

vi - bri il ciel_____ per ful - - - mi -

nar - - - - - - - - - mi

EX.12.2. A. M. Bononcini, Cantata 8/I, mm. 130–39. A long melodic line combining verses 1 and 2.

entire line of text then follows in a five-bar musical phrase. Another special device involves attrition: the repetition of gradually less and less of a line, as at the end of A in "S'io ritorno." When repeating groups of lines, he occasionally presents them in a different order, a procedure used in the coda of "Più barbaro martire."

By combining two or more lines of text, composers frequently create longer musical units. Giovanni Bononcini usually writes a separate phrase for the opening line of text, but he often groups succeeding lines in pairs. Ariosti generally splices only the penultimate and final lines of a section, especially when the text concludes with a short verse. Ziani, Badia, and Antonio Bononcini occasionally begin an individual A or B with a long melodic phrase combining two or more lines of text (see example 11.5 and example 12.2).

The Interactions of the Text with Melody and Rhythm

In many arias word and sentence intonations clearly influence the musical lines. Composers often coordinate melodic peaks and leaps with accented syllables that reinforce the declamatory effect. This technique frequently results in a striking opening theme. Badia, for example, closely observes the word accents in the initial melody of "Gelosia, furia d'Alletto." He assigns the melodic high point to the most stressed syllable of the word *Gelosia*, gives a secondary peak to the strong syllable of *d'Alletto*, and concludes with a descending fifth that deemphasizes the ending of the same word. The falling interval enables the singer to exaggerate the staccato effect of the Italian double consonant (see example 10.1). The correspondence of accented syllables and melodic peaks can also be found in opening themes by Ariosti and Antonio Bononcini. In such examples the composer focuses attention upon the

EX.12.3. Ariosti, Cantata 39/I, mm. 3–4. Coordination of an ascending leap and a melodic peak with accented syllables.

strong syllable not only by using a melodic high point but also by following it with a descending leap. Melodies like these increase the singer's opportunities to underline important words. The opening line of Ariosti's "Insoffribile tormento" includes an ascending tritone to stress the third syllable of the first word and a melodic peak for the accented syllable of the second word (example 12.3). Antonio Bononcini frequently begins an aria with a short declamatory motive perfectly matched with the initial line of text. More legato themes may also contain leaps that stress specific words. At the opening of "Al tuo bel volto," for example, the composer isolates *tuo* by using a melodic peak approached and left by a leap. To emphasize particular words or syllables he does not always rely upon disjunct lines. "Benché m'abbia" begins with an elegant melody moving entirely by steps; the top of the arch coincides with the accented syllable of *cruda*.

Of the Viennese cantata composers, Ziani most consistently incorporates leaps in his melodic lines. Occasionally the disjunct patterns clarify word rhythms. Thus, the descending seventh, rising fourth, and falling third in the opening line of "Brami e speri" neatly confirm the accented syllables of *speri, vile,* and *affetto* (example 12.4). At times, however, the composer deliberately avoids assigning strong syllables to higher pitches. The second phrase of "Brami e speri" illustrates this feature. In the series of ascending fourths the unaccented syllables occur on higher pitches and simultaneously on the weak parts of beats, producing a jaunty, syncopated effect (example 12.5). Elsewhere word and sentence intonations play less significant roles in Ziani melodies.

EX.12.4. Ziani, Cantata 18/VI, mm. 3–4. The use of leaps to clarify word accents.

EX.12.5. Ziani, Cantata 18/VI, mm. 6–8. Placement of weak syllables on higher pitches.

The poetic meter frequently influences the choice of musical meter. Of the twenty-five texts, twelve are trochaic (¯ ˘), four iambic (˘ ¯), three primarily dactylic (¯ ˘ ˘), one anapestic (˘ ˘ ¯), two mainly tribrachic (˘ ˘ ˘), and three a mixture of several meters.

For five settings of trochaic texts, the composers choose $\frac{3}{4}$ or $\frac{3}{8}$, which corresponds naturally to the trochaic swing of strong and weak syllables. Instead of slavishly observing the alternation of accented and unaccented syllables, however, the composers usually vary the surface rhythm in order to escape obvious singsong solutions. Antonio Bononcini, for example, favors a stress on the second beat as a means of avoiding strict patterning:

Using similar rhythms, Giovanni Bononcini sharpens the alliteration at the beginning of "Dio d'Amor":

He disguises the rigid trochaic meter of "Pena e soffri" with frequent displaced accents and by superposing a soprano line that moves predominantly in $\frac{3}{2}$ above a bass line that stresses the conventional accents of $\frac{3}{4}$ (see example 11.21).

Second-beat accents and bits of hemiola enable Ziani to overcome trochaic predictability in "Navicella che paventa," though he occasionally falls into the routine implied by the poetic meter:

For trochaic poems Ariosti consistently prefers duple meter. Thus, he sets the texts of "Al voler del bene amato," "Insoffribile tormento," and "È pur dolce" all in $\frac{4}{4}$. For the most part, his surface rhythms remain closely bound to the basic trochaic patterns. The constant dotted figures of "E pur dolce," for example, mostly reinforce the poetic accents:

And repetitive patterns consisting of eighths and sixteenths produce singsong results throughout "Al voler" and "Insoffribile":

A similar rhythmic monotony resulting from persistent adherence to the poetic meter can be seen in the A of Giovanni Bononcini's "Dolce amor":

By contrasting the surface rhythms slightly more than Giovanni or Ariosti, Badia achieves a bit more variety in his $\frac{4}{4}$ setting of the trochaic text "Gelosia, furia d'Alletto." Ziani does not vary the rhythm greatly in the duple-meter "Brami e speri," but his tendency to include numerous melodic skips, frequently emphasizing weak beats, prevents the trochaic swing from becoming too obvious.

Alternating strong and weak syllables are also characteristic of iambic meter (˘ ¯). To varying degrees the surface rhythms of the four settings of iambic texts confirm or conflict with the poetic meter. As in "È pur dolce," in "Nice, crudel" (trochaic at first, but predominantly iambic) Ariosti depends upon simple dotted figures that underline the word rhythms:

In "Sì vaga e sì vezzosa" Badia also makes little attempt to conceal the poetic patterning. Antonio Bononcini treats the iambic texts with considerably more freedom and elasticity in the $\frac{3}{4}$ aria "Al tuo bel volto." The vocal line begins on a downbeat rather than the upbeat implied by the iambic text; an ascending leap to e^2 on beat 2 helps to preserve the natural poetic meter without exaggerating it. Antonio confirms the poetic accents of the duple-meter aria "Amore ingannatore" melodically and rhythmically, but he frequently organizes the phrases so that the strong syllables fall on weak beats.

Three texts mix dactyls with trochees or iambs. Badia clearly derives the opening rhythms of "Basti per mio contento" from the word and sentence intonations, producing a simple theme made up of an antecedent and a consequent (example 12.6). In his $\frac{4}{4}$ setting of "Ombra del mio bel sol," he observes the initial dactyl of line 1, then confirms the swing of alternating strong and weak syllables:

The occasional placement of strong syllables on weak beats and the use of differentiated note values make "Ombra" rhythmically one of Badia's most interesting text settings. However, at times the composer's imagination flags even in this aria, as at the beginning of B.

The opening theme of Antonio Bononcini's "Sentimi, crudo Amore" correlates rhythmic and melodic elements in a more unusual text setting. The eighth and two sixteenths on the first beat conform to the poetic dactyl, but they rise melodically to a peak on the second beat, effectively creating a special emphasis for the key word *crudo*. The tie from the end of the third beat into the fourth and the brief burst of coloratura at the end of the phrase add rhythmic vitality. During the B section Antonio does not hesitate to place a weak syllable on the accented part of a beat within a rhythmic-melodic sequence; thus he stresses the second syllable of *sino* in the rising sequence of bars 54–55. The text of Antonio's "Benché m'abbia" consists mainly of anapests. One of his simpler themes, the opening melody is closely coordinated with the poetic accents.

Ba - sti per mio   con - ten - to, ba - sti per   tu - o   tor - men - to

EX.12.6. Badia, Cantata 75/III, mm. 7–9. Antecedent and consequent phrases with rhythms clearly derived from word and sentence intonations.

Badia's version of the tribrachic text of "Se sarai mio" again demonstrates his tendency to yield to the singsong patterns of the poetic meter:

Se   sa - rai   mi - o   io   tua   sa - rò

By occasionally beginning a line on the second beat in B, he varies the rhythm slightly, but he rarely departs from the basic textual rhythms:

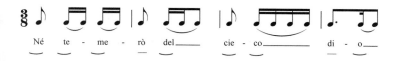

Né   te - me - rò del   cie - co   di - o

The first lines of Antonio Bononcini's "Un cor più tormentato" at first seem purely iambic ("Un cor più tormentato / di questo cor non v'è" [A heart that is more tormented than this one does not exist]), but lines 3–4 begin with tribrachs ("Langue d'Amor piagato / senza sperar mercé" [It suffers, wounded by Love, without any hope]). Musically, line 3 corresponds to line 1, while line 4 is similar to line 2. Noticing the tribrachs at the beginnings of verses 3–4, Antonio uses an appropriate rhythm in $\frac{3}{8}$; the characteristic second-beat stresses (measures 2 and 5) prevent the rhythm from sounding too conventional:

Lan - gue d'A - mor pia - ga - to   sen - za spe - rar mer - cé

Curiously, the composer applies the tribrachic formula also to the opening pair of lines:

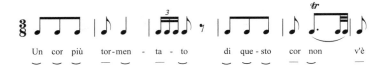

He therefore largely disguises the implicit iambic meter:

However, he gives some stress to the poetically accented syllables of *cor* and *questo* by assigning them to higher pitches (example 12.7). The use of similar melodic contours in B results in the placement of weak syllables on higher pitches. Antonio fuses rhythmic and melodic elements to create some unusually elastic lines. He does not neglect the poetic meter; neither does he treat it as a straightjacket.

EX.12.7. A. M. Bononcini, Cantata 99/II, mm. 18–23. Combination of tribrachic and iambic characteristics.

The text of Ariosti's triple-meter "Cangi Amore" combines trochees, iambs, and tribrachs. One of the composer's most effective settings, the piece retains the essential poetic accents without presenting them in an obvious manner. He achieves greater freedom by inserting long *fioriture* at the beginnings of many phrases and by concluding many vocal lines with hemiola patterns that confirm the poetic but not the musical meter. Higher pitches generally coincide with strong syllables. In Ziani's setting of "Se infelice," also a text with mixed poetic meters, the composer does not draw upon differentiated rhythms, melodic leaps, or peaks to clarify the word and sentence intonations. Proceeding in continuous quarter notes, the meandering melody nevertheless seems appropriate to the content—a detached statement from an academic cantata about a romantic problem. Antonio Bononcini's "Più barbaro martire" combines iambs with tribrachs. The composer ignores the tribrachic aspect of the text, writing several phrases in which the poetic and musical accents do not agree. As in many arias by Antonio, the numerous accents on

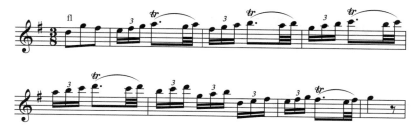

EX.12.8. A. M. Bononcini, Cantata 99/II, mm. 10–17. A playful flute obbligato used ironically.

normally weak beats contribute to the liveliness of the rhythm and enable him to avoid mechanical patterning.

TONE COLOR AND DYNAMICS

The use of specific timbres and dynamics for the evocation of particular moods can be seen in several Viennese cantatas, notably those by Antonio Bononcini. Occasionally a composer focuses upon the actual sound of a word to achieve a special effect. Badia's tendency to linger on the first syllable of *ombra* aptly allows the singer to exploit dark qualities in the word. A particular range or tessitura may also be used to recall a mood. For example, the somber effect achieved by Ariosti at the beginning of B in "Cangi Amore" can be attributed partly to the unusually low soprano tessitura used for the line "Ma sciolto in cenere il vago volto" (But who will behold the lovely face turned to ash). Antonio Bononcini's inclusion of a brilliant coloratura line leading to a high c3 in "Sentimi, crudo Amore" may have been inspired by the defiant lines "Mi toglierai la vita, ma non la libertà" (You will take my life, but not my liberty).

Though texts rarely influence the choices of instrumental timbre, Giovanni Bononcini uses the flute cleverly for echo effects in the aria "Dio d'Amor"; here the flute seems to represent the god of love, constantly responding to the questions posed by the singer. In "Un cor più tormentato," Antonio's teasing flute obbligato seems ironically suitable for the lover's complaint; the instrumental line includes rollicking triplets, trills, and turns (example 12.8). The intense solo violin obbligato of his "Benché m'abbia," with its drooping lines and frequent string crossings, ideally portrays the cruel wounds inflicted by Cupid. For "Più barbaro martire," Antonio selects paired violins (solo/tutti) and cello obbligato, marked *Andante e staccato;* the agitated string figures, biting dissonances, and frequent syncopations convincingly reflect the lover's barbarous sufferings. The larger orchestra (solo/tutti violins 1–2, viola, and basso continuo) and frequent imitative entries of "Sentimi, crudo Amore" contribute to the declaration of war on the god of love.

EX.12.9. Badia, Cantata 1/III, mm. 96–108. The use of a sustained tone for a descriptive effect.

Only Antonio Bononcini consistently exploits dynamics for textual reasons in the scores of cantatas. He uses echo dynamics, but the written-in *piano* at the end of B in his "Per non arder" seems clearly derived from the verse "E mai pace in sen non ho" (And in my breast I never have peace). The composer completes B of "Un cor più tormentato" with a final *piano* statement of the line "senza sperar mercé" (without hoping for mercy), the only specific dynamic marking in the aria. Evidently fond of concluding a section softly, he also saves a *piano* for the expressive final phrase of "Benché m'abbia." In "Al tuo bel volto" the *piano* serves both a structural and an affective purpose. It occurs only twice, underlining the penultimate phrases of A and B and thus adding a subtle detail in the symmetrical design. The soft dynamic also shades the meanings of important words such as *morrà* in A and *martire* in B. "Sentimi, crudo Amore" contains the most elaborate dynamics. Antonio not only coordinates the *piano/forte* markings with concertato contrasts but also exploits them for the combat described in the text.

DESCRIPTIVE TREATMENT OF THE TEXT

The Viennese arias include only occasional pictorial details. Obvious wordplay can be seen in arias like Ariosti's "Nice, crudel," where the word *raddoppia* invites a repetition not overlooked by the composer. Similarly, Antonio Bononcini repeats the words *mille dardi* (a thousand darts) again and again in "S'io ritorno," adding appropriate dissonances for the reiterations of *dardi*.

The composers sometimes write sustained tones to denote fidelity or stability. For example, in B of Giovanni Bononcini's "Pena e soffri," the melody twice rises to a sustained peak of f2 on the strong syllable of *costanza;* the line then descends on the words *nel morir.* Antonio repeatedly uses a sustained high point for *costante* in "Al tuo bel volto." One of Badia's rare descriptive effects comes near the end of B in "Se sarai mio," where the soprano sings the accented syllable of *stabile* on the pitch d2 for more than seven measures (example 12.9).

I lac - ci___ tuoi___ già___ fran - go   e

li - be - ro___ ri - man - go

EX.12.10. A. M. Bononcini, Cantata 8/I, mm. 45–47. Musical description of breaking bonds through a quickly rising line and a descending octave.

Conjunct and disjunct lines may also characterize specific words. Thus, Ariosti creates a smooth, florid melody for *un contento* in "Al voler del bene amato" (see example 11.15). Melodic leaps, including sevenths and octaves, musically illustrate the words *lungi vanne* in Badia's "Gelosia, furia d'Alletto" (see example 10.1). In "Più barbaro martire," Antonio Bononcini invents a musical analogue for *lontananza* by writing a jagged melody consisting of sixths and sevenths. To illustrate the action of breaking bonds in "Amore ingannatore," a rising line ends with a dramatic descending octave (example 12.10).

Images of turbulence often call forth specific musical devices. Near the end of A in Badia's "Gelosia, furia d'Alletto" a swirling pattern vividly illustrates the agitation caused by jealousy and rage. In "Navicella che paventa" Ziani paints the tempestuous sea with a twisting melodic line incorporating frequent leaps and hemiola patterns (see example 11.4). A leaping sequential melody in Antonio Bononcini's "S'io ritorno" portrays the shaking of heaven (*vibri il ciel;* see example 12.2). To create the impression of a battle in "Sentimi, crudo Amore," he uses a short motive in a rising chromatic sequence; the repetitions of the motive, separated by rests, suggest the breathlessness caused by combat.

AFFECTIVE TREATMENT OF THE TEXT

The extent to which composers exploit individual style elements for expressive purposes varies widely. Ziani rarely uses affective harmony, melody, or rhythm to enhance a particular line or word. Often delightfully unpretentious, his playful melodies and jaunty rhythms seem ideally suited to the discourses of the academic cantatas. Expressive leaps like the diminished fifth for the words *si pente* in "Navicella che paventa" occur very rarely.

Badia's arias include slightly more evocative harmony and melody than Ziani's. An ascending major seventh tellingly underlines the words *troppo crudo* in B of "Gelosia, furia d'Alletto." The composer generally uses dissonance for cadential

chi mi - re - rà sen - - - za pie - tà?

EX.12.11. Ariosti, Cantata 65/I, mm. 68–71. Affective treatment of the line "chi mirerà senza pietà": a suspension followed by a Phrygian cadence and a dramatic octave leap.

rather than affective reasons. The most consistent use of expressive harmony occurs in "Ombra del mio bel sol," which contains a chain of suspensions for the word *adorarti*. Badia also emphasizes this word melodically with a florid sequence concluding with an ascending diminished seventh.

Many pieces by Ariosti do not surpass the expressive level of text setting found in works by Ziani and Badia. However, he often delights in the melancholy color of the Neapolitan sixth, using it for words like *lascia, moro,* and *piacer*. A leap to a melodic peak followed by a cascade of thirty-second notes underline the word *barbaro* in "Nice, crudel." Now and then the composer devises a striking harmonic progression for a particularly intense text. For example, the opening ritornello of "Insoffribile tormento" includes a series of languid diminished-seventh chords and secondary dominants in various inversions as well as a melodic line with prominent tritones. "Cangi Amore" perhaps represents Ariosti's strongest effort in text setting. By using bold musical contrasts between A and B, he convincingly portrays the shift from inward acceptance of the god of love's flames (A) to outward compassion for the beloved's ashen face (B). A bright F-major Vivace contrasts with a melancholy d-minor Adagio. Moreover, the florid vocal writing used for words like *cangi* and *arda* in A largely disappears during B. The dark low range of the soprano voice seems especially appropriate for the word *cenere* at the beginning of B. Here the bass line descends by steps for two measures, while the soprano line rises gradually throughout the first eleven measures. The rich harmonies, with seventh chords in various inversions, contributes to the general intensity. For the words *senza pietà* Ariosti links an expressive suspension to the melodic high point of B. The phrase concludes with a dramatic octave descent over a Phrygian cadence (example 12.11). This beautiful passage reveals Ariosti's sensitive use of harmonic color; unfortunately, his cantatas yield very few examples of such imaginative writing.

Giovanni Bononcini exploits affective harmony and melody more frequently than Ariosti. In the long Bb-major B section of "Pena e soffri," chromaticism involving the tonic $^6_4$ chord borrowed from the parallel minor darkens the harmony for the words *nel morir,* and a drooping diminished fourth on the second syllable of *morir* further enhances the expressive writing. After the bb-minor inflection, the harmony aptly returns to the tonic major for the words *o nell'amar* (see example 11.16). Bon-

EX.12.12. G. Bononcini, Cantata 22/I, mm. 66–71. Affective suspensions for the words *eccesso* and *pene;* a falling diminished fifth on *morirò.*

oncini matches the exaggerated sentiment expressed in the verses "E l'eccesso de le pene / mi sa dir ch'io morirò" (And the excess of my pains knows how to tell me that I shall die) from "Dio d'Amor" with a languid, descending sequence. Suspensions on the accented syllables of *l'eccesso* and *pene* heighten the intensity, and a falling diminished fifth underscores the words *ch'io morirò* at the end of the phrase (example 12.12).

Like Ariosti's "Cangi Amore," Giovanni's "Dolce amor" boldly contrasts two moods through changes in tempo, meter, mode, and thematic material. The main affect of A is compassion (*pietà*), emphasized by the $\frac{4}{4}$ adagio, the g-minor mode, and the use of conjunct motion in which peaks and lows are approached gradually. The composer portrays the words *lieto* and *contento* in B with a $\frac{3}{8}$ vivace (Bb major) and with an agitated melody having many quick rises and falls. He reserves the most expressive writing for the word *pietà*. Extensive melismas on the final syllable enhance the melodic lines of both the opening section and the varied da capo. When the voice rises from c^2 to eb^2 at the beginning of the first melisma, the supporting dominant-seventh chord briefly becomes a minor ninth; near the end of the phrase the voice rises a minor seventh, then outlines a descending diminished seventh. A Phrygian cadence using the low range of the cello concludes the

EX.12.13. G. Bononcini, Cantata 82/I, mm. 47–48. Affective melody and harmony to underscore *pietà*.

A section. In A' Giovanni expands the melisma by one and one-half bars. Using a falling sequential pattern, he enriches the passage with melodic chromaticism, an affective contrast rhythm ($\quad$), and a final descending scale in thirty-seconds, again outlining a diminished seventh. The long phrase stops on vii° $^6_4$, an unstable chord inviting an additional improvised flourish. Both harmonically and melodically, the final measures of the varied da capo maintain the intensity of the penultimate phrase. A deceptive progression (i $^6_4$–V–vii°$_6$) proceeds directly to vii°$_7$ of the tonic; the soprano line ascends an augmented fourth, then rises to a peak of g² before falling a perfect fifth (example 12.13). A deceptive cadence (V–VI) provides an unusual conclusion for the final vocal phrase.

After so much evidence of effective control, it comes as no surprise that Antonio Bononcini most consistently heightens the emotional content of the poetry with affective harmony, melody, and rhythm. Though he highlights specific words with coloristic chords less frequently than his brother, he draws on a generally richer harmonic vocabulary for broad affects. Often he evokes a particular mood with dissonant or chromatic harmonies already in the introductory ritornello. Thus, the sharp dissonances in the opening of "Amore ingannatore" (see example 11.30) establish the singer's wrath against the treacherous god of love. Similarly, biting seconds and sevenths in the ritornello of "Più barbaro martire" set the stage for the barbarous sufferings described in the text. The numerous seventh chords, suspensions, and chromatic harmonies provide an intense harmonic background for "Sentimi, crudo Amore," a determined refusal to submit to Cupid's "bold right hand." And the frequent unprepared dissonances and sevenths of "Benché m'abbia" represent the aching wounds inflicted by Amor.

Although Antonio favors general affects, he sometimes paints specific verses or words with chord colors. To underscore the words *miracolo è d'Amor* (it is the miracle of Love) in B of "Più barbaro martire," he uses an abrupt modulation from c minor to d minor. He reaches the new key in just three chords: the tonic of c minor, its mediant (the Neapolitan of d minor), and the dominant of d. By placing the Neapolitan chord in second rather than the customary first inversion, the com-

EX.12.14. A. M. Bononcini, Cantata 45/I, mm. 57–59. A chromatic modulation for the words *miracolo è d'Amor.*

poser writes a smoothly descending bass line (example 12.14). Antonio's fondness for the Neapolitan chord can be seen in many arias. In "Al tuo bel volto" it provides a listless quality for *povero.* At the end of "Benché m'abbia" the composer combines it with a falling melodic line for the word *sperare.* Antonio also uses dissonance to sharpen the meaning of a particular word. Thus, the biting chord clusters used for the repetitions of *dardi* in "S'io ritorno" clearly illustrate the stings of Cupid's arrows. The weeping (*pianto*) that could move Amor's heart in "Men crudele" is accompanied by a chain of 9–8, 7–6, and 4–3 suspensions.

A host of expressive melodic figures elucidates the texts of Antonio's arias. Fiery coloratura passages culminating in brilliant peaks match the resolute mood of "Sentimi, crudo Amore" (see example 11.19). A series of rising triplets illustrates *fulminari* in "S'io ritorno" (example 12.2), and a melody undulating between d2 and eb2 affectively stresses the lines "di quel che soffre un cor" (than that which a heart suffers) and "e non morire" ([who could endure it] and not die) in "Più barbaro martire." Rapidly rising lines coordinated with syncopation perfectly portray the treachery of "Amore ingannatore." The playful turns and trills of "Un cor più tormentato" mockingly depict the torment experienced by the lover (see example 12.8). Long ascending and descending lines portray the word *morrà* in "Al tuo bel volto" (see example 11.25a). For *martire* in B of the same aria the composer writes an affective chromatic variant of the rising melody used for *morrà* in A (see example 11.25b). Recurrent rests interrupt the flow of sixteenth notes used for *sperare* in "Benché m'abbia," producing a typically baroque sighing effect.

Antonio uses affective intervals for specific textual reasons. He interpolates a characteristic diminished fourth in the long melodic line for verses 2–3 of "Men crudele": "Fate voi che più non tanto / mi tormenti il mio dolor" (Make it so that my pain does not torment me so much). Diminished thirds color words like *arder, languir,* and *morir* in "Per non arder." In measure 28 a descending diminished seventh poignantly underscores the question, "Dimmi o cor, che far dovrò?" (Tell me, O heart, what shall I have to do?). Occasionally phrases conclude with octave descents that dramatize words like *martire* and *frango.*

To evoke particular moods, Antonio also invents specific rhythmic figures. Thus, the driving syncopated rhythms of "Amore ingannatore" are ideally suited to describe the treachery of the god of love. The numerous syncopations and staccato figures in "Più barbaro martire" confirm the lover's suffering caused by the absence of the beloved. Syncopations and double-dotted patterns in "S'io ritorno" stress the anguished lover's wish to be struck dead if ever he ventures to love again.

The five composers discussed in this chapter show varying degrees of sensitivity to text. However, in details of affective harmony, melody, and rhythm, as in most aspects of style, Antonio surpasses his Viennese contemporaries.

13

Conclusion: The Interregnum
and Its Aftermath

The End of the War of the Spanish Succession

Until 1709 events in the War of the Spanish Succession seemed to favor Austria, but a series of misfortunes quickly turned the tide in favor of France. These included Charles III's inability to gain a stronghold in Spain and England's decision to open peace negotiations with France in 1710. The possibility of a Spain reunited with the Holy Roman Empire could hardly have been more palatable than the prospect of Spain and France under one crown. Queen Anne had ultimately decided that it was necessary to end the war in order to prevent the consolidation and expansion of Habsburg power. England therefore sought to persuade Charles to accept a peace treaty shortly after the death of his brother on 17 April 1711. In the spring of that year George Frideric Handel was visiting England for the first time, and soon after the success of his opera debut, *Rinaldo,* he received a commission for a festive cantata that would pay homage to Charles and reflect the English mood of rejoicing at the prospect of peace.

Handel's personal connection to Austria seems to have been very limited. It would be unwarranted speculation to suggest that he passed through Vienna en route to Italy in the second half of 1706, but definite information is known about his return journey to Germany. Following the run of performances of *Agrippina* at Venice near the end of February 1710, he traveled through Innsbruck in March on his way to Hanover. Prince Carl von Neuburg, governor of Tyrol, received Handel and offered him assistance, which the composer declined.[1]

Several theories about the origins of the cantata *Echeggiate, festeggiate, numi eterni,* HWV 119, have been advanced. That it was composed before Charles was proclaimed emperor is evident from the reference in the text to "Carlo, il rege d'Iberia." Although the cantata was once thought to have been composed in Rome, its English provenance is evident from the paper of the autograph. Thus the cantata could not have been composed earlier than the end of 1710, when Handel arrived in England. Although the precise dating remains uncertain, recent scholars have suggested that the cantata was probably composed in March and April 1711 while Handel was enjoying the success of *Rinaldo*.[2] The extant autograph lacks both a title and the opening music. The unusually lavish vocal and instrumental scoring consists of three sopranos, alto, bass, two recorders, two oboes, strings, and basso continuo.

The premature death of Joseph I dealt a heavy blow to Austria, leaving the Habsburgs with no male heir to the throne other than Archduke Charles himself. The Austrian claimant to the Spanish throne was forced to leave Barcelona on 27 September 1711. While he returned to Austria, Leopold's widow, the empress dowager Eleonora Magdalena, served as regent of the empire. Austerity measures were announced, including a reduction of expenses for musical activities and personnel. Notices about the reductions were circulated on 3 and 11 September.[3] The number of court musicians declined temporarily to eighty-six, but it had climbed to one hundred again by 1715.[4] A committee consisting of Marc'Antonio Ziani, Johann Josef Fux, and Kilian Reinhardt was charged with making recommendations for reappointments. All musicians were to be paid through September—that is, the end of the third quarter—but after 31 September only church musicians were to be retained. Many artists and musicians remained in Vienna through 1711, expecting to be reinstated after the arrival of the new emperor. Uncertainty with regard to the precise membership of the emperor's chapel persisted until a list was finally established on 31 December 1712.

Traveling from Spain through Italy to Frankfurt am Main, where he was crowned emperor on 22 December 1711, Charles arrived in Vienna on 26 January 1712. In the treaty of Rastatt (1714) Austria agreed to recognize Philip V as king of Spain; in return the Habsburgs gained control of the sections of the Netherlands formerly belonging to Spain and parts of Italy, including Naples, Milan, Mantua, and Sardinia. Having lost the prize he most earnestly desired, Emperor Charles VI cultivated a strong Spanish influence at the Viennese court. Many artists and musicians who had served him in Barcelona came to Vienna in search of employment.

The Fate of the Cantata Composers and Librettists Who Served Joseph I

During the unsettled months of the transition, cantata composers who had been employed during the reign of Joseph I (Ziani, Badia, the Bononcini brothers, and Ariosti) awaited word concerning their appointments. Joseph I had not filled the post of Kapellmeister after the death of Antonio Pancotti in 1709. As assistant Kapellmeister, Marc'Antonio Ziani assumed leadership of the chapel during the interregnum. In December 1711 he went with other members of the chapel to Frankfurt for the coronation of Charles. On 1 January 1712 he finally received the official appointment as Kapellmeister, and Fux was named his assistant. However, clarifications about the definitive membership of Charles's chapel and financial relief for many musicians did not follow immediately. In June 1712 Ziani wrote to Charles on behalf of the entire chapel.[5] A list of chapel members was eventually posted on 1 January 1713, and many applied for and received payment for the period of reorganization.

Unfortunately, Ziani was to hold the honored post as Kapellmeister for little more than three years before he died on 22 January 1715. These three years saw major changes in personnel and style at Vienna, but Ziani did not live to witness the full blossoming of music during the Fux-Caldara-Conti generation, once the scars of the War of the Spanish Succession had faded. The high esteem that he had earned can be seen from the fact that a pension was awarded not only to his wife but also to his brother Francesco, ostensibly an isolated example of this practice at Vienna.[6] At the church of San Salvatore in Venice, the renowned castrato Francesco Senesino participated in elaborate funeral music that paid homage to a native son.[7]

On 1 October 1711 both Carlo Badia and his wife were reengaged, but the situation remained temporary for them until the definitive list of musicians was posted at the outset of 1713. Once again, the Badias received new appointments. At Vienna, where opera performances were the proudest adornments of the court, Lisi Badia's reputation probably contributed to the renewal of her husband's contract as well as her own. Badia's lengthy cantata *Il sacrificio di Berenice* (text by P. A. del Negro) was commissioned in Vienna for the birthday of Empress Elizabeth Christina (28 August 1712), who had remained in Barcelona until the spring of 1713, clinging to the Habsburg claim to the Spanish throne.[8]

Circumstances following the death of Joseph brought about a complete reversal of Giovanni Bononcini's most favored position at Vienna. Giovanni, his brother, and both Stampiglias were released along with other artists, but they remained in Vienna through 1711, expecting to be reinstated after the arrival of the new emperor. While musicians such as Ziani and Badia received fresh appointments under Charles, the Bononcinis and the Stampiglias did not.

The exact reasons for Giovanni's failure to retain his post remain clouded, but they appear to be a combination of pride and financial demands unacceptable to the court. According to a petition made by Bononcini to the empress Maria Theresia in 1742, Joseph I had agreed in 1711 to give Bononcini the enormous sum of twenty thousand florins in unpaid salary. This sum represented money owed to Bononcini for the period 1698–1707. Joseph also agreed to pay Bononcini his full annual salary of five thousand florins—the total from both the court treasury and the private treasury—even after the composer's retirement.[9] Joseph's commitments were made only a few days before he contracted smallpox.

After his accession, Charles VI evidently refused to assume responsibility for the promises of Joseph I. One of the principal aims of Count Molard, who as

Musik-Oberdirektor from 1712 to 1716 was responsible for the reorganization of the Habsburg chapel, was the strict adherence to basic salaries, to be paid from the court treasury only. In other words, sums previously paid from the private imperial treasury were to be eliminated.[10] Perhaps Bononcini insisted upon the complete fulfillment of Joseph's promises. In doing so, he may well have offended Charles. Moreover, like his predecessors, Charles was undoubtedly eager to attract his own circle of artists and advisors. Many who had served Charles in Spain followed him to Austria. Such artists as Ferdinando Galli-Bibiena, Antonio Caldara, and Giuseppe Porsile, all of whom had gained favor in Barcelona, eventually received appointments in Vienna. Many others from Barcelona and southern Italy journeyed to Austria in hope of finding employment. With such a steady supply of talent, it hardly seems surprising that Charles refused to meet Bononcini's demands.[11]

Attilio Ariosti had never held an official post as a musician at the Habsburg court, but he had served as an agent-general from at least the spring of 1707. He retained this post until the end of Joseph's reign, but during the interregnum he was released by the empress dowager and appears to have resumed his clerical life in Bologna.

During the more than twenty months of confusion following the death of Joseph, Antonio Maria Bononcini probably remained in Vienna, anticipating that his contract would eventually be renewed by Charles. However, neither Bononcini was reappointed, probably because of the financial conditions set by Giovanni, which the court was unwilling to meet. The brothers may have traveled together to Rome in 1713. Antonio Maria is traceable there in 1714.[12] There is no evidence that Antonio had antagonized the emperor or that, like Giovanni, he experienced professional frustration during the years in which he hoped to be reinstated at Vienna. On the contrary, during the years 1715–21, Antonio seems to have finally become independent from his brother and to have achieved a degree of fame as an opera composer in his own right.

The theorbist Francesco Conti not only was retained by Charles VI but was to become one of the most important and prolific composers of operas, oratorios, and cantatas of the next generation. Conti traveled to Frankfurt with other court musicians for the coronation of Charles. Returning to Vienna, he was reengaged as court theorbist, with an annual salary of 1,440 florins. From at least 1714 he also held an appointment as court composer, for which he received an additional 1,440 florins, making him one of the highest paid members of the Viennese chapel.[13] Conti's reputation as the premier theorbist of his generation and his affiliation with and marriage to the prima donna Maria Landini undoubtedly strengthened his position at court during the years of transition.

The unstable period following Joseph's death also witnessed important changes for librettists. Pietro Antonio Bernardoni had served as first court poet beginning in 1705. Toward the middle of 1706 Joseph engaged Silvio Stampiglia as an additional court poet. A rivalry between the two librettists may have been responsible for Bernardoni's decisions to give up his prestigious appointment and to return to Bologna in 1710. Stampiglia remained in Vienna until at least 1714 and possibly as late as 1718.[14]

The Cantatas by Composers Residing in Vienna during the Interregnum

A small number of cantatas by composers active during Joseph's reign were probably composed in the months following the emperor's death. Cantatas of the transitional period include Badia's *Il sacrificio di Berenice* and several chamber cantatas by Giovanni Bononcini and Francesco Conti. After he was reappointed at the beginning of 1713, Badia apparently did not write any additional cantatas, though he did compose a *dialogo da cantarsi* entitled *Il bel Genio dell'Austria ed il Fato,* which was performed in November 1723 for the return to Vienna of Charles VI following his coronation as king of the Romans at Prague.[15] *Il sacrificio di Berenice* is discussed in chapters 8–9 with all the cantatas by Badia dating from Leopold's waning years and the reign of Joseph I.

Of particular interest is MS 17567 at A-Wn.[16] This manuscript contains three cantatas by Giovanni Bononcini, three by Francesco Conti, three by Antonio Caldara (1671?–1736), two by Emanuele d'Astorga (1680–1757?), and one by Andrea Stefano Fiorè (1686–1732). The cantatas by Bononcini belong stylistically with cantatas of the period 1700–1711 and are discussed in this book with the cantatas by composers of this generation. The Conti cantatas probably date from the transition year and need to be discussed with the total oeuvre of this composer's impressive contribution to the cantata literature. That Bononcini and Conti would have composed cantatas during the interregnum is not surprising, for this was a period in which commissions for large-scale dramatic works were particularly rare. By early 1713 Bononcini had already departed for Italy. The cantatas by him, therefore, and most of the others in MS 17567 probably date from the period immediately preceding the posting of the new list of chapel members of 1713.

There is strong internal evidence that MS 17567 actually dates from 1712. Caldara is known to have sojourned at Vienna from February to June 1712.[17] The second cantata in MS 17567, Caldara's *Io soffrirò tacendo,* is also preserved in an autograph copy now at D-Bsb with the dating "Fine a 7 Marzo 1712 in Vienna." No concordances have been located for the other two Caldara cantatas in MS 17567 (*Arda il mio petto* and *Senti Filli incostante*), which presumably were also composed in that year.[18] The three Caldara cantatas in MS 17567, like those of Conti, will be discussed by me in a future study dealing with the composer's total contribution to the cantata repertoire in Vienna.

Andrea Stefano Fiorè was born in Milan but spent most of his life in the service of the duke of Savoy, becoming the *maestro di cappella* at the Turin court on 13 June 1707. During the period 1704–14 Turin's Teatro Regio remained closed, but Fiorè seized opportunities to compose operas for other courts, including Vienna, where three dramatic works were produced between 1708 and 1710.[19] Because Fiorè received commissions for these operas, it has often been suggested that he also visited the imperial capital, but no documentation has emerged to verify this conclusion. Since Fiorè was active at Turin, a court closely allied with the Habsburgs at the time, the acceptance of his music in Vienna is not surprising. Evidence is also lacking to support a hypothesis that Fiorè traveled to Vienna in the hope of finding employment at the prestigious Habsburg court during the transition of 1712. Unique to MS 17567, Fiorè's *Di quel sguardo fatal* is the final cantata in this manuscript.[20]

One of the most storied and colorful figures in the history of music, Baron Emanuele (Giacchino Cesare Rincón) d'Astorga, led a peripatetic career that curiously parallels Giovanni Bononcini's.[21] Unlike Bononcini, however, Astorga came from an aristocratic family, initially preventing him from pursuing a career as a professional musician. Of Spanish lineage, the Astorga family had settled in Sicily, acquiring wealth, land, and in 1633 a baronial title. Perhaps because of quarrels with his violent father, Emanuele set out on a life of adventure sometime before 1708, making his way as a composer at first in Rome, then in Genoa, where he and the librettist for some of his cantatas, Sebastiano Biancardi, were robbed by their servant. Composer and poet assumed the names Giuseppe del Chiaro and Domenico Lalli, respectively, and were able to raise some money by composing operas for Genoa (*Dafni,* 21 April 1709) and Venice (*L'Amor tirannico,* autumn 1710). As the claimant to the Spanish throne, Charles III had summoned Astorga in 1709 to Barcelona, where the composer's *Dafni* was performed successfully in June of that year. Winning the admiration of Charles III, Astorga was granted a salary of two thousand florins annually by Emperor Joseph I,[22] a salary that he only began to receive in 1712, once Charles had become emperor.

By 9 May 1712 Astorga was in Vienna, where he stood in for the Dutch ambassador Hamel von Bruynings as godfather in the baptismal ceremonies for a daughter of Caldara.[23] Possibly because the court was slow in paying his salary, he contracted several debts, then disappeared in the late spring of 1714. Once again in Palermo by September 1714, he inherited the family estates and title following the deaths of his elder brother and father. In October 1717 he married the fifteen-year-old daughter of a baron, but in 1721 he deserted his wife and three daughters, setting out once again on a life of wandering.[24]

The two Astorga cantatas in MS 17567 (*Che ti giova* and *Quando penso a quell'ore*) are unique to this source but undated. In the thematic catalog of her dissertation, Karen Ladd cites two additional cantatas (*Quando penso agl'affanni* and *Ti parlo, e non m'ascolti*) that are dated 1712 and might therefore have been composed in Vienna.[25] Ladd lists a total of ten manuscripts that preserve *Quando penso agl'affanni*, including three that date the cantata August 1712. *Quando penso agl'affanni* is dated "Vienna Agosto 1712" in two separate manuscripts found at B-Bc and one now at D-Dl. However, it is also found on pages 196–205 in B-MAR, Cote MS 46–2, a manuscript that includes a total of twenty-two cantatas by Astroga. Marie Cornaz has described this source in detail.[26] According to Cornaz, the attribution "Del Sg.ʳ Baron d'Astorgas. 1710" is written on page 1 of the manuscript. The watermarks are those found in many British copies. If *Quando penso agl'affanni* was already copied in England by 1710, then it could not have been composed for Vienna in 1712, though Astorga might have offered it as a new cantata during his stay in Vienna.[27] Ladd inventories fourteen manuscripts that include *Ti parlo, e non m'ascolti*, only one of which, I-Nc, 33.4.25, bears the date 1712. *Ti parlo* is the fourteenth cantata in the collection and is written in a completely different hand from the thirteen cantatas that precede it and the four that follow it. At the end of this cantata, the copyist has dated it simply "1712." Without additional evidence, it remains impossible to verify whether or not *Ti parlo* was composed for Vienna. One or more of the Astorga cantatas preserved at A-Wgm may eventually prove to be of Viennese origins, but at present documentation is lacking to verify the origin of any of these cantatas. Of the nine Astorga cantatas in A-Wgm cataloged by me, only *Non deggio lagnarmi* is preserved in a manuscript that is clearly of Viennese origin (Q 4131); the copyist is a Viennese scribe of the Caldara-Conti generation (compare, for example, Conti's *Per volervi un dì*, no. 2 in VI 11845 [Q 4895]), and the watermark is of the common three-crescent variety found in numerous manuscripts of this period. *Non deggio lagnarmi* survives in only one other manuscript, I-Bc, DD27, but this source is not dated. To summarize, Astorga may have composed several cantatas for Vienna in 1712, but at present it is possible to identify only the two found in MS 17567 as compositions written for Vienna during the interregnum.

It is tempting to view MS 17567 as a special set of cantatas by composers competing for positions at the court of Charles VI in the year before the final list was posted. While there is no firm basis for this assumption, it is clear that the careers of at least four of these five composers were intimately bound up with the shifting circumstances in Vienna. The collection also gives a useful glimpse of cantata activity at an important crossroads in Viennese music history. All twelve cantatas are scored for soprano and basso continuo. Virtually all of them adhere to standard patterns of alternating recitative and aria. Nine cantatas unfold in the most common pattern, R–A–R–A, while two cantatas follow the shorter A–R–A scheme, and one illustrates a slightly expanded plan, A–R–A–R–A. All the arias illustrate the da capo or modified da capo design.

The cantatas in MS 17567 reveal the stylistic preferences of each composer. An outstanding cellist, Bononcini, for example, excels at composing idiomatic bass lines in the ritornellos, exploiting string crossings and wide leaps, often treated sequentially. Both Bononcini and Caldara offer the star singers of the period special challenges, such as long-breathed coloratura passages, sustained tones in high range, and wide melodic leaps. Conti sometimes makes similar demands, but, significantly, his cantatas nearly always feature phrases with unusually expressive chromaticism, both harmonic and melodic. All three composers highlight words such as *costanza, amor,* and *ghiaccio* with vivid melodic figuration. The arias of Bononcini received detailed stylistic analysis in chapters 9–12, and the cantatas of Caldara and Conti will be discussed in a future study.

Andrea Fiorè's single contribution to MS 17567, *Di quel sguardo fatal,* shows a rather individual approach to cantata composition. The opening recitative is followed by a thirty-three-measure arioso set in g minor and in triple meter, except for the final two measures in common time. This extraordinary arioso—the only example in MS 17567—features chromatic harmony and a jagged vocal line to express the verse "Non s'accorgon nemen del mio tormento." The bass line of the ensuing F-major aria features a vigorous thirty-second-note motive. The composer introduces this motive in the opening ritornello, reserving it for the bass throughout the aria and contrasting it with the smoother, occasionally florid soprano line. The concluding, B♭-major aria is a fascinating modified da capo. The A section begins with a brief ritornello, continues with three separate vocal sections, each repeated, and concludes with a considerably altered and extended version of the ritornello. The B section contains no repeated sections; it moves through c minor to d minor, reaching a climax on a full diminished-seventh chord followed by a dramatic pause and four measures of chromatic motion in common time before cadencing in d minor. The da capo proceeds exactly as before, including the extended ritornello at the end.

The style of Astorga's cantatas in MS 17567 needs to be understood within the context of his total output.[28] Of the three arias in *Che ti giova, Amor crudele,* the most surprising is the lengthy second aria, an Andante with constant alternation between $\frac{3}{8}$ and common time signatures. Sensitivity to text setting and rhythm is in fact one of Astorga's strengths. To adjust his rhythms to Italian prosody he employs techniques such as frequent hemiola (both within phrases and at cadences), appropriate syncopation, and notes tied across bar lines in florid passages that provide a lively, swinging effect. Astorga's bass lines and melodies are more perfunctory than those of Bononcini, Caldara, and Conti. In the first aria of *Che ti giova* the bass line does not participate in motivic ideas from the lyric vocal melody but functions purely as harmonic support. More interesting ritornellos are found in the third aria of *Che ti giova* and the second aria of *Quando penso a quell'ore.* The first aria of *Quando penso a quell'ore* ("Cessa omai pensier crudité") begins with the type of vocal motto that became popular in the early eighteenth century. Unlike arias with a *Devise,* this aria does not begin with an introductory ritornello. Instead, it commences immediately with a vocal phrase followed by a full sequential ritornello before the singer proceeds with the rest of the A section. Here the composer is more

TABLE 13.1. CANTATAS COMPOSED IN VIENNA CA. 1712

CANTATA TEXT INCIPIT	COMPOSER	VIENNESE SOURCES
Arda il mio petto	Antonio Caldara	A-Wn, 17567, 33r⁻39v
Che ti giova, Amor crudele	Emanuele d'Astorga	A-Wn, 17567, 70r⁻80v
Dimmi, o sorte nemica	Francesco Conti	A-Wn, 17567, 40r⁻46v
Io soffrirò tacendo	Antonio Caldara	A-Wn, 17567, 9r⁻17v
Lasciami Amor nemico	Francesco Conti	A-Wn, 17567, 18r⁻25v
Non ardisco pregarti	Giovanni Bononcini	A-Wn, 17567, 1r⁻8v
Quando penso a quell'ore	Emanuele d'Astorga	A-Wn, 17567, 81r⁻88v
Regina eccoci al Tempio (Title: *Il Sacrificio di Berenice*)	Carlo Badia	A-Wn, 17675, 76 fols.
Rompi l'arco	Giovanni Bononcini	A-Wn, 17567, 47r⁻53v
Senti, Filli inconstante	Antonio Caldara	A-Wn, 17567, 54r⁻61v
Sento dentro del petto	Giovanni Bononcini	A-Wn, 17567, 25r⁻32v
Tento scuotere dal seno	Francesco Conti	A-Wn, 17567, 62r⁻69v

daring than usual, drawing upon expressive word painting and an attractive rising and falling melody for "di piagar l'afflitto cor." The introductory bass line of the third aria of *Che ti giova* features tried-and-true triadic motion in anticipation of the cliché setting of the first verse, "Guerra, guerra, ardito Amore."

Table 5.1 summarizes details about the sources of the twelve cantatas known to have been written by composers residing in Vienna in 1712. With the appointment of Fux as Kapellmeister in 1715 and Caldara as his assistant in 1716, Viennese musical life entered a new period that was largely dominated by these two men and by Conti. Egon Wellesz identified the origins of the new generation as far back as 1709, the earliest year in which Caldara contributed to a large secular dramatic work performed in Vienna.[29] Caldara's influence was certainly felt in Vienna before his appointment in Vienna in 1716; some of his compositions were heard at the imperial court before he began his service as assistant Kapellmeister, and his visit to Vienna in 1712 is well documented. However, the Bononcini brothers, Ziani, Badia, and Conti remained the nucleus of the Italian faction at least until 1713, after which the winds of change blew quickly: the Bononcini brothers departed for Italy early in 1713; Ziani died early in 1715; and Badia's influence was negligible after this time. Of the earlier group, only Conti—along with Fux and Caldara—was to receive many important commissions during the reign of Charles VI.

APPENDIX A
INDEX OF CANTATA TEXT
INCIPITS AND SOURCES

The cantatas have been divided into two historical periods, 1658–1700 and 1700–1712. A few cantatas by Carlo Badia date from slightly before 1700 but belong stylistically with the later group. The cantatas are indexed alphabetically by first line of text; alphabetization is letter by letter rather than word by word. For indexing purposes, modern Italian spelling, capitalization, and punctuation have been used for the opening text of each cantata. Following each incipit, additional information is given in parentheses: the title (if one appears in the manuscript or print), the composer's name, the voicing and instrumentation, and all sources known to me, beginning with the core manuscript or print.

Each of the fifty-eight cantatas from the period 1658–1700 is preserved in a unique copy, with the exceptions of Carlo Cappellini's *Occhi miei non vi struggete* and A. M. Viviani's *Un tiranno di foco;* concerning the conflicting attribution of Viviani's cantata with Luigi Rossi, see Herbert Seifert's *Giovanni Buonaventura Viviani,* pages 170–71. Several chamber cantatas from the period 1700–1712 survive in more than one source. All the sources known to me are listed. Individual copies of Badia's *Tributi armonici* are not given for each cantata from this print; a list of them may be found in the catalogue raisonné (appendix B).

1658–1700

1. *Adorate mie bellezze quando mai vi rivedrò* (A. M. Viviani; S, bc; A-Wn, 18762, fols. 54v–55v)

2. *Agl'incendi ai legami alle ferite* (*Forza d'un bel volto;* Antonio Draghi; SSATB, bc; A-Wn, 16135, fols. 3–23)

3. *Ancor sazia non sei* (Carlo Cappellini; S, bc; A-Wn, 17768, fols. 1–13v)

4. *Cantiam, cantiamo un poco* (*Lo specchio;* Antonio Draghi; SSSSS, bc; A-Wn, 16299, fols. 1–19)

5. *Care selve, frondosi ricetti* (Filippo Vismarri; S, bc; A-Wn, 17753, fols. 77–90v)

6. *Che risolvi dunque, o core?* (G. B. Pederzuoli; S, bc; A-Wn, 18872, fols. 16–21v)

7. *Chi mi credeva instabile* (Filippo Vismarri; S, bc; A-Wn, 17753, fols. 64v–69)

8. *Cieli, non posso più* (Carlo Cappellini; SA, bc; A-Wn, 17768, fols. 95–106v)

9. *Cinto d'oscure bende* (*Che la Ruggiada è Pianto dell'Aurora;* Carlo Cappellini; S, bc; A-Wn, 17768, fols. 33–40v)

10. *Consigliatemi, che farò?* (*Accademia quarta;* G. B. Pederzuoli; A-Wn, 16909, fols. 153–168v)

11. *Così, bella, mi lasci* (Carlo Cappellini; SS, bc; A-Wn, 17768, fols. 55–75v)

12. *Deh volgetemi un guardo* (Antonio Bertali; SS, bc; S-Uu, vmhs 047:020)

13. *Di Minerva feconda* (*Prima accademia;* G. B. Pederzuoli; A-Wn, 16909, fols. 101–127)

14. *Dove Amor lungi mi tiene* (Filippo Vismarri; S, bc; A-Wn, 17753, fols. 21v–28)

15. *D'un occhio brillante* (Johann Caspar Kerll; S, bc; A-GÖ, Musikarchiv, Ms. 4089, pp. 141–49)

16. *Ecco Amor che cerca Gloria* (*Accademia quinta;* G. B. Pederzuoli; A-Wn, 16909, fols. 35–74v)

17. *Era l'aurora e le fugaci stelle* (*Di tre amanti;* Antonio Draghi; SAT, 2 treble instruments, bc; A-Wn, 16315, fols. 27–37v)

18. *Far l'amor e star lontana* (Filippo Vismarri; S, bc; A-Wn, 17753, fols. 196–205)

19. *Fra la reggia di pensieri* (Filippo Vismarri; S, bc; A-Wn, fols. 112–123)

20. *Fu che fuor di te* (Filippo Vismarri; S, bc; A-Wn, 17753, fols. 137–145v)

21. *Già dai monti* (Antonio Bertali; SSATT, vl 1–2, hpcd, basso di viola, theorbo, or basso di viola da gamba; S-Uifm, vmhs 047:022)

22. *Gioverà cangiar pensiero* (*Contro l'ambizione di donna invecchiata;* Filippo Vismarri; S, bc; A-Wn, 17753, fols. 205v–216)

23. *In amor ci vuol patienza* (Filippo Vismarri; S, bc; A-Wn, 17753, fols. 123v–136v)

24. *In che pena son io?* (*Terza accademia;* Antonio Draghi; SSA, vl 1–2, alto vla, basso di viola; A-Wn, 16027, fols. 1–42)

25. *Ingrata è la beltà* (*Seconda accademia;* G. B. Pederzuoli; SATB, bc; A-Wn, 16909, fols. 129–152)

26. *Innamoratevi del sommo bene* (Filippo Vismarri; S, bc; A-Wn, 17753, fols. 28v–37)

27. *Io son pregio di natura* (Filippo Vismarri; S, bc; A-Wn, 17753, fols. 188v–195v)

28. *La mia bella è stravagante* (*Seconda accademia;* Antonio Draghi; A-Wn, 17926, fols. 2–21v)

29. *La, muta voi fate, io il sordo farò* (Filippo Vismarri; S, bc; A-Wn, 17753, fols. 228v–245)

30. *Lasci d'amar chi non ha sorte* (Filippo Vismarri; S, bc; A-Wn, fols. 56–64)

31 *Lidio t'intendo affé* (*Dialogo a due, Lilla e Lidio;* A. M. Viviani; SBaritone, bc; A-Wn, 18762, fols. 41–47v)

32. *Luci belle, miei soli* (*In lontananza di B. D.;* Filippo Vismarri; S, bc; A-Wn, 17753, fols. 216v–228)

33. *Maledetto sia quel dì* (Filippo Vismarri; S, bc; A-Wn, 17753, fols. 15–21)

34. *Mio cor ti perdersi* (Johann Caspar Kerll; S, bc; A-GÖ, Musikarchiv, Ms. 4089, pp. 150–56)

35. *Mortali vedete* (*Lamento della Regina d'Inghilterra;* Antonio Bertali; S, bass viol, bc, B, four viols; S-Uu, vmhs 047:021)

36. *Non credete, amanti, no* (Filippo Vismarri; S, bc; A-Wn, 17753, fols. 181–188)

37. *No, nel mondo alcun non v'è* (*Accademia sesta;* G. B. Pederzuoli; SAT, bc; A-Wn, 16909, fols. 1–34v)

38. *Non ti credo, non mi fido* (G. B. Pederzuoli; T, bc; A-Wn, 18872, fols. 9–15v)

39. *Occhi miei, non vi struggete* (Carlo Cappellini; S, bc; A-Wn, 17768, fols. 15–23v; A-GÖ, MS 4091, fols. 17–20)

40. *Occhi, ohimè, qui manco e moro* (Filippo Vismarri; S, bc; A-Wn, 17753, fols. 171–180v)

41. *Occhi, se sete infidi* (Filippo Vismarri; S, bc; A-Wn, 17753, fols. 146–159v)

42. *Pensieri, amerò!* (Carlo Cappellini; S, bc; A-Wn, 17768, fols. 41–53v)

43. *Perchè, mio cor, perchè* (A. M. Viviani; B, bc; A-Wn, 18762, fols. 56–58)

44. *Prendi l'arco, o Cupido* (Carlo Cappellini; S, bc; A-Wn, 17768, fols. 25–32v)

45. *Sa il mio core* (Filippo Vismarri; S, bc; A-Wn, fols. 69v–76v)

46. *Scioglieasi baldanzoso* (Filippo Vismarri; S, bc; A-Wn, 17753, fols. 1–14v)

47. *Sensi miei, sospirate* (Carlo Cappellini; SS, bc; A-Wn, 17768, fols. 77–94v)

48. *Se troppo perfidi* (Filippo Vismarri; S, bc; A-Wn, 17753, fols. 37v–46v)

49. *Siamo in tempi sì, infelici* (*Accademia terza;* G. B. Pederzuoli; SATB, bc; A-Wn, 16909, fols. 75–99)

50. *Sì, sì, voglio morir* (Filippo Vismarri; S, bc; A-Wn, 17753, fols. 160–170v)

51. *So ben io dov'è legata* (Filippo Vismarri; S, bc; A-Wn, 17753, fols. 47–55v)

52. *Son felice, e so perchè* (G. B. Pederzuoli; S, bc; A-Wn, 18872, fols. 4v–8v)

53. *Son sembianze di quel bene* (Filippo Vismarri; S, bc; A-Wn, 17753, fols. 91–102)

54. *Sopra le proprie pene* (Filippo Vismarri; S, bc; A-Wn, 17753, fols. 102v–111v)

55. *Su la riva d'un ruscello* (A. M. Viviani; S, bc; A-Wn, 18762, fols. 50–55v)

56. *Sulle felici sponde* (G. B. Pederzuoli; A, bc; A-Wn, 18872, fols. 1–4)

57. *Una volta si decida* (*Intramezzo di musica in una accademia di dame;* Antonio Draghi; SSSS, bc; A-Wn, 16316, fols. 2–25)

58. *Un tiranno di foco* (A. M. Viviani; SA, bc; A-Wn, 18762, fols. 59–63v; attributed to Luigi Rossi, I-Fc, D 2357, fols. 162–165v)

1700–1712

1. *A Clori, che fra l'erbe* (Carlo Badia; S, 2 treble instruments, bc; A-Wn, 17721, fols. 46–58)

2. *Ahimè, ch'io son ferito!/Ahimè, ch'io son piagato!* (M. A. Ziani; TB, bc and opening sinfonia, 2 treble instruments, 1 alto instrument, bn, 1 bass instrument; A-Wn, 17650, fols. 1–23)

3. *Alli giusti miei lamenti* (anon.; SST, bc, unison violins and concluding chorus: SSATB; A-Wn, 18513, fols. 1–22)

4. *All'impero de' tuoi lumi/Al valor del tuo sembiante* (Carlo Badia; SS, bc; A-Wn, 18794, fols. 47v–65)

5. *Allor che rimirava* (Carlo Badia; S, bc; A-Wn, 17734, fols. 1–6)

6. *Al voler del bene amato* (Attilio Ariosti; S, bc; A-Wn, 17591, fols. 22–24v)

7. *Amo Clori che mi fugge* (Attilio Ariosti; A, bc; A-Wn, 17575, fols. 9–11v)

8. *Amore ingannatore, più non ti credo* (Antonio Bononcini; A, fl 1–2, bc; A-Wn, 17587, fols. 63–78v; parts in A-Wn, 15931)

9. *Augellin vago e canoro* (Carlo Badia; S, 2 treble instruments, bc; A-Wn, 17721, fols. 3–13v; a different setting attributed to "Gasparini" is in D-Bsb, Mus. ms. 30182, fols. 86–92)

10. *Begl'occhi neri m'avete colto* (Carlo Badia; S, bc; A-Wn, 17574, fols. 71–76)

11. *Bella face d'Amor* (Carlo Badia; S, bc; A-Wn, 17574, fols. 27–31v)

12. *Belle stille che grondate* (Attilio Ariosti; S, bc; A-Wn, 17591, fols. 25–28v; D-Bsb, Mus. ms. 30094, no. 22)

13. *Belli occhi amorosi vi miro* (Carlo Badia; S, bc; *Tributi armonici,* pp. 64–75)

14. *Cetre amiche, a un cor che langue* (anon.; T, bc; introductory sinfonia: vl 1–2, vla, bc; A-Wn, 18758, fols. 1–24)

15. *Che mi giova esser Regina* (Attilio Ariosti; S, 1 treble instrument, bc; A-Wn, 17591, fols. 9v–14v)

16. *Che si può far?* (Attilio Ariosti; S, bc; A-Wn, 17591, fols. 18–21v)

17. *Chi brama d'amor* (Carlo Badia; SS, bc; A-Wn, 18794, fols. 26–47)

18. *Cieco fanciul che in traccia* (M. A. Ziani; SS, bc; introductory sinfonia: vl 1–2, vla, vlc, bn, bc; A-Wn, 17635, fols. 1–24)

19. *Cieco Nume, alato Arciero* (Attilio Ariosti; S, bc; A-Wn, 17591, fols. 32v–36v; B-Bc, 15153, pp. 220–22; D-Bsb, Mus. ms. 30212, no. 36)

20. *Clori, bell'idol mio* (Carlo Badia; S, bc; A-Wn, 17574, fols. 57–64v)

21. *Clori, non più rigori* (Carlo Badia; S, bc; *Tributi armonici,* pp. 13–25)

22. *Clori, svenar mi sento* (Giovanni Bononcini; A, fl, bc; instrumental introduction: 2 treble instruments, bc; A-Wn, 17721, fols. 70v–80)

23. *Dalle rose del vago mio bene* (Carlo Badia; S, bc; A-Wn, 17574, fols. 33–38v)

24. *Dal timor d'esser tradito* (Carlo Badia; S, bc; *Tributi armonici,* pp. 140–50)

25. *D'amica selva il solitario orrore* (Carlo Badia; S, bc; A-Wn, 17574, fols. 51–56v)

26. *Dea loquace, deh non più* (Carlo Badia; S, fl 1–2, bc; A-Wn, 16308, fols. 81–101v)

27. *Dolce pace cara sei* (Carlo Badia; S, bc; A-Wn, 17734, fols. 7–10v)

28. *Ecco Amor che mi segue* (Antonio Bononcini; S, "soli e tutti" vl 1–2, vla, vlc, bc; A-Wn, 17637, fols. 1–21; parts in A-Wn, 15931; missing nineteenth-century incomplete copy from the Molitor Collection: A-Wn, 19242, vol. 1, no. 24)

29. *È pur dolce a un cor legato* (Attilio Ariosti; A, bc; A-Wn, 17575, fols. 13–15v; A-Wn, E.M. 178, fols. 1–2v)

30. *È ver, che sparge intorno* (Carlo Badia; SS, bc; A-Wn, 18794, fols. 13v–25v)

31. *Farfalletta amorosa, che intorno al caro* (Carlo Badia; S, bc; *Tributi armonici*, pp. 102–15)

32. *Filli mi disse un dì* (*Rotta fede;* M. A. Ziani; S, bc; A-Wgm, VI 13378 [A 407], pp. 1–8)

33. *Furie, che negl'abissi* (Attilio Ariosti; A, 1 treble instrument, bc; A-Wn, 17575, fols. 16–19v)

34. *Genio che amar volea* (*Genio;* Attilio Ariosti; S, bc; A-Wn, 17591, fols. 2–9; D-Bsb, Mus. ms. 30182, fols. 96v–98v; two different settings by Giovanni Bononcini: first setting in D-Bsb, Mus. ms. 30188, D-Mbs, 695, GB-Cfm, 32 G 20, GB-Lam, MS 127, GB-Lbl, 14228 and Add. MS 31518, GB-Ob, Mus. Sch. d.223, and I-Fc, B. 2376; second setting in I-MOe, Mus. F. 99)

35. *Già che intender non vole* (Attilio Ariosti; A, bc; A-Wn, 17575, fols. 37–40)

36. *Già rinascon le chiome* (Carlo Badia; S, bc; A-Wn, 17574, fols. 77–82v)

37. *Già tra l'onde il sol s'asconde* (Carlo Badia; S, bc; A-Wn, 17574, fols. 15–20v; three different settings: first setting attributed to Antonio Bononcini in D-Mbs, 696 but attributed to Giovanni Bononcini in I-Bc, DD51; second setting attributed to Giacomo Grebo in D-Bsb, Grasnick Collection; third setting attributed to Ant.io R. in D-Bsb, Mus. ms. 30186)

38. *Grazie alli Dei pur torna* (Carlo Badia; SS, bc; A-Wn, 18794, fols. 1–13)

39. *Insoffribile tormento è celar d'amor* (Attilio Ariosti; S, bc; A-Wn, 17591, fols. 37–40)

40. *I sospiri dell'aure qui soffri* (Carlo Badia; A, 2 treble instruments, 1 alto instrument, bc; instrumental introduction; A-Wn, 17721, fols. 59–64v)

41. *Là nell'arabe selve, ove la terra* (*La Fenice;* Carlo Badia; S, fl 1–2, vl 1–2, bc; A-Wn, 16308, fols. 25–63v)

42. *L'idol mio de pianti miei* (Attilio Ariosti; A, bc; A-Wn, 17575, fols. 25v–28v)

43. *Lumi che vi dirò?* (Carlo Badia; S, bc; *Tributi armonici*, pp. 1–12)

44. *Luminoso pianeta, del ciel pupilla eterna* (*Il sole;* Carlo Badia; S, vl 1–2, bc; A-Wn, 16308, fols. 1–24)

45. *Mentre al novo apparir* (Antonio Bononcini; A, vl 1–2, bc; A-Wn, 17607, fols. 55–84; parts in A-Wn, 15931)

46. *Mentre in placido sonno stanchi* (Antonio Bononcini; S, fl 1–2, bc; A-Wn, 17587, fols. 15–30; parts in A-Wn, 15931)

47. *Mi convien soffrir in pace* (Attilio Ariosti; A, bc; A-Wn, 17575, fols. 33–36v; a perfect fifth higher for S in D-Bsb, Mus. ms. 30074, pp. 110–16)

48. *Miei segreti pensieri cui spesso* (Carlo Badia; S, bc; *Tributi armonici*, pp. 116–28)

49. *Nella febbre d'Amor mi struggo* (Carlo Badia; S, bc; A-Wn, 17574, fols. 21–25v)

50. *Ne' spaziosi campi de la stellata mole* (Attilio Ariosti; A, bc; A-Wn, 17575, fols. 20–24)

51. *Non ardisco pregarti, amata bella* (Giovanni Bononcini; S, bc; A-Wn, 17567, fols. 1–8v)

52. *Non so se più mi piace* (Carlo Badia; S, bc; A-Wn, 17734, fols. 33–37)

53. *Non voglio udirti, o core* (Carlo Badia; S, bc; *Tributi armonici*, pp. 38–50)

54. *Occhi che in fronte a Filli* (Carlo Badia; A, 4 treble instruments, bc; A-Wn, 17721, fols. 31–45)

55. *Occhi più non vi fidate* (Carlo Badia; S, bc; A-Wn, 17734, fols. 29–32v)

56. *Occhi, voi che mirate l'ardor* (Antonio Bononcini; S, fl 1–2, bc; A-Wn, 17587, fols. 31–48v; parts in A-Wn, 15931)

57. *Oh miseria d'amante core* (Attilio Ariosti; A, bc; A-Wn, 17575, fols. 1–3v; D-Bsb, Mus. ms. 30188, pp. 44–48; D-SHs, Mus. B.1:3, pp. 11–16)

58. *Or nel bosco et or nel prato* (Giovanni Bononcini; S, bc; A-Wn, 17721, fols. 80v–84)

59. *Pastor, pastore, hai vinto* (Attilio Ariosti; A, bc; A-Wn, 17575, fols. 29–32)

60. *Per te sola Filli mia sentirò* (Carlo Badia; S, bc; *Tributi armonici*, pp. 129–39)

61. *Povero amante core, quanto mi fai pietà* (Carlo Badia; S, bc; A-Wn, 17574, fols. 7–14v)

62. *Pur alfine tu sei mia cara e dolce* (Carlo Badia; S, bc; *Tributi armonici*, pp. 51–63)

63. *Quai lamenti improvisi? In giorno sì felice* (*Al tempo;* Carlo Badia; S, unison lutes, bc; A-Wn, 16308, fols. 65–80)

64. *Qual in mar la navicella agitate* (Carlo Badia; S, bc; A-Wn, 17734, fols. 47–52)

65. *Quando Nice era fida* (Attilio Ariosti; S, bc; A-Wn, 17591, fols. 45–49v)

66. *Quando vedo a mille rose* (Antonio Bononcini; A, fl 1–2, bc; A-Wn, 17587, fols. 49–61v; parts in A-Wn, 15931)

67. *Questo felice giorno, che del nome di Carlo altero splende* (*La Fortuna, il Valore, e la Giustitia;* Antonio Bononcini; SAB, vl 1–2, vla, "bassi," bc; A-Wn, 17586, fols. 2–54)

68. *Qui fra l'ombre a te ritorno* (Carlo Badia; A, bc; introductory *entré* [*sic*] for 1 treble instrument, bc; A-Wn, 17721, fols. 65v–69v)

69. *Regina, eccoci al tempio della diva amorosa* (*Il sacrificio di Berenice;* Carlo Badia; SSAT, vl 1–2 ["cont:°" and "tutti"], vla, bc; introductory sinfonia and concluding SATB chorus; A-Wn, 17675, fols. 2–76)

70. *Rompi l'arco, rompi i lacci* (Giovanni Bononcini; S, bc; A-Wn, 17567, fols. 47–53v; the aria "Pupilette vezzosette" is in GB-CDp, M.C.1.5)

71. *Rotto è l'antico laccio* (Carlo Badia; S, bc; *Tributi armonici*, pp. 88–101)

72. *Rusignol che tempri il canto* (Carlo Badia; A, 2 treble instruments, bc; A-Wn, 17721, fols. 14–24)

73. *Sapesse il core almen* (Carlo Badia; S, bc; A-Wn, 17734, fols. 38–41v; a different setting attributed to "Fago" is in D-Bsb, Mus. ms. 30197, and D-MEIr, Ed109ⁱ = 82ᶜ)

74. *Scesa dal ciel superno* (*Il Tempo parta alla Fama;* Carlo Badia; T, 2 treble instruments, bc; D-Dl, Mus. 2192/J/1, fols. 1–11)

75. *Scrive a chi la tradì* (Carlo Badia; S, bc; A-Wn, 17574, fols. 83–92)

76. *Se avessi in mezzo al petto* (Antonio Bononcini; A, fl 1–2, bc; A-Wn, 17587, fols. 79–94v; parts in A-Wn, 15931)

77. *Se Giustizia è nel tuo regno, giusto Amor* (Carlo Badia; S, bc; A-Wn, 17734, fols. 25–28v)

78. *Sei tu rosa o pur sei stella* (Carlo Badia; S, bc; A-Wn, 17574, fols. 65–70)

79. *Se mai d'altra beltà* (Carlo Badia; S, bc; *Tributi armonici*, pp. 26–37)

80. *Sempre alletta, sempre incatena* (*La Pace, e Marte supplicanti avanti al Trono della Gloria;* Carlo Badia; SSA, vl 1–2, vla, tr, bc; A-Wn, 17725, fols. 2–44v)

81. *Sempre ti dissi, o cor* (Carlo Badia; S, bc; A-Wn, 17574, fols. 45–50v)

82. *Sento dentro del petto* (Giovanni Bononcini; S, bc; A-Wn, 17567, fols. 26–32v)

83. *Senza te, dolce tiranno, Lidio caro* (*Lontananza;* Attilio Ariosti; S, bc; A-Wn, 17591, fols. 50–53v)

84. *Se t'offesi, o bella Irene* (Attilio Ariosti; S, bc; A-Wn, 17591, fols. 29–32)

85. *Sia con me Fillide irata* (Attilio Ariosti; A, bc; A-Wn, 17575, fols. 41–43v; anon. in D-Bsb, Mus. ms. 30197, pp. 6–10)

86. *Sì vaga e sì vezzosa* (Carlo Badia; A, 2 treble instruments, bc; A-Wn, 17721, fols. 25–30v)

87. *Sopra l'orme d'Irene parti* (Antonio Bononcini; A, vl 1–2, bc; A-Wn, 17607; parts in A-Wn, 15931)

88. *Sovra carro di luce* (Carlo Badia; S, bc; A-Wn, 17734, fols. 42–46v)

89. *Star lungi dal suo bene* (Carlo Badia; S, bc; A-Wn, 17574, fols. 1–6v)

90. *Su l'arenoso lido del vago mar* (Carlo Badia; S, bc; A-Wn, 17734, fols. 20–24)

91. *Sul margine adorato di vago ruscelletto* (Antonio Bononcini; S, vl 1–2, bc; A-Wn, 17607, fols. 1–17v; parts in A-Wn, 15931; a different setting attributed to Giovanni del Violone in GB-Lk, R.M. 23.f.4, pp. 83–88)

92. *S'una volta io potrò intendere* (Carlo Badia; S, bc; A-Wn, 17734, fols. 11–19v)

93. *Tante e tante del ciel* (Attilio Ariosti; S, bc; A-Wn, 17591, fols. 40v–44v; a major second higher in D-DS, Mus. ms. 46, fols. 78–82)

94. *Tanto avezzo ho il core a piangere* (Antonio Bononcini; A, vl 1–2, bc; A-Wn, 17607, fols. 85–102v; parts in A-Wn, 15931)

95. *Tempo è già, che la possanza* (*L'Ercole, vincitor dell'invidia*; M. A. Ziani; SSATB, vl 1–2, ob 1–2, vla, unison bn, lute, bc; A-Wn, 17570, fols. 2–88)

96. *Tolta da un pigro sonno* (Carlo Badia; S, bc; A-Wn, 17574, fols. 93–102)

97. *Troppo conosco, o Filli* (M. A. Ziani; S, bc; D-Bsb, M Mus. Ms. Autogr. Ziani, Ant. 1, fols. 1–8)

98. *Troppo rigore, Clori* (Antonio Bononcini; S, vl 1–2, bc; A-Wn, 17607, fols. 35–54; parts in A-Wn, 15931)

99. *Tutta fiamme e tutta ardore* (Antonio Bononcini; S, fl 1–2, bc; A-Wn, 17587, fols. 1–14v; parts in A-Wn, 15931)

100. *Un barbaro rigor fa il misero mio cor* (Attilio Ariosti; S, bc; A-Wn, 17591, fols. 15–17v)

101. *Un guardo solo, o bella* (Carlo Badia; S, bc; *Tributi armonici*, pp. 76–87)

102. *Uno spirito galante tutto brio* (Carlo Badia; S, bc; A-Wn, 17574, fols. 39–44)

103. *Vorrei, pupille belle, rivedervi un momento* (Antonio Bononcini; S, vl 1–2, bc; A-Wn, 17607, fols. 19–34v; parts in A-Wn, 15931)

104. *Voti offersi al cor d'Irene* (Attilio Ariosti; A, bc; A-Wn, 17575, fols. 5–7v)

APPENDIX B
CATALOGUE RAISONNÉ OF
VIENNESE CANTATA SOURCES

A total of 39 sources containing 162 Italian cantatas by composers employed by the Habsburgs during the period 1658–1712 have been identified. Fourteen of these sources are manuscripts dating from the years 1658–1700. (For a description of the manuscript that contains two cantatas by Johann Caspar Kerll [A-GÖ, Musikarchiv, Ms. 4089], see Friedrich Wilhelm Riedel and Leonhard Riedel, "Zum Repertoire der italienischen Kantatenkomposition," 331.) Eighteen manuscripts and seven copies of a single printed collection, Badia's *Tributi armonici*, comprise the sources for cantatas dating from the years 1700–1712; these sources include a few works by Badia that date from the final years of the seventeenth century, but they belong historically and stylistically with the younger generation.

The source descriptions given below for thirteen manuscripts from 1658 to 1700 have been subdivided into dated archival copies, undated archival copies, and three manuscripts in S-Uu. No extant holographs from this period are known to me. The descriptions for the chamber cantatas from 1700 to 1712 are subdivided into five categories: two holographs, the printed collection, six dated archival copies, nine undated archival copies, and the single manuscript in D-Dl. The descriptions for the manuscripts with four grand cantatas, all preserved in archival copies, appear at the end of this appendix.

To the extent that specific information is known to me, I have indicated for each source its date or approximate date, format, dimensions, pagination and/or foliation, number of staves per page, type of binding, imprints, watermarks, and contents. Special remarks about scribes, dedicatees, poets, performers, and possible owners appear at the end of the description for each source.

1658–1700

DATED ARCHIVAL COPIES
A-Wn, 16299

Date:	23 November 1676
Format:	standard upright
Dimensions:	18.9 × 28.8 cm
Foliation:	19 fols.; modern pencil for fol. 10 and fol. 19 (blank staves) only
No. of staves:	12
Binding:	white parchment
Imprints:	front: image of Leopold I with laurel in gold; back: the Eye of God
Watermarks:	horn: Heawood 1618–19, related to 2628? (Jena, 1675?; possibly Louvain [Leuven], 1597)
Contents:	1 cantata by Antonio Draghi: *Cantiam, cantiamo un poco* (*Lo specchio*); facsimile ed. in ICSC 16
Remarks:	dedicatee: Empress Dowager Eleonora (birthday)

A-Wn, 16909
Date: 1685
Format: standard upright
Dimensions: 19.5 × 25.5 cm
Foliation: 166 fols.; modern pencil throughout; original foliation beginning with fol. 1
                 for each *accademia*
No. of staves: 10
Binding: white parchment
Imprints: front: image of Leopold I with laurel in gold; back: double-headed eagle
                 with crown in gold
Watermarks: ?
Contents: 6 *accademie* by G. B. Pederzuoli:
                 Di Minerva feconda (prima accademia)
                 Ingrata è la beltà (seconda accademia)
                 Siamo in tempi sì infelici (accademia terza)
                 Consigliatemi, che farò? (accademia quarta)
                 Ecco Amor che cerca Gloria (accademia quinta)
                 No, nel mondo alcun non v'è (accademia sesta)
Remarks: poet: Nicolò Minato

A-Wn, 17926
Date: 3 February 1693
Format: standard upright
Dimensions: 20 × 30 cm
Foliation: 21 fols.; modern pencil every 10 fols.
No. of staves: 10
Binding: white parchment
Imprints: ?
Watermarks: ?
Contents: *seconda accademia* by Antonio Draghi: *La mia bella è stravagante*
Remarks: poet: Nicolò Minato

A-Wn, 16316
Date: 15 November 1697
Format: standard upright
Dimensions: 19 × 28.5 cm
Foliation: 26 fols. in modern pencil
No. of staves: 10
Binding: white parchment
Imprints: front: image of Emperor Leopold I in gold; back: double-headed eagle with
                 crown and coat of arms in gold
Watermarks: ?
Contents: 1 *accademia* by Antonio Draghi: *Una volta si decida*
Remarks: poet: Nicolò Minato

A-Wn, 16027
Date: 11 February 1698
Format: standard upright
Dimensions: 20.5 × 30 cm
Foliation: 42 fols.; modern pencil for fols. 10, 20, 30, 40, and 42 only
No. of staves: 10

Binding:	modern heavy cardboard with tape at spine over earlier heavy red paper with gold decorations
Imprints:	none
Watermarks:	?
Contents:	*terza accademia* by Antonio Draghi: *In che pena son io?*
Remarks:	poet: Nicolò Minato

UNDATED ARCHIVAL COPIES

A-Wn, 18762

Date:	between 1667 and 1676?
Format:	oblong
Dimensions:	17.5 × 23.5 cm
Foliation:	65 fols. in modern pencil
No. of staves:	6 (nos. 1–3) or 8 (nos. 4–11)
Binding:	white parchment
Imprints:	front: image of Leopold I; back: eye of God
Watermarks:	?
Contents:	12 accompanied vocal pieces:
	Anonymous: *Un misero pastore* (cantata, S, bc)
	Alessandro Melani: *In questo mondo instabile* (*capriccio a tre*, SSA, bc)
	G. M. Pagliardi: *Ben venuto il nuovo Maggio* (*Ritorno di primavera*, duet, SB, bc)
	G. M. Pagliardi: *Godi pur d'altra beltà* (trio, ATB, bc)
	G. M. Pagliardi: *D'impuri affetti e stolti* (cantata, S, bc)
	G. M. Viviani: *copla* no. 1 (S, bc)
	G. M. Viviani: *copla* no. 2 (S, bc)
	G. M. Viviani: *Lidio t'intendo affé* (*dialogo à due: Lilla e Lidio*, SBaritone, bc)
	G. M. Viviani: *Su la riva d'un ruscello* (cantata, S, bc)
	G. M. Viviani: *Adorate mie bellezze quando mai vi rivedrò* (cantata, S, bc)
	G. M. Viviani: *Perchè, mio cor, perchè* (cantata, B, bc)
	G. M. Viviani: *Un tiranno di foco* (duet, SA, bc)
Remarks:	the MS consists of at least three different papers bound together; the eleven pieces were copied by at least seven different scribes

A-Wn, 18872

Date:	between 1677 and 1686
Format:	standard upright
Dimensions:	20.3 × 28.7 cm
Foliation:	34 fols. in modern pencil
No. of staves:	12
Binding:	white parchment
Imprints:	front: image of Leopold I; back: eye of God; floral design in gold
Watermarks:	coat of arms?
Contents:	4 *accademie* by G. B. Pederzuoli:
	Sulle felici sponde
	Son felice, e so perchè
	Non ti credo, no mi fido
	Che risolvi dunque, o core?
Remarks:	dedicatee: Empress Dowager Eleonora; facsimile ed. in ICSC 16

A-Wn, 16315

Date:	before 1682

Format: standard upright
Dimensions: 19.1 × 28.6 cm
Foliation: 38 fols. in modern pencil
No. of staves: 12
Binding: white parchment
Imprints: front and back: double-headed eagle with crown surrounded by scroll
Watermarks: horn with letter M: Heawood 2628? (Jena, 1675)
Contents: 2 vocal works by Antonio Draghi: *Agl'incendi ai legami alle ferite* (*Forza d'un bel volto*); *Era l'aurora e le fugaci stelle* (*Di tre amanti*)
Remarks: poet for each piece: Nicolò Minato?

A-Wn, 17753
Date: before 1683
Format: oblong
Dimensions: 11.5 × 24.5 cm
Foliation: 247 fols., original; 246–47 (*tavola*) in modern pencil
No. of staves: 4
Binding: dark-brown leather at one time held together with straps
Imprints: front and back: small floral designs in center and in corners
Watermarks: single crescent plus letters?; possibly Heawood 3068 (Padua, 1680)
Contents: 24 cantatas and ariettas by Filippo Vismarri:
                 Scioglieasi baldanzoso
                 Maledetto sia quel dì
                 Dove Amor lungi mi tiene
                 Innamoratevi del sommo bene
                 Se troppo perfidy
                 So ben io dov'è legata
                 Lasci d'amar chi non ha sorte
                 Chi mi credeva instabile
                 Sa il mio core
                 Care selve, frondosi ricetti
                 Son sembianze di quel bene
                 Sopra le proprie pene
                 Fra la reggia di pensieri
                 In amor ci vuol patienza
                 Fu che fuor di te
                 Occhi, se sete infidi
                 Sì, sì, voglio morir
                 Occhi, ohimè, qui manco e moro
                 Non credete, amanti, no
                 Io son pregio di natura
                 Far l'amor e star lontana
                 Gioverà cangiar pensiero (*Contro l'ambizione di donna invecchiata*)
                 Luci belle, miei soli
                 La, muta voi fate, io il sordo farò
Remarks: poets: Marc'Antonio Signorini (nos. 1, 5, 11, and 22); Giovanni Lotti (no. 4); Domenico Manzini (no. 21); Carlo Marcheselli (no. 23); and Paolo Castelli (no. 24); nos. 1–6 in ICSC 16

A-Wn, 17768
Date: before 1683

Format:	oblong
Dimensions:	11.1 × 25.7 cm
Foliation:	106 fols., original; fols. 1 (title page) and 107 (*tavola*) in modern pencil
No. of staves:	4
Binding:	white parchment at one time held together with straps
Imprints:	front and back: simple line edging
Watermarks:	anchor; similar to Heawood 2 (Venice, 1711)
Contents:	8 cantatas by Carlo Cappellini:

> *Ancor sazia non sei*
> *Occhi miei, non vi struggete*
> *Prendi l'arco, o Cupido*
> *Cinto d'oscure bende* (*Che la Ruggiada è Pianto dell'Aurora*)
> *Pensieri amerò!*
> *Così, bella, mi lasci*
> *Sensi miei, sospirate*
> *Cieli, non posso più*

Remarks:	poets: Giberto Ferri (nos. 1, 3, 4, 6, and 7); Girolamo Branchi (nos. 5 and 8); nos. 1–5 in ICSC 16

THREE ADDITIONAL CORE SOURCES

Each of three manuscripts at S-Uu contains a single cantata by Antonio Bertali: *Deh volgetemi un guardo* (vmhs 047:020), *Mortali vedete* (*Lamento della Regina d'Inghilterra;* vmhs 047:021), and *Già dai monti* (vmhs 047:022). For detailed descriptions of these manuscripts, see the Düben Collection Database Catalogue, ed. Erik Kjellberg and Kerala J. Snyder, online at http://www2.musik.uu.se/duben/Duben.php. All three compositions date from the last years of the composer's life. Archduke Leopold Wilhelm penned the text for *Mortali vedete,,* composed by Bertali in 1669 on the death of the English queen Henrietta Maria, wife of Charles I.

1700–1712

CHAMBER CANTATAS

Holographs
A-Wgm, 13378 (A 407)

Date:	between 1700 and 1715; Mandyczewski, in the *Zusatzband* of the *Geschichte der K.K. Gesellschaft der Musikfreunde,* p. 123, dated this MS ca. 1710
Format:	oblong
Foliation:	4 unnumbered fols. (fragment)
No. of staves:	10
Binding:	modern paper folder
Imprints:	none
Watermarks:	none discernible
Contents:	1 cantata by M. A. Ziani: *Filli mi disse un dì* (*Rotta fede*)
Remarks:	On the right-hand side of fol. 1, Mandyczewski has identified the MS as an original Ziani autograph

D-Bsb, M Mus. Ms. Autogr. Ziani, Ant. 1

Date:	between 1700 and 1715
Format:	oblong
Foliation:	4 unnumbered fols. (fragment)

No. of staves: 10
Binding: modern paper
Imprints: none
Watermarks: three crescents
Contents: 1 cantata by M. A. Ziani: *Troppo conosco, o Filli*
Remarks: this holograph may be a MS once owned by A-Wgm (VI 13377) but now
                  missing there; early broker or possible owner: Aloys Fuchs

Print
Carlo Agostino Badia, *Tributi armonici* (Nuremberg: Weigl, between 1699 and 1704); seven
exemplars: A-Wn, SH.Badia.1; B-Bc, D-W, 9 Musica div. (used for the description given here);
D-Dl, 2192/K/1; GB-Lbl, B.321; I-Bc, Gaspari catalogue III, p. 208; I-Rsc, AS A.CS.1.D.22; a
copy formerly at A-Wm appears to be lost
Format: oblong
Pagination: 150 pages
No. of staves: 6
Binding: original
Imprints: none
Watermarks: horse
Contents: 12 cantatas by Carlo Badia:
                  Lumi che vi dirò?
                  Clori, non più rigori
                  Se mai d'altra beltà
                  Non voglio udirti o core
                  Pur alfine tu sei mia cara e dolce
                  Belli occhi amorosi vi miro
                  Un guardo solo, o bella
                  Rotto è l'antico laccio
                  Farfalletta amorosa
                  Miei segreti pensieri
                  Per te sola Filli mia
                  Dal timor d'esser tradito
Remarks: dedicatee: Leopold I; engravings by Antonio Beduzzi; poet: Abbate Ruggieri
                  (nos. 2, 3, 6, and 9–12)

Dated Archival Copies
A-Wn, 16308
Date: 1699
Format: standard upright
Dimensions: 19.8 × 19.9 cm
Foliation: 103 fols., modern pencil
No. of staves: 10
Binding: white parchment
Imprints: likeness of Leopold I (front); two-headed eagle and crown (back); ornamental
                  gilt edging
Watermarks: coat of arms (?)
Contents: 4 cantatas by Carlo Badia:
                  Luminoso pianeta, del ciel pupilla eterna (*Il Sole*)
                  Là nell'arabe selve, ove la terra (*La Fenice*)
                  Quai lamenti improvisi? (*Al tempo*),
                  Dea loquace, deh non più

Remarks:	the opening folio of no. 4 is missing; dedicatee: Leopold I; the dedication is written in a messy hand that is not the main scribe's; poet: Donato Cupeda; performers: "Fatta della S. M. del Re de' Romani Archiduccha et Archiduchesse con cavalieri e Dame"; three court ladies are named: Contessa della Torre, Contessa Sousin, and Contessa Fünfkirchen

A-Wn, 17574

Date:	1704
Format:	oblong
Dimensions:	20.5 × 28.5 cm
Foliation:	116 fols. (1–102 in original scribe's hand; 103–16 in modern pencil)
No. of staves:	8
Binding:	reddish-brown leather
Imprints:	ornamental gilt edging
Watermarks:	fleur-de-lis in single circle
Contents:	15 cantatas by Carlo Badia:
	Star lungi dal suo bene
	Povero amante core, quanto mi fai pietà
	Già tra l'onde il sol s'asconde
	Nella febbre d'Amor mi struggo
	Bella face d'Amor
	Dalle rose del vago mio bene
	Uno spirito galante tutto brio
	Sempre ti dissi, o cor
	D'amica selva il solitario orrore
	Clori, bell'idol mio, Clori mio core
	Sei tu rosa o pur sei stella
	Begl'occhi neri m'avete colto
	Già rinascon le chiome
	Scrive a chi la tradì
	Tolta da un pigro sonno
Remarks:	poet: P. A. Bernardoni (no. 12)

A-Wn, 17635

Date:	1706
Format:	oblongDimensions: 22 × 31 cm
Foliations:	24 fols. (in modern pencil every 10 fols.)
No. of staves:	10
Binding:	?
Imprints:	?
Watermark:	?
Contents:	1 *accademia* by M. A. Ziani: *Cieco fanciful che in traccia*
Remarks:	the first of two academic cantatas from the year 1706; poet: P. A. Bernardoni; copyist is the same scribe who prepared A-Wn, 17650

A-Wn, 17650

Date:	1706
Format:	oblong
Dimensions:	22 × 31 cm
Foliation:	23 fols. (in modern pencil, for fols. 1, 7, and 23 only)
No. of staves:	10

Binding:	modern brown-and-blue paper over cardboard
Imprints:	none
Watermarks:	three crescents: Heawood 866 and 868 (Venice, 1696)
Contents:	1 *accademia* (duet) by M. A. Ziani: *Ahimè, ch'io son ferito!/Ahimè, ch'io son piagato!*
Remarks:	the second of two academic cantatas from the year 1706; poet: P. A. Bernardoni; the copyist is the same scribe who prepared A-Wn, 17635

A-Wn, 17587

Date:	1708
Format:	oblong
Dimensions:	21.7 × 29.1 cm
Foliation:	94 fols. (in modern pencil)
No. of staves:	8
Binding:	brown leather
Imprints:	none
Watermarks:	1. three crescents: Heawood 866 and 868 (Venice, 1696); 2. letters?
Contents:	6 cantatas by A. M. Bononcini:
	Tutta fiamme e tutta ardore
	Mentre in placido sonno stanchi
	Occhi, voi che mirate l'ardor
	Quando vedo a mille rose
	Amore ingannatore, più non ti credo
	Se avessi in mezzo al petto
Remarks:	probably three copyists: scribe no. 1 copied cantatas 1, 3, 4, and 6 (as well as the complete A. M. Bononcini MS A-Wn, 17607; see below); scribe no. 2 prepared cantatas 2 and 5 and the instrumental parts (A-Wn, 15931) for both 17587 and 17607; scribe no. 3 copied the conclusion of cantata no. 6 (fols. 81v–94v)

A-Wn, 17607

Date:	1708
Format:	oblong
Dimensions:	21.2 × 29.5 cm
Foliation:	120 fols. (in modern pencil)
No. of staves:	8
Binding:	brown leather
Imprints:	none
Watermarks:	1. three crescents: Heawood 866 and 868 (Venice, 1696); 2. monogram: Heawood 3225 (Vienna, ca. 1695); 3. Eagle?
Contents:	6 cantatas by A. M. Bononcini:
	Sul margine adorato di vago ruscelletto
	Vorrei, pupille belle, rivedervi un momento
	Troppo rigore, Clori
	Mentre al novo apparir
	Tanto avezzo ho il core a piangere
	Sopra l'orme d'Irene parti
Remarks:	one copyist for the entire MS, the same as scribe no. 1 of A-Wn, 17587

Undated Archival Copies
A-Wn, 18758

Date:	1702 or 1704

Format:	standard upright
Dimensions:	22.8 × 30.3 cm
Foliation:	24 fols. (in modern pencil)
No. of staves:	10
Binding:	modern cardboard envelope
Imprints:	none
Watermarks:	three crescents: Heawood 866 (Venice, 1696)
Contents:	1 anonymous cantata: *Cetre amiche, a un cor che langue*
Remarks:	the MS is undated, but it is apparent from the text that the cantata was composed for one of the victories at Landau (1702 or 1704) led by the future emperor Joseph I

A-Wn, 18513

Date:	1705
Format:	standard upright
Foliation:	22 unnumbered fols.
No. of staves:	10
Binding:	red paper over cardboard
Imprints:	gilt pattern of swirls, birds, and flowers over the entire binding, plus an elaborate version of the Habsburg seal (two-headed eagle, crown, scepter, and apple) on the back cover
Watermarks:	coat of arms; similar to Heawood 563 (1702)
Contents:	1 anonymous cantata: *Alli giusti miei lamenti*
Remarks:	the MS is undated, but it is apparent from the text that the cantata was composed for the 1705 coronation of Joseph I

A-Wn, 18794

Date:	before 1706
Format:	oblong
Dimensions:	21.5 × 29 cm
Foliation:	68 fols. (in modern pencil)
No. of staves:	8
Binding:	white parchment
Imprints:	plain black ornamental edging; designs on the crack; two-headed eagle and crown on front and back
Watermarks:	three crescents: Heawood 866? (Venice, 1696)
Contents:	4 chamber duets by Carlo Badia:
	Grazie alli Dei pur torna
	È ver, che sparge intorno
	Chi brama d'amor
	All'impero de' tuoi lumi/Al valor del tuo sembiante

A-Wn, 17734

Date:	between 1706 and 1712
Format:	oblong
Dimensions:	21 × 28.8 cm
Foliation:	53 fols. (in modern pencil); original foliation, mostly cropped, is identical with modern foliation
No. of staves:	8
Binding:	brown/black-speckled leather
Imprints:	plain black design on edges and crack
Watermarks:	three crescents: Heawood 866 or 867 (Venice, 1696)

Contents:	10 cantatas by Carlo Badia:
	Allor che rimirava
	Dolce pace cara sei
	S'una volta io potrò intendere
	Su l'arenoso lido del vago mar
	Occhi più non vi fidate
	Se Giustizia è nel tuo regno, giusto Amor
	Non so se più mi piace
	Sapesse il core almen
	Sovra carro di luce
	Qual in mar la navicella agitate
Remarks:	the attribution on the title page is written in a messy hand that is not the main scribe's

A-Wn, 17721

Date:	between 1706 and 1712
Format:	oblong
Dimensions:	20.7 × 19.4 cm
Pagination:	163 pp.; pp. 1–55 are in the hand of scribe 1; pp. 156–63 are in modern pencil; in addition, there are 18 unnumbered pp. of blank staves at the end of the MS; foliation has also been written in by a modern hand; it begins with the *tavola* and runs through the final fol. of blank staves, making a total of 93 fols.
No. of staves:	10
Binding:	dark-brown leather
Imprints:	gold seal: two-headed eagle and coat of arms
Watermarks:	three crescents: Heawood 868 (Venice, 1696)
Contents:	7 cantatas by Carlo Badia and 2 cantatas by Giovanni Bononcini:
	Augellin vago e canoro (Badia)
	Rusignol che tempri il canto (Badia)
	Sì vaga e sì vezzosa (Badia)
	Occhi che in fronte a Filli (Badia)
	A Clori, che fra l'erbe (Badia)
	I sospiri dell'aure qui soffri (Badia)
	Qui fra l'ombre a te ritorno (Badia)
	Clori, svenar mi sento (Giovanni Bononcini)
	Or nel bosco et or nel prato (Giovanni Bononcini)
Remarks:	two scribes: scribe 1 copied the seven Badia cantatas plus the first Bononcini cantata; scribe 2 added the second Bononcini cantata on staves that were part of the original MS; it is obvious that besides the 9 fols. of blank staves that follow the last cantata, even more belonged to the original source

A-Wn, 17575

Date:	between 1706 and 1712
Format:	oblong
Dimensions:	21.6 × 29.9 cm
Foliation:	44 fols. (in modern pencil)
No. of staves:	10
Binding:	reddish-brown leather
Imprints:	plain black lines along edges of the binding
Watermarks:	three crescents: Heawood 866 and 868 (Venice, 1696)
Contents:	11 cantatas by Attilio Ariosti:

> Oh miseria d'amante core
> Voti offersi al cor d'Irene
> Amo Clori che mi fugge
> È pur dolce a un cor legato
> Furie, che negl'abissi
> Ne' spaziosi campi de la stellata mole
> L'idol mio de pianti miei
> Pastor, pastore, hai vinto
> Mi convien soffrir in pace
> Già che intender non vole
> Sia con me Fillide irata

Remarks:	poet: P. A. Bernardoni (nos. 7 and 8)

A-Wn, 17591

Date:	between 1706 and 1712
Format:	oblong
Dimensions:	21.4 × 30.3
Foliation:	53 fols. (modern pencil)
No. of staves:	8
Binding:	black leather
Imprints:	gilt edging and design in each corner
Watermarks:	1. three crescents: Heawood 866 and 868 (Venice, 1696); 2. anchor: Heawood 6 (Rome, n.d.)
Contents:	12 cantatas by Attilio Ariosti:

> Genio che amar volea (Genio)
> Che mi giova esser Regina
> Un barbaro rigor fa il misero mio cor
> Che si può far?
> Al voler del bene amato
> Belle stille che grondate
> Se t'offesi, o bella Irene
> Cieco Nume, alato Arciero
> Insoffribile tormento è celar d'amor
> Tante e tante del ciel
> Quando Nice era fida
> Senza te, dolce tiranno, Lidio caro (Lontananza)

Remarks:	poet: P. A. Bernardoni (no. 2)

A-Wn, 17637

Date:	before 1713
Format:	oblong
Dimensions:	22 × 29 cm
Foliation:	22 fols. (in modern pencil, every 10 fols.)
No. of staves:	10
Binding:	reddish-brown leather
Imprints:	none
Watermarks:	1. three crescents: Heawood 868 (Venice, 1696); 2. coat of arms?
Contents:	1 cantata by A. M. Bononcini: Ecco Amor che mi segue

A-Wn, 17567

Date:	probably 1712
Format:	oblong

Dimensions:	25 × 31 cm
Foliation:	98 fols. (in modern pencil)
No. of staves:	8
Binding:	brownish-red leather
Imprints:	gold seal (front and back): two-headed eagle, coat of arms, and crown
Watermarks:	1. three crescents: Heawood 868 (Venice, 1696); 2. fleur-de-lis with crown
Contents:	12 cantatas by Giovanni Bononcini, Antonio Caldara, Francesco Conti, Emauele d'Astorga, and Andrea Stefano Fiorè:

Non ardisco pregarti, amata bella (Giovanni Bononcini)
Io soffrirò tacendo questo incendio (Caldara)
Lasciami amor nemico del riposo (Conti)
Sento dentro del petto (Giovanni Bononcini)
Arda il mio petto (Caldara)
Dimmi, o sorte amica (Conti)
Rompi l'arco, rompi i lacci (Giovanni Bononcini)
Senti, Filli incostante (Caldara)
Tento scuotere dal seno crudo (Conti)
Che ti giova, Amor crudele (Astorga)
Quando penso a quell'ore (Astorga)
Di quell sguardo fatal (Fiorè)

One Additional Core Source
D-Dl, Mus. 2192/J/1

Date:	early eighteenth century
Format:	oblong
Foliation:	11 fols. (in scribe's hand); also 22 pp. (added in a modern hand)
No. of staves:	10
Binding:	none?
Watermarks:	?
Contents:	1 cantata by Carlo Badia: *Scesa dal ciel superno* (*Il Tempo parta alla Fama*)
Remarks:	possibly holograph; the dedication to Joseph I may be spurious

GRAND CANTATAS

A-Wn, 17725

Date:	19 March 1701
Format:	oblong
Dimensions:	20.5 × 29 cm
Foliation:	44 fols.; modern pencil every 10 fols.
No. of staves:	8
Binding:	light-red paper over cardboard
Imprints:	gilt design of birds and foliage over entire binding
Watermarks:	three crescents: Heawood 868 (Venice, 1696)
Contents:	1 grand cantata by Carlo Badia: *Sempre alletta, sempre incatena* (*La Pace, e Marte supplicanti avanti al Trono della Gloria*)
Remarks:	composed for the name day of Archduke Joseph (the future Emperor Joseph I); poet: G. D. Filippeschi

A-Wn, 17570

Date:	19 March 1706
Format:	oblong
Dimensions:	22 × 30.2 cm

Foliation:	90 fols.; modern pencil every 10 fols.
No. of staves:	10
Binding:	brown leather over cardboard; worn on edges, corner, and crack
Imprints:	fleur-de-lis imprints on crack
Watermarks:	three crescents: Heawood 866 (Venice, 1696)
Contents:	1 grand cantata by Marc Antonio Ziani: *Tempo è già, che la possanza* (*L'Ercole, vincitor dell'invidia*)
Remarks:	composed for the name day of Emperor Joseph I; poet: Domenico Mazza

A-Wn, 17586

Date:	4 November 1706
Format:	oblong
Dimensions:	21.7 × 30 cm
Foliation:	54 fols.; modern pencil every 10 fols.
No. of staves:	10
Binding:	dark-brown leather
Imprints:	none
Watermarks:	three crescents: Heawood 868 (Venice, 1696)
Contents:	1 grand cantata by Antonio Bononcini: *Questo felice giorno, che del nome di Carlo altero splende* (*La Fortuna, il Valore, e la Giustitia*)
Remarks:	composed for the name day of Charles III (the future Emperor Charles VI); poet: Pietro Antonio Bernardoni

A-Wn, 17675

Date:	19 November 1712
Format:	oblong
Dimensions:	21.9 × 30.3 cm
Foliation:	76 fols.; modern pencil every 10 fols.
No. of staves:	10
Binding:	red leather; worn edges
Imprints:	small design on each corner
Watermarks:	three crescents: Heawood 868 (Venice, 1696)
Contents:	1 grand cantata by Carlo Badia: *Regina, eccoci al tempio della diva amorosa* (*Il sacrificio di Berenice*)
Remarks:	composed for the name day of Empress Elizabeth Christina; poet: Paolo Antonio del Negro

APPENDIX C
TEXTS OF ARIAS ANALYZED
IN CHAPTERS 10–12

Antonio Bononcini

Cantata 98/II

Al tuo bel volto amante
morrà fido e costante
il povero mio cor;
l'andrà dicendo poi
che sol per gl'occhi tuoi
fu martire d'amor.

Cantata 8/I

Amore ingannatore,
più non ti credo, no.
I lacci tuoi già frango
e libero rimango
da chi m'incatenò.

Cantata 91/II

Benché m'abbia la cruda saetta
di Cupido quest'alma ferita,
su quel campo la tenera erbetta
col suo verde a sperare m'invita.

Cantata 56/I

Men crudele e men severo
fate voi che più non tanto
mi tormenti il mio dolor.
0 pietoso il nume arciero
per virtù del vostro pianto
dia la pace a questo cor.

Cantata 56/II

Per non arder più d'amor
dimmi, o dimmi o cor,
che far dovrò?
Ché in soffrirsi rio tormento
io languir, morir mi sento
e mai pace in sen non ho.

Cantata 45/I

Più barbaro martire
chi mai provò
di quel che soffre un cor
per lontananza?
Provarlo e non morire,
quando si può,
miracolo è d'Amor,
non è costanza.

Cantata 28/I

Sentimi, crudo Amore,
mi toglierai la vita

	ma non la libertà.
	Combatterà il mio core
	con la tua destra ardita
	sino che spirto avrà.
Cantata 8/II	S'io ritorno a innamorarvi
	vibri il ciel per fulminarmi
	mille dardi e il cor m'uccida,
	ché non vuo' che più il mio petto
	sia soggetto
	al rigor di donna infida.
Cantata 99/II	Un cor più tormentato
	di questo cor non v'è.
	Langue d'Amor piagato
	senza sperar mercé.

Ariosti

Cantata 6/I	Al voler del bene amato
	un contento è l'ubbidir.
	Sembra un secolo di duolo
	quel momento solo
	che si lascia di servir.
Cantata 65/I	Cangi Amore
	sua face in fulgore
	e m'arda in petto
	l'empia beltà.
	Ma sciolto
	in cenere il vago volto
	chi mirerà
	senza pietà?
Cantata 29/I	È pur dolce a un cor legato
	il piacer di libertà.
	Ma il mio cor che fu legato
	tal contento più non ha.
Cantata 39/I	Insoffribile tormento
	è celar d'Amor il foco,
	né poter dir: "per te moro,"
	e fra ceppi d'un crin d'oro
	consumarsi a poco a poco.
Cantata 57/I	Nice, crudel, perché
	stillar mi vuoi nel sen
	il barbaro velen
	di gelosia?
	Sospira sol per te
	quest'alma e questo cor,
	ma il tuo novello ardor
	raddoppia il mio dolor
	la doglia mia.

Badia

Cantata 75/III	Basti per mio contento,
	basti per tuo tormento
	quanto il pensier dettò;

dirti di più non voglio
e chiudo questo foglio
con dir che Filli amò.

Cantata 64/II

Gelosia, furia d'Alletto,
lunghi vanne dal mio sen.
Stanne lunghi dal mio petto;
troppo crudo è il tuo velen.

Cantata 4/II

Ombra del mio bel sol,
finché respirerò
voglio adorarti:
e per placar il duol
almeno t'amerò
senza mirarti.

Cantata 1/III

Se sarai mio
io tua sarò,
né temerò
del cieco dio
il genio labile,
ma sempre stabile
t'adorerò.

Cantata 86/I

Sì vaga e sì vezzosa
miro la bella rosa
che bramo di sue spine
aver piagato il cor:
e tanto ella mi piace
che l'alma mia si sface
al vago suo splendor.

Giovanni Bononcini
Cantata 22/I

Dio d'Amor, deh, mi rispondi
se partendo dal mio bene
al mio ben ritornerò?
Già ti sento a dir di sì,
ma il destin risponde: "no,"
e l'eccesso de le pene
mi sa dir ch'io morirò.

Cantata 82/I

Dolce amor che sei mia vita,
poiché Filli alfin gradita
del mio cor ebbe pietà,
resta lieto in questo petto
per goder di quel diletto
che contento ugual non ha.

Cantata 51/I

Pena e soffri, o fido core,
quel rigore
che non vuole, no, cangiar.
S'en va persa la speranza,*
la costanza,
nel morir o nell' amar.

Ziani
Cantata 18/VI

Amore:
Brami e speri un vile affetto;
nulla speri Amor gentile.

Speranza:
La Speranza è del diletto
ad Amor madre e nudrice.
Amore:
Non può renderlo felice
chi l'amor render può vile.

Cantata 18/V

Speranza:
Navicella che paventa
e va lenta
in mar che freme
è l'Amor, s'io non lo guido;
l'urti vento o mar crudele
d'un disprezzo o d'un rigore;
quell'amore
che parea tanto fedele
già si pente e torna al lido.

Cantata 2/II

Se infelice, se giammai
i bei rai
ti mostra Amore
di due vaghi occhi piangenti,
in sembianza di pietà
t'entrerà
crudo nel core
ed un gel ti sembrerà
quell'ardor ch'ora tu senti.

---

* The erroneous original text reads "Serva persa la speranza."

NOTES

1. INTRODUCTION

1. "Let's sing, let's sing a little and in melodious harmonies cheerfully pass the hours of this happy day."

2. A selection of their compositions appears in Adler, *Musikalische Werke*. See also Guido Adler, "Die Kaiser Ferdinand III., Leopold I., Joseph I. und Karl VI. als Tonsetzer und Förderer der Musik," *VMw* 8 (1892): 252–74. In the appendix to the article "New Discoveries Concerning Ferdinand III's Musical Compositions," *SMw* 45 (1996): 7–31, Steven Saunders lists a total of twenty surviving compositions by Ferdinand III as well as numerous works mentioned in archival documents and inventories. Saunders's appendix, which includes nine Italian pieces, substantially augments the number of compositions known to Adler; of the nine Italian pieces, only two are extant.

3. In a recent paper Herbert Seifert has shown that a *Miserere mei Deus* attributed to Leopold I is not in Leopold's hand but very likely in the hand of his son, the young Charles. In an e-mail message dated 22 July 2011, Seifert states that he is "also convinced that Charles could not have been the composer of the music, because there is a huge gap between the awkward notation and the compositional skills. So it seems likely to me that Archduke Charles copied the piece composed by a skilled composer, maybe by his old father." Seifert's paper was delivered at the conference "Sacred Music in the Habsburg Empire 1619–1740 and Its Contexts" in Middleburg, the Netherlands, in 2009.

4. Hereafter A-Wn and A-Wgm, respectively. For a complete list of library sigla, see the front matter.

5. See the article on Cesti by David Burrows and Carl Schmidt in the NG, 4:92.

6. Fruchtman and Fruchtman, "Instrumental Scoring," 246.

7. Seifert, *Die Oper am Wiener Kaiserhof,* 444, 649.

8. See Rosand, "Barbara Strozzi," 244.

9. Klenz, *Giovanni Maria Bononcini,* 43.

10. NG, 23:115.

11. Seifert, "Neues zu Antonio Draghis," 97–98. Seifert also provides many helpful insights regarding genre designations. Ulrike Hofmann ("Die Serenata") assumes scenic representation for the seventeenth-century serenata in Vienna. For additional bibliographic details, see Hadamowsky, "Barocktheater," 69, 96.

12. For this summary of the forerunners of the cantata, I am especially grateful to Steven Saunders, who offered many helpful suggestions.

13. For more about the court of Archduke Ferdinand at Graz, see especially two studies by Hellmut Federhofer: *Musikpflege und Musiker* and "Graz Court Musicians."

14. Concerning the probability that Rasi sang the title role of *Orfeo,* see two articles in *The Cambridge Companion to Monteverdi*: Pryer, "Approaching Monteverdi," 12–13; and Steinheuer, "Orfeo (1607)," 122.

15. About this collection, see Einstein, "Ein Emissär der Monodie," 31–34. The holograph source, which belonged to the archbishop, is now in D-Rp. Einstein gives Rasi's dedication (31).

16. See RISM A/I/6, 349.

17. See Chappell White, in NG, 4:884.

18. For more about monody north of the Alps, see Seifert, "Beiträge zur Frühgeschichte"; Einstein, "Italienische Musik," 50; Flotzinger, *Eine Quelle italienischer Frühmonodie;* Racek, "Collezione di Monodie," 11 ff.; and Federhofer, "Graz Court Musicians," 168.

19. For a comprehensive study of composers active at the court of Ferdinand II, see especially Saunders, *Cross, Sword and Lyre.* About Priuli, see also Federhofer, "Graz Court Musicians," 185–91; and Einstein, "Italienische Musik," 49–52; and concerning Valentini, see also Federhofer, "Graz Court Musicians," 191–200. About Verdina, see Federhofer, in NG, 26:471; concerning Arrigoni, see Josef-Horst Lederer, in NG, 2:78.

20. Seifert, "Monteverdi und die Habsburger."

21. Mabbett, "Madrigalists." For this study I was unable to consult Mabbett's dissertation, "The Italian Madrigal, 1620–1655" (Ph.D. diss., King's College, University of London, 1989).

22. Mabbett, "Madrigalists," 295.

23. Mabbett, "Madrigalists," 301–302.

24. Holman, "'Col nobilissimo esercitio.'"

25. Two volumes of a modern edition of the *Delicie musicali* (1625), ed. Albert Biales (Graz, 1977), have appeared.

26. For a list of these collections, see Hellmut Federhofer and Steven Saunders, in NG, 26:210; and Joachim Steinheuer, in MGG, *Personenteil,* 16:1270 (2006). Selections from *Musiche a doi voci* (1622) are published in *Frühmeister des stile nuovo in Österreich* (DTOe 125); the madrigal "Vanne, o carta amorosa" from the same collection is published as no. 13 in Whenham, *Duet and Dialogue,* 2:251–55.

27. Federhofer and Saunders, in NG, 26:210.

28. Steinheuer, MGG, *Personenteil,* 16:1279–80 (2006).

29. For more about Bertali, see especially Bartels, "Die Instrumentalstücke"; Orel, "Die Kontrapunktlehren"; and Rudolf Schnitzler and Charles Brewer, in NG, 3:452–54.

30. A-Wn, Supp. Mus. 2451.

31. The Düben Collection Database Catalogue, ed. Erik Kjellberg and Kerala J. Snyder, is available online at http://www2.musik.uu.se/duben/Duben.php.

32. About Sances's career in Vienna, see especially John Whenham and Steven Saunders, in NG, 22:224–26; Antonicek, "Musik und italienische Poesie"; and two dissertations: Webhofer, "Giovanni Felice Sances," and Raschl, "Die weltliche Vokalwerke."

33. http://imslp.org/wiki/Category:Sances,_Giovanni_Felice.

34. See Weberhofer, "Giovanni Felice Sances," 35. Raschl adds: "Ebenso liessen vermutlich mehrmalige 'Bestands-überstellungen' der Musikalien der Hofmusikkapelle zahlreiche Kompositions-Überlieferungen verlorengehen" (Likewise, the multiple inventories of the court chapel's music presumably led to the loss of many compositional traditions) ("Die weltliche Vokalwerke," 10). Raschl's dissertation is a style-analytical study of the vocal chamber music that came down in the surviving printed collections available to him in 1967; on pp. 280–88 Raschl gives a thematic index of these pieces. For a list of the extant copies of Sances's prints, see RISM A/I/7, 331; see also Raschl for additional details (9–24).

35. Whenham, *Duet and Dialogue,* vol. 2, includes two multisectional works by Sances: no. 36, the aria "Occhi, sfere vivaci" (363–75), and no. 43, the dialogue "Tirsi morir volea" (438–47).

36. Steinheuer, "Zur musikdramatischen Umsetzung," 203–205.

37. See Whenham, *Duet and Dialogue,* 1:184, 226–28.

38. See Waldner, "Zwei Inventarien," 135.

2. THE POLITICAL AND CULTURAL MILIEU

1. About Austrian political and cultural history during the late seventeenth and early eighteenth centuries, see Ingrao, *The Habsburg Monarchy*, 53–149; Spielman, *Leopold I of Austria*; Spielman, *The City and the Crown*; Kann, *A History of the Habsburg Empire*, 51–155; Mayer and Kaindl, *Geschichte und Kulturlebens Österreichs*, 186–265; and Zöllner, *Geschichte Österreichs*, 246–303. Vehse's *Memoirs of the Court*, 1:471–503 and 2:1–91, contains abundant details about the life of Leopold and his relationship to the nobility; and the anonymous *Life of Leopold* gives full descriptions of seventeenth-century wars and military campaigns.

2. For more concerning Leopold's changing image, see Goloubeva, *The Glorification*, esp. 229–33. For an evaluation of Leopold the man and the emperor, see Ingrao, *The Habsburg Monarchy*, 58–59, 83–104; and Spielman, *Leopold I of Austria*, 196–203. Concerning Austrian cultural and intellectual history of the late seventeenth and early eighteenth centuries, see also Mayer and Kaindl, *Geschichte und Kulturlebens Österreichs*, 2:253–65; Kann, *A Study*, 1–136; and Hennings, *Das barocke Wien*.

3. Mayer and Kaindl, *Geschichte und Kulturlebens Österreichs*, 232–33.

4. See Hadamowsky, "Barocktheater," 65, for information about the growing importance of dancing at the imperial court during the late seventeenth and early eighteenth centuries.

5. Concerning the ensemble dances of the Schmelzers, see the article on Johann Heinrich by Adolf Layer in NG, 22:527; and the article on Anton Andreas by Rudolf Schnitzler and Thomas D. Walker in NG, 22:526. See also Nettl, "Die Wiener Tanzkomposition"; Wellesz, "Die Ballett-Suiten"; and Meyer, *Die Mehrstimmige Spielmusik*, chap. 4 and pp. 243–45. A collection of J. H. Schmelzer's ballet suites is published in DTOe 56 (Vienna, 1921). Keyboard suites of the period show a French as well as an Italian influence; see Harris, "Keyboard Music," 128–59.

6. Wolf, *The Emergence*, 245.

7. For more concerning Eleonora, see Schnitzler, "The Sacred Dramatic Music," 12; and Landau, *Die italienische Literatur*, 8–10.

8. Mayer and Kaindl, *Geschichte und Kulturlebens Österreichs*, 171; Hennings, *Das barocke Wien*, 1:14.

9. See Fiedler, *Die Relationen*, 2:48–79; Adler, "Die Kaiser Ferdinand III.," 261. There is a manuscript volume of Italian verse by Leopold in the Handschriften-Sammlung of A-Wn.

10. McGuigan, *The Habsburgs*, 182.

11. Leopold Wilhelm was regent of the Netherlands during the period 1646–56. Concerning his activities as a patron there, see Knaus, "Beiträge."

12. See Culley, *Jesuits and Music I*, 150.

13. Culley, *Jesuits and Music I*, 182–93.

14. The inventory HKA, Nö HA, 60/A/32, fols. 2r–10v, was written down by Giuseppe Zamponi and is titled *Lista de Instrumenti e libri di Su Alt:^za Ser:^ma / L'Arciducca Leopoldo Guglielmo di Austria*. The titles of secular vocal chamber music appear on fols. 6v–10v. The composers for only a tiny fraction of the secular pieces are identified: Morazzuolo (Marazzeulo), Lodovico Ciccolini, Francesco Marcaurelle (Marcorelli), and Felice Sances.

15. Seifert, "Akademien am Wiener Kaiserhof"; see also chap. 5, "Akademie," in Seifert's *Die Oper am Wiener Kaiserhof*, 195–204.

16. Leopold Wilhelm, *Diporti del Crescente Divisi*.

17. Ferdinand III, *Poesie diverse*; a copy is preserved at A-Wn, *38 Dd. 125. Some of the poetry published by Ferdinand III and Leopold Wilhelm was set as vocal chamber music by Bertali and Sances; for this information I am indebted to Steven Saunders.

18. See Seifert, "Akademien am Wiener Kaiserhof," 218.

19. For more concerning Leopold's academy, see Seifert, "Akademien am Wiener Kaiserhof," 219–21.

20. Kanduth, "Italienische Dichtung."

21. For more concerning the Viennese academies, see Hofmann, "Die Accademia am Wiener Kaiserhof"; Antonicek, "Italienische Akademien"; and Bin, "Leopoldo I."

22. See Mayer and Kaindl, *Geschichte und Kulturlebens Österreichs,* 252–53; Adler, "Die Kaiser Ferdinand III.," 261; Somerset, "The Habsburg Emperors."

23. Gmeiner, "Die 'Schlafkammerbibliothek.'"

24. Gmeiner, "Die 'Schlafkammerbibliothek,'" 207, provides a helpful diagram of the imperial apartments of the Schweizerhof.

25. In 2005 the collection was moved once again, this time to the Palais Mollard in Herrengasse.

26. Concerning Leopold's role as a patron of music, see Goloubeva, *The Glorification;* and Somerset, "The Habsburg Emperors," 204–15. Herbert Seifert's monumental study *Die Oper am Wiener Kaiserhof im 17. Jahrhundert* is indispensable for an understanding of Leopold's patronage of secular dramatic works. See also Adler, "Die Kaiser Ferdinand III.," 256–68; Hamann, "Musik am Hofe Leopold I."; and Wessely, "Kaiser Leopolds I."

27. Hadamowsky, "Barocktheater," 64, also demonstrates that singers were among the highest paid musicians.

28. Thus, for example, in autograph instructions attached to a letter dated 27 May 1687 from Draghi to the *Obersthofmeister,* Prince Dietrichstein, Leopold outlined rules for the deportment of musicians; a German translation of the letter appears in Lipsius, *Musikbriefe,* 1:122.

29. See, for example, Brown, *A Brief Account,* 141.

30. For more concerning Leopold as a composer, see especially Brosche, "Die musikalische Werke." See also Adler, "Die Kaiser Ferdinand III.," 161–63; and Somerset, "The Habsburg Emperors," 210–12. Riedel and Riedel have recently identified a group of previously unknown arias by Leopold ("Zum Repertoire," 333–35). A selection of the emperor's compositions appears in Adler, *Musikalische Werke,* 1:45–298, 2:27–226, 259–71.

31. Seifert, *Die Oper am Wiener Kaiserhof,* 204. Steven Saunders informs me that Leopold also wrote a sacred cantata text, *Cantata di S. Paulo,* preserved at A-Wn, Cod 9401*.

32. Rudolf Schnitzler (with Herbert Seifert), in NG, 14:568.

33. See the facsimile of the beginning of *Rio destin, crudo laccio* in MGG, 8:651–52 (1960).

34. For a list of musicians who held appointments at Vienna during Leopold's reign, see Köchel, *Die kaiserliche Hof-Musikkapelle,* 62–72. Further details about court musicians can be found in several archival studies: Knaus, *Die Musiker im Archivbestand;* Knaus, "Die Musiker"; Knaus, "Wiener Hofquartierbücher"; Koczirz, "Excerpte"; and Nettl, "Zur Geschichte."

35. See Köchel, *Die kaiserliche Hof-Musikkapelle,* 10.

36. Concerning the membership of Eleonora's chapel, see Knaus, "Wiener Hofquartierbücher," 202–206.

37. Seifert, "Akademien am Wiener Kaiserhof," 218.

38. Seifert, "Neues zu Antonio Draghis," 114.

39. Köchel, *Die kaiserliche Hof-Musikkapelle,* 63–68.

40. Page, "Sirens on the Danube," an unpublished paper that Dr. Page kindly sent to me on 18 April 2012.

41. Page, "Sirens on the Danube," 5.

42. Page, "Sirens on the Danube," 4.

43. Köchel, *Die kaiserliche Hof-Musikkapelle,* 64–65, 68–72.

44. See Ferrari, "Per la bibliografia," 143–45.

45. See Köchel, *Die kaiserliche Hof-Musikkapelle,* 63.

46. Not one of the poets of Vismarri's cantatas is identified by Seifert, *Die Oper am Wiener Kaiserhof,* as the author of a text for an opera in the seventeenth century.

47. See Seifert, *Die Oper am Wiener Kaiserhof,* 469, 474, 480.

48. Concerning Branchi, see Seifert, *Die Oper am Wiener Kaiserhof,* 197–98, 486.

49. For information about Minato's Venetian career, see Rosand, *Opera in Seventeenth-Century Venice.* For the details of his Viennese opera and oratorio librettos, see Seifert, *Die Oper am Wiener Kaiserhof;* and Schnitzler, "The Sacred Dramatic Music," respectively. See also Goloubeva, *The Glorification,* for copious references to Minato's role in portraying Leopold as a hero through allegorical representations.

50. Barazzoni, "Le cantate da camera," 255.

51. For a brief but helpful survey of seicento Italian poetry, see Brand and Pertile, *The Cambridge History of Italian Literature,* 301–40; Marino is described on p. 305 as a representative of the "moderate Baroque" and "the greatest [Italian] poet of the seventeenth century." The complete poems of the three cantatas in MSS 16299 and 16313 are given in Barzzzoni, "Le cantate da camera," 266–71; the text of *Lo specchio* is also published in volume 16 of the series The Italian Cantata in the Seventeenth Century, 333–34.

3. THE COMPOSERS

1. Concerning Tricarico's biography, see Rudolf Schnitzler (with Herbert Seifert), in NG, 25:726–27; and Pastore, "Giuseppe Tricarico da Gallipoli." See also EDM 6, 222–23; SchmidlD, 2:618; SchmidlS, 416.

2. A-Wn, 18716, preserves the oratorio *La Gara della misericordia e giustizia di Dio* (Vienna, 1661). Only the Draghi libretto of *La fede trionfante* (Vienna, 1662) is extant. The sacred works are found in A-Wn, 19067, a collection entitled *Opere a Cappella . . . collectio operum musicorum ecclesiasticorum, Leopoldo I° imperatori dedicatorum;* this autograph volume contains a letter of dedication in Italian by Tricarico.

3. I-Nc, 22.1.4. contains three chamber duets for SS and bc; 33.5.38 includes one solo cantata with obbligato instruments and bc; 33.4.13 preserves a chamber duet accompanied by bc. Individual arias, possibly from cantatas, survive in I-Nc, 33.4.15 and 33.5.33, and in I-Nf.

4. Concerning Cesti's biography, see especially Seifert, "Cesti and His Opera Troupe"; and David L. Burrows and Carl B. Schmidt, in NG, 5:394–97. See also Schmidt, "The Operas of Antonio Cesti," 1:1–123; Pirrotta, "Tre capitoli su Cesti"; Burrows, "Antonio Cesti on Music"; Antonicek, "Zum 300. Todestag"; Giazotto, "Nel CCC anno della morte"; Coradini, "P. Antonio Cesti"; ES, 462–68 (1956). Rosand, *Opera in Seventeenth-Century Venice,* chaps. 10–12, provides insightful observations about Cesti's musical style within the context of the broad development of opera in Venice.

5. Seifert, "Cesti and His Opera Troupe," 27.

6. For documents pertaining to Cesti's residence in Vienna, see especially Seifert, "Cesti and His Opera Troupe," 51–52; and Antonicek, "Antonio Cesti alla corte."

7. Köchel, *Die kaiserliche Hof-Musikkapelle,* 62, gives the dates 1 January 1666–69 as the period that Cesti held the position as assistant Kapellmeister simultaneously with Sances.

8. The premiere performances were actually delayed and did not take place for more than one and one-half years, finally celebrating the empress's birthday. Seifert, "Cesti and His Opera Troupe," 47, provides a complete list of Cesti's operas. For more concerning the Viennese operas, see Schmidt, "The Operas of Antonio Cesti"; Schmidt, "Antonio Cesti's *Il pomo d'oro*"; Crowther, "The Operas of Cesti"; Holmes, "Comedy—Opera—Comic Opera"; Wellesz, "Die Opern und Oratorien," 27–33; Wellesz, *Essays on Opera,* 54–81; and Nettl,

"Ein verschollenes Tournierballet." For information regarding sources and modern editions of *Il pomo d'oro,* see Burrows and Schmidt, in NG, 5:398.

9. See Seifert, "Cesti and His Opera Troupe," 41–46, concerning Cesti's final Tuscan period.

10. For an inventory of Cesti's cantatas, see the thematic index by Burrows in WECIS 1. For additional details, see Burrows and Schmidt, in NG, 5:398–99. With regard to Cesti's cantata style, see Burrows, "The Cantatas of Antonio Cesti"; and Peters, "Antonio Cesti's Solo Cantatas." Editions of Cesti cantatas appear in Burrows, *The Italian Cantata I;* Burrows, *Antonio Cesti: Four Chamber Duets;* Burrows, *Antonio Cesti: Cantatas;* and Burrows, "The Cantatas of Antonio Cesti," 160–248.

11. Seifert, *Die Oper am Wiener Kaiserhof,* 179.

12. For details about the locations of sources, see Burrows and Schmidt, in NG, 5:398–99; and WECIS 1.

13. For more about D-Mbs, Mus. ms. 1527, see Riedel and Riedel, "Zum Repertoire," 323–24. Wilhelm Friedrich Riedel, the author of the first portion of the article, points out the striking parallels in notational style and repertoire with four manuscripts in A-GÖ and one in A-Wn.

14. For more about A-GÖ, Ms. 4091, see Riedel and Riedel, "Zum Repertoire," 336–51. Leonhard Riedel provided the detailed analysis of the texts and music.

15. About the life of P. A. Ziani, see especially Antonicek, "Die *Damira*-Opern." See also Antonicek and H. S. Saunders, in NG, 27:815–16; ES, 9:2128–29 (1962); La MusicaD 2, no. 2 (1968): 1563–64. Rosand, *Opera in Seventeenth-Century Venice,* chaps. 10–12, discusses Ziani's musical style within the context of the broad development of opera in Venice.

16. No copies of opp. 4–5 appear to be extant.

17. Senn, *Musik und Theater,* 268.

18. See Antonicek, "Die *Damira*-Opern," 177. For details with regard to Ziani's operas composed for Vienna, see Deutsch, "Das Repertoire," 379; Hadamowsky, "Barocktheater," 72–73; and Antonicek and Saunders, in NG, 27:816.

19. Manuscript copies of cantatas, duets, madrigals, and arias survive at D-Kl, GB-Lbl, I-Bc, I-Nc, and I-Nf. Similar works, attributed simply to Ziani without a first name, are found at D-DS, D-Kl, F-Pn, GB-Lbl, I-Bc, I-Nc, and I-Vmc. Some of these works may have been composed by Pietro Andrea's nephew, Marc'Antonio Ziani.

20. The most detailed biography of Draghi is given in an excellent article by Seifert, "Da Rimini alla corte di Leopoldo." Draghi's date of birth has usually been given as either 1634 or 1635; Seifert offers persuasive evidence that Draghi was born in early 1634.

21. For details about Draghi's secular dramatic works composed during the period 1662–70, see especially Seifert, *Die Oper am Wiener Kaiserhof,* 451–70; and Hadamowsky, "Barocktheater," 72–76; concerning the four sacred works, see Schnitzler, "The Sacred Dramatic Music," 347–48. See also Schnitzler (with Seifert), in NG, 7:548, 550.

22. With regard to Draghi's tenure at the court of the empress dowager, see Seifert, "Da Rimini alla corte di Leopoldo," 4–7; Neuhaus, "Antonio Draghi"; and Schnitzler, "The Sacred Dramatic Music," 27–29. As Kapellmeister, Draghi succeeded Ziani, not Tricarico, as stated by Schnitzler, who indicates that Draghi may have functioned as Kapellmeister as early as 1667 because of Ziani's frequent absences from the court.

23. It is not true, as stated by Schnitzler, "The Sacred Dramatic Music," 29, that Leopold "created the position" for Draghi, since a similar title had been held by Cesti: see Burrows and Schmidt, in NG, 5:395.

24. Concerning the centralization of music in France and Lully's relationship with Louis XIV, see especially Isherwood, *Music in the Service,* 150–203, 247.

25. Seifert, "Da Rimini alla corte di Leopoldo," 8–9; and Neuhaus, "Antonio Draghi," 107–15. Seifert also demonstrates that by 1683 Draghi had become fairly affluent.

26. Schnitzler, "The Sacred Dramatic Music," 37, names Cesti as the principal figure "who may have had an influence on the style of Draghi."

27. Schnitzler, "The Sacred Dramatic Music," 277–78. See p. 103 for a concise description of the three basic types of sacred dramatic music performed at Vienna in the late seventeenth century. There is a printed copy of a libretto for a Draghi oratorio in the Houghton Library of US-CA that is not accounted for in Schnitzler's list of sources on pp. 123–25.

28. Seifert, "Da Rimini alla corte di Leopoldo," 14.

29. For lists of Draghi's works, see Schnitzler (with Seifert), in NG, 7:549–51; and Neuhaus, "Antonio Draghi," 142–73; see also Seifert, *Die Oper am Wiener Kaiserhof,* 451 ff.; and Hadamowsky, "Barocktheater," 72–96, for copious details. Neuhaus, "Antonio Draghi," 174–92, provides excerpts from several secular dramatic works. For more concerning the operas, see Seifert, "Neues zu Antonio Draghis"; Neuhaus, "Antonio Draghi," 121–40; and Wellesz, "Die Opern und Oratorien," 35–45. The most comprehensive catalog of Draghi's sacred dramatic music appears in Schnitzler, "The Sacred Dramatic Music," 342–97; extensive music examples are given on 299–341. The surviving liturgical works are published in Denkmäler der Tonkunst in Österreich 46. Schnitzler provides a thorough investigation of the sacred dramatic works, and Guido Adler discusses the liturgical pieces in Denkmäler der Tonkunst in Österreich 46, v–vi. See also Adler's "Zur Geschichte der Wiener Messkomposition," concerning the masses of Draghi and his contemporaries.

30. See Knaus, *Die Musiker im Archivbestand* 254 (1967): 159.

31. Köchel, *Die kaiserliche Hof-Musikkapelle,* 66.

32. Schnitzler (with Seifert), in NG, 7:546.

33. The sections concerning Vismarri in chaps. 3, 4, and 5 of this book were originally written by me for NG and updated in 2011 for *Grove Music Online* published by Oxford University Press; they appear on OxfordMusicOnline.com and are given here with the permission of the publisher.

34. Knaus, *Die Musiker im Archivbestand* 254 (1967): 26, 49.

35. Knaus, *Die Musiker im Archivbestand* 254 (1967): 65.

36. See Holmes, "*Orontea*: A Study"; see also Holmes's introduction to his edition of Cesti's *Orontea* in WE 9.

37. Holmes, "Yet Another '*Orontea*.'" Holmes demonstrates on p. 221 that Vismarri's *Orontea* compares unfavorably with Cesti's version in aspects such as melodic invention, structural variety, and sensitivity to text.

38. Knaus, *Die Musiker im Archivbestand* 259 (1968): 104.

39. *Giuda disperato* is preserved in I-Baf; see EitnerQ, 11:86. Concerning the sacred works, see Sehnhal, "Die Musikkapelle," 119.

40. The text of no. 6 (*So ben io dov'è legata*) may also have been set by Carissimi; see the catalog of Carissimi's cantatas compiled by Gloria Rose, WECIS 5. The text of no. 8 (*Chi mi credeva instabile*) was also set by Luigi Rossi; see the inventory of Rossi's cantatas by Eleanor Caluori, WECIS 3a.

41. The text of no. 2 (*Maledetto sia quel dì*) survives in a setting in I-Rvat, Barb. lat. 4176, and the libretto of no. 3 (*Dove amor lungi mi tiene*) comes down in a version in I-Rvat, Chigi Q.IV.8. The text of no. 1 (*Sciolieasi baldanzoso per l'oceano*) is preserved in a setting for bass in I-Nc, 33.5.18; the text of no. 7 (*Lasci d'amar chi non ha sorte*) survives in two manuscripts at I-MOe: Mus. G.258 and Mus. F.1349. I have not yet determined whether the two pieces in I-MOe have the same music.

42. The sections concerning Cappellini in chaps. 3, 4, and 5 of this book were originally written by me for NG and updated in 2011 for *Grove Music Online* published by Oxford University Press; they appear on OxfordMusicOnline.com and are given here with the permission of the publisher.

43. See Bertolotti, *Musici alla corte,* 90; EitnerQ, 2:315; FétisB, 2:179. Michelangelo Cappellini (Capollini), a singer and composer, was born at Rome in 1598 or 1599 and died at Mantua on 11 July 1627. He entered the service of the duke of Mantua as a castrato toward the end of 1612 or the beginning of 1613 and was still employed in Mantua at the time of his death at the age of twenty-eight. Fétis reported that an oratorio in *stile recitativo* by him was performed at the Chiesa dei Santi Innocenti in 1627; there is apparently no extant score of this work, entitled *Lamento di Maria Vergine, accompagnato dalle lagrime di S. Maria Maddalena e di S. Giovanni per la morte di Giesù Cristo.*

44. For more concerning Pietro Paolo Cappelini, see Roncaglia, "Di un autor"; ES, 2:1729. The only known information about the career of Pietro Paolo (fl. mid-seventeenth century) survives in the manuscript of his *cantata scenica* (in I-MOe), *La forza d'amore,* a pastoral idyll for three voices in three acts with a libretto by the Roman G. F. Apolloni (a text later set by Bernardo Pasquini). In the manuscript, two coats of arms are joined, thus suggesting that Cappellini composed the work for the marriage of members of two noble households. One of these may have been the Roman family Pietraccini, according to Roncaglia, who also stated that the style of the music appears to have been strongly influenced by Carissimi. From this it is reasonable to conclude that Cappellini was active in Rome in the middle of the seventeenth century.

45. See Seifert, "Die Rolle Wiens."

46. Knaus, *Die Musiker im Archivbestand* 254 (1967): 79–80, and 259 (1968): 21.

47. See Ferrari, "Per la bibliografia," 141.

48. Two libraries preserve other works: a *Missa Sancti Caietani* dated 1671 and now at CZ-KR, and an instrumental work for violin and basso continuo, no. 37, in a manuscript collection at GB-Lbl, *66 Solos or Sonatas.* The instrumental piece may be a composition of Pietro Paolo Cappellini's, but Carlo Cappellini's experience as a keyboard player is an indication of his interest in instrumental music.

49. The sections concerning Pederzuoli in chaps. 3, 4, and 5 of this book were originally written by me for NG and updated in 2011 for *Grove Music Online* published by Oxford University Press; they appear on OxfordMusicOnline.com and are given here with the permission of the publisher. See also *La Musica,* 589; and Schnitzler, "The Sacred Dramatic Music," 36–37.

50. Donati-Pettèni, *L'arte della musica in Bergamo,* 16.

51. Preserved at I-Nf.

52. Concerning A. M. and G. B. Viviani, see Seifert, *Giovanni Buonaventura Viviani.* See also the articles for these two composers by Seifert in NG, 26:845; and Brockpähler, *Handbuch zur Geschichte,* 233.

53. The libretto, by Diego de Lequile, is in SI-Lf.

54. See, for example, Seifert, *Giovanni Buonaventura Viviani,* 27–29.

55. Seifert, *Giovanni Buonaventura Viviani,* 29.

56. Op. 6 (*Cantate* for violin and basso continuo) was published at Bologna in 1689; op. 7 (*Veglie armoniche a 1–3 v. con V. e senza*) appeared at Florence in 1690; and op. 8 (*Solfeggiamenti a 2 v.*) was published in the same city three years later. The manuscript A-Wn, 17769, contains, in addition to one cantata by Viviani (*Care pene*), two cantatas by Cesti, six by Pier Simone Agostini, and one by Pasquini. The source is dated "Pisa, 1691," and is dedicated "al signor canonico Steffano Morandini." See Seifert, *Giovanni Buonaventura Viviani,* 154–55, for a complete list of G. B. Viviani's cantatas and their sources; see pp. 168–69 for additional details.

57. See Seifert, *Giovanni Buonaventura Viviani,* 169; and Riedel and Riedel, "Zum Repertoire," 332.

58. NG, 22:528.

59. For biographical studies of Kerll, see C. David Harris (with Albert C. Giebler), in NG, 13:491–92; and Schaal, "Quellen zu Johann Kaspar Kerll"; see also Riedel, "Eine unbekannte Quelle"; Harris, "Keyboard Music"; Giebler, "The Masses"; and Knaus, "Beiträge."

60. Riedel and Riedel, "Zum Repertoire," 332. I did not examine the manuscript A-GÖ, 4089, for this study.

61. Schaal, "Quellen zu Johann Kaspar Kerll," 23.

4. REPERTOIRE AND SOURCES

1. Concerning lost works of Bertali and Sances, see chap. 1.

2. Newman, *The Sonata in the Baroque Era*, 212, suggests that Leopold's preoccupation with opera and oratorio may also have "kept the sonata production from growing as fast as that in Germany."

3. The letter is preserved in I-Bc, cod. 66, no. 6; see Neuhaus, "Antonio Draghi," 112.

4. With regard to Leopold's musical tastes, see Wellesz, "Die Opern und Oratorien," 7; Adler, "Die Kaiser Ferdinand III.," 258–60.

5. A handful of cantatas by Carlo Agostino Badia were composed shortly before 1700. Historically and stylistically, these cantatas belong to the period 1700–1711 and will be discussed in chaps. 6–12.

6. One of the most politically and historically significant collections of cantatas dedicated to a member of the Habsburg family are the six in A-Wn, 17751, by Giovanni Varischino (fl. 1680–92), a nephew and student of Giovanni Legrenzi; these cantatas were composed "per la coronation del novo rè de Romani," probably the eleven-year-old Joseph, Leopold's first son, who was crowned king of the Romans on 26 January 1690 in Augsburg.

7. *Lo specchio* is reproduced in facsimile in The Italian Cantata in the Seventeenth Century 16:121–58; the title is given in the facsimile on p. 121, the first folio of music. The *Cantata à servitio di camera* entitled *Gli obblighi dell'universo* and attributed to Draghi in A-Wn, 17925, is listed as a doubtful work by Schnitzler (with Seifert) in NG, 7:550.

8. In the article "Le cantate di camera," 254, Beatrice Barazzoni also suggests that the cantatas in MS 16315 probably date from the 1670s because of the close stylistic similarity to *Lo specchio*. On pp. 273–87 Barazzoni gives a complete transcription of *Forza d'un bel volto*.

9. In my 1980 dissertation, "The Italian Cantata in Vienna, c.1700–c.1711," 31, I conjectured that the undated *accademia* in MS 17922 may have been the first in a series of three *accademie* composed rather late in Draghi's career, but this work is now considered doubtful, as are the examples in MSS 17923, 17924, and 17295; see Seifert, "Neues zu Antonio Draghis," 102; and Schnitzler (with Seifert), in NG, 7:550.

10. See Seifert, *Giovanni Buonaventura Viviani*, 170–71, concerning the Florentine source, which contains an additional duet probably by A. M. Viviani.

11. Cappellini's *Occhi miei non vi struggete* is also found in A-GÖ, Mus. ms. 4091.

12. Six cantatas are published in facsimile and edited by me in The Italian Cantata in the Seventeenth Century 16:1–67; a facsimile of the front cover of the binding on p. 1 of this edition gives the title of the complete collection: "Cantate e ariette per camera / à voce sola / Composte in Musica, dà / D. Filippo Vismarri Musico / di Camera / di sua Maestà Cesarea." A note at the top of the cover, written in a hand other than the main copyist's, gives information about an early owner: "Comparavit P. Lambertus Stabler, Prof. Gottw. Ao. [1]718." P. Lambert Stabler (1684–1750) worked as librarian at Stift Göttweig, a Benedictine monastery in Lower Austria. The manuscript was evidently later returned to Vienna; see Riedel and Riedel, "Zum Repertoire," 128–29.

13. The first five cantatas are published in facsimile in The Italian Cantata in the Seventeenth Century 16:68–120; a facsimile of the front cover on p. 67 supplies the title: "Cantate per Camera / à 1 e 2 voci / di / Carlo Cappellini."

14. Concerning lost sources, see chap. 1; concerning a doubtful source, D-Bsb, Mus. ms. 30186, see chap. 7.

15. See Gmeiner, "Die 'Schlafkammerbibliothek' Kaiser Leopolds I.," 204.

16. Salchi was employed at the court from 1682 and was pensioned on 1 October 1711; Abendt received an appointment in 1686 and continued to work until his death on 3 December 1729 at the age of seventy-three. See Köchel, Die kaiserliche Hofmusikkapelle, 69.

17. It is instructive to compare the handwriting found in these three pieces with the copying seen in the facsimiles given in The Italian Cantata in the Seventeenth Century 16.

5. TEXT AND MUSIC

1. See, for example, Stein, "Between Key and Mode."

2. Deh volgetemi un guardo is found in S-Uu, vmhs 047:020, and Già dai monti is preserved in vmhs 047:022.

3. S-Uu, vmhs 047:021. This work can be seen online in the Web Library of Seventeenth-Century Music, no. 11 (2008), in an excellent edition by Andrew Weaver, with introduction, text, and English translation.

4. Riedel and Riedel, "Zum Repertoire," 336.

5. The Helmholtz system of pitch notation has been used throughout this book.

6. "In love, patience is required; he who has none will be nothing. Beauty is a maiden whom you do not violate; in love, patience is required."

7. Cappellini's keyboard training may also be seen in his specific use of the word cembalo in one of the arias of his chamber opera La fama illustrata, a rare instance in the entire seventeenth-century repertoire.

8. The four cantatas in MS 18872 are reproduced in facsimile in The Italian Cantata in the Seventeenth Century 16:159–200; the facsimile of fol. 1r supplies the title: "Quattro Cantate Per / l'Accademia per Sua M.^{tà} Ces.r / Dell'Imp.^{ce} Eleonora."

9. For a clarification regarding the difference between a Devisenarie and a motto aria, see the article "Devise" by Thomas Braatz (15 October 2005) at the website http://www.bach-cantatas.com/Terms-7.htm.

10. Lo specchio is reproduced in facsimile in The Italian Cantata in the Seventeenth Century 16:121–58; the title is given in the facsimile on p. 121, the first folio of music.

11. Gmeiner, "Die 'Schlafkammerbibliothek' Kaiser Leopolds I.," indicates that the volumes of the Schlafkammerbibliothek were not for the performers but for Leopold's personal use to follow along when not at the keyboard, thus accounting for why only the beginnings of ritornellos are written out.

12. I am indebted to Brett Bogart for his help with the translations of these three cantata texts.

13. Barazzoni, "Le cantate da camera," 258–65.

6. THE POLITICAL AND CULTURAL MILIEU

1. About the reign of Joseph I, see especially two studies by Ingrao, The Habsburg Monarchy, 105–18, and In Quest and Crisis; see also Tapié, The Rise and Fall, 158–62; and Mikoletzky, Österreich, 58–96.

2. For details concerning the battles at Landau, see two studies by Heuser: Die Belagerung von Landau and Die dritte und vierte Belagerung Landaus.

3. See Lindgren, "A Bibliographic Scrutiny," 101–102. For a poetic tribute to Joseph upon his departure to the battlefront, see Bernardoni, *Rime varie*, 20. Concerning several Caldara compositions related to the War of the Spanish Succession, see Kirkendale, "The War of the Spanish Succession."

4. Concerning the role of music and theater at the court of King Charles III (the future Emperor Charles VI) in Barcelona, see especially Sommer-Mathis, "Von Barcelona nach Wien."

5. Concerning Joseph's personality and his patronage of the arts, see Elizabeth Fritz in *MGG*, *Personenteil*, 9:1203–1204 (2003); and Mikoletsky, *Österreich*, 75–77. For a much less positive evaluation of Joseph's personality and imperial objectives, see Williams, *Francesco Bartolomeo Conti*, 15–16.

6. See Fritz, *MGG*, *Personenteil*, 9:1203–1204 (2003).

7. Joseph displayed "a perfect keyboard [technique], played the flute, and practiced many other instruments with charm." Quoted from the article by Othmar Wessely in *MGG*, 7:183 (1958). About Joseph as a flutist, see also Hantsch, *Reichsvizekanzler*, 41–42.

8. For more about Joseph's musical activities, see Adler, "Die Kaiser Ferdinand III.," 269–71; and Somerset, "The Habsburg Emperors," 204–15.

9. See Lindgren, "Count Rudolf Franz Erwein von Schönborn," 264 and n37.

10. Wessely, in *MGG*, 7:183 (1958).

11. For a catalog of Joseph I's compositions, see Fritz, *MGG*, *Personenteil*, 9:1204 (2003). See also Lindgren, "A Bibliographic Scrutiny," 122. The MGG list does not include the Italian cantata *Presso allo stuol pomposo*, perhaps by Joseph, in the manuscript D-Bsb, Mus. ms. 30186; see chap. 7. About another cantata possibly by Joseph, see also chap. 7. A selection of Joseph's works is published in Adler, *Musikalische Werke*, 1:299–328, 2:227–52, 272–73.

12. Concerning Austrian cultural and intellectual history of the late seventeenth and early eighteenth centuries, see Mayer and Kaindl, *Geschichte und Kulturlebens Österreichs*, 2:253–65; Kann, *A Study*, 1–136; Hennings, *Das barocke Wien*, vols. 1 and 2; and Ingrao, *The Habsburg Monarchy*, 122–26.

13. About Burnacini, see Harald Zielske in *MGG*, *Personenteil*, 3:1317–19 (2000); and Biach-Schiffmann, *Giovanni und Ludovico Burnacini*; concerning the Theater auf der Cortina, see Klein, "Die Schauplätze der Hofoper"; and Hadamowsky, "Barocktheater," 34–37.

14. Klein, "Die Schauplätze der Hofoper," 372. The remodeling of the Komödienhaus appears to have been Francesco Galli-Bibiena's earliest commission in Vienna; a fire severely damaged the Komödienhaus on 16 July 1699, but it was renovated and reopened on 28 January 1700.

15. See Schenk, "Die Anfänge des Wiener Kärntnertortheaters"; and Klein, "Die Schauplätze der Hofoper," 374. At first the theater was used for comedies by foreign troupes and for traditional Austrian entertainments such as the Stegreifkomödien and the Hanswurst-Stücken, but from 1728 this theater also served as a public opera house.

16. Concerning Ferdinando and Francesco Galli-Bibiena, see Zielske (with Sergio Martinotti) in *MGG*, *Personenteil*, 2:1579–83 (1999); and Mayor, *The Bibiena Family*.

17. See Klein, "Die Schauplätze der Hofoper," 372–73; and Hadamowsky, "Barocktheater," 41.

18. See Kann, *A Study*, 42–43.

19. See, for example, Forment, "'La terra, il cielo e l'inferno'"; Etscheit, "Händels *Rodelinda*"; Freeman, "Opera without Drama"; Schnitzler, "The Sacred Dramatic Music," 126–89. For earlier studies of the libretto at Vienna, see Salzer, "Il teatro allegorico"; and Salzer, "Teatro italiano."

20. For the broad definition of the term *chapel* used in this book, see chap. 1.

21. Köchel, *Die kaiserliche Hof-Musikkapelle*, 10.

22. Schenk, *Kleine Wiener Musikgeschichte*, 81.

23. See Köchel, *Die kaiserliche Hof-Musikkapelle*, 65.

24. Köchel, *Die kaiserliche Hof-Musikkapelle*, 31.

25. For more about genre designations for baroque opera, see Haas, "Geschichtliche Opernbezeichnungen"; Wellesz, "Die Opern und Oratorien," 12–13; Hueber, "Die Wiener Opern," 16–17.

26. Hadamowsky, "Barocktheater," 98.

27. The Badia composition is not listed by any of the modern chroniclers (Köchel, Weilen, Hadamowsky, Bauer, or Deutsch) of Viennese dramatic works performed during the baroque era, perhaps because the only known source is preserved at D-Dl.

28. Köchel, *Johann Josef Fux*.

29. Weilen, *Zur Wiener Theatergeschichte*, no. 573.

30. Deutsch, "Das Repertoire," 385.

31. Lindgren, "A Bibliographic Scrutiny," 113n122.

32. The inventory is preserved at the Hofkammerarchiv in Vienna: HKA, Nö HA, 60/A/32.

33. Dated 14 November 1732, the holograph (A-Wgm, VI 16570 [A 404], no. 3) indicates that the cantata was performed "per servigio di tavola."

34. For more about this work, see Lindgren, "A Bibliographic Scrutiny," 113.

35. Hadamowsky, "Barocktheater," 40.

36. See chap. 9. Wessely, in MGG, 7:col. 182 (1958), indicates that Joseph participated in these Badia cantatas as a singer; however, an examination of the score reveals that all four cantatas were intended for specific sopranos. Since there are no other references to Joseph as a singer who participated in court entertainments, his participation as a flutist in Badia's cantatas seems more plausible.

37. See Hadamowsky, "Barocktheater," 60.

38. Especially in the 1680s and 1690s such aristocratic and Habsburg family performances were quite common, and Leopold himself wrote several dramatic works for Carnival season that involved members of the nobility and the imperial household. With Leopold's advancing age, the marriages of his daughters, the entrance of Joseph and Charles into world politics, and the exigencies of the War of the Spanish Succession, the Habsburg family presentations seem to have become much more rare after 1700. After this time Leopold also seems to have ended his activity as a composer.

39. See Lindgren, "A Bibliographic Scrutiny," 96–97.

40. Page, "Sirens on the Danube."

41. Köchel, *Die kaiserliche Hof-Musikkapelle*, 68.

42. See the article on Antonio Maria Bononcini by Lindgren in NG, 3:877.

43. Köchel, *Die kaiserliche Hof-Musikkapelle*, 68.

44. Lindgren, "A Bibliographic Scrutiny," 975.

45. Lindgren, "A Bibliographic Scrutiny," 972–77, 1047–49.

46. Köchel, *Die kaiserliche Hof-Musikkapelle*, 66–68.

47. During the reign of Charles VI, Caldara wrote a substantial number of cantatas for bass, but cantatas for tenor remained extremely rare. The possibility that a cantata written in soprano clef was occasionally transposed down an octave and sung by a tenor cannot be excluded.

48. For a detailed list of singers employed at the Habsburg court during the reign of Joseph I, their years of service, and the dramatic works in which they performed, see Glüxam, "Verzeichnis."

49. The remark about Bononcini's primacy as a cello virtuoso was published in the anonymous English translation of François Raguenet's *Paralele* (Paris, 1702): *A Comparison between the French and Italian Musick and Operas*, 51n35. Gasparini's praise appeared

in his *L'armonico pratico al cimbalo* (Venice, 1708); see the English translation by Stillings, *The Practical Harmonist*, 94.

50. See Lindgren's article on Antonio Maria Bononcini in NG, 3:866.

51. The cantata comes down in at least two sources: D-Bsb, Mo. 780/20, and D-DS, Mus. ms. 1046.

52. For more about Matteis, see McCredie, "Nicholas Matteis"; and Nettl, "An English Musician."

53. See, for example, the first five of eight Conti cantatas in A-Wn, 17593.

54. See Weilen, *Zur Wiener Theatergeschichte*, nos. 522, 545; and Seifert, *Die Oper am Wiener Kaiserhof*, 576, 581.

55. For more about Cupeda, see the article by Seifert in NGDO, 1:1029 (1992).

56. See S. Simonetti in DBI, 9:317 (1967). See also Lindgren in NGDO, 1:443 (1992).

57. Nava, "P. A. Bernardoni e il melodramma," 109–10.

58. Simonetti, DBI, 9:318 (1967): "Di scarso valore poetico, ad eccezione di qualche canzonetta, che sembra anticipare per melodiosità e spigliatezza di ritmo le perfette 'ariette' del melodramma metastasiano."

59. Concerning Giralomo Frigimelica Roberti (1653–1732), see Over, "'. . . sotto l'Ombra,'" 271–73.

60. See the article on Stampiglia by Lindgren in NG, 24:272.

61. About the librettos of late seventeenth-century Viennese dramatic works, see Wellesz, "Die Opern und Oratorien," 93–97; concerning the librettos of the sacred music of Draghi, see Schnitzler, "The Sacred Dramatic Music," 126–89.

62. Burrows, "The Cantatas of Antonio Cesti," 22.

63. A-Wn, 17591, no. 5, aria 1: "Nice crudel, perchè / stillar mi vuoi nel sen / il barbaro velen di gelosia? Sospira sol per te / quest'alma e questo cor, / ma il tuo novello ardor / radoppia il mio dolor, la doglia mia."

64. A-Wn, 17607, no. 4, aria 1: "Più barbaro martire / chi mai provò / di quel che soffre un cor per lontananza. / Provarlo, e non morire / quando si può / miracolo è d'Amor, non è costanza."

65. A-Wn, 17607, no. 3, aria 2: "Al tuo bel volto amante / morrà fido e costante / il povero mio cor. E andrà dicendo poi / che sol per gl'occhi tuoi / fu martire d'amor."

66. A-Wn, 17637, aria 1: "Sentimi crudo Amore, / mi toglierai la vita / ma non la libertà. / Combatterà il mio core / con la tua destra ardita / sino che spirto avrà."

67. A-Wn, 17591, no. 5, aria 1: "Al voler del bene amato / un contento è l'ubbidir. / Sembra un secolo di duolo / quel momento solo / che si lascia di servir."

68. A-Wn, 17575, no. 4, aria 1: "È pur dolce a un cor legato / il piacer di libertà, / ma il cor che fu legato / tal contento più non ha."

69. Lines of seven and eleven syllables were prescribed for oratorio recitatives by Archangelo Spagna in his *Oratorii overo melodrami sacri*, 10–11.

70. For a discussion of the poetic *canzonetta*, see Wilkins, *A History of Italian Literature*, 295–96.

71. For a discussion of the *canzonetta* form in the librettos of Draghi's sacred music, see Schnitzler, "The Sacred Dramatic Music," 184–88.

72. A-Wn, 17691, no. 9, aria 1: "Insoffribile tormento / è celar d'Amor il foco, / né poter dir per te moro; / e fra ceppi d'un crin d'oro / consumarsi a poco a poco."

73. Burrows, "The Cantatas of Antonio Cesti," 25.

7. THE COMPOSERS

1. The sections concerning Badia in chaps. 7, 8, and 9 of this book were originally written by me for NG and updated in 2011 for *Grove Music Online* published by Oxford

University Press; they appear on OxfordMusicOnline.com and are given here with the permission of the publisher. Concerning Badia's biography, see also Johann Steinecker in *MGG, Personenteil* (1999), 1:1598–1601; Nemeth, "Zur Lebensgeschichte"; and Molitor, *Biographische und kunstgeschichtliche Stoffsammlung,* no. 5. In the MGG entry, Steinecker argues that Verona rather than Venice was probably Badia's birthplace, citing an entry in the *Trauungsbuch,* where Badia is named as a native of Warona.

2. See Ademollo, *I Teatri di Roma,* 186.

3. For more about Badia's activities at Innsbruck, see Senn, *Musik und Theater,* 306–307; and Brockpähler, *Handbuch zur Geschichte,* 230–37. For details concerning the three *sepolcri,* see Senn, *Musik und Theater,* 307, 447; the librettos are preserved at A-Imf.

4. For this information, I am indebted to Eva Halfar Badura-Skoda.

5. For documents concerning Badia's Viennese appointment, see Nemeth, "Zur Lebensgeschichte," 225.

6. Nemeth, "Zur Lebensgeschichte," 226; see also Steinecker in *MGG, Personenteil,* 1:1598 (1999).

7. Nemeth, "Zur Lebensgeschichte," 225.

8. Nemeth, "Zur Lebensgeschichte," 228; for still another contemporary evaluation, see Walther, *Musikalisches Lexicon,* 65.

9. For more on Anna Maria Lisi Badia, see Nemeth, "Zur Lebensgeschichte," 227, 229–31; Köchel, *Die kaiserliche Hof-Musikkapelle,* 68, 75; Meer, *Johann Josef Fux,* 36, 63, 73; and Knaus, *Die Musiker im Archivbestand* 264 (1969): 99, 114.

10. See Fürstenau, *Zur Geschichte der Musik,* 2:71; and Brockpähler, *Handbuch der Geschichte,* 136.

11. See Allacci, *Drammaturgia,* 620; Hadamowsky, "Barocktheater," 74–97; Deutsch, "Das Repertoire," 384–87; Ferrari, "Per la bibliografia," 143–48; Weilen, *Zur Wiener Theatergeschichte,* 48–73; and the list of works given by me in NG, 2:456–57.

12. See Knaus, "Die Musiker," 14–38.

13. Wellesz, "Die Opern und Oratorien," 61–66, 133–34; about Badia's style, see also Wellesz, *Essays on Opera,* 51.

14. See the Torelli article by Anne Schnoebelen and Marc Vanscheeuwijck in NG, 25:616–17.

15. For general biographical studies of Giovanni Bononcini, see especially Lindgren, "A Bibliographic Scrutiny"; Ford, "Giovanni Bononcini"; and the article by Lindgren in NG, 3:872–77.

16. Concerning the biography of G. M. Bononcini, see Klenz, *Giovanni Maria Bononcini of Modena;* Pancaldi and Roncaglia, "Maestri di cappella"; Roncaglia, "Di insigni musicisti modenesi"; Roncaglia, *La cappella musicale,* 130–50; and Valdrighi, "I Bononcini da Modena." About G. M. Bononcini's instrumental music, see especially Barnett, *Bolognese Instrumental Music;* see also Schenk, "Osservazioni"; Newman, *The Sonata in the Baroque Era,* 144–46; and the article by me in NG, 3:870–72. Concerning G. M. Bononcini's influential modal theories, see Barnett, "Giovanni Maria Bononcini"; Barnett, *Bolognese Instrumental Music;* and Holler, *Giovanni Maria Bononcini's Musico Prattico.*

17. The confusion seems to have originated with a letter of 1686 from Giovanni to Colonna; it appears in German translation in Lipsius, *Musikerbriefe,* 1:119–20, with the incorrect date 1656.

18. For more about Giovanni's early career, see especially Ford, "Giovanni Bononcini," 695–96; Roncaglia, "L. A. Muratori"; Valdrighi, "I Bononcini da Modena"; Adelmo Damerini, "Le due 'Maddalene'"; the article by Lindgren in NG, 3:872; and Barnett, *Bolognese Instrumental Music.*

19. For a list of the fourteen libraries known to own printed copies of the *Duetti da camera,* see RISM A/I/1, 372; in addition, individual duets come down to us in as many as

seventeen manuscript copies, including the *Prachtband*. A comparison of the manuscript and printed versions reveals very few differences. I-Bc, MS X.134 contains seven *Duetti* with *passi* (ornaments) by Carlo Benati; the beginning of no. 7 appears without and with Benati's *passi* in Ferand, *Die Improvisation*, 118–22. A thematic index of all twelve *Duetti* is given in Zobeley, *Die Musikalien*, vol. 1, pt. 1, 21–22.

20. Lindgren identifies 141 solo cantatas composed in Italy before Giovanni arrived in Vienna ("Bononcini's 'agreable and easie style,'" 163).

21. Johann Wilhelm's first wife had been Archduchess Marianna, Leopold's stepsister, and his sister Eleonora Magdalena became Leopold's third wife in 1676. Alfred Ebert, discusses three letters dated 2 November 1697 from the cardinal to Johann Wilhelm (*Attilio Ariosti in Berlin*, 28). Two of these are rough drafts, and the third is an explanation of intent; all three are preserved in I-Fas. For further details, see Lindgren, "A Bibliographic Scrutiny," 52; on p. 53 Lindgren reproduces the second letter.

22. See Hueber, "Gli ultimi anni," 159. Bononcini did not go directly to Vienna. He was in Venice in February 1698, and he may have been in his native Modena during the previous month for a production of a setting of *Endimione*, possibly by Bononcini himself. See Lindgren, "A Bibliographic Scrutiny," 53–56. *Endimione* was performed at Modena during a stay there by Amalia Wilhelmina of Hanover, sister of Carlotta Felicita (wife of Duke Rinaldo I). At the time of the Modenese performance, negotiations were well under way for the marriage of Amalia to the future Emperor Joseph I. Only the libretto of the Modena version is extant; according to Lindgren, it corresponds closely to the Viennese version set by Bononcini in honor of Amalia's name day on 6 July 1706.

23. The claim is printed in Hueber, "Gli ultimi anni," 159–60.

24. The imperial order appears in Hueber, "Gli ultimi anni," 160. Hueber and Lindgren ("A Bibliographic Scrutiny," 88–92) discuss fully questions pertaining to Bononcini's salary during his first Viennese engagement (1698–1712). Like other leading musicians at the Habsburg court, Bononcini was apparently promised considerably larger sums than he ever received.

25. Hueber, "Gli ultimi anni," 159–60. Bononcini's remarks in a 1742 request addressed to Empress Maria Theresia are printed on pp. 163–65.

26. See the letter from M. A. Ziani to Emperor Charles VI on behalf of all court musicians (June 1712), which appears in Lipsius, *Musikerbriefe*, 1:128–29, and the letter from the Viennese bass G. B. Cattivelli to Giacomo Antonio Perti (I-Bc, P.144, no. 62); the pertinent passage is given by Lindgren, "A Bibliographic Scrutiny," 90.

27. The most reliable lists of dramatic works of this period appear in Lindgren, "A Bibliographic Scrutiny," 88, and the entry by him in NG, 3:874–75.

28. See the letter from Sophie Charlotte to Baron Hans Caspar von Bothmer of Hanover in Doebner, "Briefe der Königin," 10–11; for further references to Bononcini in the letters of Sophie Charlotte, see pp. 78–80. About Bononcini's stay in Berlin, see also Ebert, *Attilio Ariosti in Berlin*, 28–31. The apocryphal story of a meeting and rivalry between Bononcini and Handel at Berlin in 1698 is groundless, since Bononcini did not arrive until the end of 1701 or the beginning of 1702. The story of the Berlin rivalry appears to have originated with Mainwaring, *Memoirs of the Life*, 18, and it was frequently repeated by subsequent biographers of Handel.

29. For references to these and other artists, see Doebner, "Briefe der Königin," 78–80; and Telemann, "Autobiography," published by Johann Mattheson in his *Grundlage einer Ehren-Pforte*, 359. See Lindgren, "A Bibliographic Scrutiny," 93–101, for an annotated discussion of these and other documents related to Bononcini's Berlin residence.

30. Lindgren, "A Bibliographic Scrutiny," 96–97.

31. The paintings, along with portraits of Corelli and Pasquini, are now preserved in Sophie Charlotte's writing room at Charlottenburg. See Bose, "Ariosti und Bononcini."

32. Hadamowsky, "Barocktheater," 98, indicates that the period of mourning officially ended on 9 June 1706.

33. Lindgren, "A Bibliographic Scrutiny," 111, lists the first nine dramatic works from 1705 to 1711. Scores for all are preserved at A-Wn. Concerning the last work, *Enea in Caonia,* performed for Joseph's name day (19 March) in 1711, see Ferrari, "Per la bibliografia," 147.

34. Some details of Bononcini's personal life at Vienna have come to light. He is known to have had a *maîtresse* (perhaps a wife) who died while he was in Berlin, and a letter dated December 1702 from the Viennese bass singer G. B. Cattivelli to the composer G. A. Perti reveals Bononcini's possible involvements with two other women; see Lindgren, "A Bibliographic Scrutiny," 99. He appears to have married at some point later in his stay at Vienna, for a daughter, Anna Eleonora Mechtildis, was baptized on 21 February 1709; she died on 26 August 1711. See Hueber, "Die Wiener Opern," 7.

35. See Crescimbeni, *Comentari,* 240–41.

36. Raguenet, *Défense du paralèle,* 43–44.

37. For a list, see Lindgren, "A Bibliographic Scrutiny," 350. For a detailed discussion of the dispute between Raguenet and Jean Laurent Le Cerf de La Viéville concerning the comparative merits of Italian and French styles, see Lindgren, "Bononcini's 'agreable and easie style,'" 141–47.

38. See Stillings's English translation, p. 94, of Gasparini's *L'armonico pratico al cimbalo.*

39. Burney, *A General History,* 635–36.

40. See Selfridge-Field, *The Music of Benedetto and Alessandro Marcello.* Antonio Caldara also composed a large quantity of cantatas, but a detailed accounting of his cantatas has yet to be completed.

41. For details about the sources and chronology of Giovanni Bononcini's cantatas, see Lindgren, "Bononcini's 'agreable and easie style.'"

42. Excluding the printed compositions, some twenty-five cantatas survive in between eight and twenty-three copies. Fourteen copies of Giovanni's *Duetti da camera* (Bologna, 1691; repr., 1701) and at least twenty-six copies of the *Cantate e duetti* (London, 1721; repr., ca. 1727) are preserved. There are also numerous manuscript copies of the printed cantatas and duets.

43. It is interesting to compare Bononcini with Antonio Cesti, a leading seicento cantata composer who seems to have written few cantatas, if any, during his three-year residence at Vienna; like Bononcini, Cesti appears to have been preoccupied with the composition of large-scale dramatic works.

44. For biographical information about M. A. Ziani, see especially two articles by Antonicek: "Marc'Antonio Ziani," and "Die *Damira*-Opern." See also Saskia Maria Woyke in *MGG, Personenteil,* 17:1457–61 (2007).

45. Antonicek, "Die *Damira*-Opern," 181. Antonicek, NG, 27:812, suggests that Pietro Andrea Ziani may have been Marc'Antonio's teacher.

46. See Antonicek, "Die *Damira*-Opern," 179; and Woyke, in *MGG, Personenteil,* 17:1457 (2007).

47. Bertolotti, *Musici alla corte,* 114. According to Antonicek, NG, 27:813, "Caffi's assertion (*Storia della musica,* 1854–55) that the duke paid Ziani to give music lessons to Caldara remains unproven."

48. See Antonicek in MGG, 14:1257 (1968).

49. For a list of operas by Ziani composed before his Viennese appointment (1700), see NG, 27:813–14; and *MGG, Personenteil,* 17:1458 (2007). For more concerning Ziani's Venetian operas, see Wolff, *Die venezianische Oper,* 128–30; and Antonicek, "Die *Damira*-Opern," 182–207.

50. Köchel, *Die kaiserliche Hof-Musikkapelle,* 65.

51. At some point prior to his arrival at Vienna, Ziani had married; his wife, Ursula, died at the age of forty-two in April 1703, only one week after the death of her sixteen-year-old daughter, Margareta. In a letter of 28 July 1703 to G. A. Perti, Ziani expressed his grief; the letter is now at I-Bc. Ziani subsequently married a woman named Giacomina, probably the mother of two daughters listed among his heirs.

52. For details about dramatic works written for Vienna by Ziani, see Deutsch, Hadamowsky, Weilen, Ferrari, and Antonicek in NG, 27:814.

53. For general biographical information and documents concerning the life of Ariosti, see Lindgren in NG, 1:901–904; Ebert, *Attilio Ariosti in Berlin;* Frati, "Attilio Ottavio Ariosti"; Vicentini, "Memorie di musicisti"; Casimiri and Vicentini, "Attilio Ottavio Ariosti." Concerning Ariosti's career before he went to England in 1716, see also Lindgren, "Ariosti's London Years."

54. See Frati, "Attilio Ottavio Ariosti," 551.

55. Having noticed attributions to "Attilio Ariosti" and "Ottavio Ariosti," EitnerQ mistakenly concluded that there were actually two Ariostis, Attilio and Ottavio. Variants of the composer's first name also include "Aurelio." Attributions frequently exclude the last name; the forms "Sigr. Attilio" and "Pater Attilio" are especially common.

56. Parts are preserved at I-Bc and I-Bsp; see RISM A/I/1, 84.

57. Frati, "Attilio Ottavio Ariosti," 552, cites a letter of 18 November 1698 from Duke Carlo IV Gonzaga to Cardinal Francesco Maria de' Medici that reveals the duke's high esteem for Ariosti both as a composer and as an instrumentalist. He may have composed one act of the opera *Il Tirsi* (1696), for which Lotti and Caldara each supplied an additional act.

58. See Ebert, *Attilio Ariosti in Berlin,* 19.

59. Ebert, *Attilio Ariosti in Berlin,* 20–21.

60. In a letter of 27 March 1703 to Sophie Charlotte, the German philosopher Gottfried Leibniz offered a less than favorable estimate of Ariosti's talents: "Il peut faire seul un opéra, car il compose et fait des vers et l'une et l'autre fois passablement" (He indeed can write an opera, as he both composes and writes poetry passably). See Ebert, *Attilio Ariosti in Berlin,* appendix, letter no. 37, 90–91. However, Leibniz joined several prominent Italian clerics and noblemen in supporting Sophie Charlotte's efforts to extend Ariosti's visit to Berlin, much against the objections of the Servite order.

61. For details about the five secular dramatic works, see Ebert, *Attilio Ariosti in Berlin,* 31–37; Frati, "Attilio Ottavio Ariosti," 552–53; and Lindgren in NG, 1:902–903.

62. Ebert, *Attilio Ariosti in Berlin,* 38–62.

63. See Bose, "Ariosti und Bononcini am Berliner Hof," 55–64.

64. ES, 1:846.

65. For Ariosti's letter, see Einstein, "Italienische Musiker," 416–17; see also ES, 1:846. In the same letter, Ariosti used the opportunity to offer Johann Wilhelm a portrait. For additional letters, see Lindgren, "Six Newly Discovered Letters."

66. See ES, 1:846. Albi Rosenthal, in *MGG, Personenteil,* 1:910 (1999), indicates that the possibility that Ariosti may have been removed from his official religious position in the Servite order at some point during his sojourns in Berlin and Vienna has not been documented.

67. A facsimile of part of the letter is given by Werner Bollert in MGG, 1:625 (1949). Concerning Albergati (1663–1735) as a noble patron of music and a composer of sacred and secular music, including Italian cantatas, see Anne Schnoebelen in NG, 1:295–96. In 1687 Albergati had dedicated his *Pletro armonico,* op. 5, to Leopold I.

68. The work is a *poemetto drammatico, La Placidia* (text by Bernardoni). For further details about dramatic works written for Vienna by Ariosti during the period 1703–1709, see especially Deutsch, "Das Repertoire der Höfischen Oper," and the list by Lindgren in

NG, 1:902–903. The original version and performance of the oratorio *La Passione*, also performed at Vienna in 1709, took place at Modena in 1693; the score is preserved at I-MOe.

69. Concerning the style of Ariosti's music until 1712 and the composer's post-Viennese career, see Lindgren in NG, 1:901–902. About the composer's subsequent career in London, see Lindgren, "Ariosti's London Years," 334–48.

70. See Rosenblum, "The Viola d'amore"; Rosenblum's dating of the cantata (ca. 1690) is questionable. Copies survive in D-Bsb, Mus. ms. 780/20, and D-DS, Mus. ms. 1046. Concerning Antonio Vivaldi's possible relationship with Ariosti, see Danks, "The Influence of Attilio Ariosti." About the fifty-seven pieces for viola d'amore, see Günther Weiss, "57 unbekannte Instrumentalstücke." The manuscript that contains the pieces is S-Skma, MAB Ronr 99. Roman was a Swedish violinist and composer who studied with Ariosti and Pepusch in London during the period 1714–20; see Deutsch, *Handel*, 162.

71. For a list, see RISM A/I/1, 84.

72. Details are given by Lindgren in NG, 1:903.

73. In the appendix to the article "Ariosti's London Years," 349–51, Lindgren provides both a list of manuscripts containing Ariosti cantatas and an alphabetical list of the titles, including the twenty-three cantatas at A-Wn.

74. For general biographical studies of Antonio Maria Bononcini, see Lindgren, "A Bibliographic Scrutiny," 117–22, 133–43; the entry in NG, 3:877–79, also by Lindgren; Valdrighi, "I Bononcini da Modena," 23–67; and Valdrighi, "Cappelle, concerti e musiche."

75. See the letter of 1686 from Giovanni to Colonna, printed in German translation in Lipsius, *Musikerbriefe*, 1:119–20, where it is incorrectly attributed to Giovanni Maria Bononcini; Lipsius misread the date as 1656.

76. The score is preserved in I-Bsp, Lib.B.3. Further evidence of Antonio Maria's interest in the cello can be seen from fifteen sonatas for violoncello and basso continuo (modern edition by Lindgren in Recent Researches in the Music of the Baroque Era 77 [1996]) and from the florid obbligatos written for cantatas in A-Wn, 17607.

77. See Lindgren in "A Bibliographic Scrutiny," 27–28, and in NG, 3:877. Only the libretto is extant.

78. No references to Antonio Maria appear in the archival studies of Köchel or Knaus.

79. See Telemann, "Autobiography," 359.

80. Lindgren, "A Bibliographic Scrutiny," 98. Giovanni was undoubtedly responsible for the acceptance of other artists at Vienna, including the brothers Silvio and Nunzio Stampiglia, both librettists.

81. Lindgren, "A Bibliographic Scrutiny," 119, lists all but the earliest of the eleven dramatic works, with dates, dedicatees, and known librettists. One of these works, *La Fortuna, il Valore e la Giustitia* (4 November 1706), is a grand cantata; Lindgren includes it in the list of serenatas (NG, 3:878). Concerning Antonio Maria's first work known to have been written for Vienna, the oratorio *La Maddalena*, see Ferrari, "Per la bibliografia," 146. The performance of *La Maddalena* took place only shortly before the death of Leopold on 5 May 1705.

82. "La Maddalena. Oratorio sung at the Royal Court of Spain during the festivities celebrated by His Highness the Marquis of Pescara and Vasto, ordinary ambassador of Charles III, King of Spain, in memory of the glorious victories of the King in Catalonia with the conquest of Barcelona on the past 14 October." Quoted from Ferrari, "Per la bibliografia," 146; the libretto of *La Maddalena* is at I-Vnm.

83. Lindgren, "A Bibliographic Scrutiny," 119. Charles (1685–1740) was proclaimed Charles III of Spain at Vienna on 12 November 1703. Charles traveled from Holland and England to Portugal before conquering Barcelona on 18 October.

84. The statement is printed in Koczirz, "Exzerpte," 286–87.

85. Knaus, "Die Musiker," 32–33.

86. Nineteenth-century copies have been excluded. For details, see the list of cantatas given by Lindgren in NG, 3:878.

87. The question of conflicting Bononcini-brother attributions deserves future scrutiny. However complex the problem of ascribing individual cantatas may be, the overall question of Bononcini cantata attributions is mitigated somewhat by the limited spread of Antonio Maria's works, by a frequently helpful eighteenth-century tendency to differentiate between the two men by the use of first names, and by clear source evidence in several particular instances. On the whole, I consider cantatas ascribed simply to "Bononcini" with the list of works by the more prolific and widely known Giovanni.

88. The complete letter is printed in Montagu, *Court and Society,* 2:231–32.

89. See Harald Kümmerling, "Vorwort und Einfuhrung," in *Katalog der Sammlung Bokemeyer.* Kümmerling believes that the collection was prepared in Germany. However, Lindgren contends that many of the manuscripts belonging to the Sammlung Bokemeyer originated in England, not Germany; according to Lindgren, the appearance of these sources and the scribal style closely resemble English manuscripts of the same period, that is, shortly after 1700. It is worth noting that some of the sources do include cantatas by composers active in England at that time, including Pepusch and Giacomo Grebo.

90. Brosche, "Die musikalische Werke," 34. Brosche does not include *Presso allo stuol pomposo* in his catalog of works by Leopold; nor is it included in Guido Adler's edition, *Musikalische Werke.*

91. Copies of Bononcini's setting of *Presso allo stuol pomposo* are preserved in eight manuscripts: D-Bsb, 30197; GB-CDp, M.C.1.25; GB-Lam, MS 34; GB-Lbl, Add. 31546; GB-Lk, R.M. 24.c.17; GB-Ob, Mus.d.20 and Mus.d.22; and I-Mc, C.65.6.

92. For biographical information about Francesco Conti and the dating of his birth, see especially Williams, *Francesco Bartolomeo Conti,* 3–80.

93. See Telemann, "Autobiography," 359.

94. Köchel, *Die kaiserliche Hof-Musikkapelle,* 70.

95. See Williams, *Francesco Bartolomeo Conti,* 17–23, concerning the composer's visit to London, where Conti contributed at least the overture and five arias to the *dramma per musica Clotilda,* a pasticcio. The arias were probably taken from the first opera Conti composed for Vienna, *Clotilde* (1706), but the music of this work is lost; on p. 85 Williams states that the overture to the pasticcio was initially used for Conti's first Viennese oratorio, *Il Gioseffo* (1706).

96. Williams, *Francesco Bartolomeo Conti,* 43–44.

97. Williams, *Francesco Bartolomeo Conti,* 25.

98. About Tosi, see the entry by Malcolm Boyd and John Rosselli in NG, 25:646–47.

99. Köchel, *Die kaiserliche Hof-Musikkapelle,* 66.

100. Concerning Johann Wilhelm as patron, see Einstein, "Italienische Musiker," 398–424.

101. The original edition (Bologna, 1723) was translated into English by J. E. Galliard as *Observations on the Florid Song.*

102. For a list of libraries containing manuscripts of Tosi's cantatas and arias, see NG, 25:647.

103. Burney, *A General History,* 2:824.

104. Tagliavini, MGG, 13:582 (1966).

8. REPERTOIRE AND SOURCES

1. For a facsimile of part of the Ariosti letter, see the entry for Ariosti by Werner Bollert in MGG, 1:625 (1949); for more about Albergati, see Anne Schnoebelen and Marc Vanscheeuwijck, in NG, 1:295–96.

2. The Bononcini manuscript is A-Wn, 17579; the Lotti collection is A-Wn, 18776.

3. Supp. Mus. 2452 is entitled "Catalogo Delle Compositioni Musicali. Continente Oratori Sacri, Componimenti da Camera, Serenate, et Opere Composte, e rappresentate, sotto il Gloriosissimo Governo della S:ª Ces:a Real Catt:a M:ˢᵗᵃ di Carlo VI. Imperadore de' Romani sempre Augustto. Dall'A:° 1712. Con un' Appendice in fine, d'alcune Compositioni rappresentate in Tempo, che regnarono gl'Aug:mi Imp: Leopoldo, e Giuseppe I:ᵐⁱ di sempre gloriosa Memoria: consistente di Sepolcri, Oratori Sacri, Componomenti da Camera, et Opere. Compresovi le altre Simili Composizioni Musicali dedicate humilissimamente alla stessa Ces:ª e Real Cattolica Maestà di Carlo VI."

4. Supp. Mus. 2454 is the "Catalogo delle Opere, Serenade, Cantate, ed Oratori le quali Sua Imperiale Reale Maestà L'Imperadore Giuseppe II. Si compiaque di trasmetter nell'Archivio Musicale, dell' Imp: Reale Capella, L'Anno MDCCLXXVIII." Supp. Mus. 2455 is the "Catalogo delle Opere, Serenate, Cantate, Oratorii, Messe, Concerti, Sinfonie, e Partite le quali Sua Imp: Reale Masestà L'Imperadore Giuseppe II. Si compiaquè di trasmetter nell'Archivio di Musica della Imperiale Reale Capella. MDCCLXXVIII."

5. See Gericke, *Der Wiener Musikalienhandel*, 16–20.

6. For a detailed chronology and discussion of Giovanni Bononcini's vast cantata output, see Lindgren, "Bononcini's 'agreable and easie style,'" 135–75. Lindgren identifies 270 works for solo voice, 11 for solo voice with obbligato instruments, and 13 vocal duets. He does not include thirty-four works with conflicting attributions and twenty-eight serenatas, at least one of which (*Egeria, Dorinda e Amarilli*) is named in the source as a *cantata a 3*. This essay provides important revisions to Lindgren's list of Giovanni's cantatas in NG, 3:875–86. Lindgren identifies thirty-eight solo cantatas and four vocal duets by Antonio Maria Bononcini (NG, 3:878). At least seventeen, or nearly half, of the solo cantatas include obbligato instrumental accompaniment. The vocal duet *Clori dal colle al prato* is attributed to Antonio in three manuscripts and to Giovanni in two; Lindgren includes it only in the list of Antonio's works. Two cantatas preserved only in D-SHs, Mus. B.1:3, *Occhi del mio tesor* and *Quando lieta saria*, may have been composed for Vienna, but they are not found in core Viennese sources. Similarly, Anotnio's *Con non inteso affanno* may be of Viennese origins, but this cantata is preserved in only one source, F-Pn, X 118B. See Lindgren, "Bononcini's 'agreeable and easie style,'" 141n. For a detailed inventory of chamber cantatas and duets by Ariosti, see the list compiled by Lindgren in NG, 1:903, and in the same author's article "Ariosti's London Years," 350–51. Of the ninety-seven cantatas identified by Lindgren, three appear to be lost; there are three conflicting attributions with Giovanni Bononcini, one with Francesco Conti, and one with Luigi Mancia.

7. EitnerQ lists Badia's *Diana rappacificata con Venere e con Amore* (1700) as a cantata, but it is actually a *trattenimento musicale* and thus a stage work. Also omitted here is a one-act secular dramatic work probably intended for at least rudimentary stage performance: the *musica da camera* entitled *Il commun giubilo del mondo* (1699).

8. Copies at A-Wn, B-Bc, D-Dl, D-W, GB-Lbl, I-Bc, and I-Rsc. A copy of the print formerly in A-Wm and cited by EitnerQ appears to be lost; see Riedel, *Das Musikarchiv im Minoritenkonvent*, 110. Individual cantatas from this print are also found in several manuscript copies: all twelve survive in a mid-eighteenth-century manuscript at GB-Lgc; eleven are found in a manuscript at D-SHs; seven are in a source at D-MEIr; and one is preserved in a manuscript at D-Bsb. For details, see the index of cantata text incipits and sources (appendix A). No date of publication appears in the printed copies; the year 1699 is given by Johann Steinecker, the author of the article for Badia in *MGG, Personenteil*, vol. 1 (1999), and by Emanuel Scobel, who penned the article for the Nuremberg publisher Johann Christoph Weigel in *MGG, Personenteil*, vol. 17 (2007).

9. Torbé, "Die weltliche Solokantate," 48b.

10. *Già tra l'onde* comes down in versions by Giovanni Bononcini (in I-Bc, DD51; the same setting is attributed to Antonio Maria in D-Mbs, 696, but with the incipit *Già fra*

l'onde), "Ant.^{io} R." (in D-Bsb, Mus. ms. 30186), and Jakob Greber (in D-Bsb, a Grasnick collection, according to Alfred Wotquenne's card catalog of Italian cantatas, now owned by B-Bc). *Augellin vago e canoro* is found in a Gasparini setting (in D-Bsb, Mus. ms. 30182), and *Sapesse il core almen* was also composed by Nicola Fago (copies in D-Bsb, Mus. ms. 30197, and D-MEIr, Ed 1091 = 82c).

11. I have not included A-Wn, 17588, which preserves one short stage work with three *balli* (*L'Oracolo d'Apollo*, 1707), or A-Wgm, VI 27694 (Q 3710), which contains another brief dramatic composition, an undated serenata with the text incipit *Infelice mia sorte*. See Lindgren, "A Bibliographic Scrutiny," 473, 844.

12. See Lindgren, "Bononcini's 'agreable and easie style,'" n. 131. "Pupilette vezzo-sette," the first aria of *Rompi l'arco* (A-Wn, 17567, no. 7), is also preserved in GB-CDp, M.C.1.5.a.

13. See Haas, *Die estensischen Musikalien*.

14. Lindgren, "Bononcini's 'agreable and easie style,'" 163–65, lists all six cantatas in VI 15496 (Q 4562), VI 15497 (Q 4563), VI 15498 (Q 4564), and VI 15499 (Q 4565) under the rubric "149 works composed in 1692–98 (= phase 2, in Rome and Naples)." The copies are marked with an "R," indicating that they once belonged to Archduke Rudolph of Austria (1788–1831), the patron of Beethoven.

15. Lindgren, "A Bibliographic Scrutiny," 119, includes the grand cantata in MS 17586, *La Fortuna, il Valore, e la Giustitia* (A-Wn, 17586), in his list of dramatic works by Antonio Maria.

16. An incomplete copy of Antonio Maria's *Ecco Amor che mi segue*, found in its entirety in MS 17637, is preserved in the nineteenth-century Molitor manuscript A-Wn, 19242, vol. 1, no. 24; it begins with the second recitative, "Periglioso è il cimento." This source is missing at A-Wn.

17. A copy is preserved in GB-Lk, R.M. 23.f.4.

18. Theophil Antonicek and Jennifer Williams Brown, the authors of the M. A. Ziani article in NG, 27:814, list "Other secular cants. and arias" in D-MÜs, GB-Lam, GB-Lbl, I-BGc, and I-MOe that I have not yet seen.

19. These two works are the *accademie* of 1707; see Antonicek and Williams in NG, 27:814. The lengthy *cantata per servizio di camera* entitled *L'Ercole, vincitor dell'invidia* (A-Wn, 17570) has been included here.

20. Ziani's cantata *Aquila generosa* has a text that probably honored a member of the imperial family. The collection containing this cantata (GB-Lbl, Add. 34056) was prepared at Rome in 1709; it contains cantatas by composers active mainly in Italy at the beginning of the eighteenth century. The year in which Ziani actually composed *Aquila generosa* and the specific occasion for which he wrote it remain unclear. Two Ziani cantatas that probably did not originate at Vienna are *Stravaganze d'amor io non v'intendo?* and *Bei labri eccovi un cor*. The former is found in A-Wn, E.M. 178, and the latter comes down in I-MOe, Mus. G. 259. The attribution of *Bei labri* to M. A. Ziani is questionable; the cantata may prove to be a composition by P. A. Ziani.

21. A-Wn, 17575, no. 1 (*Oh miseria d'amante core*) is found also in D-Bsb, Mus. ms. 30188, and in D-SHs, Mus B.1:3. No. 4 (*È pur dolce a un cor*) is also preserved in A-Wn, E.M. 178, and no. 9 (*Mi convien soffrir in pace*) appears in D-Bsb, Mus. ms. 30074. The concordance for no. 11 is in D-Bsb, Mus. ms. 30197, where this cantata (*Sia con me Fillide irata*) appears as no. 2 on pp. 6–10; in the *Tavola* prepared by the main scribe at the front of the manuscript, this cantata appears to be grouped with no. 1, attributed to Fago.

22. A-Wn, 17591, no. 8 (*Cieco Nume alato Arciero*) also appears in B-Bc, 15153, pp. 220–22, a nineteenth-century German copy made from D-Bsb, Mus. ms. 30212.

23. There are actually two Bononcini settings. One survives only in I-MOe, Mus. F. 99; the other comes down in at least nine copies: D-Bsb, Mus. ms. 30188; D-Mbs, 695; GB-Cfm,

32 G 20; GB-Lam, MS 127; GB-Lbl, Add. 14228 (two copies) and Add. 31518; GB-Ob, Mus. Sch. d. 223; and I-Fc, B.2376.

24. The six anonymous cantatas in A-Wn, 18320, may date from the first decade of the eighteenth century or from the period shortly after the death of Joseph I; the internal evidence found in this manuscript leaves the question of dating open to future investigation.

25. Lindgren, "Vienna, the 'natural centro,'" 367n12.

26. The single source found in each of five of these libraries (B-Bc, D-W, GB-Lbl, I-Bc, and I-Rsc) is a copy of Badia's printed collection *Tributi armonici* (Nuremberg, between 1699 and 1704). Two other extant copies of the print are housed at A-Wn and D-Dl.

27. Many Caldara cantatas and other compositions written for Vienna from 1712 until his death in 1736 come down in holographs as well as in archival copies, providing rich source material for future studies.

28. The catalog dates from approximately 1820. It is incomplete and has many additions by men such as Sonnleithner, Pohl, Geissler, and Mandyczewski.

29. See Schaal, "Die Autographen." Schaal lists only one Ziani composition, a motet, in his inventory of works that were actually owned by Fuchs himself; see p. 190. For more details about Fuchs's activities as a manuscript collector, see Schaal, *Quellen und Forschungen.*

30. See RISM A/I/1, 193; and Vogel et al., *Bibliografia della musica italiana,* 1, no. 203. The observations given here about Badia's print are based upon a study of the copy D-W, 9 Musica div. For a list of the seven libraries that house printed copies of the *Tributi armonici,* see n. 8 above. A small number of manuscripts preserve individual cantatas; for details, see appendix A.

31. Concerning the Weigel family, see Emanuel Scobel in MGG, *Personenteil,* 17:654 (2007); and Wolfgang Spindler in NG, 27:214.

32. See Hadamowsky, "Barocktheater," 46–48. Concerning Beduzzi (1675–1735) and his long service as a decorative artist, stage designer, and painter in Habsburg lands, see Turner, *The Dictionary of Art,* 3:488.

33. The date given in the biographical articles for Badia in *MGG, Personenteil,* vol. 1 (2001), DBI, ES, and *LaMusicaD,* and in the article on Johann Christoph Weigel in *MGG, Personenteil,* vol. 17 (2007) is 1699; in the 1949 MGG entry for Badia, Eva Halfar Badura-Skoda indicates that the year of publication was "wahrscheinlich 1699."

34. Vogel et al., *Bibliografia della musica italiana,* 1, no. 203.

35. MGG, 14:375 (1968).

36. For more about copyists at the Habsburg court in the first third of the eighteenth century, see Bennett, "A Little-Known Collection," 274n25, 278. Gericke, *Der Wiener Musikalienhandel,* 102–109, gives information about court and commercial copyists active in Vienna in the eighteenth century, but it is unclear whether any of them was employed by Leopold or Joseph.

37. A preliminary list of peripheral cantata sources with music by the core composers would include three sources from D-SHs (Mus B.1:1, B.1:2, and B.1:3); four manuscripts from A-Wgm (VI 44 [Q 2679], VI 15496 [Q 4562], VI 15498 [Q 4564], and VI 15499 [Q 4565]) and one from D-DS (Mus. ms. 46); at least five from D-Bsb (Mus. mss. 30074, 30103, 30186, 30188, and 30197); three from D-MEIr (Ed 82, Ed, 109i = 82c, and Ed 123m = 82d); one from F-Pn (Vm7.2371); one from GB-Lbl (Add. 34056); two from GB-Lgc (G. Mus. 400 and 401); and one from S-L (Kat. Wenster Litt. Ä Nr. 1). The list will undoubtedly grow, but these eighteen manuscripts form a basic checklist for future investigation.

38. For bringing to my attention the three manuscripts in Sondershausen and a related source in I-MOe (Mus. F. 99), I am grateful to Lowell Lindgren.

39. See Lindgren, "Bononcini's 'agreable and easie style,'" n. 140.

40. For example, the soprano clefs resemble those found in manuscripts copied during the reign of Joseph I: they are angular and box-like, with the top half set back from the

bottom. The soprano clefs of the period after the interregnum are consistently more flowing, less angular.

41. Two are in a source of English origins, A-Wn, 17748; two in A-Wn, E.M. 178; one in A-Wgm, VI 15497 (Q 4563); and one in A-Wn, SA 67.A.25. One of the concordances in E.M. 178, *Peno e l'alma fedele*, is attributed to Albinoni there. The cantata in SA 67.A.25, *Anche i tronchi, anche le rupi*, was not copied by one of the Viennese professional scribes active during Giovanni's first residency in Vienna and may have been composed by the composer after he returned to Vienna in 1736.

42. Lindgren, "Bononcini's 'agreable and easie style,'" 169–70, names sixty-nine works composed during the period 1692–1711—in other words, during the years in which Giovanni was active in Rome, Vienna, and Berlin. Ascertaining precisely which of these cantatas were composed for each of the three courts remains a complex and difficult challenge for future research.

43. See Ladd, "The Solo Cantatas," 283.

44. Concerning D-MEIr, Ed 109i = 82c and the conflicting attributions for *Amor che far degg'io*, see Bennett, "A Little-Known Collection," 278, 294, 301.

45. For further details concerning these three Meiningen manuscripts, see Bennett, "A Little-Known Collection," 278, 293–301.

46. For a thematic index of cantatas by Mancini, see Wright, "The Secular Cantatas," 309–430. In the entry on Giovanni Bononcini in NG, 3:875–76, Lindgren provides a list of first lines of the composer's cantatas known to him. The first lines of the cantatas in MSS 17576 and 17748 are also given by Mantuani.

47. In 1705 Lotti published an enlarged version of this collection and dedicated it to Joseph I and his sons and successors; see RISM A/I/5, 364, for a list of extant copies of the print.

48. For citations of Viennese performances of dramatic works by these and other Italians of the early eighteenth century, see Bauer, Deutsch, Hadamowsky, and Weilen.

49. These two *accademie* with texts by Bernardoni are the *Introduzione per musica al problema d'un accademia* and the *Introduzione per musica per una altra accademia;* see Antonicek in NG, 27:814. Seifert, *Akademien am Wiener Kaiserhof,* 220, discusses briefly the two *accademie* of 1706 but does not mention the lost *accademie* of 1707.

50. Torbé, "Die weltliche Solo-Kantate," 48b, indicates that a search in 1920 by the librarian of A-Wgm, Eusebius Mandyczewski, failed to turn up the autograph of *Troppo conosco, o Filli* (MS VI 13377). Antonicek, in MGG, 14:1259 (1968), reports that the cantata still existed in an autograph copy at A-Wgm, but a thorough search by me in the spring of 1971 again failed to produce the manuscript.

9. STYLE OVERVIEW

1. This chapter is revised and expanded by permission of the publishers from "The Italian Cantata in Vienna, 1700–1711: An Overview of Stylistic Traits," in *Antonio Caldara: Essays on His Life and Times,* ed. Brian W. Pritchard (Farnham: Ashgate, 1987), 183–211. Copyright © 1987.

2. Wellesz, "Die Opern und Oratorien," 58.

3. See Hadamowsky, "Barocktheater," 21.

4. For the important distinction between a *Devisenarie* and a motto aria, see the article "Devise" by Thomas Braatz (15 October 2005) at the website http://www.bach-cantatas.com/Term/Terms-7.htm.

5. Obbligato instruments are found in about one-third of the cantatas written for Vienna. In contrast, fewer than 10 percent of the cantatas by Alessandro Scarlatti include obbligato or orchestral parts, while another composer active at Naples, Francesco Mancini,

drew upon concertizing instruments for only about 5 percent of his chamber cantatas and duets. See Wright, "The Secular Cantatas," 40–41, 106.

6. Fixed patterns of alternating recitatives and arias became the norm in cantatas by composers active throughout Italy during the early years of the eighteenth century. Wright, "The Secular Cantatas," 43, 67, indicates, for example, that schemes such as R–A–R–A were extremely common at Naples from about 1700.

7. For this information I am indebted to Myron Rosenblum.

8. Concerning the use of trumpet in orchestral introductions, see Brown, "The Trumpet Overture." In Table 2–3, "Trumpet Overtures to Dramatic Works, 1685–1762," p. 20, Brown does not include Badia's *La Pace, e Marte supplicanti.*

9. Concerning the use of this term in preference to the pejorative nineteenth-century term *recitativo secco,* see Heartz, foreword to the edition of Mozart's *Idomeneo,* xxvi.

10. *A tempo* sections at the ends of recitatives were especially common at Naples in cantatas by composers such as Nicola Fago and Francesco Mancini; see Wright, "The Secular Cantatas," 54, 112.

11. Tosi, *Observations,* 113–14.

12. Tosi, *Observations,* 111–12.

13. Concerning the term *continuum,* see La Rue, *Guidelines for Style Analysis,* 90.

14. At Naples the *devise* beginnings disappeared altogether after about 1725; see Wright, "The Secular Cantatas," 56.

15. One of the seminal figures of the late baroque era, Alessandro Scarlatti, did not adopt the da capo plan consistently for his opera and cantata arias until after about 1697 (curiously, at exactly the time da capo arias were becoming popular in Vienna), although three-part schemes had become common already in the Stradella generation. See Boyd, "Form and Style," 19.

10. ASPECTS OF FORM

1. The style analytical approach used in chapters 10–12 is based upon La Rue, *Guidelines for Style Analysis.*

2. While the da capo aria was almost exclusively monothematic at Vienna in the first decade of the eighteenth century, bithematic structures were beginning to appear at Naples about the same time. Thus in arias by composers like Fago and Mancini, A and B sections sometimes presented contrasting themes. After about 1715 monothematic arias were almost entirely superseded by polythematic designs; see Wright, "The Secular Cantatas," 45.

3. In most Viennese arias an actual modulation *to* the dominant takes place in the middle of A.

4. For the symbols representing sequence, coloratura, and *Fortspinnung* I am indebted to Lynch, "Opera in Hamburg," 2:303.

5. See La Rue, "Bifocal Tonality."

6. In MS 17575 several accidentals essential for melodic or harmonic minor are missing; in example 10.10 they are added above the pitches. In the original, the rhythm for the last beat of measure 9 reads ♪ 𝅘𝅥𝅯𝅘𝅥𝅯𝅘𝅥𝅮; I have altered it to ♪ 𝅘𝅥𝅯𝅘𝅥𝅮 because of insufficient text syllables. In simplifying the melody I have taken harmonic as well as melodic considerations into account.

7. See, for example, the end of the last vocal section of the aria "But Who May Abide the Day of His Coming?" (*Messiah,* no. 6). Here, as in Bononcini's "Pena e soffri," the exciting penultimate phrase ends abruptly with a deceptive cadence (i $^6_4$–V $^7_?$); likewise, a complete articulation precedes the concluding vocal phrase, which is elided with the ritornello. Hueber, "Die Wiener Opern," 240–56, contends that Bononcini's music was the principal influence upon Handel's mature style.

8. The complete separation of the climactic penultimate phrase from the broad final one can be cited as a characteristic of the mature Handelian style. Often the penultimate phrase ends with a deceptive cadence. The broadening of the last phrase may be achieved by hemiola (*Messiah*, no. 41: "Let Us Break Their Bonds Asunder"); by a decrease of surface-rhythm activity (*Messiah*, no. 44: "Hallelujah"); by a written-in adagio (*Messiah*, no. 6: "But Who May Abide the Day of His Coming?"); or by a combination of slower surface rhythm plus a written-in adagio (*Messiah*, no. 53: "Amen").

11. MELODY, HARMONY, AND RHYTHM

1. About the first prima donnas to become regular members of the imperial chapel, see chap. 6.

2. The use of high c (c3) in secular cantatas composed before 1710 appears to be extremely rare. Handel, for example, does not require such a high pitch in his cantatas, but he does require c3 in Edilia's aria "Proverai" from *Almira* (Hamburg, 1705). The use of such a high pitch may represent a regional taste north of the Alps or simply indicate that an aria was composed for a specific singer. Pitch differences in various European centers may also be relevant.

3. The use of violins as the lowest line was evidently common in French baroque music. For a recent study of the use of violins as the bass line, see Deborah Kauffman, "*Violins en basse* as Musical Allegory," in JM (2006), 153–85.

13. CONCLUSION

1. See Anthony Hicks, "Handel," in NG, 10:749.

2. See the critical commentary concerning the cantata's origins by Percy Robinson and Reinhard Strohm on pp. xix–xx of the Halle Handel Edition of *Echeggiate, festeggiate*, ser. 5, vol. 4, ed. Hans J. Marx (1995), 75–116. A facsimile is given on p. xxv; text and translations (English and German) are given on pp. xxxvii–xl.

3. See Köchel, *Johann Josef Fux*, 315–16.

4. Köchel, *Johann Josef Fux*, 10.

5. The letter is preserved at A-Ws; for a German translation, see La Mara, *Musikbriefe aus fünf Jahrhunderten*, 1:128–29.

6. Antonicek, "Die *Damira*-Opern," 180.

7. See Eberhard Preussner, *Die musikalische Reisen des Herrn von Uffenbach* (Kassel, 1949), 66.

8. *Il sacrificio di Berenice* is preserved in A-Wn, MS 17675.

9. Hueber, *Die Wiener Opern*, 7.

10. For Count Molard's suggestions, see Köchel, *Johann Josef Fux*, 316–20; and Köchel, *Die kaiserliche Hof-Musikkapelle*, 7, 40. For a list of musicians and the salaries they were to receive, see Köchel's *Johann Josef Fux*, 320–22. In practice the basic salaries were not always adhered to strictly, even after the court adopted Molard's recommendations. Fux's salary was greatly augmented simply by assigning several titles to him; see Köchel's *Johann Josef Fux*, 299–301.

11. In the years following his departure from Vienna, Bononcini was to apply repeatedly for payment of back salary and eventually for full reinstatement at the Habsburg court. He had some success in acquiring part of his back salary, but he actually never received all the money owed to him. For further details, see Koczirz, *Excerpte aus den Hofmusikakten*, 286–87; Lindgren, "A Bibliographic Scrutiny," 123–28; and Lindgren, "Vienna, the 'natural centro,'" 369–70.

12. In his autobiography, Gottfried Heinrich Stölzel stated that he became acquainted with Antonio Maria at Rome in 1714. The autobiography is printed in Mattheson's *Grundlage einer Ehren-Pforte;* Stölzel's reference to Antonio Maria appears on p. 345.

13. For further details about Conti's salaries and his troubles with the Finance Ministry, see Williams, *Francesco Bartolomeo Conti,* 32–33.

14. In the article on Stampiglia by Lindgren in NG, 24:272, the author adds that "Stampiglia retained the title of imperial poet when he returned to Italy, and he received commissions mainly from Viennese diplomats during his final years in Rome (?1718–22) and Naples (1722–25)."

15. The number of commissions Badia received for large dramatic works also declined drastically after the accession of Charles VI.

16. Concerning this manuscript, see also Lindgren, "Bononcini's 'agreable and easie style,'" 136n5, 168.

17. See the article on Caldara by Brian Pritchard in NG, 4:820. Pritchard indicates that Caldara probably petitioned Charles for the position as Kapellmeister, but by the time he arrived in Vienna, Ziani had already secured this appointment, and Fux had been assured of the post as assistant Kapellmeister.

18. The autograph copy of Caldara's *Io soffrirò tacendo* is found in D-Bsb, Mus. ms. autogr. Caldara A.10. The composer's *Arda il mio petto amante olocausto fedel* differs textually and musically from Giovanni Bononcini's *Arde il mio petto amante e nasce il foco,* found in MS 17748 at A-Wn.

19. See Sven Hansell in NG, 8:882.

20. The work list in NG, 8:883, includes five cantatas in addition to *Di quel sguardo fatal*. Possible further evidence of Fiorè's efforts as a cantata composer for Vienna may be seen from a cantata preserved at D-MEIr; this cantata, *Dite perchè begl'occhi,* is the first in a volume of thirteen cantatas, including works by Badia, Giovanni Bononcini, Alessandro Scarlatti, and anonymous composers. The inclusion of a Fiorè cantata with several by Badia and Bononcini suggests that the work predates 1715. See Bennett, "A Little-Known Collection," 264, 278.

21. Carrying out a correspondence with archivists in various European capitals, Hans Volkmann was able to construct a two-volume biography, *Emanuel d'Astorga* (Leipzig, 1911, 1919), which has served as the basis for Astorga research for nearly a century. Studies by Frank Walker ("Emanuele d'Astorga and a Neapolitan Librettist," MMR 86 [1951]: 90–96), Ottavio Tiby ("Emanuele d'Astorga: Aggiunte e correzioni da apportare alle ricerche del prof. Hans Volkmann," IMSCR V: Utrecht 1952, 198–403), Karen S. Ladd ("The Solo Cantatas of Emanuele d'Astorga," Ph.D. diss., Ohio State University, 1982), and Roberto Pagano (*Scarlatti Alessandro e Domenico, due vite in una* [Milan, 1985]) have corrected and clarified many points in Volkmann's biography of Astorga and have added important new information. For a summary of biographical information, see the article by Alfred Loewenberg and Frank Walker/Nicolò Maccavino in NG, 2:124–25.

22. NG erroneously identifies the emperor as Joseph II.

23. See Volkmann, *Emanuel d'Astorga,* 1:57; and Ursula Kirkendale, *Antonio Caldara* (Graz, 1966), 67. Concerning cantatas written by Astorga during his stay in Vienna, see Volkmann, *Emanuel d'Astorga,* 2:142, and for documents concerning his pension and debts, see 2:131–39; and Koczirz, *Excerpte aus den Hofmusikakten,* 293–94.

24. Astorga possibly traveled first to Rome but is definitely traceable in Lisbon before the end of 1721. Whether he visited London, as Hawkins asserted, has not been confirmed. The last years of his life are shrouded in mystery. Notes in the hand of Abbot Santini in volumes of Astorga cantatas now in the Santini collection at D-MÜs and at F-Pn indicate that Astorga died at Madrid in 1757, but this information has never been verified.

25. Ladd, "The Solo Cantatas," cataloged a total of 208 solo cantatas with basso continuo that have reliable attributions and 13 solo cantatas with basso continuo that have questionable or conflicting attributions. At the time of her dissertation, Ladd was unaware of a source in Meiningen (D-MEIr, Ed 82) that contains at least twelve cantatas by Astorga, including *Scorso è gran tempo,* listed by Ladd (no. 328) as one of the cantatas unavailable for her study. The work list for Astorga in the NG article identifies ten additional cantatas for solo voice with basso continuo. The NG work list also names seven duets for two sopranos with basso continuo; one duet for two sopranos, two violins, and basso continuo; one soprano cantata with cello obbligato; and two solo soprano cantatas with orchestral accompaniment.

26. Marie Cornaz, "Le fonds de musique ancienne de l'Abbaye de Maredsous," FAM 42, no. 3 (1995): 346–70.

27. For this information, I am grateful to Lowell Lindgren.

28. See Volkmann, *Emanuele d'Astorga,* vol. 2; and Ladd, "The Solo Cantatas," chaps. 4–6. In appendix A Ladd provides editions of eleven solo cantatas with basso continuo.

29. Wellesz, *Die Opern und Oratorien,* 9. For more concerning the transition with regard to music and theater in the years preceding and following the interregnum, see Sommer-Mathis, "Von Barcelona nach Wien," 355–80.

EDITIONS AND BIBLIOGRAPHY

EDITIONS

Adler, Guido, ed. *Musikalische Werke der Kaiser Ferdinand III., Leopold I. und Joseph I.* 2 vols. Vienna: Artaria & Co., 1892–93; repr., Westmead, Farnborough, Eng.: Gregg International, 1972.

Bennett, Lawrence, ed. *Facsimiles of Selected Cantatas by Filippo Vismarri, Carlo Cappellini, Giovanni Battista Pederzuoli, Antonio Draghi, and Carlo Agostino Badia.* The Italian Cantata in the Seventeenth Century 16. New York: Garland, 1985.

Bertali, Antonio. *Lamento della Regina d'Inghilterra (Mortali vedete),* edited online by Andrew Weaver in the Web Library of Seventeenth-Century Music no. 11 (2008), http://www.sscm-wlscm.org/index.php/main-catalogue?pid=18&sid=43:Lamento-della-Regina-dInghilterra.

Bononcini, Antonio Maria. *Complete Sonatas for Violoncello and Basso Continuo,* edited by Lowell E. Lindgren. Recent Researches in the Music of the Baroque Era B77. Madison: A-R Editions, 1996.

Cesti, Antonio. *Cantatas,* facsimile with modern edition, edited by David Burrows. The Italian Cantata in the Seventeenth Century 6. New York: Garland, 1986.

———. *Four Chamber Duets,* edited by David Burrows. Collegium Musicum: Yale University. 2nd ser., Y2–1. Madison: A-R Editions, 1969.

———. *The Italian Cantata I: Antonio Cesti (1623–1669).* Wellesley Edition 5, edited by David Burrows. Wellesley: Wellesley College, 1963.

———. *Orontea,* edited by William C. Holmes. Wellesley Edition 9. Wellesley: Wellesley College, 1973.

Handel, George Frideric. *Echeggiate, festeggiate.* Halle Handel Edition, ser. V, vol. 4, edited by Hans J. Marx. Kassel: Bärenreiter, 1995. 75–116.

Priuli, Giovanni. *Delicie musicali* (Venice, 1625), edited by Albert Biales. 2 vols. Graz: Akademische Druck- und Verlagsanstalt, 1977.

Sances, Giovanni Felice. The aria "Occhi, sfere vivaci" and the dialogue *Tirsi morir volea,* in John Whenham, *Duet and Dialogue in the Age of Monteverdi,* 2:363–75, 438–47. Ann Arbor: UMI Research Press, 1982.

Schmelzer, Johann Heinrich. *Ballet Suites.* In *DTOe,* Guido Adler, gen. ed., Jahrg. 28/2, vol. 56, *Wiener Tanzmusik in der zweiten Hälfte des siebzehnten Jahrhunderts,* edited by Paul Nettl. Graz: Akademische- und Verlagsanstalt, 1921.

Valentini, Giovanni. The madrigal "Vanne, or carta amorosa," in John Whenham, *Duet and Dialogue in the Age of Monteverdi,* 2:251–55. Ann Arbor: UMI Research Press, 1982.

———. Selections from *Musiche a doi voci* (Venice: Alessandro Vincenti, 1622), in *DTOe,* Erich Schenk, gen. ed., vol. 125, *Frühmeister des stile nuovo in Österreich,* edited by Othmar Wessely. Graz: Akademische Druck- und Verlagsanstalt, 1973.

BIBLIOGRAPHY

Ademollo, Alessandro. *I Teatri di Roma nel secolo decimosettimo.* Rome: Pasqualucci, 1888.

Adler, Guido. "Die Kaiser Ferdinand III., Leopold I., Joseph I. und Karl VI. als Tonsetzer und Förderer der Musik." *VMw* 8 (1892): 252–74.

———. "Zur Geschichte der Wiener Messkomposition in der zweiten Hälfte des XVII. Jahrhunderts." *SMw* 4 (1916): 5–45.

Allacci, Lione. *Drammaturgia, accresciuta e continuata fino all'anno MDCCLV.* Venice: Pasquali, 1755; repr., Turin: Bottega d'Erasmo, 1966.

Antonicek, Theophil. "Antonio Cesti alla corte di Vienna." NRMI 4 (1970): 307–19.

———. "Die *Damira*-Opern der beiden Ziani." *AnMc* 14, 176–207. Studien zur italienisch-deutschen Musikgeschichte 9. Cologne: A. Volk, 1974.

———. "Italienische Akademien am Kaiserhof." *Notring Jahrbuch* (1972), 75–76.

———. "Musik und italienische Poesie am Hofe Kaiser Ferdinands III." *Mitteilungen der Kommission für Musikforschung* 42 (1990): 1–22.

———. "Zum 300. Todestag Antonio Cesti's." *ÖMz* 24 (1969): 573–77.

Barazzoni, Beatrice. "Le cantate da camera di Antonio Draghi." In *"Quel novo Cario, quel divin Orfeo." Antonio Draghi da Rimini a Vienna: Atti del convegno internazionale,* Rimini, 1998, 253–88. Lucca: Libreria musicale italiana, 2000.

Barnett, Gregory. *Bolognese Instrumental Music, 1660–1710.* Aldershot: Ashgate, 2008.

———. "Giovanni Maria Bononcini and the Uses of the Modes." *JM* 25 (2008): 230–86.

Bartels, Isolde. "Die Instrumentalstücke in Oper und Oratorium der frühvenezianischen Zeit." Ph.D. diss., University of Vienna, 1971.

Bennett, Lawrence. "The Italian Cantata in Vienna, 1700–1711: An Overview of Stylistic Traits." In *Antonio Caldara: Essays on His Life and Times,* edited by Brian W. Pritchard, 183–211. Farnham: Ashgate Publishing Ltd., 1987.

———. "The Italian Cantata in Vienna, c.1700–c.1711." Ph.D. diss., New York University, 1980.

———. "A Little-Known Collection of Early-Eighteenth-Century Vocal Music at Schloss Elisabethenburg, Meiningen." *FAM* 48 (2001): 250–302.

Bernardoni, Pietro Antonio. *Rime varie, consagrate alla S. C. R. Maestà di Giuseppe I.* Vienna: Giovanni van Ghelen, 1705.

Bertolotti, Antonino. *Musici alla corte dei Gonzaga in Mantova dal secolo XV al XVIII.* Milan: G. Ricordi &c., 1890; repr., Bologna: Forni, 1969.

Biach-Schiffmann, Flora. *Giovanni und Ludovico Burnacini.* Vienna: Krystall, 1931.

Bin, Umberto de. "Leopoldo I. imperatore e la sua corte nella letteratura italiana." *Bolletino del Circolo Accademico Italiano, 1908–09* (Trieste, 1910), 1–78.

Bose, Fritz. "Ariosti und Bononcini am Berliner Hof: Anmerkungen zu zwei Gemälden im Schloss Charlottenburg." *AMf* 22 (1965): 56–64.

Boyd, Malcolm. "Form and Style in Scarlatti's Chamber Cantatas." MR 25 (1964): 17–26.

Braatz, Thomas. "Devise." http://www.bach-cantatas.com/Term/Terms-7.htm, 15 October 2005.

Brand, Peter, and Lino Pertile, eds. *The Cambridge History of Italian Literature.* Rev. ed. Cambridge: Cambridge University Press, 1999.

Brockpähler, Renate. *Handbuch zur Geschichte der Barockoper in Deutschland.* Emsdetten: Lechte, 1964.

Brosche, Günter. "Die musikalische Werke Kaiser Leopolds I.: Ein systematisch-thematisches Verzeichnis der erhaltenen Kompositionen." In *Beiträge zur Musikdokumentation: Franz Grasberger zum 60. Geburtstag,* edited by Günter Brosche, 27–82. Tutzing: H. Schneider, 1975.

Brown, A. Peter. "The Trumpet Overture and Sinfonia in Vienna (1715–1822): Rise, Decline and Reformulation." In *Music in Eighteenth-Century Austria,* edited by David Wyn Jones, 13–69. Cambridge: Cambridge University Press, 1996.

Brown, Edward. *A Brief Account of Some Travels in Divers Parts of Europe.* London: Printed for Benj. Tooke, 1685.

Burney, Charles. *A General History of Music from the Earliest Ages to the Present Period.* 4 vols. London: Becket and others, 1776–89; also in 2 vols., edited by Frank Mercer. London: Foulis, 1935; repr., New York: Dover, 1957.

Burrows, David. "Antonio Cesti on Music." MQ 51 (1965): 518–29.

———. "The Cantatas of Antonio Cesti." Ph.D. diss., Brandeis University, 1961.

———, ed. *Thematic Index of the Cantatas of Antonio Cesti.* Wellesley Edition Cantata Index Series 1. Wellesley: Wellesley College, 1964.

Caluori, Eleanor, ed. *Thematic Index of Cantatas by Luigi Rossi.* Wellesley Edition Cantata Index Series 3a–b. Wellesley: Wellesley College, 1965.

Casimiri, Raffaele, and A. M. Vicentini. "Attilio Ottavio Ariosti: Nuovi documenti." NA 9 (1932): 1–20.

Coradini, Francesco. "P. Antonio Cesti (5 agosto 1623–14 ottobre 1669). Nuove notizie biografiche." RMI 30 (1923): 371–88.

Crescimbeni, Giovanni Mario de'. *Comentari . . . alla sua istoria della volgar poesia* 1. Rome: Rossi, 1702.

Crowther, J. V. "The Operas of Cesti." MR 31 (1970): 106–13.

Culley, Thomas D. *Jesuits and Music I: A Study of the Musicians Connected with the German College in Rome during the Seventeenth Century and Their Activities in Northern Europe.* Sources and Studies for the History of Jesuits 2. Rome: Jesuit Historical Institute, 1970.

Damerini, Adelmo. "Le due 'Maddalene' di Giovanni Bononcini." CHM 11 (1957): 115–25.

Danks, Barry. "The Influence of Attilio Ariosti." *Consort* 12 (1955): 24–26.

Deutsch, Otto Erich. "Das Repertoire der höfischen Oper, der Hof- und der Staatsoper." ÖMz 24 (1969): 369–421.

———. *Handel: A Documentary Biography.* New York: W. W. Norton, 1979; repr., New York: Da Capo Press, 1974.

Doebner, Richard, ed. "Briefe der Königin Sophie Charlotte von Preussen und der Kurfürstin Sophie von Hannover an hannoversche Diplomaten." In *Publikationen aus den K. preussischen Staatsarchiv* 79. Leipzig: Hirzel, 1905.

Donati-Pettèni, Giuliano. *L'arte della musica in Bergamo.* Bergamo: Banca mutua popolare di Bergamo, 1930.

Ebert, Alfred. *Attilio Ariosti in Berlin (1697–1703).* Leipzig: Giesecke & Devrient, 1905.

Einstein, Alfred. "Ein Emissär der Monodie in Deutschland: Francesco Rasi." In *Festschrift für Johannes Wolf zu seinem sechzigsten Geburtstag,* edited by Walter Lott, Helmut Osthoff, and Werner Wolffheim, 31–34. Berlin: M. Breslauer, 1929.

———. "Italienische Musiker am Hofe der Neuburger Wittelsbacher (1614 bis 1716)." SIMG 9 (1907–1908): 336–424.

———. "Italienische Musik und italienische Musiker am Kaiserhof und an den erzherzoglichen Höfen in Innsbruck und Graz." SMw 21 (1934): 3–52.

Etscheit, Ulrich. "Händels *Rodelinda:* Libretto, Komposition, Rezeption." Ph.D. diss., University of Heidelberg, 1998.

Federhofer, Hellmut. "Graz Court Musicians and Their Contributions to the *Parnassus Musicus Ferdinandaeus* (1615)." MD 9 (1955): 167–244.

———. *Musikpflege und Musiker am Grazer Habsburgerhof der Erzherzöge Karl und Ferdinand von Innerösterreich, 1564–1691.* Mainz: B. Schott's Söhne, 1967.

Ferand, Ernest. *Die Improvisation in Beispielen aus neun Jahrhunderten abendländischer Musik.* Cologne: Arno Volk, 1956; rev. ed., 1961.

Ferdinand III, Holy Roman Emperor. *Poesie diverse Composte in hore Rubate d'Accademico Occupato*, n.d.

Ferrari, Luigi. "Per la bibliografia del teatro italiano in Vienna." In *Studi di bibliografia e di argomento romano in memoria di Luigi de Gregori*. Rome: Fratelli Palombi, 1949.

Fiedler, Joseph, ed. *Die Relationen der Botschafter Venedigs über Deutschland und Oesterreich im siebzehnten Jahrhundert*. Fontes rerum Austriacarum, 2nd ser., 94 vols., no. 27. Vienna: Hof- und Staatsdruckerei, 1867.

Flotzinger, Rudolf. *Eine Quelle italienischer Frühmonodie in Österreich*. Sitzungsberichte der phil.-hist. Klasse der Österreichischen Akademie der Wissenschaften 251/2. Vienna, 1966.

Ford, Anthony. "Giovanni Bononcini, 1670–1747." MT 111 (1970): 695–99.

Forment, Bruno B. "'*La terra, il cielo e l'inferno*': The Representation and Reception of Greco-Roman Mythology in Opera Seria." Ph.D. diss., Ghent University, 2007.

Frati, Lodovico. "Attilio Ottavio Ariosti." RMI 33 (1926): 551–57.

Freeman, Robert. "Opera without Drama: Currents of Change in Italian Opera, 1675 to 1725, and the Roles Played Therein by Zeno, Caldara, and Others." Ph.D. diss., Princeton University, 1967.

Fruchtman, Efrim, and Caroline Fruchtman. "Instrumental Scoring in the Chamber Cantatas of Francesco Conti." In *Studies in Musicology: Essays in the History, Style, and Bibliography of Music in Memory of Glen Haydon*, edited by James W. Pruett, 245–59. Chapel Hill: University of North Carolina Press, 1969.

Fürstenau, Moritz. *Zur Geschichte der Musik und des Theaters am Hofe zu Dresden*. 2 vols. Dresden: R. Kuntze, 1861–62.

Gasparini, Francesco. *L'armonico pratico al cimbalo*. Venice: Bortoli, 1708; English translation by Frank S. Stillings as *The Practical Harmonist, at the Harpsichord*, edited by David L. Burrows. New Haven: Yale University Press, 1963.

Gericke, Hannelore. *Der Wiener Musikalienhandel von 1700 bis 1778*. Wiener Musikwissenschaftliche Beiträge 5. Graz: H. Böhlaus Nachf., 1960.

Giazotto, Remo. "Nel CCC anno della morte di Antonio Cesti: Ventidue lettere ritrovate nell'Archivio di Stato di Venezia." NRMI 3 (1969): 496–512.

Giebler, Albert C. "The Masses of Johann Caspar Kerll." Ph.D. diss., University of Michigan, 1956.

Glüxam, Dagmar. "Verzeichnis der Sänger in den Wiener Opern- und Ortorienpartituren 1705–1711." SMw 48 (2002): 269–319.

Gmeiner, Josef. "Die 'Schlafkammerbibliothek' Kaiser Leopolds I." In *Biblos: Beiträge zu Buch, Bibliothek und Schrift* 43:199–211, edited by Österreichische Nationalbibliothek (Vienna, 1994).

Goloubeva, Maria. *The Glorification of Emperor Leopold I in Image, Spectacle and Text*. Mainz: von Zabern, 2000.

Haas, Robert. *Die estensischen Musikalien: Thematisches Verzeichnis mit Einleitung*. Regensburg: G. Bosse, 1927.

———. "Geschichtliche Opernbezeichnungen." In *Festschrift Hermann Kretzschmar zum siebzigsten Geburtstage*, 43–45. Leipzig: C. F. Peters, 1918.

Hadamowsky, Franz. "Barocktheater am Wiener Kaiserhof." In *Jahrbuch der Gesellschaft für Wiener Theaterforschung 1951/52*, 7–117. Vienna: Verlag des Notringes der wissenschaftlichen Verbände Österreichs, 1955.

Hamann, Heinz Wolfgang. "Musik am Hofe Leopold I." ÖMz 17 (1962): 453–57.

Hantsch, Hugo. *Reichsvizekanzler Friedrich Karl von Schönborn (1674–1746)*. Augsburg: B. Filser, 1929.

Harris, David C. "Keyboard Music in Vienna during the Reign of Leopold I, 1658–1705." Ph.D. diss., University of Michigan, 1967.

Heartz, Daniel. Foreword to the edition of Mozart's *Idomeneo* in the *Neue Ausgabe sämtlicher Werke*, ser. 2, vol. 11. Kassel: Bärenreiter, 1972.

Heawood, Edward. *Watermarks, Mainly of the 17th and 18th Centuries*. Monumenta Chartae Papyraceae Historicum Illustrata 1, edited by E. J. Labarre. Amsterdam: Paper Publications Society, 1950; repr., 1951.

Hennings, Fred. *Das barocke Wien*. 2 vols. Vienna: Herold, 1965.

Heuser, Emil. *Die Belagerung von Landau in den Jahren 1702 und 1703*. Landau: E. Kaussler, 1894.

———. *Die dritte und vierte Belagerung Landaus im Spanischen Erfolgekrieg 1704 und 1713*. Landau: E. Kaussler, 1897.

Hofmann, Ulrike. "Die Accademia am Wiener Kaiserhof unter der Regierung Kaiser Leopolds I." *Musicologia Austriaca* 2 (1979): 76–84.

———. "Die Serenata am Hofe Kaiser Leopold I. 1658–1705." Ph.D. diss., University of Vienna, 1975.

Holler, Karl Heinz. *Giovanni Maria Bononcini's Musico Prattico in seiner Bedeutung für die musikalische Satzlehre des 17. Jahrhunderts*. Strasbourg: P. H. Heitz, 1963.

Holman, Peter. "'Col nobilissimo esercitio della vivuola': Monteverdi's String Writing." *EMc* 221 (1993): 557–90.

Holmes, William C. "Comedy—Opera—Comic Opera." In *AnMc* 5 (1968): 92–103.

———. "*Orontea*: A Study of Change and Development in the Libretto and the Music of Mid-Seventeenth-Century Italian Opera." Ph.D. diss., Columbia University, 1968.

———. "Yet Another 'Orontea': Further Rapport between Venice and Vienna." In *Venezia e il melodramma nel Seicento*, edited by Maria Teresa Muraro, 204–205. Florence: L. S. Olschki, 1976.

Hueber, Kurt. "Die Wiener Opern Giovanni Bononcinis von 1697–1710." Ph.D. diss., University of Vienna, 1955.

———. "Gli ultimi anni di Giovanni Bononcini: Notizie e documenti inediti." *Atti e memorie dell'Accademia di Scienze Lettere e Arti di Modena*, ser. 5, no. 7 (1954): 153–71.

Ingrao, Charles. *The Habsburg Monarchy 1618–1815*. Cambridge: Cambridge University Press, 1994.

———. *In Quest and Crisis: Emperor Joseph I and the Habsburg Monarchy*. West Lafayette: Purdue University Press, 1979; rev. and expanded German ed., *Josef I.: Der "vergessene" Kaiser*. Graz: Styria, 1982.

Isherwood, Robert M. *Music in the Service of the King*. Ithaca: Cornell University Press, 1973.

Kanduth, Erika. "Italienische Dichtung am Wiener Hof im 17. Jahrhundert." In *Beiträge zur Aufnahme der italienischen und spanischen Literatur in Deutschland im 16. und 17. Jahrhundert*, edited by Alberto Martino. Chloe 9, 171–207. Amsterdam: Rodopi, 1990.

Kann, Robert A. *A History of the Habsburg Empire 1526–1918*. Berkeley: University of California Press, 1974.

———. *A Study in Austrian Intellectual History*. New York: Praeger, 1960.

Kauffman, Deborah. "*Violins en basse* as Musical Allegory." *JM* (2006): 153–85.

Kirkendale, Ursula. "The War of the Spanish Succession Reflected in the Works of Antonio Caldara." *AcM* 36 (1964): 221–33.

Kjellberg, Erik, and Kerala J. Snyder, eds. The Düben Collection Database Catalogue, online at http://www2.musik.uu.se/duben/Duben.php.

Klein, Rudolf. "Die Schauplätze der Hofoper" (introduction to Otto Erich Deutsch's article "Das Repertoire der Höfischen Oper"). *ÖMz* 24 (1969): 371–72.

Klenz, William. *Giovanni Maria Bononcini of Modena: A Chapter in Baroque Instrumental Music*. Durham, N.C.: Duke University Press, 1962.

Knaus, Herwig. "Beiträge zur Geschichte der Hofmusikkapelle des Erzherzogs Leopold Wilhelm." *Anzeiger der phil.-hist. Klasse der Österreichischen Akademie der Wissenschaften* 103 (1966): 146–59.

———. *Die Musiker im Archivbestand des Kaiserlichen Obersthofmeisteramtes (1637–1705).* Sitzungsberichte der phil.-hist. Klasse der Österreichischen Akademie der Wissenschaften 254 (1967), 259 (1968), and 264 (1969).

———. "Die Musiker in den geheimen kaiserlichen Kammerzahlamtsrechnungsbüchern (1669, 1705–1711)." *Anzeiger der phil.-hist. Klasse der Österreichischen Akademie der Wissenschaften* 106 (1969): 14–38.

———. "Wiener Hofquartierbücher als biographische Quelle für Musiker des 17. Jahrhunderts." *Anzeiger der phil.-hist. Klasse der Österreichischen Akademie der Wissenschaften* 102 (1965): 178–206.

Köchel, Ludwig Ritter von. *Die kaiserliche Hof-Musikkapelle in Wien von 1563–1864.* Vienna: Beck, 1869; repr., Hildesheim: Georg Olms, 1976.

———. *Johann Josef Fux.* Vienna: A. Hölder, 1872; repr., Hildesheim: Georg Olms, 1974.

Koczirz, Adolf. "Excerpte auf den Hofmusikakten des Wiener Hofkammerarchivs." *SMw* 1 (1913): 278–303.

Kümmerling, Harald. *Katalog der Sammlung Bokemeyer.* Kieler Schriften zur Musikwissenschaft 18. Kassel: Bärenreiter, 1970.

Ladd, Karen S. "The Solo Cantatas of Emanuele d'Astorga." Ph.D. diss., Ohio State University, 1982.

Landau, Marcus. *Die italienische Literatur am österreichischen Hofe.* Vienna: Gerold, 1879.

La Rue, Jan. "Bifocal Tonality: An Explanation for Ambiguous Baroque Cadences." In *Essays on Music in Honor of A. T. Davison,* 173–84. Cambridge, Mass.: Harvard University Press, 1957.

———. *Guidelines for Style Analysis.* New York: W. W. Norton, 1970.

Leopold Wilhelm, Archduke. *Diporti del Crescente Divisi in Rime Morali Devote Heroiche Amorose.* Brussels: Mommartius, 1656.

The Life of Leopold, Late Emperor of Germany, &c. 2nd ed. London: Newborough, 1708.

Lindgren, Lowell. "Ariosti's London Years, 1716–29." ML 62 (1981): 331–34.

———. "A Bibliographic Scrutiny of Dramatic Works Set by Giovanni and His Brother Antonio Maria Bononcini." Ph.D. diss., Harvard University, 1972.

———. "Bononcini's 'agreable and easie style, and those fine inventions in his *basses* (to which he was led by an instrument upon which he excels).'" In *Aspects of the Secular Cantata in Italy,* edited by Michael Talbot, 135–75. Williston, Vt.: Ashgate, 2009.

———. "Count Rudolf Franz Erwein von Schönborn (1677–1754) and the Italian Sonatas for Violoncello in His Collection at Wiesentheid." In *Relazioni musicali tra Italia e Germania nell'età barocca (Atti del VI Convegno internazionale sulla musica italiana nel secoli XVII–XVIII),* 257–302. Como: A.M.I.S., 1997.

———. "Six Newly Discovered Letters of Attilio Ariosti, O.S.M. (1666–1729)." *Studi storici dell'Ordine dei Servi di Maria* 30 (1980): 125–37.

———. "Vienna, the 'natural centro' for Giovanni Bononcini." In *Il teatro musicale italiano nel Sacro Romano Impero nei secoli XVII–XVIII: Atti del VII Convegno internazionale sulla musica italiana nei secoli XVII–XVIII (Contributi musicologici del Centro ricerche dell'A.M.I.S. 12),* edited by Alberto Colzani, Norbert Dubowy, Andrea Luppi, and Maurizio Paduan, 365–420. Como: A.I.M.S., 1999.

Lipsius, Ida Maria ("La Mara"). *Musikbriefe aus fünf Jahrhunderten,* 2 vols. Leipzig: Breitkopf & Härtel, 1886.

Lynch, Robert. "Opera in Hamburg, 1718–1738." Ph.D. diss., New York University, 1979.

Mabbett, Margaret. "Madrigalists at the Viennese Court and Monteverdi's *Madrigali guerreri, et amorosi.*" In *Monteverdi und die Folgen: Bericht über das international Sympo-*

sium, Detmold 1993, edited by Silke Leopold and Joachim Steinheuer, 291–310. Kassel: Bärenreiter, 1998.

Mainwaring, John. *Memoirs of the Life of the Late George Frederic Handel.* London: R. and J. Dodsley, 1760; repr., Amsterdam: F. A. M. Knuf, 1964.

Mandyczewski, Eusebius. *Geschichte der K.K. Gesellschaft der Musikfreunde in Wien . . . in einem Zusatzbande: Die Sammlungen und Statuten.* Vienna: A. Holzhausen, 1912.

Mantuani, Joseph, comp. *Tabulae codicum manu scriptorum praeter Graecos et Orientales in Biblioteca Palatina Vindobonensi Asservatorum 9–10.* Vienna: Gerold, 1897–99; also available online.

Mayer, Franz Martin, and Raimund Kaindl. *Geschichte und Kulturlebens Österreichs,* edited by Hans Pirchegger. 5th ed. Vienna: Braumüller, 1958–65.

Mayor, Hyatt. *The Bibiena Family.* New York: H. Bittner and Company, 1945.

McCredie, A. D. "Nicholas Matteis—English Composer at the Habsburg Court." ML 48 (1967): 127–37.

McGuigan, Dorothy Gies. *The Habsburgs.* Garden City, N.Y.: Doubleday, 1966.

Meer, J. H. van der. *Johann Josef Fux als Opernkomponist.* 3 vols. Bilthoven: Creyghton, 1961.

Meyer, Ernst Hermann. *Die Mehrstimmige Spielmusik des 17. Jahrhunderts in Nord- und Mitteleuropa.* Kassel: Bärenreiter, 1934.

Mikoletzky, Hanns Leo. *Österreich: Das grosse 18. Jahrhundert.* Vienna: Austria Edition, 1967.

Molitor, Simon von. *Biographische und kunstgeschichtliche Stoffsammlung.* Öesterrichische Nationalbibliothek, Music MS 19239.

Montagu, William Dropo, 7th Duke of Manchester. *Court and Society from Elizabeth to Anne.* 2 vols. London: Hurst and Blackett, 1864.

Die Musik in Geschichte und Gegenwart, 1st ed., edited by Friedrich Blume, 17 vols. Kassel: Bärenreiter, 1949–68; 2nd ed., edited by Ludwig Finscher, *Sachteil,* 10 vols., and *Personenteil,* 18 vols. and suppl. Kassel: Bärenreiter, 1994–2008.

Nava, Maria Luigia. "P. A. Bernardoni e il melodramma." *Atti e memorie della Regia deputazione di storia patria per le provincie modenesi,* ser. 7, no. 5 (1928): 88–138.

Nemeth, Carl. "Zur Lebensgeschichte von Carlo Agostino Badia (1672–1738)." *Anzeiger der phil.-hist. Klasse der österreichischen Akademie der Wissenschaften* 92 (1955): 224–36.

Nettl, Paul. "Die Wiener Tanzkomposition in der zweiten Hälfte des siebzehnten Jahrhunderts." *SMw* 8 (1921): 45–175.

———. "Ein verschollenes Tournierballet von M. A. Cesti." *ZMw* 8 (1926): 411–18.

———. "An English Musician at the Court of Charles VI in Vienna." *MQ* 28 (1942): 318–28.

———. "Zur Geschichte der kaiserlichen Hofmusikkapelle von 1636–1680." *SMw* 18 (1931): 34–35, and 19 (1932): 33–40.

Neuhaus, Max. "Antonio Draghi." *SMw* 1 (1913): 106–11.

The New Grove Dictionary of Music and Musicians. 2nd ed., edited by Stanley Sadie. 29 vols. London: Macmillan, 2001; also available online.

Newman, William S. *The Sonata in the Baroque Era,* rev. ed. Chapel Hill: University of North Carolina Press, 1966.

Orel, Alfred. "Die Kontrapunktlehren von Poglietti und Bertali." In *Kongress-Bericht Bamberg 1953,* 140–42. Kassel: Bärenreiter, 1954.

Over, Berthold. ". . . sotto l'Ombra della Regina di Pennati': Antonio Vivaldi, Kurfürstin Therese Kunigunde von Bayern und andere Wittelsbacher." In *Italian Opera in Central Europe, 1614–1780,* vol. 3, *Opera Subjects and European Relationships,* edited by Norbert Dubowy, Corinna Herr, and Alina Zórawska-Witkowska, in conjunction with Dorothea Schröder. Berlin: Berliner Wissenschafts-Verlag, 2007.

Page, Janet. "Sirens on the Danube: Giulia Masotti and Women Singers at the Imperial Court." Unpublished paper received from the author on 18 April 2012.

Pancaldi, Evaristo, and Gino Roncaglia. "Maestri di cappella del duomo di Modena: G. M. Bononcini." *Studi e documenti della Reale deputazione di storia patria per l'Emilia e Romagna: Sezione di Modena* 7 (1941): 133–51.

Pastore, G. A. "Giuseppe Tricarico da Gallipoli, musicista del sec. XVII." *Studi salentini,* nos. 5–6 (1958): 143–68, and nos. 7–8 (1959): 88–130.

Peters, Alan E. "Antonio Cesti's Solo Cantatas for Bass Voice." Ph.D. diss., University of Iowa, 1968.

Pirrotta, Nino. "Tre capitoli su Cesti." In *La scuola romana: G. Carissimi—A. Cesti— M. Marazzoli.* Chigiana 10:25–79. Siena: "Accademia Musicale Chigiana," 1953.

Pryer, Anthony. "Approaching Monteverdi: His Culture and Ours." In *The Cambridge Companion to Monteverdi,* edited by John Whenham and Richard Wistreich, 1–19. Cambridge: Cambridge University Press, 2007.

Racek, Jan. "Collezione di Monodie italiane primarie alla Biblioteca Universitaria di Praga." In *Sborník Prací Filosofické Fakulty Brenenke University 1958.* Brno: Fakulta, 1958.

Raguenet, François. *Défense du paralèle des Italiens et des François.* Paris: Bertin, 1705; repr., Geneva: Minkoff, 1976.

———. *Paralele des Italiens et des François, en ce qui regarde la musique et les opera* (Paris: Moreau, 1702); anonymous English translation, *A Comparison between the French and Italian Musick and Operas.* London: Lewis, 1709; repr., London: Gregg, 1968.

Raschl, Erich. "Die weltliche Vokalwerke des Giovanni Felice Sances, ca. 1600–1679." Ph.D. diss., University of Graz, 1967.

Riedel, Wilhelm Friedrich. *Das Musikarchiv im Minoritenkonvent zu Wien (Katalog des älteren Bestandes vor 1784).* Catalogus musicus 1. Kassel, 1963.

———. "Eine unbekannte Quelle zu Johann Kaspar Kerlls Musik für Tasteninstrumente." *Mf* 13 (1960): 310–14.

Riedel, Wilhelm Friedrich, and Leonhard Riedel. "Zum Repertoire der italienischen Kantatenkomposition am Münchner und Wiener Hof um 1700." In *Das Musikleben am Hof von Kurfürst Max Emanuel: Bericht über das internationale musikwissenschaftliche Symposium, veranstaltet von der Gesellschaft für Bayerische Musikgeschichte und dem Forschungsinstitut für Musiktheater der Universität Bayreuth,* edited by Stephan Hörner and Sebastian Werr, 323–54. Tutzing: Hans Schneider, 2012.

Roncaglia, Gino. "Di insigni musicisti modenesi: Su la famiglia dei Bononcini." *Atti e memorie della Regia deputazione di storia patria per le provincie modenesi,* ser. 7, no. 6 (1930): 13–18.

———. "Di un autor e di un'opera ignorati (P. P. Cappellini: 'La forza d'amore')." *Rivista nazionale di musica* 19 (1938): 4255–59.

———. *La cappella musicale del duomo di Modena.* Historiae musicae cultores: Biblioteca 5. Florence: Olschki, 1957.

———. "L. A. Muratori, la musica e il maggior compositore modenese del suo tempo." *Atti e memorie della Regia deputazione di storia patria per le provincie modenesi,* ser. 7, no. 8 (1933): 277–318.

Rosand, Ellen. "Barbara Strozzi, *virtuosissima cantatrice:* The Composer's Voice." JAMS 31 (1978): 241–81.

———. *Opera in Seventeenth-Century Venice.* Berkeley: University of California Press, 1991.

Rose, Gloria, ed. *Thematic Index of Cantatas by Giacomo Carissimi.* Wellesley Edition Cantata Index Series 5. Wellesley: Wellesley College, 1966.

Rosenblum, Myron. "The Viola d'amore and Its Literature." *Strad* 78 (1967): 250–53, 277.

Salzer, E. C. "Il teatro allegorico italiano a Vienna." *Rivista italiana del dramma* 3 (1939): 65–84.

———. "Teatro italiano in Vienna barocca." *Rivista italiana del dramma* 2 (1938): 47–70.

Saunders, Stephen. *Cross, Sword and Lyre: Sacred Music at the Imperial Court of Ferdinand II of Habsburg (1619–1637).* London: Clarendon Press, 1995.

———. "New Discoveries Concerning Ferdinand III's Musical Compositions." *SMw* 45 (1996): 7–31.

Schaal, Richard. "Die Autographen der Wiener Musiksammlung von Aloys Fuchs." In *The Haydn Yearbook* 6:5–191. King of Prussia, Pa.: Theodore Presser, 1969.

———. *Quellen und Forschungen zur Wiener Musiksammlung von Aloys Fuchs.* Sitzungsberichte der phil.-hist. Klasse der Österreichischen Akademie der Wissenschaften 251/1. Veröffentlichungen der Kommission für Musikforschung 5, edited by Erich Schenk. Vienna, 1966.

———. "Quellen zu Johann Kaspar Kerll." *Anzeiger der phil.-hist. Klasse der Österreichischen Akademie der Wissenschaften* 99 (1962): 14–27.

Schenk, Eleonore. "Die Anfänge des Wiener Kärntnertortheaters (1710–1748)." Ph.D. diss., University of Vienna, 1969.

Schenk, Erich. *Kleine Wiener Musikgeschichte.* Vienna: Paul Neff Verlag, 1946.

———. "Osservazioni sulla scuola modenese nel Seicento." *Atti e memorie della Accademia di scienze, lettere e arti di Modena,* ser. 5, no. 10 (1952): 3–30. German translation in *SMw* 26 (1964): 25–46.

Schmidt, Carl. "Antonio Cesti's *Il pomo d'oro:* A Reexamination of a Famous Hapsburg Court Spectacle." *JAMS* 29 (1976): 381–412.

———. "The Operas of Antonio Cesti." Ph.D. diss., Harvard University, 1973.

Schnitzler, Rudolf. "The Sacred Dramatic Music of Antonio Draghi." Ph.D. diss., University of North Carolina, 1971.

Sehnhal, Jiri. "Die Musikkapelle des Olmützer Bischofs Karl Liechtenstein Castelcorn in Kremsier." *Kjb* (1967): 79–123.

Seifert, Herbert. "Akademien am Wiener Kaiserhof der Barockzeit." In *Akademie und Musik: Erscheinungsweisen des Akademiegedankens in Kultur- und Musikgeschichte: Institutionen, Veranstaltungen, Schriften (Festschrift für Werner Braun zum 65. Geburtstag,* edited by W. Frobenius and others, 215–23. Saarbrücken, 1993.

———. "Beiträge zur Frühgeschichte der Monodie in Österreich." *SMw* 31 (1980): 14–26.

———. "Cesti and His Opera Troupe in Innsbruck and Vienna, with New Informations about His Last Year and His Oeuvre." In *La figura e l'opera di Antonio Cesti nel Seicento europeo (Convegno internazionale di studio, Arezzo 26–27 aprile 2002).* RIM 37, edited by Mariateresa Dellaborra (2003): 15–62.

———. "Da Rimini alla corte di Leopoldo." In *"Quel novo Cario, quel divin Orfeo": Antonio Draghi da Rimini a Vienna. Atti del convegno internazionale* (Rimini, 1998), edited by Emilio Sala and Davide Daolmi (ConNotazioni 7), 3–14. Lucca: Libreria musicale italiana, 2000.

———. *Die Oper am Wiener Kaiserhof im 17. Jahrhundert.* Tutzing: Hans Schneider, 1985.

———. "Die Rolle Wiens bei der Rezeption italienischer Musik in Dresden." In *Dresdner Operntraditionen,* vol. 1, *Die Dresdner Oper von Heinrich Schütz bis Johann Adolf Hasse,* 96–105. Dresden: Hochschule für Musik "Carl Maria von Weber," 1985.

———. *Giovanni Buonaventura Viviani: Leben, Instrumentalwerke, vokale Kammermusik.* Wiener Veröffentlichungen zur Musikwissenschaft 21, edited by Othmar Wessely, rev. ed. Tutzing: Hans Schneider, 1982.

———. "*Miserere mei Deus.* Eine grosse Komposition des Kaisers, aber welches?" Unpublished paper delivered at the conference "Sacred Music in the Habsburg Empire 1619–1740 and Its Contexts" in Middleburg, the Netherlands, 2009.

———. "Monteverdi und die Habsburger." In *Monteverdi und die Folgen: Bericht über das internationale Symposium, Detmold 1993,* edited by Silke Leopold and Joachim Steinheuer, 77–92. Kassel: Bärenreiter, 1998.

———. "Neues zu Antonio Draghis weltlichen Werken." *Anzeiger der phil.-hist. Klasse der Österreichischen Akademie der Wissenschaften* 115 (1978): 96–116.

Selfridge-Field, Eleanor. *The Music of Benedetto and Alessandro Marcello: A Thematic Catalogue with Commentary on the Composers, Works, and Sources.* Oxford: Clarendon Press, 1990.

Senn, Walter. *Musik und Theater am Hof zu Innsbruck.* Innsbruck: Österreichische Verlagsanstalt, 1954.

Somerset, H. V. F. "The Habsburg Emperors as Musicians." ML 30 (1949): 207–208.

Sommer-Mathis, Andrea. "Von Barcelona nach Wien: Die Einrichtung des Musik- und Theaterbetriebes am Wiener Hof durch Kaiser Karl VI." In *Musica Conservata, Festschrift zum 60. Geburtstag von Günter Brosche,* 355–80. Tutzing: Hans Schneider Verlag, 1999.

Spagna, Archangelo. *Oratorii overo melodrami sacri* (rist. Anast. Rome, 1706).

Spielman, John P. *The City and the Crown: Vienna and the Imperial Court 1600–1740.* West Lafayette: Purdue University Press, 1993.

———. *Leopold I of Austria.* New Brunswick: Rutgers University Press, 1977.

Stein, Beverly. "Between Key and Mode: Tonal Practice in the Music of Giacomo Carissimi." Ph.D. diss., Brandeis University, 1994.

Steinheuer, Joachim. "Orfeo (1607)." In *The Cambridge Companion to Monteverdi,* edited by John Whenham and Richard Wistreich, 119–40. Cambridge: Cambridge University Press, 2007.

———. "Zur musikdramatischen Umsetzung epischer Texte bei Monteverdi und seinen italienischen Zeitgenossen." *Monteverdi und die Folgen: Bericht über das international Symposium, Detmold 1993,* edited by Silke Leopold and Joachim Steinheuer, 191–213. Kassel: Bärenreiter, 1998.

Tapié, Victor-L. *The Rise and Fall of the Habsburg Monarchy,* translated from the French (*Monarchie et peuples du Danube* [Paris: Fayard, 1969]) by Stephen Hardman. New York: Praeger, 1971.

Telemann, Georg Philipp. "Autobiography." in *Grundlage einer Ehren-Pforte,* by Johann Mattheson. Hamburg, 1740; modern ed. by Max Schneider. Berlin: Kommissionsverlag von L. Liepmannssohn, 1910; repr., 1969; also available online.

Torbé, Jacob. "Die weltliche Solokantate in Wien um die Wende des 17./18. Jahrhunderts." Ph.D. diss., University of Vienna, 1920.

Tosi, Pier Francesco. *Opinioni de' cantori antichi e moderni.* Bologna: Lelio dalla Volpe, 1723; English translation by J. E. Galliard as *Observations on the Florid Song* (1742, 2nd ed., 1743; repr., London: William Reeves Bookseller Ltd., 1967).

Turner, Jane, ed. *The Dictionary of Art.* 34 vols. London: Macmillan, 1996.

Valdrighi, Luigi. "Cappelle, concerti e musiche di casa d'Este." *Atti e memorie delle Regie deputazioni di storia patria per le provincie modenesi e parmensi,* ser. 3, no. 2 (1884): 415–95.

———. "I Bononcini da Modena." *Atti e memorie delle Regie deputazioni di storia patria per le provincie dell'Emilia,* n.s., 7, no. 2 (1882): 23–67.

Vehse, Eduard. *Memoirs of the Court, Aristocracy, and Diplomacy of Austria,* vols. 1–2. London: Landon, Longman, Brown, Green and Longmans, 1856; English translation of Franz Demler, *Geschichte des österreichischen Hofs und Adels und der österreichischen Diplomatie.* Hamburg: Hoffman und Campe, 1851.

Vicentini, A. M. "Memorie di musicisti dell'ordine de' Servi di Maria." NA 8 (1931): 34–57.

Vogel, Emil, Alfred Einstein, François Lesure, and Claudio Sartori. *Bibliografia della musica italiana vocale profana pubblicata dal 1500 al 1700.* 3 vols. Pomezia: Staderini-Minkoff Editori, 1977.

Waldner, Franz. "Zwei Inventarien aus dem XVI. and XVII. Jahrhundert über die hinterlassene Musikinstrumente und Musikalien am Innsbucker Hofe." SMw 4 (1916): 128–47.

Walther, Johann Gottfried. *Musikalisches Lexicon, oder musikalische Bibliothek.* Leipzig, 1732; repr., Kassel: Bärenreiter, 1953.

Webhofer, Peter. "Giovanni Felice Sances, ca. 1600–1679: Biographisch-bibliographische Untersuchung und Studie über sein Motettenwerk." Ph.D. diss., University of Innsbruck, 1964; published privately, 1965.

Weilen, Alexander von. *Zur Wiener Theatergeschichte: Die vom Jahre 1629 bis zum Jahre 1740 am Wiener Hofe zur Aufführung gelangten Werke theatralischen Characters und Oratorien.* Schriften des Österreichischen Vereines für Bibliothekswesen 2. Vienna: A. Hölder, 1901.

Weiss, Günther. "57 unbekannte Instrumentalstücke (15 Sonaten) von Attilio Ariosti in einer Abschrift von Johan Helmich Roman." *Mf* 23 (1970): 127–38.

Wellesz, Egon. "Die Ballett-Suiten von J. H. Schmelzer und A. A. Schmelzer." *Sitzungsberichte der Kaiserlichen Akademie der Wissenschaften in Wien* 176 (1914): 1–84.

———. "Die Opern und Oratorien in Wien von 1660–1708." *SMw* 6 (1919): 5–138.

———. *Essays on Opera,* trans. Patricia Kean. London: Dennis Dobson, 1950.

Wessely, Othmar. "Kaiser Leopolds I. 'Vermeinte Bruder- und Schwesterliebe': Ein Beitrag zur Geschichte des Wiener Hoftheaters in Linz." *SMw* 25 (1962): 586–608.

Whenham, John. *Duet and Dialogue in the Age of Monteverdi.* 2 vols. Ann Arbor: UMI Research Press, 1982.

Wilkins, Ernest B. *A History of Italian Literature,* rev. ed. by Thomas G. Bergin. Cambridge, Mass.: Harvard University Press, 1974.

Williams, Hermine. *Francesco Bartolomeo Conti.* Aldershot: Ashgate, 1999.

Wolf, John B. *The Emergence of the Great Powers 1685–1715.* New York: Harper, 1951.

Wolff, Hellmuth Christian. *Die venezianische Oper in der zweiten Hälfte des siebzehnten Jahrhunderts.* Berlin: O. Elsner, 1937.

Wright, Josephine. "The Secular Cantatas of Francesco Mancini." Ph.D. diss., New York University, 1975.

Zobeley, Fritz. *Die Musikalien der Grafen von Schönborn-Wiesentheid; Thematisch-bibliographisches Katalog (Veröffentlichungen der Gesellschaft für Bayerische Musikgeschichte e. V,)* vol. 1, pt. 1. Tutzing: Hans Schneider, 1967.

Zöllner, Erich. *Geschichte Österreichs.* 7th ed. Munich: R. Oldenbourg Verlag, 1984.

INDEX

In the index, page numbers with "m" suffix refer to musical examples and diagrams, "t" to tables, "n" to notes, and "s" to archival sources. Page numbers in italics refer to illustrations. Where possible, works by composers are listed in chronological order. Works whose dates of composition are unknown are listed alphabetically at the bottom with the designation "n.d." ("no date").

Much of the discussion of compositional style for the period 1700 to 1711 is focused on twenty-five sample arias by five composers. This content is indexed under the aria titles and cross referenced from the composer as indicated below:

LAWRENCE BENNETT is Professor Emeritus of Music and former Chair of the Music Department at Wabash College. He founded The Western Wind, a vocal ensemble that has toured professionally throughout North America, Europe, and Asia. Bennett has edited two collections of early American music and written often about the music of the Renaissance and the Baroque Era. In 2009 Bennett prepared an edition of the opera *Hypermnestra* by Ignaz Holzbauer, which he found in Meiningen, Germany. With Indiana University's Early Music Institute he coproduced performances of this opera at Wabash College and at Indiana University in 2009, the first since the opera's premiere at Vienna in 1741.